Challenges to China's Economic Statecraft

Challenges Facing Chinese Political Development

Series Editor: Sujian Guo, Ph.D. San Francisco State University

In an attempt to reflect the rapidly changing political environment of the People's Republic of China, editor Sujian Guo has assembled a book series to present specialized areas of research in current Chinese political studies. Incorporating theoretical, empirical, and policy research on contemporary Chinese politics both domestically and internationally, this series contemplates the Chinese past, present, and future by utilizing interdisciplinary perspectives to approach issues related to Chinese politics, economy, culture, social development, reform, the military, legal system, and foreign relations. Aimed at bringing a greater understanding of the current Chinese political climate to Western audiences, this series is focused on the emerging voices of Chinese scholars and their perspectives on the ever-changing Chinese diaspora.

Recent Titles in Series

Challenges to China's Economic Statecraft: A Global Perspective, edited by Yi Edward Yang, with Wei Liang

Governance Innovation and Policy Change: Recalibrations of Chinese Politics under Xi Jinping, edited by Nele Noesselt

Confucianism in Contemporary Chinese Politics: An Actionable Account of Authoritarian Political Culture, by Shanruo Ning Zhang

China's Agrarian Transition: Peasants, Property, and Politics, by René Trappel

The Rise of China and Chinese International Relations Scholarship, by Hung-jen Wang

Theorizing Chinese Citizenship, edited by Zhonghua Guo and Sujian Guo

Chinese Models of Development: Global, Local, and Comparative Perspectives, edited by Tse-Kang Leng and Yu-Shan Wu

State–Society Relations and Governance in China, edited by Sujian Guo

The Failure of China's Democratic Reforms, by Zaijun Yuan

Taiwan and the Rise of China: Cross-Strait Relations in the Twenty-first Century, edited by Baogang Guo and Chung-chian Teng

Participation and Empowerment at the Grassroots: Chinese Village Elections in Perspective, by Gunter Schubert and Anna L. Ahlers

Organizing Rural China—Rural China Organizing, edited by Ane Bislev and Stig Thøgersen

A Path for Chinese Civil Society: A Case Study on Industrial Associations in Wenzhou, China, by Jianxing Yu, Jun Zhou, and Hua Jiang

The Chinese Labyrinth: Exploring China's Model of Development, edited by Baogang Guo and He Li

New Frontiers in China's Foreign Relations: Zhongguo Waijiao de Xin Bianjiang, edited by Allen Carlson and Ren Xiao

Reviving Legitimacy: Lessons for and from China, edited by Zhenglai Deng and Sujian Guo

China's Quiet Rise: Peace Through Integration, edited by Baogang Guo and Chung-chian Teng

China's Quest for Political Legitimacy: The New Equity-Enhancing Politics, by Baogang Guo
Thirty Years of China–U.S. Relations: Analytical Approaches and Contemporary Issues, edited by Sujian Guo and Baogang Guo
"Harmonious World" and China's New Foreign Policy, edited by Sujian Guo and Jean-Marc F. Blanchard
Environmental Protection Policy and Experience in the U.S. and China's Western Regions, edited by Sujian Guo, Joel J. Kassiola, and Jijiao Zhang
Multidimensional Diplomacy of Contemporary China, edited by Simon Shen and Jean-Marc F. Blanchard
Dancing with the Dragon: China's Emergence in the Developing World, edited by Dennis Hickey and Baogang Guo
Online Chinese Nationalism and China's Bilateral Relations, edited by Simon Shen and Shaun Breslin
Dynamics of Local Governance in China During the Reform Era, edited by Tse-Kang Leng and Yun-Han Chu
Greater China in an Era of Globalization, edited by Sujian Guo and Baogang Guo
Toward Better Governance in China: An Unconventional Pathway of Political Reform, edited by Baogang Guo and Dennis V. Hickey
New Dimensions of Chinese Foreign Policy, edited by Sujian Guo and Shiping Hua
China in Search of a Harmonious Society, edited by Sujian Guo and Baogang Guo
The Dragon's Hidden Wings: How China Rises with Its Soft Power, by Sheng Ding
Challenges Facing Chinese Political Development, edited by Sujian Guo and Baogang Guo

To see a full list of titles in the series please visit:
https://rowman.com/Action/SERIES/LEX/CHSCFC

Challenges to China's Economic Statecraft

A Global Perspective

Edited by
Yi Edward Yang, with Wei Liang

LEXINGTON BOOKS
Lanham • Boulder • New York • London

Published by Lexington Books
An imprint of The Rowman & Littlefield Publishing Group, Inc.
4501 Forbes Boulevard, Suite 200, Lanham, Maryland 20706
www.rowman.com

6 Tinworth Street, London SE11 5AL, United Kingdom

Introduction: Journal of Chinese Political Science, Online First
Chapter 3: Journal of Chinese Political Science, Online First
Chapter 4: Journal of Chinese Political Science, Online First
Chapter 6: Journal of Chinese Political Science, Online First
Chapter 7: Journal of Chinese Political Science, Online First
Chapter 9: Chapter nine was previously published as Zhongzhou Peng and Sow Keat Tok, 2016, "The AIIB and China's Normative Power in International Financial Governance Structure," *Chinese Political Science Review* 1(4), pp 736–753.
Chapter 10: Chapter ten was previously published as Marcia Don Harpaz, "China's Coherence in International Economic Governance," *Journal of Chinese Political Science* (2016) 21:123–147.

British Library Cataloguing in Publication Information Available

Library of Congress Cataloging-in-Publication Data Is Available

ISBN 978-1-4985-8344-2 (cloth)
ISBN 978-1-4985-8345-9 (electronic)

Contents

List of Abbreviations

ADB	Asian Development Bank
AIIB	Asian Infrastructure Investment Bank
APEC	Asia-Pacific Economic Cooperation
BRI	Belt and Road Initiative
CA	Central Asia
CCP	Chinese Communist Party
CDB	China Development Bank
EAEU	Eurasian Economic Union
EU	European Union
FDI	Foreign Direct Investment
GDP	Gross Domestic Product
GNP	Gross National Product
HSR	High-Speed Rail
IMF	International Monetary Fund
M&A	Mergers and Acquisitions
MSR	Maritime Silk Road
NMD	National Missile Defense
NSR	New Silk Road
OBOR	One Belt One Road
PKO	UN Peacekeeping Operation
PLA	People's Liberation Army
PRC	People's Republic of China
ROK	Republic of Korea
RoO	Rule of Origin

SASAC	State-owned Assets Supervision and Administration Commission
SCO	Shanghai Cooperation Organization
SOE	State-owned Enterprise
SREB	Silk Road Economic Belt
SRIF	Silk Road Infrastructure Fund
THAAD	Terminal High Altitude Area Defense System
TMD	Theatre Missile Defense
UN	United Nations
WTO	World Trade Organization

Introduction

Yi Edward Yang and Wei Liang

Statecraft refers to the use of policy instruments to satisfy the core objectives of nation-states in the international system (Baldwin 1985; Norris 2016; Reilly 2016). One of its crucial components—economic statecraft—entails the purposeful selection of economic resources by national leaders to pursue strategic and security interests (Pu 2017). As such, economic statecraft's emphasis on politics makes it distinguished from commercially motivated actions as well as economic diplomacy, whose primary goal is to promote a state's business/commercial interests (Reilly 2016, 2017). Economic statecraft is by and large an exercise and pursuit of power through economic means. In practice, economic statecraft encompasses a host of policy tools, in the form of positive inducements or negative sanctions, including foreign direct investment (FDI), foreign aid, preferential trade agreement, sanction, embargo, freezing foreign assets, and so on.

Leaders of the People's Republic of China (PRC) are no strangers to economic statecraft. As a target, Beijing faced enduring Western sanctions during the Cold War. As a practitioner, Beijing provided generous foreign aid in the 1960 to 1970s to many third world countries to build a "united front" against imperialism (Zhang 2014). During the early decades of the reform era, economic statecraft mainly took the form of economic diplomacy, underscoring Beijing's desire to maintain a friendly external environment conducive to its sustained economic growth. Between 1990 and 2008, China joined all major international economic institutions and deeply integrated itself into the global economy.

China's relative economic success during the 2008–2009 global financial crisis, in contrast to Western nations, injected more confidence and ambition into its economic statecraft. Under President Xi Jinping, Beijing rolled out many concrete economic initiatives intended to achieve its strategic and security goals. To demonstrate the leadership in reforming existing global financial institutions, China created the Asian Infrastructure Investment Bank (AIIB). The "Going Out" strategy that started in the late 1990s was repackaged and rebranded into a sweeping Belt and Road Initiative (BRI), President Xi's signature foreign policy project (Wong 2019).

China's growing confidence in economic statecraft is also seen in its more frequent and blatant use of negative sanction tools such as boycott and trade barriers against countries with whom it had political or territorial disputes, mostly in Asia (Blackwill and Harris 2016; Glasser 2012). For instance, in 2010, amid the dispute over the Diaoyu/Senkaku Islands in the East China Sea, Beijing imposed export restrictions on rare earth metals to Japan (Bradsher 2010). When the 2010 Nobel Peace Prize was awarded to imprisoned political dissident Liu Xiaobo, China promptly canceled a ministerial trade delegation to Norway and launched an economic sanction to cut half of Norwegian salmon exports to Chinese market in 2011 (Baker 2014). In March 2012, China banned the import of bananas from the Philippines after a flare-up in contested waters around Scarborough Shoal in order to pressure the Philippines to give up its claim (Higgins 2012). In 2017, South Korea also faced punitive retaliations on trade, tourism, and retail after Seoul agreed to deploy the American Terminal High Altitude Area Defense (THAAD) system despite Beijing's strong opposition (Yan 2017).

China's embrace of a comprehensive and multifaceted economic statecraft as part of its grand strategy signifies a paradigm change in its foreign policy. This change has certainly captured scholarly attention—a small but growing body of research on China's economic statecraft has emerged in recent years (e.g., Blanchard and Ripsman 2013; Blackwill and Harris 2016; Li 2017; Norris 2016; Reilly 2016, 2017). This edited volume presents a fresh selection of chapters on China's economic statecraft. What distinguishes these studies from existing literature on this topic is that these chapters collectively seek to explore the following important and yet understudied questions: (1) What are the challenges China faces in implementing its economic statecraft strategies? (2) Why is China sometimes able to achieve its foreign policy objectives via economic statecraft and sometimes not? (3) How do foreign countries, particularly the targets of China's economic statecraft, respond to China's strategies? In addition, as much of the existing research has looked to China's domestic factors and dynamics (particularly its state-centric approach and the relationship between the state and firms) to explain the selection among various economic tools and the success or failure of China's economic statecraft, contributors to this volume highlight the role played by domestic factors within the target states. China's economic statecraft is critically examined in the context of more than a dozen nations and international organizations across four continents in the world, thus providing a truly global perspective.

This book consists of four parts. The first part examines China's economic statecraft in bilateral relations, including key pairings such as China-Russia, China-South Korea, China-New Zealand, and China-Canada. The second part explores China's economic statecraft in regional settings—cases include China-Africa, China-the Gulf Cooperation Council (GCC) region, China-Europe, and China-Latin America. The third part explores China's economic statecraft in creating new international institutions and shaping existing ones. Notable cases include the Asian Infrastructure Investment Bank (AIIB), the International Monetary Fund (IMF), the World Trade Organization (WTO), and the United Nations (UN).

BRI can be considered the culmination of a number of positive tools of economic statecraft. How is the project received overseas? How does this project influence major bilateral relations that will take part in the project, such as that of China and Russia? Laura Bunting's chapter examines the advancement of the BRI in Central Asia where the successful realization of China's vision in the region faces one key challenge: Russia. China needs the Central Asian states as a conduit to Europe and seeks to benefit politically and strategically from improved economic integration. China's expanding economic engagement with the region however increasingly challenges Russia's historic sphere of influence. Bunting contends that for now China and Russia each has complementary strengths in the region, with China stressing economic engagement and Russia being keen to amplify its military presence across the region. In the long run, however, China's accelerating military modernization may substantially disrupt the current Sino-Russia balance of power in Central Asia. Until then, China's economic statecraft will serve its strategic goals well in the region.

If initiatives such as the BRI highlight the importance of positive tools in China's economic statecraft, coercive measures such as sanctions are not the natural inclination of the Chinese government. For much of the PRC's history, efforts at using positive inducements were valued more than negative sanctions. Beijing consistently denounced the use of coercive economic measures such as embargo and sanctions by Western powers in the Cold War era (Li 2017). In recent years, the frequency of Beijing's utilization of economic sanctions for political/security purposes is on the rise—though with mixed results. James F. Paradise's chapter examines the most recent "unofficial sanctions" China imposed against South Korea to punish its decision to deploy the US THAAD system in the aftermath of North Korea's nuclear and missile tests. Paradise finds that explanatory frameworks emphasizing sanctioning state's (China) strategies and priorities cannot adequately explain South Korea's evolving approach to handling the THAAD case. Target state's (South Korea) considerations need to be taken into account. What mattered in Seoul's decision-making calculus include the identification of North

Korea's missile and nuclear weapons tests as a critical national security issue, the transition from a conservative to a liberal national government, and South Korea's military alliance with the United States. Theoretically, this chapter highlights the importance of target states' domestic factors in explaining the effectiveness of economic statecraft.

An important puzzle in China's economic statecraft is whether Beijing sees distinctive geopolitical values in countries that share very similar characteristics (e.g., in terms of geographic location, size of economy), and if it does, how is it reflected in China's economic statecraft strategies? With a comparative case study of China's respective economic statecraft toward Canada and New Zealand, Stephen Noakes and Charles Burton contend that there are clear differences in the strategic value of these two middle powers for China. Canada, due to its membership in influential organizations such as the G7 and its historic and ongoing ties with the United States, is a more consequential target for China's economic statecraft. Paradoxically, however, the complications present in Canada's domestic political landscape makes New Zealand an easier and quicker target for China's economic influence.

In implementing economic statecraft, the Chinese government has deliberately chosen different policy instruments determined by the combination of its own strategic goals and the political/economic characteristics of the target state. For example, China hopes to cultivate strategic alignment with African countries on the world stage. The primary strategy to achieve this goal is through strengthening economic ties with three policy tools: trade, FDI, and aid. The question is how has each policy tool fared in achieving China's strategic goals? Pippa Morgan's chapter unpacks the distinctive effects of these three tools in promoting China's strategic interests in Africa, particularly in terms of projecting soft power. Building off the principal-agent model, Morgan argues that the principal-agent problem is more pronounced in China-Africa trade than in China-Africa FDI and aid, which in turn affects how the African public views Chinese economic activities. Analyzing recent Afrobarometer survey data, Morgan's findings reveal that negative perceptions of China among African citizens are primarily associated with trade-related issues, whereas Chinese investment and aid are much more positively received. By comparing the severity and consequences of the principal-agent problem between the three major tools, Morgan's chapter makes notable contributions to literature employing the principal-agent theory to understand China's economic statecraft in Africa and elsewhere.

Wei Liang's chapter reflects on China's economic statecraft and the responses of Latin American countries (LAC) in the economic and diplomatic realms. The primary research question Liang seeks to answer is: Why China is more effective in utilizing its economic power to pursue political and strategic goals in some LAC countries, but less so in others. In the last two decades, China's economic statecraft worked more effectively with Brazil than Mexico. Brazil has become China's most important ally in the region, standing side-by-side with China on a number of global fronts (e.g., both are members of the BRICS). On the other hand, Mexico continues to see China more as a competitor in global economy and rarely sides with China on foreign policy issues important to leaders in Beijing. Liang argues that a number of critical domestic factors in the target states account for these rather varied outcomes. Specifically, the current level of trade dependence on and complementarity with Chinese market, proximity to the United States (both economically and politically), existence of alternative free trade agreements/investors to the target countries, and shared vision and interest on global governance are important factors that have affected the effectiveness of China's economic statecraft.

Jonathan Fulton's chapter explores China's economic statecraft in the GCC region, a crucial hub of the BRI initiative. China's presence in the GCC region has quietly intensified in recent years, and in the process, it has become the region's most important trade partner. This in turn has enhanced China-GCC cooperation in diplomatic, political, and security realms. Fulton notes that China's expanding ties with the GCC member states greatly benefited from the security architecture provided by the US regional presence. China's approach to economic statecraft in this case thus reflects a pragmatic and realistic assessment of its current capabilities relative to the United States in the region. In the long run, sustained growth in China-GCC economic relations will pay increasing political and strategic dividends to China as the BRI takes shape, giving China a greater degree of influence in the region.

Using FDI to acquire strategic resources and technologies has become a prevalent approach in China's economic statecraft. Bas Hooijmaaijers's chapter studies China's outward FDI in Europe and the drivers behind this "going out" strategy. By studying the recent efforts by two Chinese companies to acquire German firms, KUKA and Aixtron, Hooijmaaijers makes a strong case for "state manipulation of international economic activities for strategic purposes" and how European countries have responded. Hooijmaaijers's chapter presents a policy paradox of Chinese economic statecraft today. China's unique party-state structure has generated growing political suspicion and hostilities among European countries targeted by Chinese economic statecraft. Aggressive and hostile bidding actually backlashed and compromised the initial policy objectives of China's economic statecraft to acquire key technologies through mergers and acquisitions (M&A).

China's investment in overseas infrastructure has expanded, including in the critical infrastructure sector such as nuclear power. Biao Zhang's chapter critically evaluates whether nuclear infrastructure investment has, as claimed by some foreign observers, become China's new tool of economic statecraft.

Specifically, his chapter answers two questions: (1) Is China using nuclear infrastructure investment to induce the target countries to change their policies? (2) Are the target countries changing their policies in order to attract Chinese nuclear investment? Comparing two recent nuclear investment cases involving China-UK and China-the Czech Republic, Zhang concludes that China's nuclear infrastructural investment in fact lacks the strategic intent frequently ascribed to them. Rather, in both cases, the commercial actor and its economic motivation play a more important role. His conclusion is congruent with the "development model" view that in studying China's economic statecraft, which at least for the current phase may be driven more by economic considerations than by political ones (Bräutigam and Tang 2012).

In October 2013, the AIIB was unveiled by Chinese president Xi Jinping and premier Li Keqiang during their respective visits to Southeast Asia. The objective of this bank, as claimed by Chinese leaders, is to provide support to Asian infrastructure construction (*China Daily* 2013). Zhongzhou Peng and Sow Keat Tok's chapter emphasizes the normative implications of the AIIB. Through the lens of normative power concept, this chapter argues that the AIIB contributes to enhancing China's normative power in financial governance since it not only practices Chinese norms in the financial governance area but also serves as a broader platform of Chinese normative projection. Therefore, the AIIB represents a case of Chinese economic statecraft for the purpose of advancing its normative influence in global financial governance. However, as cautioned by Peng and Tok, while the AIIB may serve as a new vehicle for Chinese normative diffusion, the inclusion of developed Western economies, the interactions with other institutions, and the internal governance structure might also challenge and shape China's normative approach in global financial governance.

What are China's policies vis-à-vis the rules and norms of the prevailing international economic order? Marcia Don Harpaz's chapter sets out to assess China's profile within three dimensions of the international economic order: trade, investment, and development aid. Harpaz observes in international trade and investment that China has neither sought nor brought about significant change. In the global development aid regime, however, China is offering an alternative to the long dominant Western norms. What factors, then, account for this variance? Harpaz's analysis finds China's behavior can be explained by three complementary theoretical approaches: rationalist state centric, liberal institutionalist, and normative. In conclusion, the author expects that China will by and large uphold existing international economic order while trying to push for modest and incremental efforts from within.

Min Ye and Quan Li's chapter turns to an understudied area in China's economic statecraft—China's growing presence in UN peacekeeping operations (PKOs). Using formal modeling and statistical data analysis, Ye and

Li's chapter generates several interesting findings. Unlike bilateral economic diplomacy, China has only limited choices in UN PKOs because the location, size, and mandates of PKOs all are determined by the UN Security Council (UNSC). These constraints, however, have the benefits of pooling together scarce resources to achieve something that beyond the means of individual countries. By contributing to these operations, China is able to expand its global influence with relatively lower costs. This chapter also highlights that while pursuing national self-interests underscores China's participation in UN PKOs, China's actions are also motivated by the desire to create global public goods.

CONCLUSION

Through empirically examining Beijing's use of its economic power and tools in areas such as trade, investment, finance, foreign aid, and global economic governance to pursue its strategic, political and security objectives, this volume draws some important findings. First, China has indeed tried to apply economic tools strategically, determined by the specific goals and the unique political/economic characteristics of the target state/regions. China primarily relied on economic inducement in the forms of trade, FDI, and aid when targeting the developing countries. In developed countries, China has frequently used mergers and acquisitions to secure crucial resources and technologies. Secondly, the different geopolitical values of the target state play an important role in determining how they can respond to China's economic statecraft. Countries with higher strategic values to China tend to have more policy space to maneuver when dealing with China's economic penetration than those with lower strategic values. Thirdly, the existence (or lack) of alternative market and finance will also shape the policy options available to the target countries. Target countries with better alternatives can more confidently resist China's economic statecraft or negotiate more favorable terms in the economic exchanges. Fourthly, China's economic statecraft has achieved mixed results. While China has frequently used the access of its market to induce positive policy change in the developing world, it has not always worked. Even when the target country holds a trade surplus, there is always domestic concern in the target states on the grounds of de industrialization, primarization, or trade and policy dependency. FDI as a tool for China's economic statecraft is also controversial. Among the developing countries there are growing concerns about China's "extractive diplomacy" and how Chinese investment has compromised good governance and undermined the social and environmental standards in the target states. Chinese investment in the developed countries has increasingly triggered deep suspicions on China's state capitalism and how its party-state structure has caused unfair competition in a market economy. Fifth, contrary to a view held by many China critics that Beijing only seeks to maximize its own interest by taking advantage of the current international system, analysis of China's contributions to UN PKOs suggests that China is seriously committed to be a global public goods provider and through this, to promoting its global image and status. Finally, when studying China's role in international economic governance, it is helpful to dissect China's interests, priorities, and experiences in different policy dimensions (e.g., trade, investment, and development aid) in order to account for the variation in policy choices.

BIBLIOGRAPHY

Baker, Benjamin David. "Soul or Salmon? Norway's Chinese Dilemma." *The Diplomat*, May 9, 2014. https://thediplomat.com/2014/05/soul-or-salmon-norways-chinese-dilemma/.

Baldwin, David. *Economic Statecraft*. Princeton, NJ: Princeton University Press, 1985.

Blackwill, Robert D., and Jennifer M. Harris. *War by Other Means: Geoeconomics and Statecraft*. Cambridge, MA: Harvard University Press, 2016.

Blanchard, Jean Marc F., and Norrin M. Ripsman. *Economic Statecraft and Foreign Policy: Sanctions, Incentives, and Target State Calculations*. New York: Routledge, 2013.

Blanchard, Jean Marc F., Edward D. Mansfield, and Norrin M. Ripsman. *Power and the Purse: Economic Statecraft, Interdependence, and National Security*. New York: Routledge, 2000.

Bradsher, Keith. "Amid Tension, China Blocks Vital Exports to Japan." *New York Times*, September 22, 2010. http://www.nytimes.com/2010/09/23/business/global/23rare.html.

Bräutigam, Deborah, and Tang Xiaoyang. "Economic Statecraft in China's New Overseas Special Economic Zones: Soft Power, Business or Resource Security?" *International Affairs* 88 (12) (2012): 799–816.

Chin, Gregory. "Two-Way Socialization: China, the World Bank, and Hegemonic Weakening." *The Brown Journal of World Affairs* 19 (1) (Fall/Winter 2012): 211–30.

China Daily. "China Proposes Establishing Asian Infrastructure Investment Bank." October 3, 2013. http://www.chinadaily.com.cn/xinhua/2013-10-03/content_10245894.html.

Ching, Frank. "China Has all But Ended the Charade of a Peaceful Rise." *South China Morning Post*, August 26, 2016.

Glaser, Bonnie S. "China's Coercive Economic Diplomacy: A New and Worrisome Trend." *Center for Strategic and International Studies*, Commentary, August

6, 2012. http://csis.org/publication/ china's-coercive-economic-diplomacy-new-and-worrying-trend.

Higgins, Andrew. "In Philippines, Banana Growers Feel Effect of South China Sea Dispute." *Washington Post*, June 10, 2012. https://www.washingtonpost.com/world/asia_pacific/in-philippines-banana-growers-feel-effect-of-south-china-sea-dispute/2012/06/10/gJQA47WVTV_story.html?utm_term=.4691f8f90cd5.

Interview with MOFCOM officials in Beijing, July 2017.

Li, Mingjiang. *China's Economic Statecraft: Co-optation, Cooperation, and Coercion*. Singapore: World Scientific Press, 2017.

Norris, William J. *Chinese Economic Statecraft: Commercial Actors, Grand Strategy, and State Control*. Ithaca, NY: Cornell University Press, 2016.

Pu, Xiaoyu. "Interdependent Rivals: China's Economic Statecraft towards Japan." In *China's Economic Statecraft: Co-optation, Cooperation, and Coercion*, edited by Mingjiang Li, 97–115. Singapore: World Scientific Press, 2017.

Reilly, James. "China's Unilateral Sanctions." *The Washington Quarterly* 35 (4) (Fall 2012): 121–33.

Reilly, James. "China: Turning Money into Power." In *Connectivity Wars: Why Migration, Finance and Trade are the Geo-Economic Battlegrounds of the Future*, edited by Mark Leonard, 189–196. London: European Council on Foreign Relations, 2016.

Reilly, James. "China's Economic Statecraft in Europe." *Asia Europe Journal* 15 (2017): 173–85.

Xinhua. "Peaceful Rise: Strategic Choice for China." April 25, 2004. http://www.china.org.cn/english/features/93939.htm.

Yan, Sophia. "China Seeking to Punish South Korean Firms on Missile Defense Plans." *CNBC*, February 28, 2017, https://www.cnbc.com/2017/02/28/china-seeking-to-punish-south-korean-firms-on-missile-defense-plans.html.

Zhang, Shuguang. *Beijing's Economic Statecraft during the Cold War, 1949–1991*. Baltimore: Johns Hopkins University Press, 2014.

Part I

CHINA'S ECONOMIC STATECRAFT IN BILATERAL RELATIONS

Chapter 1

The New Great Game in Central Asia?

The Belt and Road Initiative and Its Implications for Sino-Russian Relations

Laura Bunting

Ambitious in intensity and scale, the Belt and Road Initiative (BRI) is widely considered the cornerstone of China's regional and increasingly global economic policy. A fundamentally positive instrument of economic statecraft, approximately 1.46 trillion dollars, has been earmarked by the Chinese Communist Party (CCP) for investment and development in cultural, linguistic, and most centrally trade ties worldwide. Currently, this is predominantly in the form of infrastructure projects across Eurasia and in particular Central Asia. Given the central role that Chinese businesses and Chinese funds are to play, from a geopolitical perspective, the BRI constitutes China's attempt to reorient and reshape global trade in order to maximize their own strategic, political, and economic interests in the long term. Consequently, engagement with, as well as general views of, the initiative often runs parallel with perspectives toward China's rise more broadly. Countries eager for cheap loans and infrastructure support see the project as an opportunity to access funds without the fear of heavy-handed political interference often associated with the United States or the International Monetary Fund (IMF). This perceived erosion of US power has similarly sparked negative and occasionally alarmist responses from Western media outlets and officials who view the BRI as a channel through which Beijing hopes to realize a new form of "global commerce on China's terms" (Perlez and Huang 2018). The highly charged and political nature of these responses makes understanding the initiative of prime importance to better understand how China's economic statecraft is both conducted and received. Moreover, it provides insight into the motivations behind economic statecraft more generally and helps discern which methods are preferable and to what degree these tools are effective.

This chapter will examine the advancement of the BRI in Central Asia to explore these key issues. The successful realization of China's vision in the region faces one key challenge—Russia; thus the relationship between the two powers will be addressed as a central point of consideration. Their dynamic reveals much about China's preferred method of negotiation, and the implications of the project on their future partnership overtime reveals to some extent the trends of Chinese policy prioritization more holistically. Indeed, how China balances the interests of Central Asia states against the regional hegemon Russia underscores the benefit of bilateral forms of negotiation and the utility of economic statecraft in pursuing its localized geopolitical objectives. This has broader implications for how China will advance the BRI across other regions, such as the Pacific, where it faces a much stronger hegemon—the United States.

WHAT IS THE BRI?

The Chinese-led BRI is a transformational project of immense scale, nominally amounting to seven times the adjusted value of the Marshall Plan (Balhuizen 2017). It consists of both land and maritime elements. The land component or SREB (Silk Road Economic Belt) is aimed at facilitating land-based trade across the Eurasian landmass through the creation and strengthening of a number of economic corridors.

This is principally to be achieved through the rapid modernization and expansion of existing rail networks—an industry in which China is increasingly taking a leading role. Indeed, with over 12,000 miles of track laid, China now has more high-speed rail (HSR) than the rest of the world combined (Wilson 2016). Through the BRI, China plans to export this technology en masse through Central Asia and connect its markets with Europe. The maritime component, the "twentieth-century Maritime Silk Road," (MSR) although currently less advanced is intended to complement the land initiative through the construction and further development of a number of coastal ports stretching through the South China Sea and the Indian Ocean to Europe. It will also extend to developing infrastructure in Africa, and Oceania and the Pacific to link the Chinese economy with Latin America. Investment into the transitory small states of the Pacific, in particular Papua New Guinea, has been ramped up "as part of Beijing Belt and Road initiative" (Wembridge 2018).

Despite this, to date the BRI is concerned principally with the land component and China is actively pursuing regional development both bilaterally and multilaterally. It can currently be considered predominantly a "neighborhood policy, aimed at integrating Central Asian countries with China's western regions . . . intended primarily to manage economic and geopolitical competition" (Economist Intelligence Unit 2015) and boost regional cooperation and trade. However, in the long term, the Silk Road projects are ultimately global in scale and "will connect countries that represent 55 percent of world GNP, 70 percent of global population, and 75 percent of known energy reserves" (Godement et al. 2015), dramatically affecting the balance of global trade. Consequently, it is difficult to view the project outside the lens of broader regional and territorial politics of all those states involved, particularly China. The project is financed principally by China, through the Asian Infrastructure Investment Bank (AIIB), Silk Road Infrastructure Fund (SRIF), and the China Development Bank (CDB). These funds are increasingly complemented by regional governments such as Singapore and the partnership of the AIIB with the Eurasian Economic Union (EAEU). Chinese capital, however, remains the central driver (Wilson 2016). Thus, both economically and politically, this is fundamentally a Chinese project—stressing "win-win" outcomes and "mutually beneficial cooperation to a new high and in new forms" (National Development and Reform Commission, Ministry of Foreign Affairs, and Ministry of Commerce 2015)—through the exporting of Chinese technologies abroad. The asymmetry of economic leverage held by the Chinese in this project is viewed with a similar level of apprehension as Chinese direct investment elsewhere. Indeed, some are prone to view BRI as the key feature of a broader Chinese strategy to realize the suzerain system in Central Asia.[1] Such a view is compounded by the ambiguity regarding the terms of Chinese investment and dispute resolution (Dezan Shira & Associates 2018) along the BRI projects, and to what extent it constitutes a new form of global trade.

A DISTINCTIVELY CHINESE INITIATIVE

China aims to advance both its political and economic objectives through the BRI. Therefore, Chinese economic statecraft cannot be viewed in isolation from broader political and security policy. While, William J. Norris's notion that "economic tools of national power can be used to pursue strictly economic objectives" (Norris 2016, 13) has credibility, his suggestion that security concerns are mere externalities discounts the fundamental trade-offs that policymakers face when considering economic policy. In the Chinese case, political and economic objectives are invariably linked, not least due to the prioritization of stable and equitable economic growth domestically by the CCP. Distinctions are further blurred by the heavy hand the CCP plays in the market, and the domination of outward foreign investment by state-owned enterprises (SOEs), in particular large "National Champions" in the resource and infrastructure sectors (Milhaupt and Zheng 2015, 665). This is compounded by the growing eminence of the BRI in the economic agenda and public domain (Ministry of Commerce of the People's Republic of China and National Bureau of Statistics of the People's Republic of China 2016). Consequently, the initiative should be considered as a key element of economic statecraft within the context of broader national interests—centrally advancing economic growth through the diversification of the economy[2]; fostering a growing respected role for China on the global stage; and bolstering security and political stability domestically. Economically, the initiative is an opportunity for China to diversify their economy and establish outlets for excess production capacity. "Having overbuilt in many domestic industries—such as coal, cement and even solar panels" (Wilson 2016), it is increasingly important to redirect capital abroad and secure trading partners to absorb these goods. Further, the need to maintain high levels of Gross Domestic Product (GDP) growth and employment puts pressure on "local Chinese officials to keep factories going" (Timmons and Huang 2016), and as a large share remains state owned, the ability to export to foreign markets renders it the most politically desirable solution for the CCP. Developing trade routes and increasing trade with Central Asia through BRI projects represents a unique opportunity to achieve a number of these goals and further Chinese interests through an avenue above purely bilateral relations under the guise of cross-country cooperation. On a domestic geostrategic level, the initiative can be considered a tool as part of a broader policy to encourage regional integration, combating what Beijing terms the "three evils"—"terrorism, separatism, and fundamentalism" (Ooi and Trinkle 2015). The proposed trade routes traverse a number of Chinese provinces, some that have the weakest economic and ethnic ties with the center and the "transport links being built between Xinjiang province and Central Asia will significantly increase China's influence in that region" (Garver 2006, 206). Indeed, the Xinjiang Uygur Autonomous Region is considered relatively politically unstable and the violent crackdown on protestors and separatists in 2009 attracted embarrassment for, and international critique of, China. As a non-majority Han region with a majority Muslim population, it has "long inspired fighters from Central Asia (and Afghanistan) to support them," in their separatist struggle against China, (Garver 2006) an unacceptable outcome for Beijing. The priority placed on territorial integrity renders this issue as one of the critical concerns to the central leadership. The potential for increased political oversight as a result of trade, in combination with employment and economic opportunity, will drive, according to Beijing, greater dependency on the central government, and therefore stability in the region. In such a way Beijing is able to utilize economic incentives to progressively achieve a strategic outcome that would otherwise require stronger military intervention.

Politically, the successful realization of the New Silk Roads is complementary to the political objectives of the Chinese leadership and the current leader Xi Jinping. It is an opportunity for Xi to demonstrate his global leadership skills and his ability to project Chinese power abroad, thus emboldening his popularity domestically. Furthermore, it serves as a tool to achieve his "Chinese dream" of self-rejuvenation, both in driving economic growth and through invoking the tradition of the ancient Han Dynasty's silk roads. This link to traditional Chinese legacies further strengthens the CCPs claims to historical legitimacy (Vickers 2009, 525). Once again all roads will lead to Beijing (Palmer 2016). It is therefore problematic to consider the BRI outside of the broader implications of China's rise, as it plays such a central part. As an element of foreign policy, the initiative tilts China westward, reducing its dependency on the American market and American secured trade routes. This is particularly true of the maritime routes which the US military utilizes to justify their military presence in the South China Sea. Therefore, through strengthening alternative routes of trade, China is indirectly undercutting America's global dominance and the monopoly the US holds as the safeguard of free trade and trade laws. This allows Beijing to strengthen an alternative to what it views as an US-led hegemonic world order, promoting, instead, a multipolar world (Herd 2015, 22). China's MSR seeks to further corrode this influence through the development of alternative trade routes through the Pacific. More apparent though, particularly in the short term, is the power of the initiative to strengthen Beijing's regional position; to lead regional economic affairs, and to translate economic dominance into political dominance. In becoming the strongest power in Central Asia, China will have the power to shape regional forums in their interests, which has profound security benefits, particularly in the face of the increasing risk of terrorism and separatism. Therefore, China stands to benefit hugely from the project, in both the short term and the long term. The public emphasis on economic benefits downplays the political, security, and diplomatic gains China hopes to realize, all factors which help to explain the enthusiasm of the current leadership for the project, and a preference of the CCP for the use of economic statecraft over other methods. Consequently, with a high level of political will it is unlikely that Beijing will give up on the realization of the initiative any time in the near future.

THE BRI AS ECONOMIC STATECRAFT

The BRI itself can be considered the culmination of a number of positive tools of economic statecraft. Considering China's doctrine of "noninterference" and its championing of "win-win" solutions, it is clear that Beijing, at least nominally, has a strong preference for positive inducements rather than negative tools such as economic sanctions. Making use of Blackwell and Harris's neat classification of the composite elements of economic statecraft (Blackwill and Harris 2016, 49–92), we can clearly identify the following instruments being utilized to varying degrees. Most obviously, *developing trade* links and favorable *investment polies* form the foundations of the BRI in its entirety. Chinese-led intuitions seek to promote and finance trade on a transformative scale. Through such policies, China is able to induce countries to comply with Chinese policy more broadly. "Dollar diplomacy" has successfully encouraged a number of nations to formally recognize China and cut ties with Taiwan. Panama is but the latest example (Sands 2017). As a *financial* tool, the BRI has the ability to further promote the Renminbi to international status by increasing the number of transactions that require its conversion. The initiative advances *national policies governing energy and commodities* by ensuring direct and secure access to raw materials. Indeed, China has signed a "string of energy deals" (Blackwill and Harris 2016, 85) with Kazakhstan. And lastly the BRI contains elements of *economic assistance*, as the CDB "under orders to develop a customer base outside their domestic borders" (Blackwill and Harris 2016, 73), is increasingly seeking partners abroad. It is worth noting that these tools are in many respects complimentary and work together to increase Chinese soft power collectively. The promotion of Chinese-led trade invariably strengthens the position of Renminbi and is likely to include trade to resource rich areas. However, the fact that these objectives are able to be sought under the broader strategy of trade development and investment underscore the strength of the BRI. Beijing clearly seeks to pursue strategies that minimize negative externalities; thus, the flexibility afforded by the ambiguity of the BRI constitutes a further benefit.

The increasing popularity and wide scale endorsement of the BRI can be considered as evidence of the initiatives success. Beijing has largely succeeded in painting the initiative as a positive rather than a negative or coercive form of power politics. Globally, leaders have been eager to champion the project, with heads of state and trade representatives from Serbia to Australia praising the initiative ("Quotes from Leaders at China's New Silk Road Meeting" 2017) Some vast, and obscure, exaggerations have been made; the president of Turkey, Recep Tayyip Erdogan, went so far as to state that it is "the kind of initiative that will put an end to terrorism" ("Quotes from Leaders at China's New Silk Road Meeting" 2017), but more importantly it is increasingly adopted as an accepted feature of global commerce. Even the West has softened its stance, with Donald Trump sending a US representative to the recent BRI forum (Hsu 2017). A further geopolitical success of the BRI is the momentum that is has built around itself—becoming an established feature of business and academic discourse. In 2017, the University of

Cambridge became the first in the West to establish a center concerning itself solely with the initiative. The co-founder David De Cremer sees this as mere prudence as "whether you like it or not, China stands out now to show global leadership" (*China Daily* 2017).

This has geostrategic implications as it promotes China's preferred conceptualization of a multipolar world—one in which bilateral negotiations are elevated as the necessary method of negotiation. China seeks to engage one-on-one with potential economic partners in order to maximize their bargaining position. Indeed, the success of the BRI has largely been achieved on bilateral grounds and its future is contingent on Beijing's ability to ensure mutually beneficial bilateral relations over time. Indeed, so long as China is able to engage with the Central Asian states and Moscow independently, it is unlikely to have its vision of the BRI challenged. Consequently, should perceptions of the initiative continue to shift in China's favor, and their growing assertiveness on the global stage normalized, the BRI is likely to remain the cornerstone of a highly effective Chinese economic statecraft, enabling to China to realize both her political and economic objectives.

CHINA'S BRI ENTERS CENTRAL ASIA

The modern conceptualization of the BRI began in Central Asia, and the region itself is a necessary partner for its realization. Fittingly, it was in Kazakhstan on September 2013 that Xi Jinping launched his plan to restore the historic Silk Road trade routes connecting the European markets to Asia. China needs the Central Asian states as a conduit to Europe and seeks to benefit politically and strategically from improved economic integration. The focus on connective and large-investment opportunities in infrastructure under the BRI represents a renewed push in China's regional economic statecraft. Strategically, China shares extensive and occasionally disputed land boundaries with Kazakhstan, Kyrgyzstan, and Tajikistan (Shen 2012) and greater economic power would improve their leverage. Furthermore, a stronger economic role would facilitate higher levels of strategic oversight, in the pursuit of regional stability. The risk of terrorism and separatism continue to plague the region (Santen 2018). This objective can theoretically and similarly be pursued through the use of other positive tools of economic statecraft, such as aid; however, politically the BRI offers an additional benefit. As countries become more dependent on Chinese finance, under uniquely Chinese terms of trade and investment, the relative strength of the Chinese economic model of trade is strengthened overall and as such erodes the ability of foreign states, such as Russia, to utilize their own tools of economic weaponry.

It is therefore unsurprising that China's amplified economic engagement with the region increasingly challenges Russia's historic sphere of influence. Invoking the historic narrative of great power rivalry, the accelerating economic and military competition between the two in Central Asia is nominally referred to as the new "Great Game in Central Asia" (Cooley 2012). Beijing's interests are predominantly economic; while Moscow seeks to preserve their monopoly over military and political affairs, they also want to enjoy their status as preferred trade partner. The distinction between economic and political spheres is increasingly murky. Economic investments need to be secured, and thus require political and military support—this has led China to seek a greater security role. China has become a key supplier of military and surveillance technology and is increasingly participating in joint military exercises to a number of the regions governments. Chinese troops were presenting at military bills with Tajik forces in 2016 and Kyrgyz forces in 2017 (Lemon 2018). Furthermore, Chinese fears of separatism and terrorism "leaking" over the borders have heightened Chinese military interests. Russia is increasingly hostile to Chinese activity in the region as it sees China's economic incursions as challenging their historic claim to regional dominance; despite China's strategic imperative not to overtly challenge Russian national interests, the risk of Russian retaliation remains considerable. The agency of the Central Asian states themselves further strains relations. While they remain historically linked to Russia, the prioritization of economic interests rather than security renders the Central Asian states increasingly at the behest of Chinese leadership. China therefore needs to balance its growing integration in Central Asia with its strategic relationship with Russia. The fear of being isolated makes it more likely that Russia with retaliate sporadically and indiscriminately.

THE RUSSIAN PERSPECTIVE

The Russian Federation views the initiative as both an opportunity and a threat, particularly at the regional level. Economically, Russia stands to benefit enormously from the influx of Chinese capital, through improved bilateral ties and broader regional growth. An increase in trade will also help energize Russia's own sluggish domestic growth and provide the resources and infrastructure to integrate their economy more closely with those of Central Asia and Eurasia. This will bolster Russia's pivot, somewhat out of necessity, away from Europe and toward Asia. Politically, however, Moscow is apprehensive of China's rise, and, in some cases, views it as a direct threat. Russia is wary of Chinese regional influence, which it perceives as "an attempt to pull Central Asia away from Russia's orbit" (Korostikov 2016). Indeed, mistrust of Chinese intentions permeates through Russian society.

Despite standing to gain from the Silk Road Fund a Russian railway company is rejecting it on "a position of principle" (Korostikov 2016) and called on other Russian companies to follow suit. From a regional perspective, the rise of China is at the expense of Moscow, as the Central Asian states are no longer dependent on Russia for both their economic and military needs. This is despite Russia being a strategic partner against US hegemony and beneficiary of China's vision for a multipolar world order.

Irrefutably, Russia hopes to gain economically from the initiative and "increasingly wants in on the action" (Feige 2016). China is now Russia's second largest trading partner after the EU, and between 2000 and 2006, "bilateral trade volumes [with China] rose from 8 billion $USD to 33 billion" (Eder 2014). This accounts for a large portion of Russian trade, and through the BRI, Russia could potentially reduce its net-trade deficit of approximately 11 billion $USD with China by boosting exports. The current state of the economy makes integration with Central Asia and China essential. "Crushed by Western sanctions and the global plunge in oil prices" (Gusovsky 2016), Russia is suffering from a prolonged period of stagnation, and the "Russian economy needs powerful external stimuli" (Prokopenko and Papchenkova 2016) if it is to recover. Furthermore, the 2007–2008 financial crisis and a slow recovery in Europe, amplified by an uncertain Brexit, and sanctions resulting from Russian military actions in Crimea and the Ukraine have rendered the Central Asian and Chinese markets increasingly important to the Russian economy. Indeed, "the stand-off with the West over Ukraine has transformed its relationship with China into an axis of necessity" (Economist Intelligence Unit 2015). However, Russian bilateral trade with China is to a strong extent "limited to gas, oil and arms" (Herd 2015), and as Russia suffers from a large trade deficit, it is in Russia's interests to pursue stronger economic integration with the Central Asian states to avoid strategic dependency on Chinese trade in the long term.

THE CRITICAL ROLE OF CENTRAL ASIA

Made up of five states—Kazakhstan, Kyrgyzstan, Tajikistan, Turkmenistan, and Uzbekistan—Central Asia has been a key supporter of the initiative and is strategically poised to play a large role in the project's future. Indeed, in its current stage, the New Silk Road (NSR) developmental projects are clustered in and around the region with Central Asia forming the "Belt" ("Our Bulldozers, Our Rules" 2016). Economically, the project offers a much-needed influx in capital and investment; however, it also raises skepticism of China's role in the region in both the short and long term. In particular, to what extent their domestic populations will benefit from the initiative with respect to Chinese firms and what China's intentions are concerning their future longer-term role in the region.

Despite the fact that Kazakhstan, the largest economy and the most successful of the "Stans," overtook Russia's GDP per capita last year ("Stans undelivered" 2016), the region is far from developed. The collapse of the ruble and oil and gas prices has placed an incredible strain on the region's economies which depend highly on the export of raw minerals. A number of ambitious development projects remain unfinished due to a lack of capital and unemployment; youth unemployment remains stubbornly high. In both Uzbekistan and Tajikistan, it is above 20 percent ("Our Bulldozers, Our Rules" 2016). Kazakhstan's "future economic growth depends heavily on transport infrastructure and regional trade" (Runde 2015); thus, the BRI and Chinese funding offer a much-needed economic boost. Due to Russia's economic decline, China is increasingly considered an indispensable strategic partner; both as an investor and an importer. With a developing economy dependent on mineral imports, China is and will remain the "largest commodities importer in the region" (Gabuev 2016) for some time. And "reversing this trend is . . . more likely than not, infeasible" (Gabuev 2016). Therefore, for their domestic economies, engagement with the initiative is inescapable.

On a domestic scale, the BRI is advantageous as it addresses the concerns over lax development and provides an opportunity to diversify their economies in order to avoid over-reliance or dependence on Russia, or for that matter, China. Building the right roads in the right places will allow for the emergence of a stronger, more assertive Central Asia. Indeed, in some cases Central Asia has been able to play off the two powers for their own economic gain (Cooley 2012). However, the nature of Chinese investment and trade suggests some serious concerns for the Central Asian governments. Chinese money tends to flow toward Chinese owned and managed businesses, bringing with them an influx of Chinese workers. Clashes have already taken place; in 2015, a brawl broke out in a Chinese run copper mine in Kazakhstan resulting in the hospitalization of sixty-five men ("65 hurt in mass China-Kazakhstan mine brawl" 2015). Despite official insistence that the conflict was not ethnically motivated ("65 hurt in mass China-Kazakhstan mine brawl" 2015), it is consistent with other xenophobic protests that have broken out across the region. Such protests tend to take a uniquely anti-Chinese flavor. In 2016, "anti-Chinese slogans" (Bayer 2016) were employed in protests across the country concerning a revision to Kazakhstan's land code; such protests threaten both the success and employees of Chinese companies and contribute to a backlash toward Chinese investment generally. This constitutes a limit to China's economic statecraft more broadly; China can encourage firms to invest but cannot direct them to do so. Moreover, from the perspective of

Central Asia governments, public protests of this kind are of concern to the authoritarian regimes who rely to some extent on nationalism for legitimacy.

Politically, all the Central Asia states "suffer under repressive cronyist governments" ("Stans undelivered" 2016), largely unchanged from their socialist past. Therefore, their leaders have a heightened fear of public activism triggering independence movements along the lines of those that "toppled regimes in the former Soviet countries of Ukraine and Georgia" ("Stans undelivered" 2016). This fear of disorder, as well as domestic political threats to state rule, is amplified by the growing threat of Jihadi terrorism. As majority Muslim states, they are growing targets of Islamic propaganda and recruitment campaigns. The fear of locally grown terrorism is not exaggerated. According to the International Crisis Group, as many as 4,000 citizens have gone to fight for Islamic State. This justifies Chinese concerns, but also strengthens Russia's position in the region as the key supplier of arms and defense.

Consequently, while the Central Asia states are increasingly turning toward China for economic growth, the mounting threat of independence movements and Islamic terrorism enhances their need for a strong security relationship with Russia. The Stans are therefore very much at the mercy of both superpowers in this regard. Furthermore, they have a vested interest in ensuring that the relationship between the two remains amicable so as to avoid being pressured by one against the other.

THE LEGACY OF CHINESE AND RUSSIAN ENGAGEMENT IN CENTRAL ASIA

In modern history, Russia has dominated Central Asia at the expense of China. The "Great Game" between Britain and Russia saw the Central Asian states carved up due to imperial whim. Indeed, it was Russia's "expansion to the Far East that marked the beginning of the end of a Sinocentric East Asian system of tributary states" (Yu 2006, 228). First conquered by Tsarist Russia, they were established as Soviet states in the 1930–1940s along ethnic lines and remained under the close control of Moscow. Critically, the Central Asian states all contain large ethnic Russian populations and "Russian remains the *lingua franca*" ("Stans undelivered" 2016). Russian cultural ties to the region are closely engrained, as are their military and economic relations. Thus, Russia is bound more closely to the Stans, both culturally and structurally than China. Furthermore, China's former role as a great central power sparks fear of a resurgence in Central Asia and thus engagement with Central Asian states is one marred by mistrust—between both Russian and the Stans and between Russia, the Stans, and China.

Russian despotic tendencies in the past have encouraged Central Asian states to seek closer ties with China to avoid Russian bullying. Thus, the Stans have always kept one eye on the east. Russia's willingness to use resource diplomacy, through their control over infrastructure, has particularly sharpened this impulse. In 2009, Gazprom, Russia's largest gas firm, shut off supplies to Ukraine, arguably due, in some part, to the Ukrainian shift toward the European Union. Subsequent military incursions have only accelerated fears of Central Asian states. Consequently, the Stans have both an economic and political incentive to diversify. In 2013, Kazakhstan promoted the Nurly Zhol initiative and constructed "Special Economic Zones" on the Kazakh-Chinese border in an aim to foster trade (Gabuev 2016), thus promoting trade away from Moscow.

Ultimately, however, Russia's historic role in the region, even though associated with bullying, is of strategic advantage to Moscow at the expense of Beijing. The Chinese are generally viewed as more foreign and less trustworthy than the Russians. Furthermore, Russia is seen to more closely represent the interests of Central Asia. As for the two major powers, their historic inability to see eye-to-eye has meant that their relationship is burdened by high levels of mistrust restricting the success of their partnership. Despite this, the two powers remain relatively pragmatic as to their strengths and limitations.

RUSSIA IN CENTRAL ASIA

Russia is Central Asia's second largest trading partner and remains dominant in some strategic clusters of economic activity—for example, the civilian nuclear industry and arms. Despite China emerging in 2010 as the "largest trading partner with Central Asia" (Gabuev 2016, 220), the fate of their economies is still closely tied to Russia and the ruble. Indeed, "the ruble's moribund fortunes could absolutely devastate Central Asian economies," as its sharp decline would cause average consumer wealth to "drop precipitously" (Panda 2015). Russia has taken a leading role in regional reintegration and in 2014 established, with Kazakhstan as a founding member, the EAEU. This is essentially a customs union and is intended to "become some kind of European Union, with unified legislation and the free circulation of goods, capital and people" (Laurell 2014). This has broader geopolitical implications and is arguably a more political than economic project, intended to prevent the economic breakup of Eurasia and thus support Russian regional leadership (Laurell 2014).

Diplomatically, Russia expects to maintain its historically dominant role in Central Asia and perceives the territory as one "whose fate should be determined by neighboring superpowers" (Gabuev 2016). In this case, major decisions are to be the result of negotiations between China and Russia. As the current dominant regional superpower, Russia hopes to mitigate the diplomatic gains afforded to the Chinese as a result of their growing economic power in order to maintain their position. Indeed, although Russia is not in a position to compete with China economically, their "military capacities surpass its economic ones by far" (Eder 2014), and Moscow remains the key security guarantor and dominant military power in Central Asia. Thus, although regional partners, they are also regional rivals. Beyond the region however, "in geostrategic terms, Russia strives for a multipolar world with itself as one of the independent poles" (Herd 2015) and considers China a geostrategic partner in this context. Therefore, China is seen as an ally against US unilateralism as evidenced by the increased integration of their regional defense programs, the National Missile Defense System (NMD) and Theatre Missile Defense (TMD) (Eder 2014). Thus, while "China's economic rise presents a development opportunity for Russia that Vladimir Putin is keen to exploit . . . in the longer-term Russia will struggle to maintain a rough parity" (Economist Intelligence Unit 2015) with Beijing. Thus, Russia's enthusiasm for the NSR is mitigated by the risk of the realization of political concerns that are the product of a more dominant and assertive China. Consequently, Moscow is keen to be directly involved in the BRI in order to affect its direction. Additionally, Russia also seeks to maintain an active security role in the region in order to balance Chinese economic preeminence.

THE FUTURE OF CHINA AND RUSSIA COOPERATION IN CENTRAL ASIA

In the near future China and Russia are, in all likelihood, to remain nominative partners in Central Asia. The short-term key priorities of the two states are distinct and relatively isolated; thus, they are unlikely to come into direct conflict. While China stresses economic engagement, Russia is keen to amplify its military presence across the region. Furthermore, they have complementary strengths—Russia needs Chinese funds and China needs Russian military technology (Economist Intelligence Unit 2015). As a senior Russian official put it "Russia would provide security, while China would bring its fiscal muscle" (Denyer 2015). Therefore, the two are increasingly comfortable working together to achieve their objectives. A key example of this was in 2015 when China and Russia declared the integration of the EAEU and the BRI—linking the two bodies economically. Additionally, the growing role of Russia within the Shanghai Cooperation Organization (SCO) indicates their willingness to pursue multilateral, rather than bilateral security. However, how these broad mutual objectives translate into effective policy is still to be adequately addressed and what form their realization will take is not yet clear. This could potentially threaten their strategic partnership—particularly in the long term.

Announced with much fanfare the linking of the EAEU with the BRI is at this stage largely honorific. It is riddled with logistical issues as what is most favorable economically to China is not most favorable to Russia. Ultimately, China wants the construction of uninterrupted rail corridors directly linking the Chinese market to Europe that could potentially rival naval transportation costs (Korostikov 2016). Russia, as well as the Central Asian states, meanwhile favors a more intermittent journey with a greater number of checkpoints. This is in order to provide an opportunity to benefit from transit fees and associated costs and to provide technical and construction jobs and ultimately encourage more trade in the region. Kazakhstan alone "aims to capture 10 per cent of the 600 billion trade volume between China and Europe" (Frolovskiy 2016) and hopes to "benefit beyond transit fees" (Frolovskiy 2016). Thus, despite a number of independent routes being proposed, "only three are seriously considered in the framework of the EAEU" (Frolovskiy 2016). The difficulty of merging the two programs is amplified by "ambiguous wording, and the language about coordination [being] limited to trying to find a link between the two initiatives" (Yan 2016). In effect what was proposed was not a merger but rather a linking up (Yan 2016).

Consequently, how this project will take shape is ill-determined and the fact that Russia's interests better align with the Central Asian states could potentially fuel an escalation of Russia's assertiveness. If Russia is able to fortify its "common interests with Central Asian states" (Gabuev 2016), this would present a significant bargaining chip in negotiations with China and thereby embolden Russia, particularly as they continue their relative decline.

The issue of the growing power imbalance between Russia and China is not lost on either party. Despite its lagging economy, at great cost, Russia continues to modernize its military and increase its presence in the region. Recently striking "deals with both Tajikistan and Kyrgyzstan to extend its bases till 2042 and 2032 respectively" (Abdurasulov 2015). The recourse to military clout is becoming the only powerful tool left in Vladimir Putin's arsenal. Alarmingly for Russia's neighbors he is increasingly willing to use it. Russia's military intervention in the former Soviet states of Ukraine and Crimea and the Russian Armed Forces (RAF) display of military might in Syria have illustrated both the sophistication of the Russian military and the extent to which Putin will utilize military methods to achieve political goals. Putin himself embodies the "Russian neo-imperial self-styled 'Master of the Taiga' mantra" (Herd 2015, 225); thus as a nationalist military strongman, the likelihood of a tactical show of military force is further increased. Indeed, at a domestic level, Putin utilizes assertive security policies "to compensate and distract" (Herd 2015, 215) for economic weakness. The growing threat of regional terrorism is therefore of tactical benefit to Russia as it strengthens the demand for their necessary security role. However, the growth in regional terrorism and separatism has also heightened Chinese concerns prompting them to be more involved in the security needs of the region. This has occurred directly through the SCO and more broadly through the evolution of China's military overall. As China's economy continues to grow, they are in the process of modernizing their army, and have the "capacity to match or eventually surpass Russian capabilities" (Kim and Indeo 2013, 278) this century. This move will "substantially disrupt the current balance of power" (Frolovskiy 2016) and how Russia reacts to this will ultimately determine the nature of their partnership. Consequently, so long as neither China nor Russia directly, or abruptly, threaten the other's broader, national interests' relations are likely to remain amicable. Therefore, the notion of a New Great Game is largely hyperbole.

CONCLUSION

A geopolitical analysis reveals two key lessons concerning Chinese economic statecraft; First, that China prefers to pursue their policy bilaterally through a purportedly multilateral forum, and secondly that the coercive power of Chinese economic statecraft can be highly successful at achieving both economic and political policy objectives.

A closer examination of the BRI enables us to categorize and better identify the priorities behind and nuance of China's economic statecraft. While the BRI has been a political success, its economic performance has been mixed—the governments firm commitment to the project emphasize the importance of its broader strategic value. The true value in BRI to China lies in its global transformative power to shift economic relations toward bilateral rather than multilateral terms and improve China's broader prestige. Since 2012 the number of countries nominally involved in the BRI has grown to sixty-nine and it is increasingly integrated into international parlance. Yet while US$304.9 billion in contracts have been signed between China and the economies along the route (Jing 2017), investment in Central Asia has actually dwindled. In 2015, direct foreign investment declined year on year to Central Asia by almost 20 percent (Ministry of Commerce of the People's Republic of China and National Bureau of Statistics of the People's Republic of China 2016). This is in no small part due to the limited economic viability of many of the projects, due to the economies of the Central Asia states themselves. Chinese investors have been put off "building roads to nowhere" (Overland and Vakulchuk 2018), limiting China's use of investment as a tool of economic statecraft. By contrast, in regard to noneconomic engagement the BRI has been more effective, over eleven Confucius institutes have been set up in Central Asia and some 23,000 students from the region have studied at Chinese universities (Overland and Vakulchuk 2018). This represents an over fourfold increase in four years (Overland and Vakulchuk 2018). The BRI has been more effective as a tool of soft rather than hard economic power. This soft power is important in the long term in Central Asia as Russia continues to carry "a strong political and cultural weight" (Corre 2018), and can in part be considered a mediating factor to the EAEU which has not been able to muster an economic alternative to China's BRI. Therefore, the true power of BRI is in its enabling ability for China. It facilitates greater connectivity such that China is able to gradually transform countries "into an open market for primarily China," under Chinese terms of trade and investment. This bolsters Chinese economic statecraft overall and erodes the ability of foreign states, in particular the United States to utilize their own tools of economic weaponry. In the context of Trump's looming trade war, this is more important than ever.

NOTES

1. The Suzerain, or tributary system, was an administrative system used by China to dominate the region politically and economically.
2. In Tandem with Made in China 2025 (MIC2025), for more information, see Kennedy (2015).

BIBLIOGRAPHY

"65 Hurt in Mass China–Kazakhstan Mine Brawl." *China Daily USA*, September 14, 2015. Accessed October 7, 2016. http://usa.chinadaily.com.cn/world/2015-07/14/content_21279776.htm.

Balhuizen, Arnoud. 2017. "China's Belt and Road Initiative, Episode Two: A Vision Encased in Steel." September 26. https://www.bhp.com/media-and-insights/prospects/2017/09/belt-and-road-initiative.

"Belt and Road Int'l Center Officially Launches at University of Cambridge." 2017. *Xinhua*, September 30. http://www.chinadaily.com.cn/china/201709/30/content_32674950.html.

Blackwill, Ambassador Robert D., and Jennifer M. Harris. 2016. *War by Other Means: Geoeconomics and Statecraft*. Cambridge, MA: Belknap Press: An Imprint of Harvard University Press.

China Daily. 2017. "Belt and Road Int'l Center Officially Launched at University of Cambridge." September 30. http://www.chinadaily.com.cn/china/2017-09/30/content_32674950.htm.
Cooley, Alexander. 2012. "The New Great Game in Central Asia." *Foreign Affairs*, August 7. https://www.foreignaffairs.com/articles/central-asia/2012-08-07/new-great-game-central-asia.
Corre, Kemal Kirişci, and Philippe Le. 2018. "The New Geopolitics of Central Asia: China Vies for Influence in Russia's Backyard." *Brookings* (blog), January 2. https://www.brookings.edu/blog/order-from-chaos/2018/01/02/the-new-geopolitics-of-central-asia-china-vies-for-influence-in-russias-backyard/.
Dezan Shira & Associates. 2018. "Confusion over Dispute Resolution at China's New Belt and Road Courts." *China Briefing News*, February 2. http://www.china-briefing.com/news/2018/02/02/bilateral-confusion-dispute-resolution-chinas-new-belt-road-courts.html.
Economist Intelligence Unit. 2015. "Russia/China Politics: China and Russia: An Unequal Partnership." *Country Views Wire*, May 14.
Eder, Thomas Stephan. 2014. *China-Russia Relations in Central Asia*. Berlin: Springer Verlag.
Frolovskiy, Dmitriy. 2016. "Kazakhstan's China Choice." *The Diplomat* (blog), July 6. https://thediplomat.com/2016/07/kazakhstans-china-choice/.
Gabuev, Alexander. 2016. "Imagined Integration: How Russia Can Maintain Its Influence in Central Asia." *Carnegie Moscow Center* (blog), January 7. https://carnegie.ru/commentary/63993.
Garver, John W. 2006. "China's Influence in Central and South Asia: Is It Increasing?" In *Power Shift: China and Asia's New Dynamics*, edited by David Shambaugh, 205–225. Berkeley: University of California Press.
Godement, Francois, Agatha Kratz, David Cohen, and Raffaello Pantucci. 2015. *"One Belt, One Road": China's Great Leap Outward*. Edited by Justine Doody. http://www.ecfr.eu/page/-/China_analysis_belt_road.pdf.
Gusovsky, Dina. 2016. "Vladimir Putin Is Not 'Strong' When It Comes to Russia's Economy." *CNBC*, September 9. https://www.cnbc.com/2016/09/09/vladimir-putin-is-not-strong-when-it-comes-to-russias-economy.html.
Herd, Graeme P. 2015. "Living the 'Chinese Dream' in the 'Russkiy Mir': Central Asia between Sino-Russian Strategic Trilemmas?" In *Russia, Eurasia and the New Geopolitics*, edited by M. Sussex, 208–233. Basingstoke, UK: Palgrave Macmillan.
Hsu, Sara. 2017. "Trump's Support for China's One Belt, One Road Initiative Is Bad For U.S., Good For World." *Forbes*, May 18. https://www.forbes.com/sites/sarahsu/2017/05/18/trumps-support-for-chinas-one-belt-one-road-initiative-is-bad-for-u-s-good-for-world/.
International Labour Organization. 2018. "Unemployment, Youth Total (% of Total Labor Force Ages 15–24)." *The World Bank*. Accessed June 18, 2018. https://data.worldbank.org/indicator/SL.UEM.1524.ZS.

Jing, Shuiyu. 2017. "Belt and Road Initiative Exceeds Initial Expectations." *China Daily*, November 4. http://www.chinadaily.com.cn/bizchina/2017-04/11/content_28878446.htm.

Kennedy, Scott. 2015. "Made in China 2025." *Center for Strategic and International Studies*, June 1. https://www.csis.org/analysis/made-china-2025.

Kim, Younkyoo, and Fabio Indeo. 2013. "The New Great Game in Central Asia Post 2014: The US 'New Silk Road' Strategy and Sino-Russian Rivalry." *Communist and Post-Communist Studies* 46 (2): 275.

Korostikov, Mikhail. 2016. "Logistics, Mistrust Hinder Extension of Silk Road into Eurasia." *Russia Beyond the Headlines*, May 27. https://www.rbth.com/business/2016/05/27/logistics-mistrust-hinder-extension-of-silk-road-into-eurasia_597475.

Laurell, Marlene. 2014. "Russia and Central Asia." *European National Policies Series* 17: 1–5. http://www.eucentralasia.eu/uploads/tx_icticontent/National-PB17-RU.pdf.

Lemon, Edward James. 2018. "China, Russia and Security in Central Asia." *Rising Powers in Global Governance* (blog), February 26. http://risingpowersproject.com/china-russia-security-central-asia/.

Milhaupt, Curtis J., and Wentong Zheng. 2015. "Beyond Ownership: State Capitalism and the Chinese Firm." *Georgetown Law Journal* 103 (3): 665–722.

Ministry of Commerce of the People's Republic of China, and National Bureau of Statistics of the People's Republic of China. 2016. *2015 Statistical Bulletin of China's Outward Foreign Direct Investment*. Beijing: China Statistics Press.

National Development and Reform Commission, Ministry of Foreign Affairs, and Ministry of Commerce. 2015. "Vision and Actions on Jointly Building Silk Road Economic Belt and 21st-Century Maritime Silk Road." March. http://en.ndrc.gov.cn/newsrelease/201503/t20150330_669367.html.

Norris, William J. 2016. *Chinese Economic Statecraft: Commercial Actors, Grand Strategy, and State Control*. London: Cornell University Press.

Ooi, Su-Mei, and Katie Trinkle. 2015. "China's New Silk Road and Its Impact on Xinjiang." *The Diplomat* (blog), March 5. https://thediplomat.com/2015/03/chinas-new-silk-road-and-its-impact-on-xinjiang/.

"Our Bulldozers, Our Rules." July 2, 2016. https://www.economist.com/china/2016/07/02/our-bulldozers-our-rules.

Overland, Indra, and Roman Vakulchuk. 2018. "China's Belt and Road Gets a Central Asian Boost." *The Diplomat* (blog), May 3. https://thediplomat.com/2018/05/chinas-belt-and-road-gets-a-central-asian-boost/.

Palmer, Richard. 2016. "All Roads Lead to Beijing." *The Trumpet* (blog), October. https://www.thetrumpet.com/14180-all-roads-lead-to-beijing.

Perlez, Jane, and Yufan Huang. 2018. "Behind China's $1 Trillion Plan to Shake up the Economic Order." *The New York Times*, January 20, sec. Business Day. https://www.nytimes.com/2017/05/13/business/china-railway-one-belt-one-road-1-trillion-plan.html.

Prokopenko, Alexandra, and Margarita Papchenkova. 2016. "Experts Predict 'Lost Decade' for Russia's Stagnating Economy." August 19. http://themoscowtimes.com/articles/experts-proclaim-lost-decade-for-russias-stagnating-economy-55039.

"Quotes from Leaders at China's New Silk Road Meeting." *Fox Business*, May 14, 2017. https://www.foxbusiness.com/markets/quotes-from-leaders-at-chinas-new-silk-road-meeting.

Runde, Daniel. 2015. "Kazakhstan: The Buckle in One Belt One Road." *Forbes*, June 29. https://www.forbes.com/sites/danielrunde/2015/06/29/kazakhstan-buckle-one-belt-one-road/#b5634ae6b5bc.

Sands, Gary. 2017. "Using Economic Muscle, Beijing Sways Panama over Taiwan." *Foreign Policy Association* (blog), July 10. https://foreignpolicyblogs.com/2017/07/10/using-economic-muscle-beijing-sways-panama-over-taiwan/.

Santen, Emma van. 2018. "Combatting Organised Crime and Terrorism in Central Asia." *Journal of Financial Crime* 25 (2): 309–19.

Shen, Wenwen. 2012. "China and Its Neighbours: Troubled Relations." *Eu-Asia Centre*, March 1. http://www.eu-asiacentre.eu/pub_details.php?pub_id=46.

"Stans Undelivered: The Five Former Soviet Republics Struggle to Survive the New Great Game." *The Economist*, July 2, 2016. http://www.economist.com/news/asia/21701522-five-former-soviet-republics-struggle-survive-new-great-game-stans-undelivered?zid=306&ah=1b164dbd43b0cb27ba0d4c3b12a5e227.

Timmons, Heather, and Zheping Huang. 2016. "Charted: How China Turned the Global Steel Industry Upside Down in Just 15 Years." *Quartz* (blog), June 7. https://qz.com/699979/how-chinas-overproduction-of-steel-is-damaging-companies-and-countries-around-the-world/.

Vickers, Edward. 2009. "Selling 'Socialism with Chinese Characteristics' "Thought and Politics" and the Legitimisation of China's Developmental Strategy.'" *International Journal of Educational Development* 29 (5): 523.

Wembridge, Mark. 2018. "Australia Lashes out at China's 'Useless' Pacific Projects." *Financial Times*, January 10. https://www.ft.com/content/9bd0cb6a-f5a6-11e7-8715-e94187b3017e.

Wilson, William T. 2016. "China's Huge 'One Belt, One Road' Initiative Is Sweeping Central Asia." *The National Interest*, July. http://nationalinterest.org/feature/chinas-huge-one-belt-one-road-initiative-sweeping-central-17150.

Yan, Dongjie. 2016. "China and Russia to Promote One Belt, One Road." *China Daily Europe*, June 20. http://europe.chinadaily.com.cn/china/2016-06/20/content_25772641.htm.

Yu, Bin. 2006. "China and Russia: Normalizing Their Strategic Partnership." In *Power Shift: China and Asia's New Dynamics*, edited by David Shambaugh, 13–25. Berkeley: University of California Press.

Chapter 2

Sanctions Effectiveness in the China-South Korea THAAD Dispute

The Importance of Target State Considerations

James F. Paradise

Relations between South Korea and China were on a recovery track—at least temporarily—in 2018. Three summits were held between newly elected South Korean president Moon Jae-in and Chinese president Xi Jinping the prior year—two on the sidelines of international meetings in Berlin, Germany, in July where a G20 summit was held and in Danang, Vietnam, where an Asia-Pacific Economic Cooperation (APEC) summit meeting was held in November, and one in Beijing in December on a state visit to China by Moon. Exchanges between governmental entities were resuming after months of virtual suspension in 2016 and 2017. And punitive Chinese economic measures against South Korea were showing signs of being eased after South Korea-China relations had deteriorated to their lowest point since formal diplomatic relations between the two countries had been established in 1992.

Triggering the downslide was a decision by the United States and the Republic of Korea (ROK) in July 2016 to deploy an US antiballistic missile system to South Korea known as the Terminal High Altitude Area Defense System (THAAD). China saw the system as a threat to its security because of its powerful radar that could be used for spying on Chinese territory and the effect the system would have on increasing US power in Northeast Asia. For South Korea, however, the system was seen as bolstering its defense against North Korea, which had been carrying out many ballistic missile and nuclear weapons tests.

The issue ramped up when China engaged in an intense retaliatory campaign against South Korea whose purpose was to force a rethink on the

THAAD deployment decision. Actions included consumer boycotts of South Korean products sold in China, removal of South Korean dramas on Chinese television, non-approval of charter flights between the two countries during the busy Chinese New Year, bans on Chinese travel agencies selling group tours to South Korea, and postponement of an international sport event that was to be held north of Seoul. There were also various measures that affected China-bound South Korean exports in industries including food and cosmetics that looked like they went beyond ordinary customs clearance procedures and tax audits and safety checks of some South Korea companies in China that raised questions because of their unexpectedness and severity. Particularly hard hit was Lotte, which had supplied land in South Korea for the deployment of THAAD at the behest of the South Korean government. Other activities of a noneconomic sort included the entry of Chinese military aircraft into South Korea's air defense identification zone that stood out because of the presence of bombers and the large number of planes (Kim and Lee 2017), live fire-drills (Johnson 2017), and "an operational test for its new-type missile weapons in waters of the Bohai Sea" to "efficiently deal with national security threats" (China Military 2017).

Faced with the onslaught and having its own views of how relations should be conducted with China, the government of Moon Jae-in, who was elected president of South Korea on May 9, 2017, embarked on a new policy approach. In October, Foreign Minister Kang Kyung-wha enunciated before the South Korean parliament the "three no's"—South Korea would not enlarge the existing THAAD system, it would not join a US missile defense network and it would not participate in a military alliance with the United States and Japan (Jung Min-kyung 2017a). It also agreed with China in December on four principles for dealing with North Korea—war is not to be permitted, denuclearization is to be attained, the nuclear issue should be dealt with through dialogue and negotiations, and improvement in inter-Korean ties is helpful for addressing Korean Peninsula issues (Jun Min-kyung 2017b). These events happened after zigzagging developments during the first few months of the Moon administration, which included South Korean government participation in China's Belt and Road Summit in Beijing in May, a pledge by Moon that same month for South Korea to contribute more money to the China-led Asian Infrastructure Investment Bank, the decision by Moon in July to deploy four more THAAD launchers after North Korea conducted a Hwaseong missile test, heated exchanges between South Korean and Chinese academics in "1.5" forum talks and low-key ceremonies between South Korea and China to mark twenty-five years of diplomatic relations in August 2017, and the extension of a currency swap agreement between the two countries in October. As 2018 dawned, relations between Seoul and Beijing appeared on a recovery track—save for an apparent reinstitution of a ban on sales of South Korean tour packages in China after a partial lifting of it in November 2017—with Chinese consumers showing a new willingness to buy South Korean products. But the Chinese government was not too quick to put the THAAD issue behind it, and seemed determined to make further improvement contingent on "good behavior" by the South Korean government.

At one level, the THAAD dispute between China and South Korea can be seen as one among many foreign policy challenges Beijing has faced over the past several decades. At another level, it can be seen as a recent instance of coercive economic diplomacy which has become increasingly important in Beijing's foreign policy toolkit as its power has grown. In the second sense, many questions arise: What has Beijing being trying to accomplish by waging economic war against South Korea? Has it been successful in achieving its objectives? What factors contributed to the outcome of the sanctions episode? How does the episode fit into the broader experience of economic statecraft as practiced by many powerful countries?

This chapter attempts to answer these questions. Different than some analyses of Chinese statecraft, I focus much of my attention on the target state because doing so has often been neglected, both in the Chinese statecraft literature and the statecraft literature in general. Whether the findings of this chapter—which have to do with importance of national security, domestic politics and international alliances in promoting or inhibiting target state compliance with sender demands—can be generalized to other cases is a matter that has to be investigated. The only claim of this chapter is that China has not fully achieved its objective of getting South Korea to repudiate THAAD because of target state-related forces that have gone against it. Thus, this chapter has more of an inductive quality than deductive quality. It is more theory suggesting than theory testing.

To unravel these issues, I proceed in the following way: first, I consider a number of preliminary matters including whether the THAAD episode really is an instance of Chinese economic statecraft, how to measure the outcome of a statecraft episode, and how to characterize the dependent variable; secondly, I examine the literature on economic statecraft for insights on what makes statecraft effective and also for clues on how to proceed in my analysis; thirdly, I look at the specific factors operative in the China-South Korea THAAD case, which is interesting not only because of the issue with which it is bound up—North Korea nuclear weapons development—but because it is one of the most dramatic recent instances of Chinese power projection; finally, I wrap the piece up by summarizing the findings, making a few tentative generalizations and suggesting where further research is needed.

PRELIMINARY CONSIDERATIONS

An immediate issue concerns the fact the Chinese government does not say it is carrying out economic retaliatory measures against South Korea. This is important because if the retaliatory actions are not a specific policy of the Chinese state, the THAAD issue cannot be an instance of Chinese economic statecraft. One might think that the Chinese government is applying economic pressure on South Korea, but it is really the result of spontaneous and voluntary activities by entities within China or affiliated with it.

One reason for doubting this is that there are many things that have happened that appear to be out of the ordinary. Among the words used to describe Chinese actions in the South Korean English-language press are "unusual," unexpected," "unprecedented," "sudden," "abrupt," and sometimes occurring without explanation or following a normal pattern. Examples are the huge number of Lotte Group affiliates in China that have been subjected to inspections in a "sudden" and "simultaneous" way (Ye and Jin 2016; Park 2016), the absence of South Korean films on a preliminary screening list for the 7th Beijing International Film Festival in April 2017 after several had been invited (Yun 2017), and the cancellation of an invitation for South Korea's trade minister to attend China's Boao Forum for Asia. While none of this constitutes definitive proof of Chinese state involvement in economic retaliation, it does raise suspicions, especially when the Chinese government is linking the resolution of the THAAD dispute to an improvement in relations between Beijing and Seoul and the Chinese state media was whipping up anti-Korean sentiment by calling for a boycott of South Korean products and saying that "South Korea must pay the price for its arrogance" (*Global Times* 2017).

A second reason for thinking there may be Chinese state involvement in the THAAD episode—beside the fact that there are many government organizations that have engaged in behavior that has raised suspicions, such as the China National Tourism Administration,[1] which reportedly issued verbal instructions to travel agencies in China to stop selling tours to South Korea, the Civil Aviation Administration of China which did not approve requests by three South Korea airlines for more flights in January and February 2017; the State Administration of Press, Publication, Radio, Film and Television which is responsible for the regulation of television programs in China, including imported shows; and the General Administration of Quality Supervision, Inspection and Quarantine, which, among other things, deals with entry-exit commodity inspection matters—is that Chinese behavior fits into a pattern where the Beijing government has applied diplomatic pressure on countries whose actions have displeased it in an effort to foster change. Instances of this include China's economic pressure against the Philippines in a South China Sea dispute, the stoppage of Chinese rare earth mineral exports to Japan after a fishing trawler incident, suspension of Free Trade Agreement (FTA) negotiations with Norway and increased inspections of Norwegian salmon imports after the Nobel Peace Prize was awarded to Chinese dissident Liu Xiaobo, and various actions against countries that have entertained visits by the Dalai Lama. Common to many of the incidents is a policy statement or expression of unhappiness by the Chinese government but an unwillingness to acknowledge the means through which it aims to achieve its policy goals. This fits in with what James Reilly has said about China's punitive economic measures which is that "Unlike US sanctions, which are formalised through domestic law and/or presidential decisions, China rarely openly declares its economic sanctions" (Reilly 2013, 8). It also sheds lights on why South Korean media, such as Arirang TV or the *Korea Times*, refer to China's economic measures in the THAAD case as "unofficial sanctions."

Two reasons why the Chinese government may not be more forthcoming about its involvement in economic retaliation episodes are that it does not want to acquire a reputation as a bully and it does not want to open itself up to international legal challenges. The second reason may have been operative in the THAAD case because the South Korean government did raise the issue of Chinese economic retaliation in World Trade Organization (WTO) bodies and had been considering making a formal complaint.

A second issue concerns how to define a successful economic sanctions episode. In this chapter, I follow Hufbauer, Schott, Elliot, and Oegg (2009) in defining a successful sanctions episode in terms of whether the sender, or user of the sanctions, is able to achieve its policy goals and the goals are achieved because of the sanctions, both which are a matter degree and involve subjective evaluations. In regard to the first issue, analysis of the THAAD episode is facilitated by the clear statements by the Chinese government that THAAD should not be deployed in South Korea and now that equipment has been deployed it should be withdrawn. Other objectives are to prevent additional deployments and to prevent South Korea from tying up with the United States and Japan in a more formal military alliance. In regard to the second issue, one avenue of investigation is counterfactual analysis which in the THAAD case would involve asking, "If China had not retaliated economically as it did, would the Moon Jae-in government still have moved to strengthen relations with China and embrace a more dovish military policy?" There are reasons for thinking it might have because Moon is more favorably predisposed toward China than his predecessor Park Geun-hye and his views of how to deal with the North Korean threat are more in line with China than conservatives in South Korea with his emphasis on dialogue, negotiation, and peaceful resolution. Also relevant here is whether the "three no's" represented a deviation from policy positions the Moon government had previously supported because if they did not there is an indication that the economic sanctions employed by China were not of great importance on this particular matter. According to one account, Moon was already against additional THAAD deployments and staying out of a US-led missile system and had previously stated that "while South Korea and the US have a firm alliance, alliances with the US and Japan or with Japan alone are out of the question" (Lee 2017). Another analysis also doubts that South Korea made big concessions with the "three no's," in part because an alliance with the United States and Japan was "never on the cards" (*The Economist* 2017). On the other hand, there are reasons for thinking that China's economic retaliation did have an effect on normalizing relations between Seoul and Beijing for both economic and non-economic reasons. On the economic side, the sanctions had a well-publicized effect on the South Korean economy through loss of exports to China, fewer Chinese visitors to South Korea, stock market declines, and hardship for individual companies in sectors such as automobiles and retail operating on the Chinese mainland. Indicative that economic considerations were important to the Moon administration is a statement from a South Korean government official after the foreign ministries of South Korea and China agreed in October 2017 to normalize relations between the two countries that "for the Moon administration, it was urgent to make a breakthrough because of economic damage incurred by the THAAD row" (official, as quoted by Yi 2017b). On the noneconomic side as well, economic sanctions may have had effects by focusing attention on the THAAD issue and even stoking South Korean political opposition to THAAD deployment. As David Baldwin has astutely observed, "Economic sanctions may have diplomatic, psychological, military, or other effects even when their economic effect is nil. Ignoring this fact severely impairs one's ability to evaluate the costs and effectiveness of economic sanctions as instruments of foreign policy" (Baldwin 1985, 63). Further complicating the issue is that economic sanctions are often used in conjunction with other measures such as military activities or cutbacks in diplomatic cooperation. Saying how much a target states' behavior is the result of the sanctions component is not easy. This is a matter than can benefit from statistical analysis or a careful qualitative study. It need not be the case that the senders' objectives are achieved only because of the sanctions to qualify as a successful sanctions episode; what matters is simply that the sanctions played a modest or significant role in bringing about a positive outcome for the sender.

A third issue has to do with how to characterize the dependent variable of this analysis which is the extent to which China's economic retaliation constituted a successful sanctions episode. It is perhaps best to characterize it as partly successful because it did encourage the Moon administration to reach out to China in a way it might not have absent the economic sanctions and make it very wary about further deployments. But it could also be characterized as partly unsuccessful because the Moon administration did not remove the existing THAAD launchers (on the contrary it increased the number of launchers from two to six to complete a battery) and may already have agreed with China on some basic principles for dealing with Northeast Asian security issues. Examples of both characterizations can be found in media headlines such as "China Wins Its War Against South Korea's US THAAD Missile Shield—Without Firing A Shot" (Volodzko 2017), "Gov't Has Capitulated to Chinese Bullying" (*The Chosunilbo* 2017b), and "Gov't Must Stop Kowtowing to China" (*The Chosunilbo* 2017c) and, on the other side, "China Blinks on South Korea, Making Nice After a Year of Hostilities" (Perlez and Choe 2017), "Chinese Concessions on THAAD Speak to Fears of Losing Influence on Korean Peninsula" (Kim 2017c), and "SK Foreign Minister Refutes Suggestions That THAAD Operations Will Be Restricted" (Jung In-hwan 2017). Each of these headlines captures an element of the truth, which is that South Korea "agreed to accept military constraints in return for the lifting of . . . sanctions" (Volodzko 2017), the South Korean government made itself vulnerable to further pressure from Beijing by linking economics to politics and national security (Volodzko 2017), South Korea did not dismantle the THAAD system and China eased some of its economic pressure on Seoul. What is different about them is their emphasis, the issues they latch on to and the political lens through which they arise. The purpose of this chapter is to view the THAAD issue as neutrally as possible and to explain why Chinese economic retaliation was both partly successful and partly unsuccessful. In other words, I am explaining one reality but doing so in ways that focuses on both "a half-full glass and half-empty glass" in different parts of this chapter. How I will proceed is the subject of the next section.

APPROACHES TO THE STUDY OF THE PROBLEM

There are different ways to study coercive economic diplomacy. One prominent account from Hufbauer et al. distinguishes between political variables and economic variables that affect the costs of compliance and defiance. Political variables include "companion policies used by the sender country or coalition," "the extent of international cooperation in imposing sanctions," "the involvement of an international organization," "the presence of international assistance to the target country," "the warmth of prior relations," and the "type of target country government" (Hufbauer et al. 2009, 55). Economic variables include "the cost imposed on the target country," "commercial relations between sender and target countries," "the relative economic size of the countries," the economic and political condition of the target, "the type of sanctions used," and "the cost to the sender country" (Hufbauer et al.

2009, 55–56). These variables are important—or potentially so in individual cases—because Hufbauer and his co-authors state that "the political and economic costs to the target from the sanctions must be greater than the political and security costs of complying with the sender's demands" for a sanctions effort to be successful (Hufbauer 2009, 50). By requiring both the policy changes must have occurred in the target state so that the senders' goal was at least partly realized and that sanctions must have made a substantial or decisive contribution to the outcome, Hufbauer et al. have a fairly high standard for success, which nonetheless is met in 34 percent of the cases they examined, which was enough for them to declare that the view "sanctions never work" is not correct (Hufbauer et al. 2009). For them to work, however, policymakers in sender countries should set modest goals, target allies, and close trading partners rather than adversaries who are less likely to comply, be wary of autocratic regimes, impose sanctions to maximum effect, and avoid sanctions that "inflict concentrated costs on particular domestic groups" (Hufbauer et al. 2009, 177). One final point that Hufbauer and colleagues state is that sender countries may have different foreign policy goals (e.g., regime change, changing target country policies, or degrading military potential of adversaries), which gives their analysis a context-specific quality because of their focus on one objective—the most difficult one—for one target country.

Another important analysis from David Baldwin distinguishes between property concepts and relational concepts. Property concepts as used in international relations have to do with particular features of states that "can be defined and measured without reference to other countries" (Baldwin 1985, 22) and include things such as population, territory, policies, influence attempts, and techniques of statecraft while relational concepts "say something about an actual or potential relationship between two or more actors" (Baldwin 1985, 22) and include things such as war, power, influence, and results. The problem, according to Baldwin who couches his analysis in terms of economic statecraft which includes not only coercive measures but also positive inducements, is that studies often confuse the two kinds of concepts as, for example, when capabilities such as power bases are viewed as property concepts instead of relational concepts and the instruments of statecraft "are often "classified according to the kind of 'power base' being 'employed'—e.g., economic, military, propaganda, or diplomatic" (Baldwin 1985, 23). That is problematic for Baldwin because "economic techniques of statecraft may also be used to exercise noneconomic forms of power. Thus, economic sanctions may be effective not because of their economic impact, which may be nil, but rather because of the signal they send about the intentions of the state imposing the sanctions" (Baldwin 1985, 24). What this means is sanctions need not change the behavior of a state engaged in objectionable action to be effective because there may be many target states and many goals such as the expression of displeasure. A conclusion of Baldwin's analysis is that "the utility of economic techniques of statecraft has been systematically underestimated by most analysts since 1945" (Baldwin 1985, 4), one which he arrives at by conceptualizing the effectiveness of statecraft in broad terms.

A third way of thinking about coercive economic diplomacy is in terms of sender and target state considerations. Sender considerations include the relationship between a state and the entities that carry out the state's policies (which in some cases include government agencies), intergovernmental rivalries, and domestic market size while target state considerations include the party in power and the degree of citizen activism. This distinction is important in thinking about Chinese economic statecraft because much of the analysis of coercive diplomacy episodes other than THAAD have focused on sender considerations, which suggests that more attention needs to be given to target state factors. That will be the focus of the next sections of this chapter in relation to THAAD, which begin by reviewing major works on Chinese economic statecraft and sketching out a few ideas for thinking about target state factors in general. Doing these things will make clear that some sender state factors and some target state factors, to use the language of Baldwin, involve property concepts and others relational concepts.

Emphasis on the Sender State

One book that focuses on the sender state is *Chinese Economic Statecraft: Commercial Actors, Grand Strategy, and State Control* by William J. Norris. Using a principal-agent framework, Norris attempts to understand the conditions under which states are able to achieve their goals using economic statecraft, which he defines as "state manipulation of international activities for strategic purposes" (Norris 2016, 3). The conditions he mentions are "compatibility of goals between the state and the commercial actors that carry on the activity of the state" (Norris 2016, 7), neither too few nor too many commercial actors, the ability of the state to act in a unified way, the existence of commercial actors that are connected to the state through ownership or management, and "relative resource endowments between the principal and the agent" in favor of the former (Norris 2016). These conditions are tested and illuminated in individual case studies, including one on cross-strait relations in which China's efforts to influence Taiwan presidential elections through coercive measures against pro-independence Taiwanese businesspeople in mainland China were found to have failed because of different goals between them—the commercial actors—and the Chinese state and the inability of the state to act in a uniform way because of different views between the central and local governments about punishing the Taiwanese businesspeople, and another case in which the Chinese government's efforts to get the State Administration of Foreign Exchange to buy Costa Rican bonds at below-market prices as part of a drive to win Costa Rica's diplomatic recognition were found to have succeeded because of new competition in the Chinese sovereign wealth fund industry and agreement among Chinese state actors on matters of strategic purpose. Another book that highlights sender state considerations is *China's Economic Statecraft: Co-Optation, Cooperation and Coercion*, edited by Mingjiang Li. Four of its main conclusions are that China lacks a highly thought out approach to economic statecraft; limitations to the effectiveness of China's economic statecraft are rooted in problems of strategic design, coherence, inter-agency coordination and export dependence; China tends to use to positive economic statecraft more than negative economic statecraft; and coercive diplomacy is becoming a more important instrument in China's foreign policy toolkit. These points are borne out in the chapters by individual authors such as Reuben Wong's piece on China's human rights disputes with the European Union which finds that "since the late-1990s, China has changed its strategic doctrine, and begun to use economic diplomacy as a coercive tool" (Li 2017a, xx), Xue Gong's piece on China and Vietnam which notes that China has preferred economic incentives to economic coercion on thorny South China Sea disputes, and Xiahe Cheng's piece on China and North Korea which states that Beijing has switched to a more economically hardline policy toward Pyongyang because of its nuclear provocations, while at the same time offering economic carrots. Another book that discusses sender state considerations is *War by Other Means: Geoeconomics and Statecraft* by Robert D. Blackwill and Jennifer M. Harris. More about the decline of economic power in US foreign policy than its use in other countries, the book has much to say about China which is described as "the world's leading practitioner of geoeconomics," or "the systematic use of economic instruments to accomplish geopolitical objectives" (Blackwill and Harris 2016, 93, 1). Noting that "Beijing has been playing the new economic game at the maestro level, staying out of wars and geopolitical confrontations and zeroing in on business" and that "nations do not fear China's military might; they fear its ability to give or withhold trade and investments" (Gelb, as quoted by Blackwell and Harris 2016, 93), the authors argue that China's economic statecraft has often been successful because of its "geoeconomic endowments" such as its large domestic market and the ability to control access to it, a large amount of domestic capital and mechanisms for investing it in foreign countries, and an important, and growing role, in the global financial system. They also note that China has been a good learner, making adjustments when necessary or seeking to understand problems when they have occurred as with a milkfish buying episode in Taiwan involving a mainland Chinese company that did not produce sought after political benefits. A fourth book that touches on sender state considerations is *China's Economic Diplomacy: The PRC's Growing International Influence in the 21st Century* by Zhang Xiaotong, Wang Hongyu, and many other authors. Two of its chapters deal with China's economic diplomacy in different policy areas such as international finance, energy cooperation, environmental protection, and foreign aid and its activities in international organizations. Another is forward looking, highlighting obstacles that China faces as it seeks to up its diplomatic game, such as a lack of grand strategy, inadequate cooperation between government agencies, and a shortage of economic diplomacy experts. The chapter also highlights emerging challenges for China, including advancement of the Belt and Road Initiative, realization of new free trade initiatives, and increasing participation in global economic governance.

Each of these books has strengths. Norris's work identifies the important role that commercial actors play in carrying out government policy and illuminates the conditions under which states may not be able to control them to achieve strategic objectives. Li and Hong's edited volume latches on to the idea that China's economic statecraft may be changing in such a way that the Chinese state is more willing to use economic coercion to pursue foreign policy goals. Blackwill and Harris's book rightly states the important role that economic statecraft has for China and specifies the conditions under which it is likely to be effective, which include not only structural factors but also "deliberate policy calculations by Chinese leaders" (Blackwill and Harris 2016, 134). The Zhang and Wang multiauthor volume provides a lot of useful factual information on matters such as the actors of China's economic diplomacy, which include government bodies—including the State Council, the Ministry of Commerce, the Ministry of Finance, the People's Bank of China, and the National Development and Reform Commission—local governments, industrial associations, research institutions, and the media; the way in which China has conducted economic diplomacy in international organizations such as the WTO, the International Monetary Fund, and the World Bank; and China's economic diplomacy toward different geographical areas, such as Central Asia where energy issues loom large.

The books also have weaknesses. One of the shortcomings of the Norris book is that it does not talk about conditions in the target state, such as its politics, or the target state's relations with third world countries, which in the case of the THAAD issue between China and South Korea are highly significant. It is possible that even if all the conditions that Norris mentions for the effective practice of economic statecraft having to do with state control of commercial actors are fulfilled, state goals are not met. Another problem with Norris's work is its discussion of commercial actors being focused exclusively on firms, which are no doubt major players in carrying out, or potentially carrying out, government policy, but are not the only ones. As we will see, consumers matter as well, which Norris might agree with because he lists the "buying and selling of commodities" as an example of international economic transactions that commercial actors carry out, but he does not talk about them, which is problematic because they figure prominently in the THAAD story. Similar problems exist in the Blackwill and Harris book whose conditions for the successful practice of geoeconomics have little or nothing to do with the domestic and international politics of the target state. Never mind the possibility that the book's main argument that the United States has neglected the art of geoeconomics is overstated; the problem is that the book's analytical framework is focused on conditions in the country practicing statecraft and not the target state, which generally plays a lesser explanatory role in the rich case studies the book contains. Lacking in the Zhang, Wang, et al. book is the existence of an analytical framework at all, unless one considers comments about the "unique" features of China's economic diplomacy such as possession of abundant strategic and political resources as constituting a framework. Common to many of the books is too little attention to identifying the conditions of when positive and negative statecraft are used or how countries decide the mix of diplomatic, economic, and military measures to achieve strategic objectives. Chapters in the Li and Hong edited volume do attempt to do this, including the one by Cheng which notes that Beijing's addition of punitive economic measures on Pyongyang came after North Korea's third nuclear test and a chapter by Roman Muzalevsky that predicts that China's expansion in Central Asia will take on a greater military character.

None of this is to say that conditions in the sender state are unimportant for understanding the outcome of economic statecraft episodes. Matters such as state-society relations, coordination between government agencies, and ownership of the media may have a bearing of whether a state is able to achieve its foreign policy objectives. At the same time, it is important to consider the circumstances of the target state for understanding why statecraft episodes end up as they do. This is very important for China because much of the literature on Chinese economic statecraft has focused largely on China. This is understandable, but it still leaves an incomplete picture of China's increasingly prominent coercive economic diplomacy which needs to be rectified.

Bringing the Target State In

Some of the variables mentioned by Hufbauer et al. have to do with the target state such as the "political character of the target country's government" and the "economic health and political stability of the target" (Hufbauer et al. 2009, 55–56). And the main focus of the analysis is the degree to which the target state complies with the demands of the sender. Yet the analysis they provide does not always dig deeply into target state considerations (this is because the case studies on which their judgments are made have been done by others), and it may be that they have not captured all the target state variables of importance. There are also problems with Baldwin's analysis which looks at statecraft episodes more from a sender state perspective, omitting information that may be important for judging an economic sanctions episode.

Two people that do put focus on the target state are Jean-Marc F. Blanchard and Norrin M. Ripsman. In a 1999 paper, they argue that economic sanctions are likely to be most effective when there are high political costs to the target state for not doing what the sender demands. Factors that affect costs include compound sanctions, including political and military action; domestic factors, including political stability and the presence of a strong political opposition before the imposition of sanctions; the international threat environment for the target state; and economic, political, and diplomatic assistance from third parties (Blanchard and Ripsman 1999). In a 2008 article that develops their ideas further, Blanchard and Ripsman focus on the idea of "stateness" in a discussion of when economic statecraft succeeds. Among its components are "(1) *autonomy*, or a state's ability to take decisions in the face of domestic political opposition; (2) *capacity*, or the state's capability either to compensate or coerce those who stand to lose from defying the sender; and (3) *legitimacy*, or the ability of the state to rally disaffected domestic groups" (Blanchard and Ripsman 2008, 372). In spelling out their argument, the authors write: "When economic statecraft co-opts domestic interest groups, high stateness will interfere with an economic statecraft attempt by allowing leaders to ignore pressures to comply. Conversely, when economic statecraft resonates with the target government, rather than domestic interest groups, stateness can actually foster compliance by allowing the leadership to overcome domestic resistance to compliance" (Blanchard and Ripsman 2008, 372).

From these analyses, there are several insights that we can glean. The first insight is that target state considerations include both domestic and international factors. Second is that economic pressure may not be effective unless it translates into political costs for the target state for noncompliance and even then it may not be successful because of "confounding factors" such as decision-making autonomy. Third is that economic sanctions may work best when combined with other types of action, such as diplomatic pressure.

What, then, are the considerations that matter in the China-South Korea THAAD case? Based on a study of evolving developments, the ones that are salient are the nature of the issue, the domestic politics of South Korea, and the military alliance between Seoul and Washington. By "nature of the issue," I mean whether the THAAD deployment arises out of national security concerns or something of lesser significance. One would expect that if THAAD is related to national security, South Korea would have a harder time giving in to economic pressure from China. As Hufbauer et al. have written, "Sender demands that threaten national security or internal regime stability are obviously ambitious; in many cases, it is simply impossible to make sanctions costly enough to gain the target's acquiescence" (Hufbauer et al. 2009, 52). By "the domestic politics of South Korea," I am referring to things such as the political party in power, the strength of the political opposition and the degree of citizen—and business—activism on the THAAD issue. One might expect if the party in power is more dovish in its foreign policy toward North Korea, it would be less supportive of THAAD and more supportive of policies that avoiding antagonizing China, which has an important role to play in resolving or ameliorating the North Korean nuclear issue. One might also expect that an activist citizenry would play a role in determining whether THAAD is dismantled, kept at the present level or increased. By "alliance considerations," I am referring to the US-ROK alliance which dates backs to the early 1950s when the United States and other countries constituting United Nations forces came to the defense of South Korea after North Korea launched an invasion of its southern neighbor. Here, one would expect that the alliance, "forged in blood," would limit Seoul's decision-making autonomy and make it more partisan to its alliance partner, making it more difficult to comply with Beijing's demands.

I turn now to an examination of each of these factors. As we will see, all of them play important roles in the China-South Korea THAAD dispute, but they do not play out exactly as one would expect.

EMPIRICAL ANALYSIS

One point to make at the beginning is that the THAAD dispute is not simply an issue between China and South Korea; it also involves third parties, including North Korea, whose actions are the reason for the THAAD deployment, the United States, which is the one doing the deploying and even Japan and Russia, which are important parts of the Northeast Asia security equation and to stretch things a bit more the international community which is weighing in on Korean Peninsula issues through the United Nations Security Council (which has passed resolutions against North Korea's nuclear and missile tests) and the International Olympic Committee which signed off on North Korea's participation in the 2018 Pyeongchang Winter Olympics. This makes the issue different than some other foreign affairs episodes of China such as a cooling of relations between London and Beijing after UK Prime Minister David Cameron met with the Dalai Lama in 2012 or the cessation of rare earth material exports to Japan after the captain of a Chinese fishing vessel was detained because of activities in waters around islands claimed by Tokyo. It also means that South Korea's actions have to be embedded in a larger framework along the lines suggested by Blanchard and Ripsman where to have a full explanation of the dynamics of economic statecraft one "must not only consider the internal dynamics of the target state, but also international political variables that can alter the political costs facing the regime" (Blanchard and Ripsman 2008, 393). The argument of this chapter is not that the target state is the only thing that matters, or that the target state should be viewed in purely domestic terms; it is that the kinds of variables mentioned in the Chinese economic statecraft literature such as state control of economic agents do not seem to best illuminate the China-South Korea THAAD episode. What matters more is the nature of the issue, the domestic politics of South Korea, and the military alliance between Seoul and Washington. Articulating them, explaining how they are connected and identifying whether they are forces for compliance or noncompliance with Chinese demands is critical.

Nature of the Issue

The THAAD issue for South Korea is very much about national security. Indications of this come from Korean and non-Korean sources, such as South Korea's president Moon Jae-in who has said on different occasions that the deployment of THAAD was "inevitable" because of North Korean behavior (The Chosunilbo 2017d), the US Department of Defense, which said that the deployment of THAAD to South Korea was "a defensive measure to ensure the security of the ROK and its people, and to protect alliance military forces from North Korea's weapons of mass destruction and ballistic missile threats" (Department of Defense 2016), and Vincent K. Brooks, then Combined Forces Command, US Forces Korea commander, who said "North Korea's continued development of ballistic missiles and weapons of mass destruction require the Alliance to take this prudent, protective measure to bolster our layered and effective missile defense" (United States Forces Korea 2016). Private analysts have also chimed in, including Bruce Klingner who noted that "enough unclassified evidence is available to conclude that the [North Korean] regime has likely achieved warhead miniaturization—the ability to place nuclear weapons on its No Dong-medium range ballistic missiles—and can threaten Japan and South Korea with nuclear weapons" (Klingner 2015) and Bruce W. Bennett, who has stated that THAAD—deployed in Seongju—can "attempt to protect the large South Korea urban areas of Pusan, Kwangju, Pohang, and Daegu, as well as many other cities in the southern part of South Korea" (Bennett 2017).

How militarily effective THAAD will be in protecting South Korea is a topic of frequent analysis. One analysis states that THAAD is attractive because it can be repositioned, it has a longer range than some other ballistic missile defense systems, it can "intercept a wider range of threats," and it "can also be used against weapons of mass destruction, i.e., chemical, nuclear and biological warheads" (Institute for Security & Development Policy 2017). On the other hand, there are weaknesses of THAAD, such as challenges in dealing with missiles that do not have regular or stable trajectories and distinguishing between real warheads and decoys (Institute for Security & Development Policy 2017). Klingner notes that THAAD can be part of a "multilayered defensive shield for South Korea" (Klingner 2015) along with the Patriot missile system, which is currently deployed in South Korea. Part of the assessment has to do with the THAAD system itself and part with how many THAAD systems are deployed in South Korea. With one system deployed as of February 2018, "it could be theoretically possible for a North Korean submarine to travel beyond and fire outside of [the radar having a 120-degree] field of view" (Institute for Security & Development Policy 2017, 3).

One can also ask what impact THAAD will have on South Korea's national security if "national security" is defined in terms that include an economic component. As numerous reports have revealed, China's economic retaliation against THAAD has damaged South Korea's economy, with some industries being particularly hard hit such as automobiles, whose major manufacturers Hyundai and Kia suffered big sales declines in China during the height of the pressure, retail, which saw moves by Emart and Lotte Mart to withdraw from China, which may also have been the result of intense Chinese competition, tourism, which was hit by a big decline in Chinese travelers to South Korea, and related industries, including airlines. One report said 0.4 percentage point would be shaved off South Korea's expected economic growth in 2017 (Lee and Kim 2017), another that South Korea's overall services deficit more than doubled in the first half of 2017 to US$15.74 billion on a provisional basis, in large part because of the Chinese government's prohibition on sales of group tours to South Korea (Kim 2017a), and another that South Korean businesses had lost more than $10 billion in China because of the THAAD dispute (*The Chosunilbo* 2017b). These considerations shaped the discourse in South Korea, acting as a force for adjusting policies to satisfy China, unlike the military considerations, which were more a force for non-adjustment.

Interpretations differ on whether the "three no's" constitute a violation of South Korean sovereignty. One view is that in accepting constraints on further THAAD deployments and other military activities, South Korea is allowing China to decide its defense policy in a significant way. Another is that the "three no's" "should be seen not as an act of kowtowing to China but confirmation of Korea's basic principles of diplomacy" (*The Korea Times* 2017). It is probably the case that both views are correct—Seoul is allowing outside interference on a sensitive military matter but the Moon government is doing something that it might have done anyhow. Interestingly, when the Moon government decided to deploy additional THAAD launchers following North Korea's launch of an Inter-Continental Ballistic Missile, it came under domestic criticism for "flip flopping" on THAAD and also criticism from China, which does not support the idea that it is weak on national security and willing to outsource its defense policy to Beijing.

From these considerations, we cannot conclude that economics trumps defense on the national security front. Economics is an important consideration in the THAAD case for South Korea, but so too is the North Korean threat. What is perhaps a bit surprising is that the Moon government would tie its hands at all on the military side by agreeing with China (though not promising as Seoul has said) not to increase its THAAD deployments when some are saying that it should do so to enhance its security. To understand why it has done so, one needs to examine developments in South Korean politics. Doing so will also shed light on why South Korea increased the deployment of THAAD launchers prior to issuing the "three no's."

The South Korean Political Scene

The most important development in South Korea affecting the THAAD issue in 2017 when China began to ease sanctions was the transition from conservative to liberal rule. This happened on May 10 when Moon Jae-in became the 19th president of South Korea with around 41 percent of the popular vote. Moon had run on a platform of strengthening relations with major allies and countries in Asia, improving relations with North Korea and reviewing the THAAD decision of Park which had resulted in the deployment of two THAAD launchers shortly before the South Korean presidential election. In each of these areas, Moon took action in the early months of his administration; he sent special envoys to China, Japan, the United States, and Russia; he traveled to Washington to meet US president Donald Trump and invited him to South Korea, he met Xi Jinping, Vladimir Putin, and Shinzo Abe; he offered aid to North Korea, encouraged it to participate in the 2018 Pyeongchang Winter Olympics (which it did), and pressed for talks between Seoul and Pyongyang; and he ordered a full environmental assessment of THAAD launchers deployed in Seongju. Efforts to normalize relations with China were welcomed by Beijing, which began to ease economic sanctions in late 2017. In Washington, there was less joy because of fears that Moon's "balanced diplomacy" was starting to tilt in favor of Xi Jinping.

Moon, however, was not acting in a domestic political vacuum as he had to contend with opposition political parties, a vibrant media, public opinion, and business displeasure which had arisen from the damage that was being done to corporate profits and stock prices. One poll of early August 2017 found that 72 percent of South Korean respondents supported the temporary deployment of four additional THAAD launchers (Kim 2017b). This was understandable given that North Korea had tested many ballistic missiles after Moon had come to power, even after he had offered an olive branch to Pyongyang. It was also significant in that Moon has made public deliberation of important issues a hallmark of his government. This was seen on many issues including the future of nuclear power, renegotiation of a FTA between South Korea and the United States, and the THAAD issue where Moon had said in the early days of his government he would seek parliamentary ratification for the deployment of launchers. Moon was also facing criticism by conservatives, who said that Seoul was giving up too much control of its defense policy, liberals, who believed that Moon was betraying them by allowing the deployment of more THAAD launchers, which was completed in September, and others of unidentified political affiliation who stated that the Moon government was "being pushed around and losing the initiative" in the THAAD dispute (analysts, as quoted by Yi 2017a). In January 2018, the approval rating for Moon, who had bent over backward to accommodate North Korea in the Pyeongchang Winter Olympics, which some were calling the "Pyongyang Olympics," fell to 59.8 percent (Kim 2018b), a highly respectable figure but way down from the 80 percent range of Moon's early days in office. As the *New York Times* reported, some people thought that Moon had gone too far in courting North Korea, with many of the skeptics being of younger age (Choe 2018).

One interpretation of Moon's actions—both to deploy and not to deploy—is that political costs were mounting, both because of Moon's "about-face" and "heartbreaking reversal" on THAAD deployment which alienated his political base and also residents of Seongju who engaged in fierce clashes with police and soldiers when additional launchers were being deployed, and also economic pressure from China which contributed to Moon cutting a deal with Beijing to normalize relations. There is truth to this interpretation as Moon was feeling the political heat as he sought to accommodate citizen opinion and that of other relevant actors in an extremely difficult decision-making process. Yet one should not take this interpretation too far because Moon was only allowed a single five-year term under South Korea's constitution, which meant that he did not have to think about reelection unless the constitution was changed to allow a longer term in office, which Moon sought along with other matters. What he did have to think about, however, was the continuation of his party in power, the Democratic Party of Korea. Another consideration is that much of the discontent in the THAAD dispute was directed at China, which was the one tightening the screws on South Korea and doing damage to its economy. Some of this discontent found expression in a resolution adopted by South Korea's parliament before Moon became president, which expressed "concern and regret over the suspension of South Korean businesses in China and the apparent ban on Chinese tour packages to South Korea," according to a characterization of it (Yonhap 2017), and urged China "to protect South Korean nationals in the country and actively participate in international efforts to halt North Korea's nuclear and missile development" (Yonhap 2017). In the business community, companies were "losing patience" in the middle of 2017 but were divided over how to respond to Chinese economic retaliation, with some companies favoring a low-key approach because of the possibility of more retaliation and others favoring a more pro-active approach (Jin 2017; Kwack 2017). Another thing that was happening was that South Korea was seeking to reduce its economic dependence on China, which was its largest foreign market, accounting for 24.7 percent of its exports in the January to September period of 2016 (Kim 2016). Ideas being bandied about or acted upon were increasing trade with Southeast Asian countries and expanding flights to Japan. One of the reasons these developments are important is that they fit in with what Hufbauer and his colleagues have said which is that sanctions sometimes fail because they "unify the target country both in support of its government and in search of commercial alternatives" (Hufbauer et al. 2009, 8).

A different interpretation of Moon's behavior puts emphasis on Moon himself. A human rights lawyer who worked in the liberal Roh Moo-hyun government of the 2000s, Moon has a very strong vision of how domestic decision-making should be made, where South Korea should be going and how inter-Korean foreign affairs should be conducted. At the same time, he is very pragmatic, responding to the North Korean threat and responding to the country that has shaped his response to the North Korean threat on THAAD—the United States.

The US-ROK Alliance

The alliance between the United States and South Korea is a constraint on Moon. As much as Moon would presumably like to have policy autonomy, he is under intense pressure from Washington to follow US preferences on THAAD. This makes it more difficult for South Korea to do what China wants on THAAD, which is that the system ultimately be withdrawn. Complicating the situation are internal strains in the alliance, North Korea diplomacy, and pressure from Beijing, all of which put Moon between "a rock and a hard place."

On many occasions, the United States and South Korea have tried to present a picture of alliance unity. In a joint statement between the presidents of the two countries after Moon had visited the White House in June 2017, the two leaders were said to have "heralded the exemplary nature of the U.S.-ROK alliance, from strengthening our security by deterring and defending against the North Korea threat, to enhancing strong regional relations, to advancing our economic relationship and expanding our global partnership, and stated their expectation that the friendship and partnership between the two countries will continue to strengthen and grow for many decades to come" ([Full Text] 2017). On the US side, Donald Trump has expressed support for inter-Korean dialogue on more than one occasion, including during Moon's US visit and in January 2018 when expectations that it might happen were increasing, and the US State Department indicated in November 2017 that it was "pleased" that relations between Seoul and Beijing were starting to improve (Kim 2017d). On the South Korean side, Moon stated in an interview during his trip in Washington in June 2017—when the South Korean press published articles with titles such as "Ironclad Alliance"—that doing an environmental study did not mean that South Korea would "cancel or reverse the decision to deploy" THAAD (Weymouth 2017), and in January 2018 even went so far as to give Trump "huge credit" for bringing about talks between South and North Korea on Olympics-related issues (Fifield 2018).

Beneath the surface, however, and sometimes above the surface when disputes became public, were tensions in the alliance. Some of them were initiated by Trump, who raised the possibility of ending US participation in the US-South Korea FTA (later Seoul and Washington entered into difficult negotiations on its revision) and also said he wanted South Korea to pick up the tab for the THAAD deployment. South Korea added to the tensions, notably when an adviser to President Moon famously suggested to reporters after a speech in Washington not long after Moon had assumed office that if there could not be debate on the THAAD issue the alliance was not worthy of the name (*The Chosunilbo* 2017a) and when it brought a case for defensive reasons against the United States at the WTO after the Trump administration decided to take safeguard measures against imports of large washing machines and solar cells and modules, which South Korean companies manufactured. This created an interesting situation where South Korea was "suing" its alliance partner who offered it defense protection but not challenging China, which was retaliating against it on the THAAD issue, the simple explanation being that it thought it could win its case against the United States if it could not be resolved through consultations whereas the Chinese case would be difficult to prove.

Pressure on the alliance was also coming from non-alliance members, namely, North Korea, whose Olympics-related diplomacy was widely interpreted to be trying to drive a wedge between Washington and Seoul, and Beijing, whose unfriendly diplomacy was followed by something different after Moon became president and especially after the party congress in October

2017 when Xi was given a second term as General Secretary of the Communist Party of China. As Chinese responses evolved, Seoul had to carefully calculate the costs and benefits of going along with Washington's hardline position on South Korean defense matters. Among the benefits to consider were those that might come from South Korean participation in China's Belt and Road Initiative, expansion of the China-South Korea FTA to services and investment, and technological cooperation.

All of this has implications for the THAAD issue. With the alliance under strain, it means that Washington may have less leverage overall. Already, there are indications of this—at the start of the Moon administration, further deployments of THAAD launchers were put on hold pending the result of the full environmental study and Washington has not been able to prevent South Korea, which in a somewhat schizophrenic way wants to assume more control over its own defense under Moon, from becoming closer to Beijing.

In the end, however, the alliance, which some people are saying needs to be updated, is still extremely important. As a former South Korea foreign minister has said:

> Those who predict that a Moon presidency will disrupt South Korean relations with the US and Japan are surely mistaken. After all, it was during the liberal Roh presidency that South Korea concluded the South Korea-US Free Trade Agreement, allowed for US troops to be redeployed within its borders, and dispatched its own troops to fight alongside the US in Iraq. Moon will affirm that legacy and attempt to revive another, an updated and renewed version of the Sunshine Policy, which embodies South Korea's most fundamental long-term aspiration. (Yoon 2017)

Evidence that this is happening is a summit meeting between Moon and North Korean leader Kim Jong-un on April 27, 2018 which resulted in the Panmunjeom Declaration whose objectives include "declaring an end to the [Korean] War, turning the armistice into a peace treaty, and establishing a permanent and solid peace regime" in meetings between the two Koreas and the United States or the two Koreas, the United States and China, and denuclearizing the Korean Peninsula (Panmunjeom Declaration 2018). Against the view of one of his advisers that if a peace treaty were to be concluded there would be no need for US forces to remain in South Korea, President Moon stated through a spokesperson that "U.S troops stationed in South Korea are an issue regarding the alliance between South Korea and the United States" and "has nothing to do with signing peace treaties" (Cited by Kim 2018a).

Ultimately, the fate of THAAD in South Korea is likely to be determined less by China's unofficial sanctions and more by the resolution of the North Korea nuclear problem over which a multiplicity of factors, including the determination of President Moon to pursue a path of peace in inter-Korean affairs, the bite of international sanctions against North Korea, Donald Trump's threats of force against Pyongyang, and great power relations, is affected. As an indication that just such a thing could happen, a report ahead of the summit meeting between Trump and Kim Jong-un in Singapore in June 2018 said that the "U.S. and China are discussing a possible withdrawal of a U.S. missile defense system from South Korea as part of a grand bargain over North Korea's nuclear program" (Na and Yi 2018).

CONCLUSION

This chapter aims to explain why the THAAD episode between China and South Korea has evolved as it has with both sides backing off of undiluted self-centered policies and traveling some distance to meet the concerns of each other, China by easing economic pressure on South Korean companies and industries such as tourism and South Korea by providing military- and geopolitical-related assurances to Beijing which some believe infringe Seoul's decision-making authority and others believe were in line with Moon's thinking anyhow, though seemingly a deviation from the preferences of Moon's predecessor Park Geun-hye.[2] What has been learned is that the national security nature of the issue for South Korea stemming from North Korea's ballistic missile and nuclear tests and Seoul's roughly seventy-year alliance with Washington have made it difficult for South Korea to forego THAAD deployment, even though Moon favors more of an engagement approach toward Pyongyang and better relations with Beijing, for both of which he has moved toward. Put together, these factors provide an explanation of the outcome of the THAAD dispute—still ongoing—in which China's economic coercion against South Korea has been partly successful in influencing policy evolution in Seoul but partly unsuccessful in triggering any major changes.

The claim of this chapter is not that the target state is the only thing that matters. It may be that the considerations that apply to the target state also apply to the sender state such as the nature of the issue and domestic politics. Reasons for thinking this is that Xi Jinping also regards the THAAD dispute as one affecting core interests and he may need to continue enunciating a hardline stance to quell any doubts about his leadership. Other considerations may be more specific to China such as the need to avoid reputational damage from appearing as a bully, which might embolden conservative forces in South Korea, and a realization that cooperation with Seoul Korea is critical in resolving the North Korean nuclear issue.

Whether the ideas generated from the analysis of the THAAD case—that national security considerations make it more difficult, though not impossible, for the target to comply with the sender's demands, that economic sanctions are especially effective when they entail high political costs, and that military alliances between target states and third parties can be an obstacle to resolving sanctions disputes, especially when the third party plays an important role in providing for its alliance partner's defense—apply to other cases, either ones in which China is involved or other countries are entangled is a matter of investigation. As a first step, we can simply make the general observation that for a sanctions episode to be "successful," things not only have to line up in the sender in a way in which agents go along with principal objectives, but also have to line up in the target in a way that domestic and international considerations are compliance promoting.

NOTES

1. This organization was merged into the newly created Ministry of Culture and Tourism inaugurated in April 2018.

2. According to a source at the Seoul-based Institute for National Security Strategy, quoted by *Hankyoreh*, "During the Lee Myung-bak and Park Geun-hye administrations, there was a movement toward a military alliance between South Korea, the U.S. and Japan, both domestically and overseas" (Jung, Seong, and Kim 2017). Such a situation is as odds with the Moon administration's commitment not to develop a trilateral military alliance, which was one of the "three no's" enunciated by Kang Kyung-wha.

BIBLIOGRAPHY

Baldwin, David A. 1985. *Economic Statecraft*. Princeton, NJ: Princeton University Press.

Bennett, Bruce W. 2017. "Why THAAD Is Needed in Korea." *The Korea Times*, August 8. http://www.koreatimes.co.kr/www/opinion/2017/08/197_234268.html.

Blackwill, Robert D., and Jennifer M. Harris. 2016. *War by Other Means: Geoeconomics and Statecraft*. Cambridge, MA: The Belknap Press of Harvard University Press.

Blanchard, Jean-Marc F., and Norrin M. Ripsman. 1999. "Asking the Right Question: When Do Economic Sanctions Work Best?" *Security Studies* 9 (1–2): 219–53.

———. 2008. "A Political Theory of Economic Statecraft." *Foreign Policy Analysis* 4: 371–98.

China Military. 2017. "PLA Rocket Force Test-Fires New-Type Missile Weapons." *Ministry of National Defense of the People's Republic of China*, May 9.

Choe, Sang-hun. 2018. "Olympic Dreams of a United Korea? Many in South Korea Say, 'No, Thanks.'" *The New York Times*, January 28. https://www.nytimes.com/2018/01/28/world/asia/koreas-olympics-reunification.html.

Department of Defense. 2016. "Republic of Korea and the United States Make Alliance Decision to Deploy THAAD to Korea." Release No: NR-254-16, July 7.

Fifield, Anna. 2018. "South Korean President Credits Trump with Bringing North Korea to the Table." *The Washington Post*, January 10. https://www.washingtonpost.com/world/asia_pacific/south-korean-president-credits-trump-with-bringing-north-korea-to-the-table/2018/01/10/ae0ee266-f606-11e7-91af-31ac729add94_story.html?utm_term=.7c3905acefb8.

Global Times. 2017. "THAAD Puts S. Korea's Prosperity at Stake." April 26. http://www.globaltimes.cn/content/1044328.shtml.

Hufbauer, Gary Clyde, Jeffrey J. Schott, Kimberly Ann Elliott, and Barbara Oegg. 2009. *Economic Sanctions Reconsidered*, 3rd Edition. Washington, DC: Peterson Institute for International Economics.

Institute for Security & Development Policy. 2017. "THAAD on the Korean Peninsula." October 2017. http://isdp.eu/publication/korea-thaad/.

Jin, Eun-soo. 2017. "Firms Losing Patience on THAAD." *Korea Joongang Daily*, July 8. http://koreajoongangdaily.joins.com/news/article/article.aspx?aid=3035588.

Johnson, Jesse. 2017. "China Conducts Live-fire Drills, Weapons Tests in Waters Near Two Koreas." *The Japan Times*, May 9. https://www.japantimes.co.jp/news/2017/05/09/asia-pacific/china-conducts-live-fire-drills-weapons-tests-waters-near-two-koreas/#.WzhCF3mmrIU.

Jun, Ji-hye. 2017. "Chinese Fighters Keep Violating Air Defense Zone." *The Korea Times*, January 10. https://www.koreatimes.co.kr/www/nation/2018/03/113_221784.html.

Jung, In-hwan. 2017. "SK Foreign Minister Refutes Suggestions that THAAD Operations Will Be Restricted." *Hankyoreh*, November 28. http://english.hani.co.kr/arti/english_edition/e_international/821100.html.

Jung, In-hwan, Yeon-cheol Seong, and Ji-eun Kim. 2017. "'Balanced Diplomacy' Becomes Fundamental to President Moon's Foreign Policy." *Hankyoreh*, November 6. http://english.hani.co.kr/arti/english_edition/e_national/817686.html.

Jung, Min-kyung. 2017a. "Seoul Not Considering Joining US Missile Defense System: FM Kang." *The Korea Herald*, October 30. http://www.koreaherald.com/view.php?ud=20171030000817.

———. 2017b. "Moon-Xi Summit Showed Willingness to Mend Strained Ties." *The Korea Herald*, December 15. http://www.koreaherald.com/view.php?ud=20171215000713.

Kim, Kyung-ho. 2016. "Economic Overreliance on China Poses Multiple Risks for South Korea." *The Korea Herald*, October 24. http://www.koreaherald.com/view.php?ud=20161024000975.

Kim, Kyung-rok. 2017a. "THAAD Deployment Causes South Korea's Biggest Ever Services Deficit with China." *Hankyoreh*, August 6. http://english.hani.co.kr/arti/english_edition/e_national/805682.html.

Kim, Nam-il. 2017b. "72% of South Koreans in Favour of Decision to Temporarily Deploy THAAD Launchers." *Hankyoreh*, August 6. http://english.hani.co.kr/arti/english_edition/e_national/805679.html.

Kim, Oi-hyun. 2017c. "Chinese Concessions on THAAD Fears of Losing Influence on Korean Peninsula." *Hankyoreh*, November 1. http://www.hani.co.kr/arti/english_edition/e_international/817030.html.

Kim, Sarah. 2017d. "U.S. Is 'Pleased' Korea and China Back on Track." *Korea Joongang Daily*, November 2. http://koreajoongangdaily.joins.com/news/article/article.aspx?aid=3040215.

Kim, Christine. 2018a. "South Korea Says It Wants U.S. Troops to Stay Regardless of Any Treaty With North Korea." *Reuters*, May 2. https://www.reuters.com/article/us-usa-southkorea-northkorea/south-korea-says-it-wants-us-troops-to-stay-regardless-of-any-treaty-with-north-korea-idUSKBN1I305J.

Kim, Rahn. 2018b. "Moon's Approval Rating Dips Below 60% for First Time." *The Korean Times*, January 2. http://www.koreatimes.co.kr/www/nation/2018/03/356_243071.html.

Kim, Sarah, and Chul-jae Lee. 2017. "Chinese Planes Penetrate Korea's ADIZ." *Korea Joongang Daily*, January 11. http://koreajoongangdaily.joins.com/news/article/article.aspx?aid=3028512.

Klingner, Bruce. 2015. "South Korea Needs THAAD Missile Defense." *The Heritage Foundation*, June 12.

Kwack, Jung-soo. 2017. "South Korean Businesses Mulling Stronger Response Against China's THAAD Retaliation." *Hankyoreh*, July 7. http://english.hani.co.kr/arti/english_edition/e_business/801911.html.

Lee, Jong-seok. 2017. "Three No's Policy Reinforces South Korea's Sovereignty." *Hankyoreh*, November 6. http://english.hani.co.kr/arti/english_edition/e_editorial/817693.html.

Lee, Joyce, and Christine Kim. 2017. "South Korean Firms Flock to Beijing Hoping Summit Will Hasten Thaw With China." *Reuters*, December 13. https://www.reuters.com/article/us-southkorea-china-companies/south-korean-firms-flock-to-beijing-hoping-summit-will-hasten-thaw-with-china-idUSKBN1E714V?il=0.

Li, Mingjiang. 2017a. "Introduction." In *China's Economic Statecraft: Co-optation, Cooperation, and Coercion*, edited by Mingjiang Li, xvii–xxv. Singapore: World Scientific Publishing Co.

———, ed. 2017b. *China's Economic Statecraft: Co-optation, Cooperation, and Coercion*. Singapore: World Scientific Publishing Co.

Na, Jeong-ju, and Whan-woo Yi. 2018. "US, China in Talks Over THAAD Withdrawal." *The Korea Times*, May 4. https://www.koreatimes.co.kr/www/nation/2018/05/120_248454.html.

Norris, William J. 2016. *Chinese Economic Statecraft: Commercial Actors, Grand Strategy, and State Control*. Ithaca, NY: Cornell University Press.

"Panmunjeom Declaration for Peace, Prosperity and Unification of the Korean Peninsula." 2018. https://www.koreatimes.co.kr/www/nation/2018/04/731_248077.html.

Park, Jae-hyuk. 2016. “China Intensifies Economic Retaliation Against Korea.” *The Korea Times*, December 2. http://www.koreatimes.co.kr/www/news/biz/2016/12/123_219418.html.

Perlez, Jane, Mark Lander, and Sang-hun Choe. 2017. “China Blinks on South Korea, Making Nice After a Year of Hostilities.” *The New York Times*, November 1. https://www.nytimes.com/2017/11/01/world/asia/china-south-korea-thaad.html.

Reilly, James. 2013. *China’s Economic Statecraft: Turning Wealth into Power*. Sydney: Lowy Institute for International Studies.

The Chosunilbo. 2017a. “Making Trouble in the Alliance Is Unhelpful at This Point.” June 19. http://english.chosun.com/site/data/html_dir/2017/06/19/2017061901482.html.

———. 2017b. “Gov’t Has Capitulated to Chinese Bullying.” November 1. http://english.chosun.com/site/data/html_dir/2017/11/01/2017110101595.html.

———. 2017c. “Gov’t Must Stop Kowtowing to China.” November 24. http://english.chosun.com/site/data/html_dir/2017/11/24/2017112401466.html.

———. 2017d. “Moon Vows THAAD Doesn’t Hurt China’s Military Interests.” December 12. http://english.chosun.com/site/data/html_dir/2017/12/12/2017121201411.html.

The Economist. 2017. “South Korea Is Making Up with China, But a Sour Taste Remains.” November 9. https://www.economist.com/china/2017/11/09/south-korea-is-making-up-with-china-but-a-sour-taste-remains.

The Korea Times. 2017. “Korea’s Doghouse Blues.” November 20. https://www.koreatimes.co.kr/www/opinion/2018/03/202_239572.html.

The Korean Times. 2017. “Joint Statement of Presidents of South Korea and the United States.” July 1. http://www.koreatimes.co.kr/www/nation/2017/07/120_232241.html.

United States Forces Korea. 2016. “ROK-U.S. Alliance Agrees to Deploy THAAD.” July 7.

Volodzko, David Josef. 2017. “China Wins Its War against South Korea’s US THAAD Missile Shield – Without Firing a Shot.” *South China Morning Post*, November 18. http://www.scmp.com/week-asia/geopolitics/article/2120452/china-wins-its-war-against-south-koreas-us-thaad-missile.

Weymouth, Lally. 2017. “South Korea’s New President: ‘Trump and I Have a Common Goal.’” *The Washington Post*, June 20. https://www.washingtonpost.com/outlook/south-koreas-president-trump-and-i-have-a-common-goal-in-dismantling-north-koreas-nuclear-program/2017/06/20/cd422e08-55bc-11e7-a204-ad706461fa4f_story.html?utm_term=.38417032064b.

Ye, Young-June, and Eun-soo Jin. 2016. “Lotte Suffering Wrath of China over Thaad.” *Korea Joongang Daily*, December 5. http://koreajoongangdaily.joins.com/news/article/article.aspx?aid=3027008.

Yi, Whan-woo. 2017a. “Moon, Xi to Hold Summit Next Week.” *The Korea Times*, October 31. https://www.koreatimes.co.kr/www/nation/2017/12/120_238542.html.

———. 2017b. “THAAD Conflict Not Over Yet.” *The Korea Times*, November 26. http://www.koreatimes.co.kr/www/nation/2017/11/120_239929.html.

Yonhap. 2017. "Parliament Urges China to Stop Retaliation Over THAAD." March 30. https://en.yna.co.kr/view/AEN20170330012100315.

Yoon, Young-kwan. 2017. "Moon's South Korean Ostpolitik." *Project Syndicate*, May 9.

Yun, Suh-young. 2017. "China's THAAD Retaliation Spreads to Big Screens." *The Korea Times*, March 29. https://www.koreatimes.co.kr/www/art/2018/04/689_226614.html.

Zhang, Xiaotong, Hongyu Wang, et al. 2015. *China's Economic Diplomacy: The PRC's Growing International Influence in the 21st Century*. London: ACA Publishing Ltd.

Chapter 3

Middle Powers and China's Economic Statecraft

Charting Variance in "Strategic Value"

Stephen Noakes and Charles Burton[1]

Conventional wisdom would suggest that middle powers, being hyper-attuned to great power politics, can be expected to bandwagon with their traditional allies. In a unipolar world, Canada and New Zealand could thus be expected to play follow-the-leader with the United States. However, the rise of China has a confounding effect on the US-led unipolar order and thus on our traditional expectations of American middle power allies as well. In this chapter we probe the apparent variation in what we term "strategic value" for China of New Zealand and Canada. While the two hold a great deal in common, we find that the Canadian case is made considerably more complicated by both the range of strategic considerations present and the potential payoff for China of one in particular—closeness to the United States, China's prime geostrategic rival. These higher stakes in the Canadian case not only make strategic inroads in New Zealand relatively easy for China but also suggest that Chinese economic policy is selectively sculpted to suit the higher strategic purposes of People's Republic of China (PRC).

This chapter is motivated by a single principal concern—what explains the apparent differences in the strategic value of two middle powers New Zealand and Canada—for China. Our conception of middle powers is based on the "technical and entrepreneurial capacities" of these states, rather than categorizations based on absolutes of size, power, or geography (Cooper, Higgott, and Nossal 1993). Indeed, it precisely is this pound-for-pound parity in capacities, we argue, that makes comparisons of Canada-China and New Zealand-China relations both possible and fruitful. As noted in our previous study of the two countries' foreign policies toward China, both are ex-British colonies with legal structures descended from UK common law. Together, they form two of the "five eyes" intelligence community and share similar sensibilities regarding the defense of human rights internationally, even if these sometimes take a backseat to perceived economic gains in the forging of new commercial relationships. Moreover, the two countries have approximately similar trade profiles, with a heavy basis in primary industries. Both are pro-free trade—Free Trade Agreements (FTAs) have their discontents in both countries, but neither has adopted an anti-free trade stance as official policy. New Zealand has enjoyed free trade with its largest trading partners (Australia and China) for several years, and Canada has been a party to the North American FTA since it came into force on January 1, 1994.[2] Finally, they also share a proximity to and affinity for a much larger neighbor which shapes their own outlooks, culturally and commercially.

The trouble with the "middle powers" framework, however, is that it obscures a great deal of intra-category variation. Middle powers are conventionally thought to behave in quite predictable ways, being hyper-attuned to geopolitical exigencies. For example, one study considering the behaviors of middling and small states argues that "middle powers, closer to the top level of international politics, tend to be particularly sensitive to the conditions that prevail there . . . despite all subjective influence, the reactions of middle powers in comparable international situations may be expected to show some similarities" (Holbraad 1984). Another suggests that "if the concept of middle powers were to be reformulated, it would clearly demonstrate the leader-follower dynamic of international politics" (Cooper, Higgott, and Nossal 1993). In other words, middle powers like New Zealand and Canada are not only sensitive to changes in the international system wrought by China's rise but usually expected to bandwagon with established allies (Gilley 2003). However, China's rise and international status-seeking complicates this theoretical orthodoxy since, as Gilley and O'Neill write, the "middle power modus operandi was predicated upon reinforcing American hegemonic world order, and this order is progressively dissolving" (Wilkins 2014). Accordingly, recent works have attempted to clarify points of difference in the way middle powers respond to China. Yet much room remains to explore key points of differentiation among middle powers in their response to China's economic statecraft, which in turn is shaped by strategic value of middle power countries to Chinese diplomacy. By virtue of much being held constant within the two cases, the comparison undertaken here brings such differences into greater relief.[3]

Economic statecraft can be broadly understood as state manipulation of international economic activities for strategic purposes (Baldwin 1985). Norris defines five factors that reflect the business government conditions under which states will be able to control commercial actors (and thus direct their activities to generate the desired strategic effects.) These determinants of whether a state will be able to mobilize and direct its economic power are (1) compatibility of goals between the state and the commercial actors that carry on the economic activity of the state, (2) commercial market structure, (3) unity of the state, (4) the reporting relationship between the commercial firms and the state, and (5) relative distribution of resources between the state and commercial actors (Norris 2018).

In the case of China, factor 4, "the reporting relationship between the commercial firms and the state," is established by the presence of Chinese Communist Party Committees that typically occupy a superior position above boards of directors and management teams of Chinese enterprises. This would also affirm factor 3, "unity of the state," due to strictly maintained hierarchical discipline of China's Leninist system of political economic organization (Huang 2017). Regarding "compatibility of goals between the state and commercial actors" a distinction between state-owned enterprises and enterprises that are not under the State-owned Assets Supervision and Administration Commission (SASAC) could be drawn (SASAC 2018), in that the state-owned enterprises could be more amenable to undertaking nonprofitable investments to serve Chinese state strategic purposes as their operational deficits can be absorbed by state revenue. But the distinction between state-owned enterprises (SOEs) and large Chinese multinationals that are not deemed SOEs such as Huawei cannot be as clearly drawn (Johnson 2018). In general, the capacity of the PRC to engage in economic statecraft through manipulation of international economic activities for strategic purposes benefits considerably from its unitary Communist Party institutions and high degree of state participation in China's domestic economy (Reilly 2013).

The abovenamed factors might explain the Chinese end of its statecraft, but what of conditions present in receiving countries? We maintain that Canada and New Zealand's categorization as middle powers makes both particularly amenable to China's economic statecraft policies. While middle powers typically seek to protect themselves from great power domination by allying with other middle powers via commitment to multilateralism through global institutions, China's preference for bilateral engagement leads to an asymmetrical power imbalance favoring China's strategic pursuits in both cases considered here. China is no more or less able to exploit the liberal democratic openness of Canada or New Zealand in engaging in remunerative and coercive tactics through its United Front Work strategy (Lampton 2008). Moreover, as Jordaan points out, middle powers "seek also to construct identities distinct from those of the weak states in their region" by attempting to distance themselves culturally and economically from their more powerful neighbors (Jordaan 2003). In the case of both New Zealand and China, this factor makes both nations more amenable to China's economic statecraft as an alternative to traditional relationships with Britain and dominant larger neighboring nations.

While market access is obviously a driving factor behind China's economic statecraft in both the Canadian and New Zealand cases, we maintain that the Canadian case is made more complicated by a range of other strategic considerations for China, which are not present—or at least not to the same degree—in New Zealand. Such factors include Canada's membership in the G7 and China's desire to cultivate stronger ties with that organization, concessions on the SCS decision, the DPRK, and various human rights claims. China expects that if it extends fairer access to its markets in Canada, then Canada will reciprocally allow the transfer of restricted technologies (including those with military applications) (Blatchford and Blanchfield 2017), as well as remove the current restrictions on Chinese state firms acquiring ownership of Canadian energy companies and mines (Wiliams 2017). In the longer term, because Canada is overall the major economic partner and strategic ally of the United States (its southern bordering neighbor), Canada's economic integration with China through a comprehensive trade agreement is seen by China as offering considerable geopolitical advantage. Gaining political economic influence in Canada is part and parcel of the PRC fervent long-term comprehensive ambition to displace the core components of the US-led "outmoded" liberal global governance system under Xi Jinping's international relations doctrine of "the community of the common destiny of humankind" by which China will eventually inevitably succeed the United States as the dominant global superpower (Xi 2017). Simply put, China may in the long run have more to gain in geostrategic terms from engaging in economic statecraft in Canada than it does in New Zealand. However, the fact that Canada is a higher-stakes affair for China also makes New Zealand an easier, quicker target for China's economic statecraft, which explains the more advanced state of Chinese penetration there.

In the pages that follow, our argument is affected methodologically by tracing two dyadic processes, centered respectively on China-New Zealand and China-Canada bilateral ties. In essence, we find that the Canadian case contains more numerous and politically salient instances of "punctuated equilibrium" than does the New Zealand case.[4] We conclude that this variance evinces the adaptability of Xi Jinping's "China Dream" to different foreign contexts—that is, of the malleability of Chinese economic policy in the pursuit of higher strategic gains.

***

THE CONTEXT OF CHINA'S ECONOMIC STATECRAFT WITH CANADA AND NEW ZEALAND

Canada

After China's Communist Revolution in 1949 the initial focus of the PRC regime was import substitution. Most foreign nationals in China had left or were expelled by the early 1950s in the wake of confiscation and nationalization of factories and businesses associated with foreign capital. But China still faced an existential threat from the US-backed KMT and severe economic disruption due to the US embargo of trade with the mainland. In the early years, and despite implementation of Leninist institutional xenophobia, the PRC sought to cultivate "foreign friends" in advanced industrialized nations for their political and economic support.

China, led by Chairman Mao Zedong, also had a larger plan to unify all of the nations of world into a China-led international soviet of the human race (Lin 2008). It would be led by China because the Soviet Union had abrogated this role by its lapse into hegemonistic revisionist betrayal of Marx and Lenin's scientific socialism after the death of Josef Stalin. China saw itself as the true leader of the nonaligned third world nations in the first instance. Due to China's own poverty and lack of resources it had limited economic statecraft initiatives in those years, but did support revolutionary movements in South East Asia and some international development projects: notably the TanZam Railway in East Africa to "build solidarity" with the "emerging peoples" (TAZARA 2017). In Canada, China provided modest support to pro-China Communist groups and established Canada-China Friendship Associations to raise awareness of the intentions of China's Great Proletarian Cultural Revolution and other Maoist political initiatives, as well as to set the stage for eventual Marxist revolutionary transformation in Canada (About Us 2017).

While significant conservative constituencies in Canada opposed engagement with the "Godless Communists" (in particular the Roman Catholic Church in Quebec), there was considerable sympathy for China's Communist regime among leftists in Canada. China's Henan and Sichuan provinces were the focus of Canada's Protestant foreign missionary enterprise for almost 100 years up to the early 1950s. The missionaries had direct experience of the weak, corrupt, and inept government of Chiang Kai-shek. They were therefore prime candidates for the Chinese Communist Party's (CCP) United Front Work assurances that the PRC would promote the interests of common people, through good government based on principles of social justice. The former missionary "China hands" were influential in shaping Canadian public opinion in favor of support for China's new Communist regime (Burton 2011).

Chester Ronning, born in China to missionary parents and Canada's Chargé d'affaires at the time of the establishment of the PRC, negotiated the purchase of a building just inside Beijing's city wall in 1950. It would have been ideal as the Canadian Embassy venue in preparation for diplomatic recognition of the PRC, but he had to leave China in February 1951 when the Korean War made it impossible for diplomatic relations to continue (Evans 1991).

The postwar rise of United States to power was a source of unease to Canadian Tories. Conservative Canadian nationalists were concerned that US economic domination and the "cultural imperialism" of the social values implicit in US popular music, radio, TV, and Hollywood movies threatened Canada's identity as a sovereign nation loyal to the British monarchy. In 1961, John Diefenbaker's Progressive conservative government agreed to ship $422 million dollars' worth of Canadian wheat and barley to China over a thirty-month period when China was suffering from a severe food shortage (due to the disastrous policies of the "Great Leap Forward" Campaign). This major Canadian trade initiative with China amounted to an audacious challenge to the anti-Chinese Communist economic embargo policy of the United States. It was a popular measure affirming Canadian humanitarianism as well as demonstrating that Canadian foreign policy would not be subject to the geopolitical imperatives of United States. In subsequent years, Canada benefited from considerable Chinese wheat purchases. From an economic statecraft perspective, China was able to exploit a rift between Canada and United States. The purchase of Canadian wheat was also of overall benefit to China economically. The wheat off-loaded in Tianjin was sold over a wide area north of the Yangtse. Chinese rice was in return exported to Southeast Asia; this more than compensated for the import cost of the Canadian wheat, as well as taking pressure off China's weak transportation infrastructure that strained to move grain from South to North (Li 2004).

While Canadian forces fought bravely in the US-led UN forces in the Korean War in the 1950s, Canada refused to join the United States in the Vietnam War in the 1960s (and indeed offered asylum to US "draft dodgers"). The election of Pierre Elliot Trudeau as prime minister of Canada in 1968 led Canada to new heights of anti-Americanism, as Trudeau initiated measures to limit and restrict both US investment, and US. music and television broadcasting in Canada.

At the same time, Trudeau was instrumental in Canada's diplomatic recognition of the PRC in 1970, which paved the way for the PRC establishing relations with dozens of nations prior to Mao's death in 1976. Trudeau was strongly supportive of China's Cultural Revolution policies; this was interpreted as China maintaining cultural sovereignty by rejecting both Russian hegemonism and US economic and cultural imperialism, through export of liberal democratic institutions (Burton 2011).

The Canadian Communist doctor, Norman Bethune, died in China during 1939 under heroic circumstances. He was subject to one of Mao's most famous short writings and began to be commemorated throughout Canada. His childhood home in Gravenhurst, Ontario, was converted to an interpretive museum managed by Parks Canada (Parks Canada 2017). York University established a college in his name (Bethune College 2017), statutes were raised, plaques mounted, and a Montreal city square renamed after Bethune (Norman Bethune 2017). All Canadians were called upon to learn from Bethune's selfless sacrifice on behalf of the Chinese people and to follow his example of support for the CCP cause, which exemplified Canada-China friendship.

After the repudiation of Mao's continuous Marxist revolution policies in the late-1970s in favor of "seek the truth from facts" with the pragmatic Deng Xiaoping at the helm, Canada enthusiastically supported China's post-ideological reform and opening up program. The Communist Party was under pressure to grow the economy, in order to deliver improved living standards and stave off popular discontent with the failings of the party's promises that socialism would deliver real benefits to the masses of ordinary Chinese citizens.

In retrospect, China's economic statecraft with Canada came fully into play starting in the 1980s. Communist Party of China officials, identified by Western diplomats as "progressive agents of change" cum liberalizers, used mostly fluent English to assure the Canadian government and business interests that China's reform and opening would inevitably lead to China evolving to a multiparty democratic state consistent with UN governance norms (Public Services 2002). In 1998, China signed the UN's International Covenant on Civil and Political Rights (ICCPR) and began a series of government-to-government bilateral dialogues on human rights (Burton 2006). Canada participated in multilateral concessional financing for Chinese development and reorientated a significant portion of Canadian International Development Agency programming to the PRC. Canada also agreed to China's entry into the World Trade Organization (WTO) in 2001.

However, Canadian offers of assistance to bring Chinese laws and practices into compliance with the ICCPR and approaches to share expertise with UN requirements were rebuffed. Moreover, Canada's modest trade surplus with China due to wheat exports turned to a 3-to-1 trade deficit over these years. The Chinese promise that significant economic benefits would accrue to "friendly nations" who assisted China in the early stages of reform and opening, by China developing rule of law and fair access to the Chinese market, failed to materialize (Burton 2009). However, from an economic statecraft perspective, China was able to leverage Canadian aid for infrastructure development and technology and intellectual property transfer. As

Canadian scholar David Zweig expounds at length with reference to Canadian International Development Agency programming, "In the 1980s, many countries were very positive towards China, so they willingly helped China in those sectors that China considered as its own priorities" (Zweig 2002). This was sometimes obtained through deception of Canadian partners, in order to achieve the CCP's larger regime goals of strengthening economic performance and thereby consolidating popular support (O'Brien 2000).

New Zealand

When compared with that of Canada, New Zealand's bilateral relations with China from the mid-twentieth century onward have been relatively harmonious. Although New Zealand did not formally recognize the People's Republic until 1972, as in Canada, the discussion over whether to recognize Mao's regime began almost immediately after his seizure of power. The available historiography recounts, "a number of considerations had to be weighed up, but by December 1949 the balance of the argument was shifting towards recognition." It was only the UN's designation of China as an aggressor in the Korean War that shifted the calculus of the then-National Party government into withholding recognition (New Zealand's China Policy 2015, 12).

Despite the lack of official recognition, however, friendly-if-informal links remained. For example, on October 1, 1959, a *kahu huruhuru* (ceremonial feather cloak) was presented to Chairman Mao by Ramai Hayward on behalf of King Karoki, the fourth Maori king, during a National Day celebration in Tiananmen Square. Arrangements for the gift were made by the New Zealand-China Friendship Society (NZCFS).[5] As an expression of *Mana Taonga* (the ongoing connection of communities to their gifted cultural treasures), the cloak retained its spiritual value due to its connection to the king. This value was maintained in the connection—the *muka* (flax fiber cord) used in its creation was intended to symbolize the interconnectedness of China and New Zealand. The Mana Taonga was expressed when NZCFS oversaw repatriation of the cloak to New Zealand in 2013, when it was placed on temporary loan to Te Papa, Wellington, by the National Museum of China, still holding its value and connection decades later (Powhiri for the Chairman 2013).

Beyond "Maori-Mao relations," Communist China had prominent ideological New Zealand sympathizers as well. After serving New Zealand on the front lines in World War I, Canterbury-born Rewi Alley travelled to China, gaining work as a factory inspection warden for the Shanghai Municipal Council in 1932.[6] In 1937, Alley was instrumental in creating the *Gongye Hezuoshe*—Chinese Industrial Cooperatives (CICs)—which aimed to promote grassroots economic development following the annexation of much of China's industrial heartland to the Empire of Japan.[7] Through his experience with the CICs and having observed the crushing poverty of ordinary Chinese individuals during the 1930s and early 1940s, Alley became radicalized. After 1949 he remained in China, ingratiating himself into the company of Mao Zedong and Zhou Enlai. Deeply committed to the Communist cause, Alley authored several notable pieces of propaganda for the CCP, such as *China's Hinterland in the Leap Forward* (Alley 1961), and later was a vocal supporter the Viet Cong in the Vietnam conflict. Interestingly, however, his ideological inclinations appear to have had relatively little impact on Alley's legacy in subsequent decades. From the point of view of both the PRC and New Zealand governments, Alley was a humanitarian who had done China a great service in its hour of need.[8] Upon his being made a Companion of the Queen's Service Order in 1985, then-New Zealand prime minister David Lange said of Alley, "New Zealand has had many great sons, but you, Sir, are our greatest son" (Mahon 2013).

Apart from Alley, Victor Wilcox, who served as secretary-general of the Communist Party of New Zealand during the 1970s, also advanced favorable impressions of New Zealand in China. Wilcox headed one of only a few fraternal parties to side with China in the Sino-Soviet split, a group that also notably included Albania's Enver Hoxha. In recognition of this show of solidarity, and because New Zealand did not enforce a travel prohibition to China, Wilcox met personally with Chinese leaders, too much fanfare, even appearing on page one of a March 1973 issue of *People's Daily*, while news of an official ministerial visit by Hon. Joe Walding was relegated to page three. As one reflection puts it, Wilcox "was routinely received in Beijing as if he were a head of state and his writings were given worldwide distribution by the Chinese" (New Zealand's China Policy 2015, 14).

Two key factors underpinned New Zealand's decision to recognize the PRC and the deepening of ties that followed. The first and most significant in geopolitical terms was New Zealand's acceptance of the One China policy. A joint communiqué, issued on December 21, 1972, formally affirmed New Zealand's backing for the official PRC position that it was the sole legitimate government of all China and that Taiwan was an inalienable part of it (Joint Communiqué 1972). As Minister of Foreign Affairs N. E. Klirk remarked in February 1973, China was unwilling to accept the 'take note' [of the PRC's claim to sovereignty over Taiwan] formula used by Canada when negotiating terms of diplomatic relations with New Zealand (New Zealand Parliament 1973, 246).

The second key factor concerned shifting trade considerations, in particular the need for New Zealand to broaden its relationships with overseas markets. Although the UK has accounted for some 80 percent of all New Zealand exports prior to economic deregulation in the 1980s (Huang and Young 2013, 65), the development of closer trade links within Europe and especially the

UK's accession to the European Economic Community led the Kirk government in to adopt the view that New Zealand should be less reliant on the UK market in the future, and that it should begin to cultivate political and trade relationships with a number of nontraditional partners. As part of this process, Wellington reopened its embassy in Moscow, which had been closed in 1950, and in 1973 established a new embassy in Vienna to facilitate closer trade relationships in eastern Europe, namely with Hungary, Romania, Poland, and Czechoslovakia. While the balance of trade between China and New Zealand initially remained small, and was in any case likely to be asymmetrical given the relative size of the two countries, it turned out that the smallness and isolation of New Zealand came with diplomatic benefits for China. These would be increasingly important for China as the 1970s wore on.

Robert Muldoon, having assumed the office of prime minister in July 1974, was keen to continue to deepen the relationship with China established by his predecessor. This view was influenced in no small part by Victor Percival, a Kiwi businessman and personal friend of Muldoon, who had recognized early the commercial potential of China. As one biography of Percival tells it, "The fresh New Zealand leader [Muldoon] shared Percival's enthusiasm for closer ties between China and New Zealand. He accepted that there would be excellent trade opportunities and scheduled an official visit to Beijing for late April/early May of 1976 as part of an overseas tour to the United Kingdom, Europe, and Northeast Asia" (Kohn 2008, 138). As it turned out, Muldoon was the last world leader to see Mao Zedong alive when the two met at a ten-minute meeting in early September that year. Following the chairman's death, the subsequent comeback of Deng Xiaoping within the CCP, and the accompanying prospects for reform and opening up, Chinese officials began to seek new opportunities to travel abroad. According to one report, "New Zealand provided a low-key environment for Chinese leaders to be exposed to the West after the long years in which China had largely been closed off to the outside world." The report goes on to state that New Zealand was an "early beneficiary" of China's outward-bound approach during this period, receiving Zhao Ziyang and Hu Yaobang in 1983 and 1985, respectively (New Zealand's China Policy 2015, 17–18).

The 1990s marked a key turning point in New Zealand-China bilateral ties, initiating what both sides now commonly refer to as the "Four Firsts"—milestones that set New Zealand apart from other Western countries in its relations with China. The first "First" came in July 1997, when New Zealand became the first developed Western country to agree to bilateral terms on China's WTO accession. With chief Chinese negotiator Long Yongtu under mounting pressure from the home front to demonstrate progress toward a deal, and with New Zealand's major sticking point being the interests of its dairy sector, "Long had a meeting with the New Zealand delegation in

Geneva and deliberately made an offer that was aimed at getting New Zealand to be the first to conclude those access talks" (Browne 2012). While the precise details of tariff quotas were not finalized until 2000, the two parties agreed to market access terms in principle. Of course, talk of market access requires the recognition of the existence of markets. The 1997 talks therefore laid the groundwork for the second "First"; in 2004 New Zealand became the first Western country to formally acknowledge China's status as a market economy. The same year, the third "First" was announced. New Zealand had become the first developed Western country to enter into free trade negotiations with China. It was not until 2008, however, that the fourth "First" was finalized, when New Zealand announced that it had successfully concluded a high-quality and comprehensive FTA with China, becoming the first Western nation to do so (but hardly the last).[9]

CHINA'S ECONOMIC STATECRAFT WITH CANADA AND NEW ZEALAND IN THE XI JINPING ERA

Canada's relationship with China cooled appreciably under conservative prime minister Stephen Harper. An annual government-to-government bilateral human rights dialogue, which had been the centerpiece of Prime Minister Chrétien's "quiet diplomacy" on non-trade issues, was suspended. With regard to expansion of Canada-China trade relations, Prime Minister Harper in an impromptu press briefing on board his jet en route to the Asia-Pacific Economic Cooperation (APEC) summit in Vietnam in 2006 said "I think Canadians want us to promote our trade relations worldwide and we do that. But I don't think Canadians want us to sell out important Canadian values. They don't want us to sell that out to the almighty dollar" (Edwards 2016).

Late in 2012, the Harper government approved a $15 billion sale of the Canadian oil firm Nexen to the China National Offshore Oil Corporation. But it was under the proviso that there would be no further sales of Canadian oil companies to state-owned firms approved, except in "exceptional circumstances." The logic behind this was that Canada's national sovereignty would be threatened if China accumulated a critical mass of economic power in the Canadian energy and mineral sectors, telecommunications network and other infrastructure development (Burton 2012).

Chinese authorities welcomed the return to power of the liberals under Justin Trudeau (Luo 2016). In opposition, Trudeau had expressed support for enhanced Chinese state investment in Canada's energy and resources sectors (Trudeau 2012). With liberals back in power China expected that an approach to initiate an early FTA would be favorably received. Once in power, Trudeau significantly upgraded Canada's representation to Beijing by shuffling one of the Government's most senior ministers, John McCallum, out of cabinet to appoint him as Canada's ambassador to China. In an interview with the Chinese press on assuming his diplomatic post, Mr. McCullum indicated that his mission to China could be summed up in three words: "more, more, more" (Na 2017). This fit with earlier statements by Justin Trudeau which implied that China would be the new "Third Option" for Canada to diversify its political and economic dependence on the United States (Trudeau 2012). Soon thereafter, Canada acceded to the Chinese government's very high volume and persistent urging that Canada and China begin exploratory talks toward a Canada-China FTA.

Nevertheless, the fact is Beijing does not need an FTA with Canada as such. China already has excellent access to the Canadian market due to Canada's low tariffs, fair, and transparent business regulations and impartial rule of law to adjudicate contract disputes. However, it is not reciprocal. Canada has nowhere near a level playing field in China, where many sectors are closed to Canadian goods, services, and investment.

The Canadian side anticipates that free trade will promote Canadian prosperity, opening the huge Chinese market to Canadian oilsands petroleum, minerals, wood products, manufactured goods and services. In contrast, Beijing understands free trade economic integration as a tool to facilitate its overall strategic geopolitical interests, as part and parcel to China's comprehensive rise to power. So, it is to be expected that in an interview with Canadian journalists, the Chinese ambassador to Canada would urge hasty negotiation of a Canada-China FTA claiming: "The earlier the Canadian side signs the FTA, the earlier you get the benefits" (Blatchford and Blanchfield 2017). However, in December 2017 in Beijing, Prime Minister Justin Trudeau attempted to impose conditions on labor and gender issues, before agreeing to initiate formal binding negotiations. Prime Minister Trudeau thus squared the circle on the conundrum of trade versus protecting Canadian values in Canada-China relations. However, Chinese Premier Li Keqiang rebuffed this initiative to add noneconomic factors to a trade agreement. As a consequence, the FTA negotiations stalled (Hall 2017; Burton 2017).

In terms of explicit economic statecraft, prior to initiation of exploratory talks on free trade, Beijing had complained that Canada's national security review process of foreign takeovers of Canadian firms under the Investment Canada Act unfairly targets China. China's ambassador Lu Shaye characterized it as "tantamount to trade protectionism" (Fife and Chase 2017). China's Premier Li Keqiang engaged Prime Minister Trudeau on this issue in a personal telephone call (Chase and Fife 2017a). Subsequently, in an interview with the Canadian news agency, the ambassador (while committing to China opening its markets "a little more" and facilitating "mutual investment" once the FTA was signed) indicated that from the Chinese government's perspective, aside from acquisition of advanced technologies and products, there are few enticing opportunities for Chinese investors in Canada (Blatchford and Blanchfield 2017). So access to high-tech currently restricted from export to China is evidently what the Chinese regime hopes to get out of Canada. This is consistent with the priorities of China's current five-year plan.

In March 2017, the liberal government overturned the previous government's cabinet order (following the advice of the Canadian Security Intelligence Service), that barred a Hong Kong company, O-Net, (partly owned by the Chinese government) from taking over ITF Technologies, a Montreal firm developing technology applicable to fiber-laser directed energy weapons (Chase 2017). Shortly thereafter, the government of Canada permitted a Shenzhen firm, Hytera, to acquire Norsat International, a provider of satellite communication systems used by military customers, including the Pentagon and the Government of Taiwan, without apparently doing an in-depth national security review (Chase and Fife 2017c). This may have created an impression in the PRC that military technologies shared by NATO and its allies can be sourced through Canada in exchange for promise of trade concessions to Canadian companies with political influence in Ottawa.

Canadian companies with close relationships with Chinese Communist business networks have been pressing the Canadian government to move full steam ahead on negotiating a FTA with China because it will bring economic benefits to these Canadian companies. The asymmetrical power relationship between China and Canada has in the past led to a lot more *take* than *give* on the Chinese side. In addition to allowing the above high-tech transfers, Ottawa is unlikely to spoil the FTA talks by reiterating its support for the Permanent Court of Arbitration's decision that declared China's expansive claims over the South China Sea as illegal under the UN Convention of the Law of the Sea; or demanding China halt its pervasive cyber-espionage of Canadian government and business servers; or by expelling Chinese security agents alleged to be furthering Beijing's interests by harassment and intimidation in Canada, or anything else that criticizes China's domestic or international policy.

There are other incentives to comply with China's demands of Canada. China threatened in 2016 to halt $2 billion in annual imports of Canadian canola seed, by imposing new regulations regarding dockage (impurities) so stringent as to be economically infeasible for Canadian producers to meet. Frantic negotiations by two Canadian cabinet ministers sent as supplicants to Beijing ensued. Just prior to an official visit to China by Prime Minister Trudeau, the matter was deferred for further study. Canadian free trade negotiators know that the agreement (whereby China keeps accepting Canadian canola under the existing dockage standard) expires in 2020 (Hui 2016).

New Zealand's experience and prevailing impressions of China under Xi Jinping are quite different from that of Canada. The year 2012 marked forty years of diplomatic relations between the two. Economic and social ties have developed rapidly both broaden and deepening considerably since the China-New Zealand FTA came into effect in 2008. The original agreement had its detractors, of course, most notably New Zealand's First leader and then-foreign minister Winston Peters, who felt that the deal was less advantageous to New Zealanders than it could have been, and a slew of Kiwi manufacturers who fretted over their ability to compete with less expensive Chinese labor (Burton and Noakes 2016, 848). However, according to Statistics New Zealand (StatsNZ), New Zealand's trade relationship with China has nearly tripled over the past decade, with two-way trade rising from $8.2 billion in the year ended June 2007 to $23 billion in the June 2016 year (see Figure 3.1). Annual exports to China have quadrupled and annual imports from China have doubled since the June 2007 year. This means that China is now New Zealand's second largest trading partner for export, with dairy and lumber products leading the way (see Figure 3.2).[10]

At the same time, China is now the third largest importer to New Zealand, with clothing and high-tech gear (mostly cell phones, tablets and laptops) predominating (see Figure 3.3). Reflecting on the successes of the 2008 agreement, New Zealand's Ministry of Foreign Affairs and Trade concluded, "We have traded more with China since the FTA entered into force in 2008 than in all our previous history, and growth is faster with China than any of our other major trading partners" (International Travel and Migration 2016).

It is little wonder then that both sides have sought to renew and expand the 2008 FTA. Jointly announced by President Xi Jinping and Prime Minister John Key in November 2016, the New Zealand-China FTA upgrade

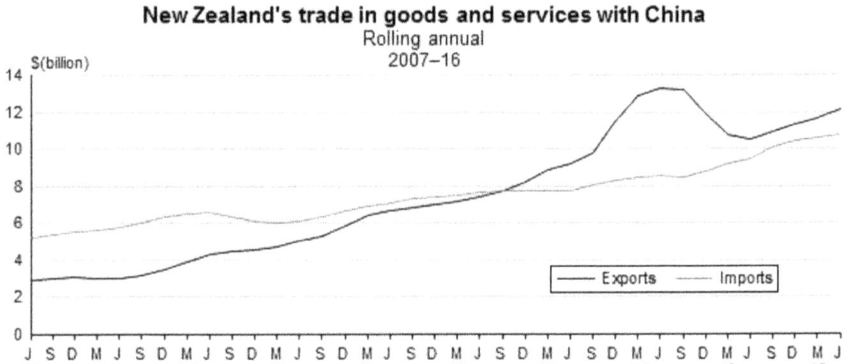

Figure 3.1 New Zealand's Trade in Goods and Services with China. Rolling Annual 2007–16. *Source*: Statistics New Zealand.

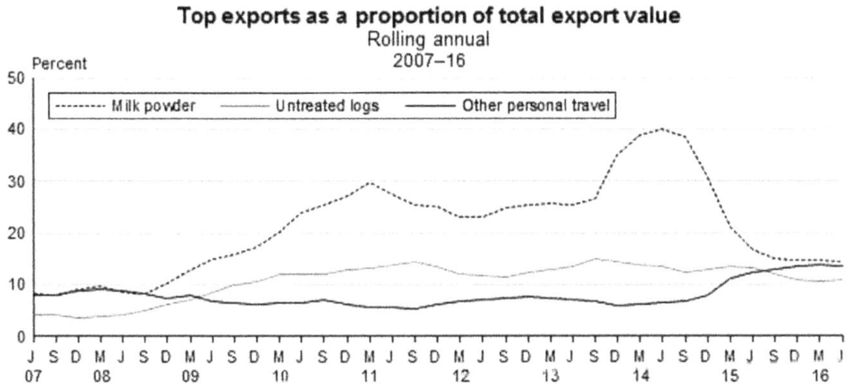

Figure 3.2 Top Exports as a Proportion of Total Export Value. Rolling Annual 2007–16. *Source*: Statistics New Zealand.

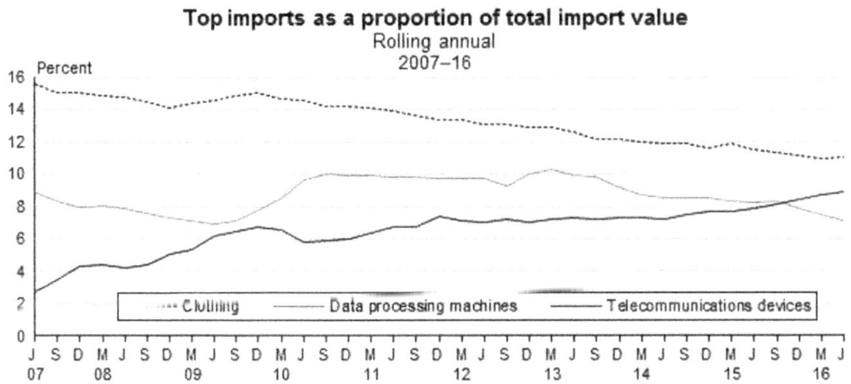

Figure 3.3 Top Imports as a Proportion of Total Import Value. Rolling Annual 2007–16. *Source*: Statistics New Zealand.

agreement "provides an opportunity to modernise the FTA and make improvements that further free up trade for goods and services to help exporters reach $30 billion in two-way trade by 2020—the target set by leaders in 2014" (NZ-China FTA Upgrade 2017). In their joint statement, Xi and Key laid out nine specific areas for negotiation and future cooperation, including technical barriers to trade (TBT); customs procedures, cooperation, and trade facilitation; rule of origin (RoO); competition policy; e-commerce; agricultural cooperation; environment; and government procurement, with further issues to be discussed as they may arise. Though final details are not yet decided, two rounds of talks have been held. The first took place in April 2017 and the second on July 3–6, 2017 in Beijing. Working groups on all nine items met on both occasions, though the second round provided greater opportunity for in-depth discussion of national priorities on both sides. As of this writing, no timetable has been set for the conclusion of talks, though New Zealand's Ministry of Foreign Affairs and Trade expects a third round of negotiation to take place in late 2017 (ibid).

As a corollary to the deepening of two-way trade, much recent discussion has emphasized the broader connections to be facilitated by the Belt and Road Initiative (BRI). Early in 2017, New Zealand notched yet another "first" when it inked a memorandum of agreement with China on the BRI. Stephen Jacobi of the New Zealand-China Council argues that in New Zealand's case the deal "is less about infrastructure and more about connecting up with China through the flow of goods, services, and people" (Sachdeva 2017). More recently, Jacobi, a former diplomat who is currently executive director of the New Zealand-China Council, has referred to the BRI "connectivity agenda" to highlight the fact that the memorandum of agreement has as much to do with facilitating people-to-people connections as anything else (Jacobi 2017). Similarly, David Wang, who is CEO of Bank of China operations in New Zealand, says that the BRI is about promoting cooperation and working to build a community of shared interests and responsibility, and points specifically to people-to-people connections as a key element of unlocking what he calls a "unique mutual opportunity" (Wang 2017). BRI thus represents the positive and natural next step in the already strong interrelationships of Chinese and New Zealand societies, one that envisages the freer movement across borders. StatsNZ figures indicate that between 1986 and 2006, the population of New Zealand residents born in Asia increased sevenfold, and that the China-born segment of that population rose by a staggering 800 percent (Bedford and Ho 2008, 12). The steady increase in Chinese migrants has continued since BRI was launched in 2013. In the year ending April 2013 there were 7,894; in 2014, 8,636; and in 2015, 10,126 (Trade with China 2018).

The influx of Chinese migrants and money to New Zealand has brought with it new worries over influence in New Zealand politics. Such fears first caught the public eye during the 2017 election campaign, when Jian Yang, a list MP for the National Party and former University of Auckland lecturer, made headlines for his alleged failure to properly disclose his record of military service in China, and in particular his role at the Luoyang Language Institute, otherwise known the People's Liberation Army-Airforce Engineering College. "National Party MP trained by Chinese Spies," the headline read (Jennings and Read 2017). While both Yang and then-prime minister Bill English made public statements affirming Yang's loyalty to New Zealand, the story spawned a series of journalistic probes into the National Party's connections to China and Chinese foreign influence activities. Professor

Anne-Marie Brady of Canterbury University in Christchurch is at the forefront of the investigation, having written a paper widely recirculated online and in the New Zealand media throughout the latter half of 2017 on the "magic weapons" (法宝) employed by China in an effort to gain influence in New Zealand. Among the specific PRC influence activities she elaborates in New Zealand are "maintaining oversight" of ethnic Chinese political figures, community organizations, and language schools, particularly in the Auckland region; "harmonization" of print and broadcast Chinese-language media outlets with official PRC Embassy priorities; and the forging of a pro-China strategic bloc through business and cultural exchanges under the BRI (Brady 2017). However, newly elected prime minister Jacinda Ardern has so far been publicly dismissive of fears over Chinese meddling in New Zealand politics. "When it comes to some of the issues that have been raised in Australia [fears over Chinese influence] I haven't seen evidence of the kinds of issues they are talking about here in New Zealand. That's not to say we should be complacent. We have to be vigilant and we are," she said (New Zealand Herald 2017).

***

THE FUTURE OF CHINA'S ECONOMIC STATECRAFT WITH NEW ZEALAND AND CANADA

In his report to the Communist Party's 19th Congress in October 2017, General Secretary Xi Jinping made clear a new basis for China's economic statecraft on Chinese terms. First of all, he explicitly repudiated liberal democratic political reform as a regime goal for the PRC. Instead, he affirmed that China would remain true to the legacy of Leninism and Stalinism that has informed China's political, social, and economic policy since 1949 (Full Text 2017). In the same report, Xi assumed the "mandate of history" to implement the "magnificent plan" of realizing the "Chinese dream of glorious Chinese national restoration" by 2050 (ibid). Proceeding from 2020, this plan is divided into two 15-year parts. By 2035, China will be fully developed and technologically advanced. It will then embark on taking its rightful place as the world's unassailable economic and cultural leader, playing "an important role in the history of humanity" (ibid). The "Belt and Road initiative" is a central part of this; it proposes trillions of yuan in investment to build world infrastructure, with the aim of bringing natural resources and other economic inputs to China and facilitating Chinese goods reaching foreign markets. Xi envisions a post-2050 new world order he dubs "a community with a shared future for mankind" (ibid) (which the *People's Daily* newspaper allows is "superior to Western mainstream international relations theory") (Wang 2017). Mao Zedong's initial revolutionary dream was the realization of socialism and communism, an ideal society without oppression or inequality, with material plenty for all. Later this dream was expanded by Mao to extend to all of humanity. As Zheng Wang has noted, "During the Cultural Revolution, Mao produced another dream of China as the center of the global revolution" (Zheng 2018).

Xi Jinping's dream of national rejuvenation is not just a redressing of the humiliations on China of nineteenth-century Western and Japanese imperialism, but extension to contemporary Chinese Marxist development of Chairman Mao Zedong's larger plan to unify all of the nations of the world into a China-led international soviet of the human race and traditional Chinese versions of "Great Unity" (*da tong)* (Allison 2017). The assumptions of this vision are that the downward spiral of United States under President Donald Trump continues unabated, and with it the end of Western liberal internationalism based on democracy and values of human rights and citizenship. Indeed, Xi hailed China as a model for "nations that want to speed up their development while preserving their independence" (ibid).

State authoritarianism and global power politics are how Beijing sees its rise to dominance playing out through the prism of global power politics and state authoritarianism—human rights and multicultural cooperation have no part in it. The same week as Xi's report was delivered, China also announced the termination of its senior-level human rights dialogue with Australia (Sheridan 2017). Shortly thereafter, the Canadian government initiated legislation to release funds for Canada's initial contribution of up to $480 million to the China-backed Asian Infrastructure Investment Bank, which is focused on the financing for the Chinese Belt and Road infrastructure development (Curry 2017).

China's economic statecraft is now based in foreign acceptance of the inevitability of China's comprehensive rise to power displacing the United States as the world's superpower. Chinese soft power is seen as following Chinese economic, military, and strategic hard power. Canada and New Zealand as weaker global players are expected to conform to the new international norms developed by China's Communist regime or suffer isolation and economic decline. Yet, as we have shown here, the two are not on equal footing with regard to their strategic value for China. Because of its historic and ongoing ties to the United States, Canada is a more challenging but consequential site for China's economic statecraft. All the more reason, then, why Canada ought to be attuned to New Zealand's early experiences of that process, and for the two middle powers to engage in free and frank dialogue over new and old international alliances.

NOTES

1. Research assistance from Lisa Maya Jagoe is acknowledged with gratitude, as are words of guidance on New Zealand-China relations from Jason Young at the New Zealand Contemporary China Research Centre at Victoria University of Wellington.

2. For a concise overview of Australia-New Zealand Closer Economic Relations (CER), consult https://www.mfat.govt.nz/en/trade/free-trade-agreements/free-trade-agreements-in-force/nz-australia-closer-economic-relations-cer/, accessed September 6, 2016.

3. A similar approach is taken by in Bruce Gilley and Andrew O'Neill, eds., in *Middle Powers and the Rise of China* (Washington, DC: Georgetown University Press, 2014); and James Manicom and Andrew O'Neill, "China's Rise and Middle Power Democracies: Canada and Australia Compared," *International Relations of the Asia-Pacific* 12, no. 2 (2012): 199–228.

4. Such data points are also commonly referred to as critical junctures or causal process observations. See Paul Pierson, "Increasing Returns, Path Dependence, and the Study of Politics," *American Political Science Review* 94, no. 2 (June 2000): 251–67; and David Collier, "Understanding Process Tracing," *PS: Political Science and Politics* 44, no. 4 (October 2010): 823–30.

5. There are some factual inaccuracies in the NZCFS source material on this event, including the attribution of a crucial role to Princess Te Puea. The Princess died in 1952, and thus could not have facilitated the gifting. We are indebted to Hirini Kaa for his clarifying comments on this issue.

6. The American journalist Edgar Snow was a contemporary of Alley's, was likewise instrumental in setting up Industrial cooperatives in China, and extensively chronicled the formation of the Communist insurgency, most notably in his 1937 book *Red Star Over China* (New York: Grove Press, 1961).

7. CICs were organized around the China Industrial Cooperatives Association, better known outside China by its less formal name, the Gung Ho International movement.

8. For a much more critical view of Alley's life and times, see Anne-Marie Brady, *Friend of China: The Myth of Rewi Alley* (London: Routledge Curzon, 2003).

9. The Australia-China free trade agreement was concluded November 17, 2014 and came into force on December 20, 2015.

10. For a more complete breakdown of the statistics, see "Trade with China Nearly Tripled in Past Decade," *Stats NZ*, September 7, 2016, accessed December 6, 2017, http://archive.stats.govt.nz/browse_for_stats/industry_sectors/imports_and_exports/trade-china-tripled-decade.aspx?url=/browse_for_stats/industry_sectors/imports_and_exports/trade-china-tripled-decade.aspx.

BIBLIOGRAPHY

"About Us." *Canada–China Friendship Society* site. Last modified 2017. http://www.ccfso.org/about-us.

Alley, Rewi. *China's Hinterland in the Leap Forward.* Peking: New World Press, 1961.

Allison, Graham. "What Xi Jinping Wants." *The Atlantic*, May 31, 2017. https://www.theatlantic.com/international/archive/2017/05/what-china-wants/528561/.

Baldwin, David A. *Economic Statecraft*, Revised edition. Princeton, NJ: Princeton University Press, 1985.

Bedford, Richard, and Elsie Ho. *Asians in New Zealand: Implications of a Changing Demography*. Asia New Zealand Foundation, 2008: 12.

"Bethune College." *York University* site. Accessed November 4, 2017.

Blatchford, Andy, and Mike Blanchfield. "China Sees Free Trade with Canada as Way to Avoid Future Norsat-like Uncertainty." *CBC News*, July 5, 2017. http://www.cbc.ca/news/politics/china-norsat-free-trade-canada-1.4190712.

Brady, Anne-Marie. "Magic Weapons: China's Political Influence Activities under Xi Jinping." In *Conference on the Corrosion of Democracy under China's Global Influence*, September 16–17, 2017. Arlington, Virginia, USA: Woodrow Wilson Centre, 2017.

Browne, Tony. "Managing the Relationship." In *Forty Years On: New Zealand China Relations Then, Now, and in the Years to Come*, edited by Chris Elder, 25–26. Wellington: Victoria University Press, 2013.

Burton, Charles. *Assessment of the Canada-China Bilateral Human Rights Dialogue (Report)*. Ontario: Department of Foreign Affairs and International Trade, 2006.

Burton, Charles. *A Reassessment of Canada's Interests in China and Options for Renewal of Canada's China Policy (Report)*. Canadian International Council, July 28, 2009.

Burton, Charles. "The Canadian Policy Context of Canada's China Policy Since 1970." In *The China Challenge: Sino–Canadian Relations in the 21st Century*, edited by Cao Huahua and Vivienne Pov. Ottawa, 32–46. Ontario: University of Ottawa Press, 2011.

Burton, Charles. "Stephen Harper's Decision on CNOOC Finally Gets the China Connection Right." *Toronto Star*, November 9, 2012. https://www.thestar.com/opinion/editorialopinion/2012/12/10/stephen_harpers_decision_on_cnooc_finally_gets_the_china_connection_right.html.

Burton, Charles. "Canada–China Relations Are Now Ready for a Rethink." *Ottawa Citizen*, December 14, 2017. http://ottawacitizen.com/opinion/columnists/burton-canada-china-relations-are-now-ripe-for-a-rethink?_utm_source=1-2-2.

Burton, Charles, and Stephen Noakes. "Forging Free Trade with China: The Maple Leaf and the Silver Fern." *Pacific Affairs* 4, no. 89 (2016): 839–58.

Chase, Steven. "Liberals Reverse Course on Chinese Takeover of Montreal High-Tech Firm." *Globe and Mail*, March 27, 2017. https://www.theglobeandmail.com/news/politics/liberals-waive-security-review-for-chinese-takeover-of-high-tech-firm/article35246673/.

Chase, Steven, and Robert Fife. "Critics Oppose Liberals' Handling of Chinese Investor's Norsat Takeover." *The Globe and Mail*, June 8, 2017a. https://www.theglobeandmail.com/news/politics/critics-oppose-liberals-handling-of-norsat-takeover/article35258716/.

Chase, Steven, and Robert Fife. "Liberals Waive Security Review for Chinese Takeover of High-Tech Firm." *The Globe and Mail*, June 8, 2017b. https://www.theglobeandmail.com/news/politics/liberals-waive-security-review-for-chinese-takeover-of-high-tech-firm/article35246673/.

Chase, Steven, and Robert Fife. "China's Premier Urges Trudeau to Relax Controls on High-Tech Exports." *Globe and Mail*, April 17, 2017c. https://www.theglobeandmail.com/news/politics/chinas-premier-urges-trudeau-to-relax-controls-on-high-tech-exports/article34746356/.

Cheng, Li, ed. *China's Changing Political Landscape*. Washington, DC: Brookings Institute, 2008.

Cooper, Andrew F., Richard A. Higgott, and Kim Richard Nossal. *Relocating Middle Powers: Australia and Canada in a Changing World Order*. Vancouver: University of British Columbia Press, 1993: 7.

Cungang, Wang. "The Concept of 'the Community with a Shared Future for Mankind' Leads Human Civilization in a Progressive Direction." *Chinadaily.Com.Cn*, November 4, 2017. http://theory.people.com.cn/n1/2017/0727/c40531-29430933.htm.

Curry, Bill. "Liberals Table Budget Bill to Join China's Asian Infrastructure Investment Bank." *The Globe and Mail*, October 27, 2017. https://www.theglobeandmail.com/news/politics/liberals-table-budget-bill-to-join-chinas-asian-infrastructure-bank/article36758568/.

Edwards, Fred. "PM's Beijing Trip—More Hype than Hope." *Toronto Star*, November 29, 2009. https://www.thestar.com/news/world/2009/11/29/edwards_pms_beijing_trip_more_hype_than_hope.html.

Evans, Brian. "Ronning and Recognition: Years of Frustration." In *Reluctant Adversaries: Canada and the People's Republic of China, 1949–1970*, edited by Paul M. Evans and Michael Frolic, 148–67. Toronto: University of Toronto Press, 1991.

Fife, Robert, and Steven Chase. "Critics Oppose Liberals' Handling of Chinese Investor's Norsat Takeover." *Globe and Mail*, June 8, 2017. https://www.theglobeandmail.com/news/politics/critics-oppose-liberals-handling-of-norsat-takeover/article35258716/.

"Full Text of Xi Jinping's Report at 19th CPC National Congress." *Chinadaily.Com.Cn*, November 4, 2017. http://www.chinadaily.com.cn/china/19thcpcnationalcongress/2017-11/04/content_34115212.htm.

Gilley, Bruce. "Middle Powers during Great Power Transitions: China's Rise and the Future of Canada–US Relations." *International Journal* 66, no. 2 (2011): 245–64.

Hall, Chris. "Free Trade Talks with China Will Not Yet Begin." *CBC News*, December 4, 2017. http://www.cbc.ca/news/politics/trudeau-china-meeting-1.4431136.

Holbraad, Carsten. *Middle Powers in International Politics*. London: Macmillan, 1984: 5.

Huang, Cary. "'Communist' China Has Embraced Capitalism but Remains Leninist." *South China Morning Post*, November 15, 2017. http://www.scmp.com/comment/insight-opinion/article/2119839/how-communist-china-has-embraced-capitalism-remains-leninist.

Hui, Ann. "What's Really behind China's Decision to Restrict Canola: Science or Politics?" *Globe and Mail*, August 30, 2016. https://www.theglobeandmail.

com/news/national/whats-really-behind-chinas-decision-to-restrict-canola-science-or-politics/article31625635/.

"International Travel and Migration." *Statistics New Zealand*. http://archive.stats.govt.nz/browse_for_stats/population/Migration/international-travel-and-migration-info-releases.aspx. Last modified April 2015.

Jacobi, Stephen. "Belt and Road and the New Zealand–China Connectivity Agenda: A New Zealand Perspective." Address to the Belt and Road Forum, Auckland, New Zealand, October 26, 2017. http://nzchinacouncil.org.nz/people/executive-director-stephen-jacobi/.

Jennings, Mark, and Melanie Read. "National Party MP Trained by Chinese Spies." *Newsroom*, September 13, 2017. https://www.newsroom.co.nz/2017/09/13/46657/national-mp-trained-by-chinese-spies.

Johnson, Tim. "Citing 'Unacceptable Risk,' Pentagon Halts Sales of Chinese Smartphones on Military Bases." *Government Technology*, 2018. http://www.govtech.com/security/Citing-Unacceptable-Risk-Pentagon-Halts-Sales-of-Chinese-Smartphones-on-Military-Bases.html.

Joint Communique on the Establishment of Diplomatic Relations between the People's Republic of China and New Zealand. *The Embassy of the People's Republic of China in New Zealand*. December 21, 1972. http://www.chinaembassy.org.nz/eng/zxgxs/t39440.htm.

Jordaan, Eduard. "The Concept of a Middle Power in International Relations: Distinguishing between Emerging and Traditional Middle Powers." *Politikon: South African Journal of Political Studies* 30, no. 2 (November 2003): 165.

Kohn, Bruce. *The Kiwi Pathfinder: Opening Mao's China to the West*. Wellington: Grantham House, 2008: 138.

Lampton, David M. *The Three Faces of Chinese Power: Might, Money, and Minds*, 1st edition. Berkeley: University of California Press, 2008.

Li, Jiechuan. "The Impact of the Wheat Trade between China and Canada in the 1960s." *World History* 1, no. 8 (2004). http://en.cnki.com.cn/Article_en/CJFDTOTAL-HIST200401008.htm.

Lin, Hai. "The East Wind Prevails Over the West Wind." *Peking Review*, March 13, 1958. https://www.marxists.org/history/erol/uk.hightide/red-star-mao.htm.

Luo, Zhaohui. "Opening a New Chapter." *China Daily*, January 9, 2016. http://usa.chinadaily.com.cn/world/2016-01/09/content_23008728.htm.

Mahon, David R. "Afternoons with Rewi Alley." *North & South*, no. 331 (October 2013): 126–27.

Mardell, Jacob. "The 'Community of Common Destiny' in Xi Jinping's New Era." *Diplomat*, 2017. https://thediplomat.com/2017/10/the-community-of-common-destiny-in-xi-jinpings-new-era/.

Na, Li. "Envoy Wants 'More, More, More' from Ties." *Chinadaily.Com.Cn*, February 23, 2017. http://usa.chinadaily.com.cn/world/2017-02/23/content_28310602.htm.

Nathan, Andrew J. *Chinese Democracy*. Berkeley: University of California Press, 1986.

New Zealand Herald. "PM Jacinda Ardern Discounts Chinese Influence." December 7, 2017.

New Zealand Contemporary China Research Centre, Australia-China Relations Institute. "New Zealand's China Policy: Building a Comprehensive Strategic Partnership." *Australia–China Relations Institute/New Zealand Contemporary China Research Centre*, July 12, 2015. https://www.australiachinarelations.org/content/new-zealand%E2%80%99s-china-policy-building-comprehensive-strategic-partnership-0.

"New Zealand Parliament, House of Representatives." *Parliamentary Debates,* February 23, 1973: 246.

"Norman Bethune." *Ville de Montréal* site. Last modified 2017. http://ville.montreal.qc.ca/portal/page?_pageid=5437,25107567&_dad=portal&_schema=PORTAL.

Norris, William J. *Chinese Economic Statecraft: Commercial Actors, Grand Strategy, and State Control.* Ithaca, NY: Cornell University Press, 2018.

Nottingham Communist Group. "Mao on Revisionism." *Red Star*, no. 3, February 1980. https://www.marxists.org/history/erol/uk.hightide/red-star-mao.htm.

"NZ-China FTA Upgrade." *New Zealand Ministry of Foreign Affairs and Trade*, 2017. https://www.mfat.govt.nz/en/trade/free-trade-agreements/free-trade-agreements-in-force/nz-china-free-trade-agreement.

O'Brien, Maire. "The Flexible Implementation of CIDA's China Program: Resolving the Disjuncture Between Structure and Process." Doctoral dissertation, York University, 2000.

Parks Canada, Gravenhurst. "Bethune Memorial House National Historic Site." Central East Ontario, Canada, 2017.

"Powhiri for the Chairman Mao Feather Cloak." *New Zealand China Friendship Society*, May 5, 2013.

Public Services and Procurement Canada Government of Canada. *Governance – CIDA's Program in China.* Government of Canada Publications, July 1, 2002.

Reilly, James. *China's Economic Statecraft: Turning Wealth into Power.* Sydney: Lowy Institute Analyses, 2013.

Sachdeva, Sam. "What Does China's Belt and Road Mean for NZ?" *Newsroom*, July 21, 2017. https://www.newsroom.co.nz/2017/07/20/39400/what-does-chinas-belt-and-road-mean-for-nz.

"SASAC." *State-owned Assets Supervision and Administration Commission of the State Council of the People's Republic of China.* Accessed May 18, 2018. http://en.sasac.gov.cn/.

Sheridan, Greg. "China to Be Most Powerful: Xi." *The Australian*, October 18, 2018. http://www.theaustralian.com.au/national-affairs/foreign-affairs/beijing-pulls-out-of-human-rights-dialogue-with-canberra/news-story/e944dc3a59ad6e8518068c94961f71c3.

"TAZARA; Tanzania-Zambia Railway Authority." *Tazara* site. Last modified November 4, 2017. https://tazarasite.com/index.php?option=com_content&view=article&id=70&Itemid=80.

"Trade with China Nearly Tripled in Past Decade." *Statistics New Zealand* site. Last modified September 7, 2016. http://archive.stats.govt.nz/browse_for_stats/industry_sectors/imports_and_exports/trade-china-tripled decade.aspx?url=/browse_for_stats/industry_sectors/imports_and_exports/trade-china-tripled-decade.aspx.

Trudeau, Justin. "Why the CNOOC-Nexen Deal Is Good for Canada." *Canada.com*, November 20, 2012. http://o.canada.com/news/national/justin-trudeau-why-the-cnooc-nexen-deal-is-good-for-canada.
Wang, David. "One Belt, One Road the Way forward for New Zealand." *Newsroom*, August 3, 2017. https://www.newsroom.co.nz/@boardroom/2017/08/02/40946/one-belt-one-road-the-way-forward-for-new-zealand.
Wilkins, Thomas S. "Australia: A Traditional Middle Power Faces the Asian Century." In *Middle Powers and the Rise of China*, edited by Bruce Gilley and Andrew O'Neill, 149. Washington, DC: Georgetown University Press, 2014.
Williams, Nia. "Canada Sees Opportunities for Chinese Investment in Oil Sands." *Reuters*, June 8, 2017. https://uk.reuters.com/article/canada-china-oilsands/canada-sees-opportunities-for-chinese-investment-in-oil-sands-minister-idUKL1N1J50QB.
Xi, Jinping. "Secure a Decisive Victory in Building a Moderately Prosperous Society in All Respects and Strive for the Great Success of Socialism with Chinese Characteristics for a New Era Delivered at the 19th National Congress of the Communist Party of China." *China Daily*, October 18, 2017. http://www.chinadaily.com.cn/china/19thcpcnationalcongress/2017-11/04/content_34115212.htm.
Xiaoming, Huang, and Jason Young. "China and the World Economy: Challenges and Opportunities for New Zealand." Discussion Paper 13/01, Victoria University of Wellington, New Zealand Contemporary China Research Centre, 2013, 65.
Zheng, Wang. "The Chinese Dream from Mao to Xi." *Diplomat*, May 7, 2018. https://thediplomat.com/2013/09/the-chinese-dream-from-mao-to-xi.
Zweig, David. *Internationalizing China: Domestic Interests and Global Linkages*, 1st edition. Ithaca, NY: Cornell University Press, 2002.

Part II

CHINA'S ECONOMIC STATECRAFT IN REGIONAL RELATIONS

Chapter 4

Can China's Economic Statecraft Win Soft Power in Africa?

Unpacking Trade, Investment, and Aid

Pippa Morgan

China, its amazing reemergence and its commitments for a win-win partnership with Africa, is one of the reasons for the beginning of the African renaissance.

—Meles Zenawi (2012), then Ethiopian prime minister (2012)[1]

We want the Chinese to leave and the old colonial rulers to return . . . at least they took good care of us . . . the Chinese are only out to exploit us.

—Michael Sata (2007), then Zambian opposition leader and former Zambian president[2]

CHINA'S AFRICAN IMAGE PROBLEM

Improving China's soft power—its ability to attract and influence without resorting to "hard" military or other coercive measures—is an important strategic goal (Ding 2010). In Africa, China's primary instrument for charming other nations is economic statecraft: through maneuvering of trade, aid, and investment, China hopes to win over African citizens and leaders, and thus improve its influence over the continent (Liang 2012). Although culture, values, and institutions are typically considered the primary instruments of soft power, African opinions on China are primarily driven by China's economic activities, making aid, trade, and investment fundamental to Chinese efforts to build soft power on the continent (Hanauer and Morris 2014, 60–63). However, its success is mixed, as China's growing economic linkages have attracted highly polarized responses among Africans. On the one hand, China is seen as an important partner, an alternative to traditional Western donors that lacks colonial baggage, and an example of a successful development model. But on the other hand, China is also perceived to be an exploitative plunderer of natural resources, supporter of non-democratic regimes, and supplier of shoddy (even dangerous) products.

What explains the polarized range of views among Africans on China? This chapter addresses this question through empirically unpacking the distinctive impacts of China's three primary tools of economic statecraft—trade policies, investment policies, and aid—on African perceptions of China. In all three of these areas China attempts to use economic policies to win over African leaders and citizens, but with varying degrees of success. Why?

To answer this question, this chapter explores the role of the Chinese state's oversight of the commercial actors on which China's economic "charm offensive" (Kurlantzick 2007) is reliant. The Chinese government is frequently assumed to wield a strong hand over all of the commercial actors on which its economic statecraft depends. However, in reality, it suffers from a principal-agent problem in which the state (the principal) cannot effectively oversee all of its agents (Norris 2016; Gill and Reilly 2007). In this chapter, I argue that the nature and extent of the principal-agent problem varies across China's three major tools of economic statecraft in Africa. China particularly struggles to monitor the behavior of the large number of private sector operators that dominate small-scale investment and China's exports to Africa. For these businesses, the overall reputation of "Made in China" is secondary to short-term financial gains, causing reputational damage where their profit motives conflict with China's soft power goals. On the other hand, China's foreign aid projects and large-scale investments in infrastructure and resources are typically carried out by major state-owned enterprises (SOEs) with strong state linkages and on-the-ground oversight from Chinese Embassies and Economic and Commercial Counselor (ECC) offices. Even though the companies serving as aid contractors or making large-scale investments are also commercial actors, their greater oversight means they are more accountable and more likely to fall in line with state goals.

This chapter assesses these contentions using data from the Afrobarometer Round 6 survey (2016) and evidence from secondary literature and media sources. The Afrobarometer surveyed almost 54,000 respondents across 36 countries, representing 76 percent of the African population. The survey asked respondents about their views of Chinese influence, Chinese aid, and factors contributing to positive and negative views of China. The evidence confirms that negative perceptions of China among Africans are fueled primarily by trade and small-scale investment-related issues, in particular trading of poor-quality, cheap Chinese manufactures. Contrary to popular Western perceptions, China's extraction of resources is not the major source of resentment for African citizens. Moreover, China's aid and large state-led investments in infrastructure generally make a positive contribution to China's image in the region, consistent with the prediction that these engagements suffer less from the principal-agent problem. Interestingly, the data suggest that on balance China is viewed positively within Africa, suggesting that the benefits of aid and investment outweigh other negative aspects of engagement with China. Despite the problems and critiques, China's use of economic statecraft to increase its soft power in Africa has been generally successful.

Of course, Africa is a large and diverse continent, and the dynamics addressed in this chapter may have different implications across varying economic, political, and societal contexts. In this chapter, I focus on the African continent as a whole, but in the concluding section discuss prospects for future research comparing Chinese economic statecraft and soft power across and within different African countries.

This chapter is organized into five parts. The following section conceptualizes economic statecraft and soft power, and reviews existing evidence on Chinese soft power in Africa. The third section outlines an analytical framework based on the principal-agent model to explain the differing effects of aid, investment, and trade tools. The fourth section provides empirical evidence, and the fifth section concludes.

"THE TOOLS OF BUSINESS": ECONOMIC STATECRAFT AND SOFT POWER

Economic Statecraft

Economic statecraft is the use of economic means to achieve political, strategic, or security goals—"waging geopolitics with capital" (Blackwill and Harris 2016, 4; Baldwin 1985). This volume is part of a growing body of literature that aims to understand the features of Chinese economic statecraft and appraise its successes and failures (Blackwill and Harris 2016; Li and Hong 2016; Norris 2016). Given its relative abundance of economic resources compared to military strength, China is particularly prone to using economic means to achieve political goals, either cooperatively or coercively depending on the context. For example, China has used boycotts and trade barriers as weapons in its historical and territorial disputes with Japan and the Philippines (Lai 2017), and generous transfers of foreign aid to isolate Taiwan diplomatically (Lin 2001; Rich 2009; Atkinson 2010). President Xi Jinping's flagship Belt and Road Initiative (BRI) is the latest and largest manifestation of modern China's economic statecraft (Yu 2017).

Soft Power

Soft power—the power to attract and co-opt—is a critical component of power in the twenty-first century (Nye 2004). Joseph Nye (1990, 166–67, 2004) originally identified "cultural attraction, ideology, and international institutions" as the key resources of soft power. Based on this conceptualization, some have concluded that China's soft power remains feeble compared to that of Western countries, due to its non-democratic political institutions and strong government hand in cultural output (Gill and Huang 2006; Shambaugh 2013, 2015). However, Chinese scholars and practitioners broaden the concept of soft power beyond the "tools of culture" to include what Joshua Kurlantzick calls "the tools of business"—economic dimensions of attractiveness (Kurlantzick 2007, 6, 2009, 167). These broader Chinese conceptualizations define soft power by its outcomes rather than the nature of the resources used to achieve it, in line with former Singaporean leader Lee Kuan Yew's definition: "when other nations admire and want to emulate aspects of that nation's civilization" (cited in Blanchard and Lu 2012, 567). In practice, contemporary China draws on both cultural (e.g., Confucius Institutes and Chinese television networks) and economic (aid, trade, and investment) tools to build its soft power. In Africa, where China has extensive economic clout but little historical or cultural affinity to draw upon, economic instruments are particularly important (Liang 2012).

Chinese Economic Statecraft and Soft Power in Africa

Modern China's economic statecraft in Africa dates back to the 1950s, when China offered technical and material assistance to socialist and postcolonial countries. Chinese trade, aid, and investment have increased in line with its own economic development, and attention on the China-Africa relationship ballooned rapidly after 2006, when China held a pivotal summit of the Forum on China-Africa Cooperation (FOCAC) for forty-eight African leaders, themed "friendship, peace, cooperation and development," in which Beijing pledged to scale-up imports and exports to unprecedented levels, cancel debt, and increase aid and investment. China's economic engagements are closely connected to political and security goals. According to its 2015 Africa Policy Paper, contemporary China hopes to promote not only common economic development, but also "mutual assistance in security," "solidarity and coordination in international affairs," and an increase in the "representation and voice" of non-Western countries on the global stage (Xinhua 2015). Given the central importance of China's economic activities to African opinions on China (see Hanauer and Morris 2014, 60–63), the soft power impacts of Chinese aid, trade, and investment are vital to the success of China's broader goals on the continent.

However, views of Chinese economic engagement among Africans vary widely: on the one hand, China is criticized for flooding local markets with poor-quality products, destroying local environments, and extracting natural resources; while on the other hand, it is seen as a new development model and partner lacking the colonial baggage of Western countries.[3] How can researchers unpack these competing perspectives? Some studies point to differences between the internal contexts of African countries. Fijałkowski (2011) emphasizes the extent to which African states are "willing to buy" Chinese attempts to influence, while Sautman and Yan (2009) highlight the degree to which politicians raise the "Chinese problem" for political ends, and the extent of Western media penetration. Others point to individual-level differences in experiences and outlooks (Keuleers 2015), or class or social differences within specific African states (Esteban 2010). An alternative perspective is offered by Marek Hanusch (2012), who uses earlier Afrobarometer Round 4 data to empirically compare the differing effects of trade and Foreign Direct Investment (FDI) on opinions of China across the African continent. Hanusch (2012) finds that exports from China to Africa have a negative effect on opinions, while FDI fosters positive views on China. This chapter sheds additional light on China's complex relationship with Africa by building on Hanusch's (2012) work in two ways: First, through incorporating China's extensive aid to Africa into the analysis; and second, by utilizing an analytical framework based on principal-agent theory to explain the differing effects of aid, trade, and investment.

WIELDING THE "TOOLS OF BUSINESS": THE PRINCIPAL-AGENT PROBLEM

Blackwill and Harris (2016) identify seven tools of economic statecraft: trade policy, investment policy, aid, sanctions, cyber-attacks, financial and monetary policies, and national governance of energy and commodities. As outlined elsewhere in this volume, economic statecraft can be used coercively or cooperatively. However, the pursuit of soft power naturally requires noncoercive economic tools: principally the provision of aid, policies to manage and guide investment, and preferential trade policies.[4] In some cases, the pursuit of soft power is a direct and primary goal of these instruments, as in China's funding of training programs for African officials, or attempts to improve views on Chinese brands. In other cases, growing soft power is an indirect, secondary aim. Nevertheless, building China's image and attractiveness is a goal that underpins its overall strategy of economic engagement in Africa (Liang 2012).

Figure 4.1 illustrates the overlap between tools of economic statecraft and soft power resources. Positive tools of economic statecraft (aid, trade, and investment) serve not only as instruments of economic policy, but also as tools for increasing a country's attractive power. How do these three tools compare in Chinese soft power building efforts in Africa, and what explains the difference in their effectiveness? Existing literature points to the severity of the principal-agent problem as a key explanatory variable in the success or failure of China's economic statecraft. The principal-agent problem arises when two conditions are fulfilled: First, principals and agents have divergent interests; and second, there is asymmetric information, so that principals lack the information to verify what agents are doing and to keep them in check (Jensen and Meckling 1976; Eisenhardt 1989, 58). Under these conditions, agents may pursue actions that run counter to the interests of the principal. By definition, the state's (the principal's) primary motives when carrying out economic statecraft are political, strategic, or security oriented.[5] However, the corporate agents' main motivations remain financial. These diverging incentives give rise to a principal-agent problem, as the state faces monitoring difficulties and has less information than the corporate implementers about their behavior.

For example, Zhang and Smith (2017) find that profit-motives of Chinese corporate actors present a challenge to successful implementation of aid projects. Likewise, Reilly (2014) argues that principal-agent issues aggravate diplomatic tensions and erode border security in China's economic strategy

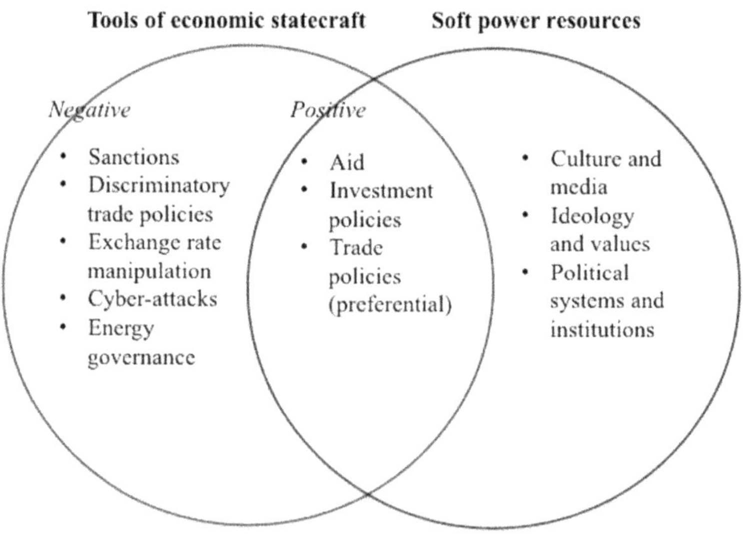

Figure 4.1 Overlap between Economic Statecraft and Soft Power Resources. *Source*: Author's own compilation.

together North Korea. Gill and Reilly (2007) hypothesize that the profit motives of Chinese corporate agents hinder Beijing's political interests in Africa, as companies' pursuit of profit encourages them to break local rules and deliver poor-quality services. However, Gill and Reilly (2007) do not directly compare the severity of the principal agent problem between trade, investment, and aid, nor do they give a systematic empirical study of their effects on African citizens' opinions of China. In one of the most important recent works on Chinese economic statecraft, Norris (2016) asks why in certain cases the Chinese state can overcome the principal-agent problem and successfully exercise economic statecraft, while in other contexts it fails. Norris identifies a series of relational factors that determine the level of state control over agents, including the market structure, state unity, the reporting relationship, and the relative distribution of resources between state and corporate actors.

This chapter contributes to these literatures through an exploration of how the severity of the principal-agent problem differs between aid, trade, and investment—the three major tools of economic statecraft in China-Africa relations—and how this in turn affects China's success in building soft power in Africa.

Aid is typically implemented by approved contractors (usually SOEs) with close state ties. Likewise, China's large-scale investments in infrastructure and resources are usually carried out by large SOEs with close state links, and may be supported by (and therefore monitored by) China's policy banks. In these contexts, the Chinese state is more easily able to monitor corporate actors to ensure their behavior does not damage China's image, and the principal agent problem is limited.

Smaller private sector investors, however, although also encouraged to "go global," are more difficult for the state to monitor and may operate under the radar and against local rules. Moreover, although China has tried to structure trade policies to "win friends" in Africa (e.g., with favorable tariffs for poorer countries), in practice much trade is carried out by small-scale private companies. The profit motives of these companies, in the context of the respective economic comparative advantages of Africa, may incentivize them to flood local markets with cheap, poor-quality manufactures that damage China's reputation.

CHINESE AID, TRADE, AND INVESTMENT: INSTRUMENTS OF ECONOMIC STATECRAFT

Aid

Foreign aid has a long history as a tool of economic statecraft (Morgenthau 1962). The aid literature typically defines foreign aid as financial flows that meet the OECD's definition of Official Development Assistance (ODA),[6] although there are some differences between the OECD and Chinese government conceptualizations.[7] China has given aid to Africa since 1956,[8] and has used its aid program to achieve specific political goals such as winning the Chinese UN seat from the Republic of China (ROC) in 1971 (Bräutigam 2008, 202), supporting socialist allies during the Mao era (Morgan 2018), mitigating international isolation following the 1989 Tiananmen incident (Taylor 1998), and persuading African countries to switch diplomatic recognition from the ROC to the People's Republic (Bräutigam 2009, 71; Tseng 2008). The scope and scale of China's aid program has increased in line with China's own economic growth, and since 2000, China has committed an estimated 46,052 million USD in aid[9] to Africa, covering over 1,800 separate projects (Dreher et al. 2017). Figure 4.2 shows the number of Chinese aid projects in Africa recorded by AidData's "Global Chinese Official Finance Dataset" from 2000 to 2014.

Some Chinese aid projects are implemented directly by line ministries or provincial governments. For example, Chinese provinces dispatch medical teams under the auspices of the Ministry of Health;[10] while Chinese government scholarships are administered by the China Scholarship Council (CSC), a nonprofit organization affiliated to the Ministry of Education, with a coordinating role for Chinese Embassies in recipient countries (Dong and Chapman 2008). However, projects in other sectors—in particular China's major infrastructure and construction projects—are typically implemented by commercial contractors who are paid using grants or soft loans from the Chinese government or policy banks. China does not

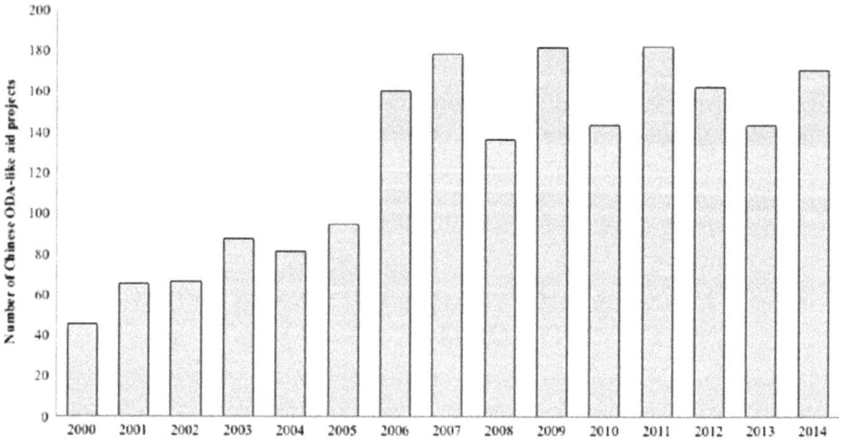

Figure 4.2 Chinese Aid Projects in Africa. *Source*: Compiled by author using data from Dreher et al. (2017).

release official data on firm type and aid projects. However, multiple pieces of existing research suggest that the largest proportions are SOEs, such as China State Construction Engineering Corporation (CSCEC), China Civil Engineering Construction Corporation (CCECC), and China Railway Construction Corporation (CRCC) (Ohashi 2013, 91–92; Buckley and Weng 2016). Of the African projects in AidData's database of Chinese official finance that list an implementing organization, 58 percent list a Chinese SOE as implementer, with eighteen out of the top twenty projects by monetary value implemented by an SOE.[11] Warmerdam and Dijk's (2013, 285) survey of Chinese companies in Kampala, Uganda found that only 12 percent of private Chinese companies were motivated to come to the country for a Chinese government project, compared to 56 percent for SOEs, and 33 percent for state-private hybrids. Chen, Goldstein, and Orr's (2009, 79) survey of major Chinese contractors[12] in the African market found that all thirty-five firms surveyed were state-owned. Finally, McKinsey's survey of over 10,000 Chinese firms across Africa found that 83 percent of Chinese government policy–linked finance went to state-owned enterprises, while just 17 percent went to private firms (Yuan Sun, Jayaram, and Kassiri 2017, 35).

Since China's SOE reforms of the 1980s and 1990s, the companies that typically serve as aid contractors are profit-seeking enterprises concerned with commercial rather than political or strategic motives. However, their behavior is comparatively easy to monitor for two reasons. First, their large size makes them highly visible to the authorities. Second, administrative structures exist for monitoring their activities. Monitoring of aid implementers occurs in two main ways. First, SOEs are directly supervised by relevant administrative authorities. China's central SOEs are monitored by the State-Owned Assets Supervision and Administration Commission (SASAC), which sits under the State Council, China's primary administrative authority. The SASAC appoints central SOEs top executives, sets wage-related policies, dispatches supervisory panels, and inspects legal compliance (among other functions).[13] Provincial SOEs face similar monitoring by provincial-level authorities that perform analogous functions to the SASAC. Among some large SOEs there remains overlap between the bureaucracy and senior management, with senior managers holding administrative ranks. Existing research suggests that SOEs in Africa have high levels of awareness of Chinese government policies, and are more likely than private firms to strictly follow local regulations, reflecting their closer monitoring from the state (Buckley and Weng 2016).

Secondly, all aid contractors—regardless of ownership structure—are supervised through their application to MOFCOM's list of approved overseas contractors, and through monitoring of progress for specific projects during the aid project cycle. In recipient countries, aid implementers have regular direct contact with Chinese Economic and Commercial Counselors (ECCs). ECCs serve as MOFCOM's in-country representatives and undertake day-to-day oversight of Chinese assistance. Project cycles vary depending on the nature of the finance and the relationship between China and the recipient government, but follow a basic pattern of: (1) submission of request(s) by the recipient government, either to the local Chinese Embassy (for grants) or to the EXIM bank (for concessional loans); (2) evaluation of the request and submission to China's Ministry of Commerce (MOFCOM) for agreement; (3) signing of an agreement and appointment of an approved Chinese contractor; (4) payment and monitoring of progress by MOFCOM, and/or the EXIM bank, and/or a monitoring company (Davies et al. 2008, 15–18; Bräutigam 2009, 143). Throughout this process, ECCs serve as a practical bridge between MOFCOM in Beijing, the local government, and Chinese contractors.

Investment Policies

Since the launch of the 1999 "Go Global" strategy, stimulating outward commercial investment by Chinese businesses has been a key facet of China's international strategy, and an important part of its efforts to "charm other nations" (Kurlantzick 2007, 84). While much attention is concentrated on Chinese SOEs outward direct investment (ODI), encouraging private sector ODI is another key part of China's strategy (Luo, Xue, and Han 2010, 3). As shown in Figure 4.3 Chinese outward investment has risen alongside China's own economic development.

According to MOFCOM data there were 2,946 investment approvals in 50 African countries from 2000 to 2015, around 17 percent of which were made by Central State-Owned Enterprises (CSOEs), with remainder by provincial SOEs and privately run firms (Morgan and Zheng 2018b, 19–20). SOEs dominate investment in the resource and infrastructure sectors,[14] while smaller-scale private sector businesses dominate in manufacturing and services. In general, SOEs make much larger investments than private firms. For example, Warmerdam and Dijk (2013) found that the majority of SOEs they surveyed in Kampala, Uganda, invested over 10 million USD. In contrast, only 29 percent of private firms invested more than 1 million USD.

Chinese firms investing abroad are required to register with MOFCOM or their relevant provincial branch, and until 2014 were required to seek official approval.[15] In addition to processes to monitor where Chinese firms are making investments, the government has promulgated various regulations to manage the behavior of the myriad Chinese investors in Africa and elsewhere. These include provisions for corporate social responsibility, social policies, environmental management, fair competition, risk management, and

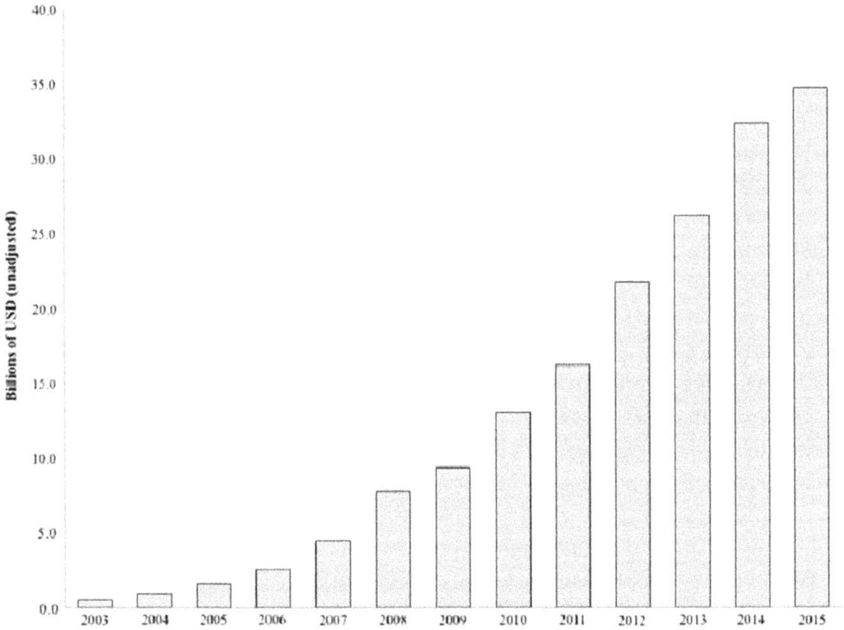

Figure 4.3 Chinese FDI Stock in Africa. *Source*: Compiled by author using data from Johns Hopkins University SAIS China-Africa Research Initiative, http://www.sais-cari.org/data-chinese-and-american-fdi-to-africa.

security management (CAITEC et al. 2015). China's ODI regime is explicitly designed to ensure that economic interests of outward investors do not harm China's reputation in and relations with host countries; and principle five of the State Council's 2007 "Nine Principles on Encouraging and Standardizing Foreign Investment" requires Chinese companies to follow local laws and maintain social and environmental responsibility (Maurin and Yeophantong 2013, 287). The Chinese government and affiliated research bodies have also strengthened research efforts in this area: in 2015 the Chinese Academy of International Trade and Economic Cooperation (CAITEC), MOFCOM's research arm, released a report on the sustainable development of Chinese enterprises overseas alongside China's State-Owned Assets Supervision and Administration Commission (SASAC) and UNDP China (CAITEC et al. 2015). A further report on the same topic was released in 2017, linking the UN 2030 Agenda for Sustainable Development and China's Belt and Road Initiative (CAITEC et al. 2017). These reports aim to serve as an information source and guide for Chinese companies on appropriate and sustainable behavior, as well as offering suggestions for the Chinese government and other stakeholders on how to effectively oversee and manage the behavior of

Chinese outward investors. The Chinese government is also directly encouraging large Chinese investors to undertake corporate social responsibility initiatives, for example, through using their corporate training schools to offer classes to the local population.[16]

The success of these oversight initiatives is highly dependent on the type of company involved. Large State-Owned Enterprises (SOEs) have close in-country connections with Chinese Embassies and Economic and Commercial Counselor (ECC) offices, and—as outlined above—are also subject to a high degree of political supervision at home through central and local State-Owned Assets Supervision and Administration Commissions.

Moreover, similarly to aid, in practice China's commercial official finance for investment is primarily targeted at SOEs, who use their political capital to compete in market settings (Liou 2014; Buckley and Weng 2016). The mechanisms for seeking official finance for investment thus constitute an important method by which the Chinese government monitors the activities of companies operating in Africa, isolating those who are distant from these processes to official oversight.

While the government is by no means fully successful in monitoring SOEs and ensuring their commercial interests don't harm China's wider political goals (see, Liou [2009] or Maurin and Yeophantong [2013] for examples of the oversight challenges), the comparatively small number of large SOEs are much easier to manage than the plethora of smaller private investors. Communication between private enterprises and the Chinese government is poor, and there is a tendency for small private entrepreneurs to avoid registering with the embassy or ECC at all—with little chance of securing official investment funding, they do not see a value in registration (Buckley and Weng 2016; Gu 2016, 164). Chinese ECCs in Africa are frequently staffed by a small number of people with a large number of duties,[17] and have neither the administrative capacity or the structures and policies in place to monitor the behavior of the myriad of small private Chinese investors. Indeed, the Chinese government is simply unaware of the existence of many small-scale private companies. McKinsey's survey of 10,000 Chinese firms found huge discrepancies between the number of companies in Chinese (and local) government databases across all African countries surveyed, and in particular discovered an unexpectedly large number of small private firms engaged in manufacturing and trade (Yuan Sun, Jayaram, and Kassiri 2017).

Without knowing which private Chinese investors are actually operating in their jurisdictions, it is very difficult for Chinese officials to hold them accountable. Moreover, poor communications with the private sector also leads to lower policy awareness. In interviews with fifty-eight personnel of Chinese companies in Africa, Buckley and Weng (2016, 17) found that over half of SOE interviewees had some level of awareness of Chinese policies and guidelines, compared to only one-third of private sector respondents.

Trade Policies

Like aid and investment, Chinese trade with Africa has soared in recent years, and China is now Africa's number one trading partner (see Figure 4.4). In line with the respective comparative advantages and economic structures of China and most African economies, China mainly exports manufactured products and imports primary commodities and raw materials from a small number of resource-rich countries (FOCAC 2010; Haugen 2011).

The Chinese government has instituted several measures to improve the quantity and quality of Sino-Africa trade relations with the aim of boosting its economic and political linkages with the continent. Since 2003, China has offered tariff-free access to the huge Chinese market for the least developed African countries, and has tried to rebalance its imports through expanding the proportion of manufactures from Africa, for example, through opening an African Products Exhibition Center in China's light manufactures trading hub in Yiwu City, Zhejiang Province (PRC State Council 2013). In addition, China has taken steps to improve the quality of products exported to Africa, and to shut down Intellectual Property (IP) violations and counterfeiting. For example, from December to March 2011 Chinese authorities launched a special crackdown on poor quality and counterfeit products, including pre-shipment inspections (PRC State Council 2013), and in 2015 the Chinese government announced its intention to increase the manpower involved in monitoring the quality of Chinese exports, and urged Economic and Commercial Counselor offices to set up teams to ensure the reputation of Chinese products and Chinese brands (Nan 2015).

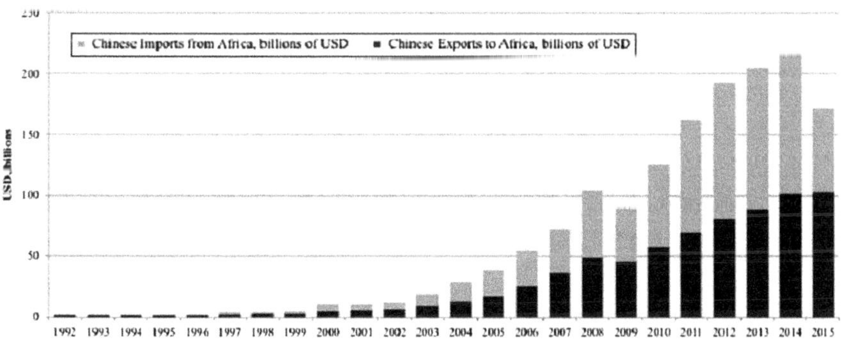

Figure 4.4 Chinese Trade with Africa. *Source*: Data from Johns Hopkins University SAIS China-Africa Research Initiative, http://www.sais-cari.org/data-china-africa-trade.

China's manufacturing commodity export boom, including to Africa, has been driven mainly by a large number of small- and medium-sized private firms, operating primarily on China's East and South coast (Chen 2006, 142). The Sino-African manufactures trade is thus characterized by a large number of small- or medium-sized private enterprises that have limited official contact. Many small-scale private businesses are involved in what Lee (2014, 13–14) terms "globalization from below"—cash trade, often in used or copied goods, without "lawyers or copyright laws . . . through more informal and at times illegal structures." Difficulties in monitoring trade overlap with the challenges of supervising smaller private investors: many Chinese manufactured products in African markets are sold by individual- or family-run Chinese enterprises, which are typically off the radar of the authorities (Dobler 2008; Mohan and Tan-mullins 2009). Shen (2015, 88) finds that only 9 percent of Chinese companies in Africa that are engaged in the trade sector are state owned. In addition to small-scale Chinese enterprises, networks of African traders are also involved in exports of "made in China" manufactures to Africa, with large communities concentrated in the manufacturing hubs of Yiwu in Zhejiang Province, and Guangzhou, capital of Guangdong province (Cissé 2015).

In sum, the level of state control over the corporate implementers of China's three major tools of economic statecraft in Africa varies significantly. The large SOEs that typically implement aid projects and large-scale investments in infrastructure and resources have close government linkages and higher awareness of government policies. Smaller-scale private traders and investors, on the other hand, are much harder to monitor and typically operate at arm's length from the authorities. This discussion leads to the following related propositions, which I test empirically in the next section:

1. Due to higher levels of state oversight, Chinese aid and large-scale infrastructure investments are more likely to make a positive contribution to Chinese soft power than other types of economic engagement.
2. Due to lower levels of state oversight, Chinese trade and small-scale investments are less likely to make a positive contribution to Chinese soft power than other types of economic engagement.

AFRICAN VIEWS ON CHINA: UNTANGLING THE IMPACTS OF AID, TRADE, AND INVESTMENT

Public Opinion, Foreign Policy, and Soft Power

Soft power's intangibility makes it inherently tricky to measure. Nye (2004, 17–18) argues that opinion polls, although imperfect, are a useful way of measuring soft power. Existing studies have used opinion polls conducted in foreign countries to measure the success of China's Confucius Institutes (Paradise 2009) and assess African views of Chinese aid (Han and Huang 2016) and general perceptions of China in Africa (Sautman and Yan 2009).

Whitney and Shambaugh (2009) use public opinion polls to assess soft power across the Asian continent. However, whether and how public opinion actually translates into soft power depends on whether or not public opinion affects foreign policy.

Several studies find that public opinion on the United States in foreign countries has substantive impact on their policies toward the United States (Datta 2009; Goldsmith and Horiuchi 2012). Tomz, Weeks, and Yarhi-Milo (2017) propose two mechanisms through which popular views affect foreign policy in democracies: "sanctioning," in which leaders are punished by the electorate for policies the public disagrees with, and "selection," where prospective leaders propose policies they believe the public will favor and carry them out while in office, and find empirical evidence for both mechanisms. Africa contains a spread of democratic, hybrid, and nondemocratic regimes, and it is unclear whether these specific mechanisms can translate to non-democracies. However, there is evidence within the literature that public opinion affects foreign policy in authoritarian states such as China (Li and Chen 2018); and in their study of public opinion and foreign policy across fifty-eight democratic and nondemocratic countries, Goldsmith and Horiuchi (2012) find no significant differences between democracies and non-democracies.

These literatures suggest that the views of African citizens on China matter for African foreign policies toward China. Public opinion is an important constituent of China's soft power because populations with positive images of China are likely to be supportive toward their own leaders when they pursue policies favorable to China. In democratic countries, citizens express their support in elections, giving leaders a strong incentive to respond to public opinion. However, even in nondemocratic countries publics may put pressure on leaders through traditional and social media, protests, or formal official channels [47]. Thus, favorable images of China (as measured by public opinion surveys) increase China's ability to attract and co-opt African governments (i.e., its soft power).

To unpack the impacts on Chinese soft power of aid, investment, and trade, this study uses data from Afrobarometer Round 6,[18] combined with evidence from media and secondary sources. Afrobarometer is a nonpartisan African research network that carries out public opinion surveys on political and economic issues in Africa. The Round 6 survey covered surveyed almost 54,000 respondents across 36 African countries, representing 76 percent of the African population, and asked substantially more detailed questions about China than earlier rounds. Compared to other major opinion surveys such as the Pew Global Attitudes survey, the Afrobarometer offers a much wider coverage of African countries (the latest Pew surveyed only seven African states), as well as more detailed information about views on China's economic impact.[19] Respondents were questioned on their views of Chinese aid, the factors contributing to positive and negative perceptions of China, including aid, investment, and trade, and related issues such as natural resource extraction, the conduct of Chinese citizens, and the quality of Chinese products.

"Charm offensive": Factors Contributing to a Positive Image of China

Figure 4.5 shows responses to the question "which of the following factors contributes most to positive [*sic*] image of China in [your country]?"

As expected, the factor that contributes most to positive views on China is China's support for African infrastructure and development, which includes both aid and investment in infrastructure. Responses to further questioning on Chinese aid confirm its positive contribution to Chinese soft power in Africa. When asked to evaluate whether or not Chinese development assistance did a good or bad job in meeting their countries' needs, over 50 percent of respondents said that it did a very good or somewhat good job, compared to less than 20 percent who thought Chinese aid did a bad job (see Figure 4.6).

Positive views on Chinese aid run counter to popular Western narratives of shoddy Chinese roads, railways, and buildings made by corner-cutting companies (see, e.g., French 2014, 366–67), and to arguments that Chinese aid harms African citizens by enabling corrupt elites and poor governance

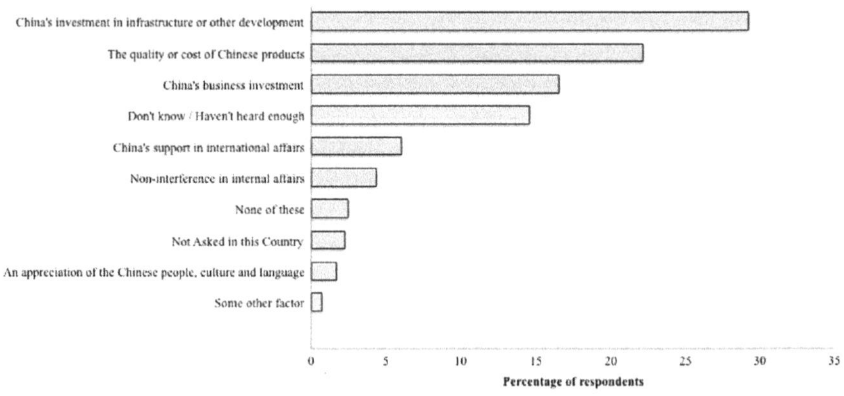

Figure 4.5 Factors Contributing to a Positive Image of China. *Source*: Afrobarometer Round 6 (Responses to Question 81c).

(Naím 2007). Data on the quality of Chinese-funded aid projects are not officially available, but the performance of Chinese contractors employed to deliver World Bank aid projects provides a useful proxy. Jamie Farrel (2016) quantitatively compared the outcomes of seventy-two Chinese and thrity-six OECD World Bank aid contracts. Like Chinese aid contracts, Chinese firms that win World Bank contracts tend to be large State-Owned Enterprises (77 percent of the contracts in Farrel's study were won by just seven SOEs). Farrel found no statistically significant difference between the quality of OECD companies' work and that of Chinese contractors, suggesting that major Chinese SOEs generally operate on par with those of developed countries. Moreover, the World Bank reported environmental and social problems in the execution of only two of seventy-two contracts signed with Chinese firms (Farrel 2016, 7). These patterns are consistent with the explanation offered in this chapter, that the SOEs carrying out aid projects are closely connected to and well-monitored by China's bureaucracies and policy banks. Although they are profit-seeking enterprises operating under contract, their behavior is generally in line with China's foreign policy aims. As an official of the Zambia's Development Agency (ZDA) remarked, large Chinese firms are seen to "have standards," but smaller firms—typically involved in trade or small-scale manufactures—sometimes do not follow local laws.[20] These findings are also consistent with a survey of African university students and faculty in nine African countries carried out by Sautman and Yan (2009, 739, 742), which finds that the views of firms working on large Chinese projects are generally positive, while views of small Chinese businesses are mixed. These

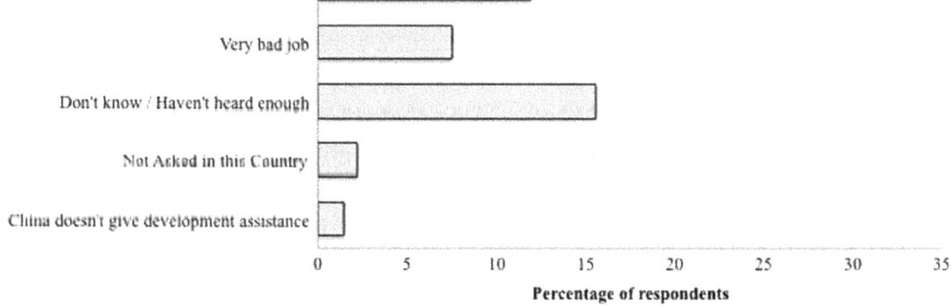

Figure 4.6 Opinions on China's Development Assistance. *Source*: Afrobarometer Round 6 (Responses to Question 81e).

findings suggest that Gill and Reilly's (2007) emphasis on SOEs as troublesome agents in China-Africa relations is somewhat misplaced.

Interestingly, the low cost of Chinese products is welcomed by Africans: Figure 4.5 shows that over 20 percent of respondents reported low-cost products as the variable contributing most to positive images of China. For African consumers, it appears that Chinese manufactures are an affordable and therefore welcome option. However, as discussed below, African opinions of the quality of Chinese products are extremely low, and are the key factors contributing to negative perceptions of China in Africa. This points to paradoxical attitudes to Chinese products, which could possibly be driven by differences in incomes. For the very poor, cheap Chinese products could represent welcome access to goods they previously could not afford. But for many others, the poor quality of Chinese products could be a source of resentment and—as outlined below—do major damage to opinions on China.

Rogue Elements: What Damages China's Image in Africa?

In 2014, Chinese Aabassador to Tanzania Liu Xinsheng gave an interview in which he criticized the "bad habits" of Chinese traders and their tendency to engage in unlawful behavior such as smuggling of counterfeit goods (Kaiman 2014). The same interview triggered China's foreign ministry to condemn the "unlawful behaviour of a small number of Chinese people in Tanzania and other African countries [which] has harmed China's image," and "had a negative impact on friendly . . . relations" (Kaiman 2014).

The Afrobarometer Round 6 data confirm that the Chinese government is right to be concerned about the impact of Chinese traders and small-scale investors on its image. Figure 4.7 shows responses to the question "Which of the following factors contributes most to negative images of China in [your country]?"

The poor quality of Chinese products is by far the largest factor, with 35 percent of respondents identifying it as the major cause of negative opinions of China. Despite their competitive prices—affordable for African citizens on low incomes—Chinese exports have a significantly detrimental impact on how Africans perceive China. Poor-quality and counterfeit medical drugs have attracted particular attention, as have shoddily made electronic goods, which carry fire risks (Lee 2014, 91). For example, in June 2012, 1.4 million packets of counterfeit malaria medication—containing none of the active ingredient necessary to make the drug effective—were discovered hidden in a shipment of speakers imported from Guangzhou to Angola (Lee 2014, 90). Uganda's then head of Interpol Uganda described fake Chinese drugs as "crimes against humanity" (Jocelyne 2013). African media lament the continent's status as a "dumping ground" for counterfeit products from China.

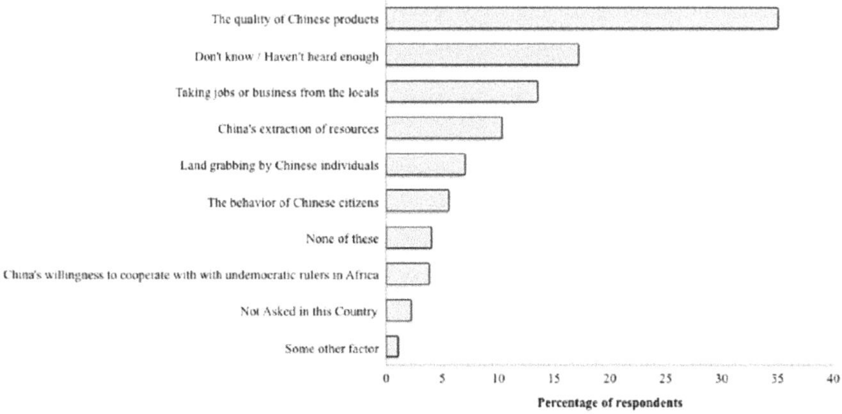

Figure 4.7 Factors Contributing to a Negative Image of China. *Source*: Afrobarometer Round 6 (Responses to Question 81d).

(Thomas 2015), and cheap Chinese manufactures have attracted derogatory nicknames around the continent—in Naiorbi's Eastleigh trading hub, for example, they're known as "one-time" (Kuo 2017). Small private Chinese firms have also been found to lag behind SOEs in environmental and social responsibility, as Chinese central authorities' increasingly progressive attitude toward environmental responsibilities of Chinese firms operating abroad struggles to filter through to small private enterprises (Compagnon and Alejandro 2013; Aklilu 2014).

The second largest problem damaging African views of China—Chinese businesses taking jobs from locals—is also primarily related to low-cost Chinese manufactures, although is more a function of economic fundamentals than failure on the part of the state to control commercial actors. Both private and state-owned Chinese firms invested in Africa employ a significant majority of locals (Yuan Sun, Jayaram, and Kassiri 2017, 43). However, imports of cheap Chinese products, typically sold by small-scale Chinese or African traders, have crowded out domestic manufacturing industries in sectors such as textiles, resulting in job losses for local citizens (Bräutigam 2009, 218–19; Thomson 2010, 174). For example, competition from Chinese manufactured copies of traditional African printed fabrics "badly battered" textile firms across the continent (Bräutigam 2009, 218–19). In South Africa, by the mid-2000s more than 600 textile firms had closed and 60,000 workers had been made unemployed as a result of competition with China's manufacturing sector (Hanusch 2012, 5).[21]

All these factors add up to a perception among Africans that China benefits more than local economies from the trading relationship.[22] Issues with small Chinese trading firms have even sparked popular protest: in April 2017, hundreds protested against the presence of Chinese traders in Kampala, Uganda, calling for Chinese trade to be restructured to large-scale investments (Muhumza 2017).

On the other hand, the issues that are commonly critiqued in conventional narratives on the China-Africa relationship, such as natural resource extraction and support for undemocratic leaders (see, e.g., Naím [2007]), appear comparatively unimportant for African citizens, earning only 10 and 4 percent of responses, respectively. Of course, large state-owned firms have at times been caught in high-profile controversies, in particular in the extractive sector, and these can have strongly negative impacts in individual country contexts.[23] Nonetheless, the empirical data suggest that at the aggregate level, these are relatively minor contributors to negative African views on China.

Overall Perceptions

On balance, how do the benefits and drawbacks of aid, investment, and trade on African views on China weigh out? Overall, the data suggest that the scales tip in China's favor (Lekorwe et al. 2016). Figure 4.8 shows responses to the question "Do you think that China's economic and political influence [on your country] is mostly positive, or mostly negative, or haven't you heard enough to say?" Over 60 percent of respondents had somewhat or very positive views of China, compared to 37 percent negative, unsure or ambivalent views. It seems that overall the positive effects of Chinese aid and investment

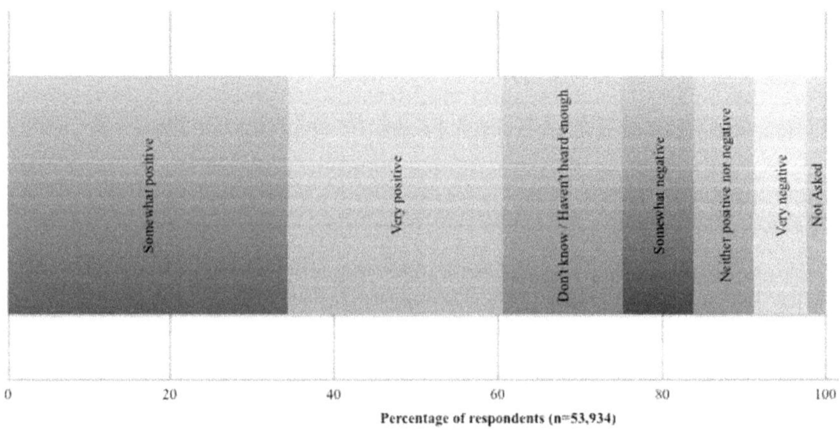

Figure 4.8 Overall Opinions of China. *Source*: Afrobarometer Round 6 (Responses to Question 81b).

in infrastructure outweigh the negative impacts of poor-quality goods and crowding out of local markets.

Conclusions and Wider Implications

This chapter has explored China's deployment of trade policies, investment policies, and aid to build soft power on the African continent, deploying principal-agent theory to understand in what situations, and why, Chinese economic statecraft in Africa succeeds or fails in this aim. Like Norris (2016), I argue that the degree of state control over the corporate implementers of economic statecraft is important to understanding its outcomes. China's aid projects and large-scale investments in infrastructure and resources are typically implemented by SOEs that, due to their size and ownership structure are comparatively easy for Chinese Embassies and other state actors to communicate with and monitor. On the other hand—although China has encouraged both public and private investors to "go global," and has tried to implement trade policies that will help it "win friends" in Africa—in practice they are much more difficult for the state to supervise (or even to keep track of) because private investments and exports of manufactured goods from China to Africa are typically carried out by small-scale commercial actors. Data from the Afrobarometer Round 6 survey, combined with qualitative evidence from a variety of sources, support this argument. Overall, for African citizens, the factors that cause the most damage to China's image are primarily related to the behavior of small-scale traders and investors in Chinese manufactures, while China's aid and infrastructure investments are generally welcomed.

This analysis makes two main contributions to research on Chinese economic statecraft and wider foreign policy. First, by comparing the severity and consequences of the principal-agent problem between the three major tools of aid, trade, and investment, it contributes to literature employing the principal-agent theory to understand China's economic statecraft in Africa and elsewhere. Second, through analysis of Afrobarometer survey data from almost 54,000 respondents across 36 African countries, this chapter contributes to understanding on the understudied views of ordinary citizens of African countries on Chinese economic engagement. Contrary to popular perceptions in Western media and scholarship, Chinese aid and infrastructure investments are generally viewed in a positive light and contribute to China's soft power "charm offensive" in Africa, and China's resource extraction and support for nondemocratic governments are not dominant sources of criticism. Instead, residents of African countries care first and foremost about flooding of poor-quality Chinese manufactures into African markets.

These findings suggest that to understand the implications of Chinese economic engagement in Africa, more attention is needed both on the underemphasized and understudied behavior of small-scale Chinese commercial actors, and on the opinions of African citizens directly affected by China's growing presence on the continent. This chapter focuses on public opinions over African continent as a whole, but its findings imply that the impacts of Chinese economic statecraft on soft power will differ across countries, as the nature of Chinese economic engagement varies depending on development levels, resources, and other variables. This chapter is intended to open the door to further research that compares opinions on Chinese economic statecraft across and within different country contexts.

NOTES

1. Speech at the opening of the African Union headquarters (see https://www.ft.com/content/86cbd2ba-4b60-11e1-a325-00144feabdc0?mhq5j=e5).

2. Comments made in 2007 while Michael Sata was leader of the opposition party Patriotic Front (see http://www.telegraph.co.uk/news/obituaries/11195960/Michael-Sata-obituary.html).

3. See, for example, Manji and Marks (2007).

4. Other positive instruments, such as non-devaluation of the *renminbi* during the 1997 Asian Financial Crisis, are sometimes employed (Ding 2010).

5. Of course, China's activities in Africa also have economic motivations, and many analyses focus on Africa's economic importance to China, in particular as a source of natural resources. However, Africa represents a very small proportion of Chinese global economic activity. In 2016 just 4 percent of Chinese trade (imports plus exports) was with Africa (see International Trade Map: https://www.trademap.org/Index.aspx), and just 1 percent of Chinese foreign direct investment went to Africa (see Chinese official statistics: http://data.stats.gov.cn/easyquery.htm?cn=C01). In reality, Africa is likely of more geopolitical and strategic importance to China than economic importance (although for Africa, China is of course economically extremely significant). Moreover, where the state does have an economic interest it is in long-term stable development, not short-term profit (see http://www.china.org.cn/english/features/China-Africa/82055.htm). On balance, therefore, it is reasonable to conclude that the interests of the principal and agents are divergent.

6. To be classed as ODA, financial flows must "have as their main objective the promotion of the economic development and welfare of developing countries." Loans must be concessional and have a grant element of at least 25 percent. See http://stats.oecd.org/glossary/detail.asp?ID=6043.

7. See Bräutigam (2011) for a detailed comparison of Chinese and OECD definitions of aid.

8. For an overview of the historical evolution of Chinese aid modalities and sectors in Africa, see Morgan and Zheng (2018a).

9. These figures include only financial flows that meet the OECD's definition of Official Development Assistance (ODA).

10. See A. Li (2011); and Shen and Fan (2014) for a detailed overview of Chinese medical teams.

11. These figures refer to Chinese Official Finance projects in Africa that AidData list as "recommended for research," and which contain details of an implementing organization.

12. In addition to Chinese aid contracts, these firms also implement contracts from other aid donors such as the World Bank, as well as projects funded by local governments.

13. A full list of functions is available from the SASAC website. See http://en.sasac.gov.cn/2018/07/17/c_7.htm.

14. Although some Chinese officially financed infrastructure construction in Africa is aid—that is, concessional in nature—much is funded by commercial investments from the China Development Bank (CBD) and other state financial apparatuses. See Dreher et al. (2017) for an overview of the various classifications of Chinese official finance.

15. See http://www.loc.gov/law/foreign-news/article/china-rules-revised-to-facilitate-overseas-investments/.

16. For example, at the encouragement of both the local and Chinese government, Sinhohydro, has opened their Kafue Gorge Lower project to the local community and offers loans to help local people unaffiliated with the company to study at the school. Author interview with representative of PowerChina (parent company of Sinohydro), Lusaka, June 2018.

17. Author interviews with a diplomat at the Chinese Embassy, Lilongwe; and representative of the Chinese ECC, Lusaka, June 2018.

18. The data and codebook can be downloaded from here: http://afrobarometer.org/data/merged-data.

19. See http://www.pewglobal.org/database/indicator/24/survey/19/map/.

20. Author interview with official in the Investment Promotions Office, Zambian Development Agency, Lusaka, June 2018.

21. However, this trend may reverse as wages rise in China and manufacturing moves from "made in China" and "sold in Africa" to "made in Africa." In Ethiopia, for example, Chinese-invested manufacturers in Chinese-built Special Economic Zones (SEZs) have become significant job creators. For this reason, public opinions on China's impact on jobs may change in future.

22. As one local consultant in Lilongwe, Malawi, put it; after China-Malawi trade accelerated following the establishment of diplomatic relations in 2008, there was a perception that China was turning Malawi into a "dumping ground" for cheap Chinese products. Author interview, Lilongwe, June 2018.

23. For example, difficult conditions and worker-management clashes at the Chambishi coal mine in Zambia, owned by a subsidiary of China Nonferrous Metal Mining (Group) Co. Ltd. (CNMC), a central SOE—were used by then opposition leader Michael Sata in Zambia to whip up anti-Chinese fervor in the 2006 general election (Sata later went on to win the 2011 general election on a similarly anti-China platform) (Gonzalez-Vicente 2011, 408).

BIBLIOGRAPHY

Afrobarometer Data. 2016. "All Countries, Round 6." http://www.afrobarometer.org.

Aklilu, Negusu. 2014. "Greening Africa–China Relations: African Agents Punching Below Their Weight?" *JCIR* 2 (1): 26–48.

Atkinson, Joel. 2010. "China–Taiwan Diplomatic Competition and the Pacific Islands." *The Pacific Review* 23 (4): 407–27.

Baldwin, David A. 1985. *Economic Statecraft*. Princeton, NJ: Princeton University Press.

Blackwill, Robert D., and Jennifer M. Harris. 2016. *War By Other Means: Geoeconomics and Statecraft*. Cambridge, MA: The Belknap Press of Harvard University Press.

Blanchard, Jean Marc F., and Fujia Lu. 2012. "Thinking Hard About Soft Power: A Review and Critique of the Literature on China and Soft Power." *Asian Perspective* 36: 565–89.

Bräutigam, Deborah. 2008. "China's Foreign Aid in Africa: What Do We Know?" In *China into Africa: Trade, Aid and Influence*, edited by Robert I. Rotberg, 197–296. Washington, DC: Brookings Institution Press.

———. 2009. *The Dragon's Gift*. Oxford: Oxford University Press.

———. 2011. "Aid 'With Chinese Characteristics': Chinese Foreign Aid and Development Finance Meet the OECD-DAC Aid Regime." *Journal of International Development* 23 (5): 752–64.

Buckley, Lila, and Xiaoxue Weng. 2016. "Chinese Businesses in Africa: Perspectives on Corporate Social Responsibility and the Role of Chinese Government Policies." Discussion Paper. doi:http://pubs.iied.org/pdfs/17581IIED.pdf.

CAITEC, MOFCOM, SASAC, and UNDP China. 2015. "2015 Report on the Sustainable Development of Chinese Enterprises Overseas." http://images.caitec.org.cn/file/20160118/9441453104112616.pdf.

———. 2017. "2017 Report on the Sustainable Development of Chinese Enterprises Overseas." http://images.caitec.org.cn/file/20170525/7696149570054902 6.pdf.

Chen, Chuan, Andrea Goldstein, and Ryan J. Orr. 2009. "Local Operations of Chinese Construction Firms in Africa: An Empirical Survey." *International Journal of Construction Management* 9 (2): 75–89.

Chen, Jia. 2006. "Development of Chinese Small and Medium-sized Enterprises." *Journal of Small Business and Enterprise Development* 13 (2): 140–47.

Cissé, Daouda. 2015. "African Traders in Yiwu: Their Trade Networks and Their Role in the Distribution of 'Made in China' Products in Africa." *The Journal of Pan African Studies* 7 (10): 44–64.

Compagnon, Daniel, and Audrey Alejandro. 2013. "China's External Environmental Policy: Understanding China's Environmental Impact in Africa and How It Is Addressed." *Environmental Practice* 15 (3): 220–27.

Datta, Monti N. 2009. "The Decline of America's Soft Power in the United Nations." *International Studies Perspectives* 10 (3): 265–84.

Davies, Martyn, Hannah Edinger, Nastasya Tay, and Sanusha Naidu. 2008. *How China Delivers Development Assistance to Africa*. Centre for Chinese Studies, University of Stellenbosch.

Ding, Sheng. 2010. "Analyzing Rising Power from the Perspective of Soft Power: A New Look at China's Rise to the Status Quo Power." *Journal of Contemporary China* 19 (64): 255–72.

Dobler, Gregor. 2008. "From Scotch Whisky to Chinese Sneakers: International Commodity Flows and New Trade Networks in Oshikango, Namibia." *Africa* 78 (3): 410–32.

Dong, Lili, and David W. Chapman. 2008. "The Chinese Government Scholarship Program: An Effective Form of Foreign Assistance?" *International Review of Education* 54 (2): 155–73.

Dreher, Axel, Andreas Fuchs, Bradley Parks, Austin Strange, and Michael J. Tierney. 2017. "Aid, China, and Growth: Evidence from a New Global Development Finance Dataset." AidData Working Paper. http://aiddata.org/publications/aid-china-and-growth-evidence-from-a-new-global-development-finance-dataset.

Esteban, Mario. 2010. "A Silent Invasion? African Views on the Growing Chinese Presence in Africa: The Case of Equatorial Guinea." *African and Asian Studies* 9 (3): 232–51.

Farrel, Jamie. 2016. "How Do Chinese Contractors Perform in Africa? Evidence from World Bank Projects." SAIS-CARI Working Paper. http://www.sais-cari.org/s/Working-Paper_Jamie-Farrell.pdf.

Fijałkowski, Łukasz. 2011. "China's 'Soft Power' in Africa?" *Journal of Contemporary African Studies* 29 (2): 223–32.

FOCAC. 2010. "China–Africa Trade and Economic Relationship Annual Report 2010." http://www.focac.org/eng/zxxx/t832788.htm.

French, Howard W. 2014. *China's Second Continent: How a Million Migrants Are Building a New Empire in Africa*. New York: Alfred A. Knopf.

Gill, Bates, and Yanzhong Huang. 2006. "Sources and Limits of Chinese 'Soft Power.'" *Survival* 48 (2): 17–36.

Gill, Bates, and James Reilly. 2007. "The Tenuous Hold of China Inc. in Africa." *The Washington Quarterly* 30 (3): 37–52.

Goldsmith, Benjamin E., and Yusaku Horiuchi. 2012. "In Search of Soft Power: Does Foreign Public Opinion Matter for US Foreign Policy?" *World Politics* 64 (3): 555–85.

Gonzalez-Vicente, Ruben. 2011. "The Internationalization of the Chinese State." *Political Geography* 30 (7): 402–11.

Gu, Jing. 2016. "China's Private Enterprises in Africa and the Implications for African Development." In *The Power of the Chinese Dragon: Implications for African Development and Economic Growth*, edited by Spencer Henson and O. Fiona Yap, 149–73. London: Palgrave Macmillan UK.

Hanauer, Larry, and Lyle J. Morris. 2014. "Chinese Engagement in Africa: Drivers, Reactions, and Implications for U.S. Policy." RAND Corporation. http://www.rand.org/content/dam/rand/pubs/research_reports/RR500/RR521/RAND_RR521.pdf.

Hanusch, Marek. 2012. "African Perspectives on China–Africa: Modelling Popular Perceptions and Their Economic and Political Determinants." *Oxford Development Studies* 40 (4): 492–516.

Haugen, Heidi Østbø. 2011. "Chinese Exports to Africa: Competition, Complementarity and Cooperation between Micro-Level Actors." *Forum for Development Studies* 38 (2): 157–76.

韩冬临 (Han, Donglin), and 黄臻尔 (Zhen'er Huang). 2016. "非洲公众如何评价中国的对非援助" (How Do African Citizens Evaluate China's Foreign Aid)." 世界政治 (*World Politics*) 第6期 (6): 1–17.

Jensen, Michael C., and William H. Meckling. 1976. "Theory of the Firm: Managerial Behavior, Agency Costs and Ownership Structure." *Journal of Financial Economics* 3 (4): 305–60.

Jocelyne, Sambira. 2013. "Counterfeit Drugs Raise Africa's Temperature." *Africa Renewal*, May. http://www.un.org/africarenewal/magazine/may-2013/counterfeit-drugs-raise-africa%E2%80%99s-temperature.

Kaiman, Jonathan. 2014. "China–Africa Relations Hurt by Bad Chinese Behaviour, Says Ambassador." *The Guardian*, July 17. https://www.theguardian.com/world/2014/jul/17/chinese-ambassador-tanzania-china-africa-relationship-ivory-smuggling-counterfeit.

Eisenhardt, Kathleen M. 1989. "Agency Theory: An Assessment and Review." *The Academy of Management Review* 14 (1): 57–74.

Keuleers, Floor. 2015. "Explaining External Perceptions: The EU and China in African Public Opinion." *JCMS: Journal of Common Market Studies* 53 (4): 803–21.

King, Kenneth. 2013. *China's Aid and Soft Power in Africa*. Suffolk, UK: Boydell and Brewer. http://www.jstor.org/stable/10.7722/j.ctt2tt1tp.

Kuo, Lily. 2017. "The Best Days of Selling Cheap Chinese Goods in Africa Are Over." *Quartz*, May 3. https://qz.com/africa/950377/the-best-days-of-selling-cheap-chinese-goods-in-africa-are-over/.

Kurlantzick, Joshua. 2007. *Charm Offensive: How China's Soft Power Is Transforming the World*. New Haven, CT: Yale University Press.

———. 2009. "China's Soft Power in Africa." In *Soft Power: China's Emerging Strategy in International Politics*, edited by Mingjiang Li, 165–84. New York: Lexington Books.

Lai, Christina. 2017. "Acting One Way and Talking Another: China's Coercive Economic Diplomacy in East Asia and Beyond." *The Pacific Review* 31 (2): 1–19.

Lee, Margert C. 2014. *Africa's World Trade: Informal Economies and Globalization from Below*. London: Zed Books.

Lekorwe Mogopodi, Anyway Chingwete, Mina Okuru, and Romaric Samson. 2016. "China's Growing Presence in Africa Wins Largely Positive Popular Reviews." *Afrobarometer*, Dispatch No. 122. http://afrobarometer.org/sites/default/files/publications/Dispatches/ab_r6_dispatchno122_perceptions_of_china_in_africa1.pdf.

Li, Anshan. 2011. "Chinese Medical Cooperation in Africa: With Special Emphasis on the Medical Teams and Anti-Malaria Campaign." Discussion Papers: Nordiska Afrikainstitutet, Uppsala. http://nai.diva-portal.org/smash/get/diva2:399727/FULLTEXT02.

Li, Mingjiang, and Nathalie Yan Hong, eds. 2016. *China's Economic Statecraft: Co-Optation, Cooperation, and Coercion*. Singapore: World Scientific Publishing Co.
Li, Xiaojun, and Dingding Chen. 2018. "Public Opinion, International Reputation, and Audience Cost in an Authoritarian Regime." Working Paper. https://www.researchgate.net/profile/Xiaojun_Li25/publication/323486247_Public_Opinion_International_Reputation_and_Audience_Cost_in_an_Authoritarian_Regime/links/5a98160fa6fdccecff0c10f1/Public-Opinion-International-Reputation-and-Audience-Cost-in-an-Authoritarian-Regime.pdf.
Liang, Wei. 2012. "China's Soft Power in Africa: Is Economic Power Sufficient?" *Asian Perspective* 36: 667–92.
Lin, Richard C. 2001. "Complementary Measures To Foreign Aid: Taiwan and the PRC Under Diplomatic Rivalry." *Contemporary Economic Policy* 19 (3): 360–68.
Liou, Chih-shian. 2009. "Bureaucratic Politics and State-Owned Oil Companies: Illusory Champions." *Asian Survey* 49 (4): 670–90.
———. 2014. "Rent-Seeking at Home, Capturing Market Share Abroad: The Domestic Determinants of the Transnationalization of China State Construction Engineering Corporation." *World Development* 54: 220–31.
Luo, Yadong, Qiuzhi Xue, and Binjie Han. 2010. "How Emerging Market Governments Promote Outward FDI: Experience from China." *Journal of World Business* 45 (1): 68–79.
Muhumza, Rodney. 2017. "Hundreds Protest in Uganda Capital against Chinese Traders." *AP*, April 19. https://apnews.com/f1fa7c0ca5ca44f493d6912c42fe8e2b/hundreds-protest-uganda-capital-against-chinese-traders.
Manji, Firoze, and Stephen Marks, eds. 2007. *African Perspectives on China in Africa*. Oxford: Fahamu.
Maurin, Cristelle, and Pichamon Yeophantong. 2013. "Going Global Responsibly? China's Strategies Towards 'Sustainable' Overseas Investments." *Pacific Affairs* 86 (2): 281–303.
Mohan, Giles, and May Tan-mullins. 2009. "Chinese Migrants in Africa as New Agents of Development? An Analytical Framework." *European Journal of Development Research* 21 (4): 588–605.
Morgan, Pippa. 2018. "Ideology and Relationality: Chinese Aid in Africa Revisited." *Asian Perspective* 42 (2): 207–38.
Morgan, Pippa, and Yu Zheng. 2018a. "Old Bottle New Wine? The Evolution of China's Aid in Africa 1956–2014." Working Paper.
———. 2018b. "Tracing the Legacy: China's Historical Aid and Contemporary Investment in Africa." Working Paper.
Morgenthau, Hans. 1962. "A Political Theory of Foreign Aid." *The American Political Science Review* 56 (2): 301–9.
Naím, Moisès. 2007. "Rogue Aid." *Foreign Policy* 159 (March/April): 95–96.
Nan, Zhong. 2015. "China to Stop Counterfeits from Being Exported." *China Daily*, November 10. http://www.chinadaily.com.cn/bizchina/2015-11/10/content_22415380.htm.
Norris, William J. 2016. *Chinese Economic Statecraft: Commercial Actors, Grand Strategy, and State Control*. Ithaca, NY: Cornell University Press.

Nye, Joseph S., Jr. 1990. "Soft Power." *Foreign Policy* 80: 153–71.

———. 2004. *Soft Power: The Means to Success in World Politics*. New York: Public Affairs.

Ohashi, Hideo. 2013. "The Link between Aid and Non-Aid Activities: A Distinguishing Feature of China's Engagement." In *A Study of China's Foreign Aid: An Asian Perspective*, edited by Hideo Ohashi and Yasutami Shimomura, 82–103. London: Palgrave Macmillan.

Paradise, James F. 2009. "China And International Harmony: The Role of Confucius Institutes." *Asian Survey* 49 (4): 647–69.

PRC State Council. 2013. "White Paper on China-Africa Economic and Trade Cooperation." http://www.china.org.cn/government/whitepaper/node_7189938.htm.

Reilly, James. 2014. "China's Economic Engagement in North Korea." *The China Quarterly* 220: 915–35.

Rich, Timothy S. 2009. "Status for Sale: Taiwan and the Competition for Diplomatic Recognition." *Issues and Studies* 45 (4): 159–88.

Sautman, Barry, and Hairong Yan. 2009. "African Perspectives on China–Africa Links." *The China Quarterly* 199: 728–59.

Shambaugh, David. 2013. *China Goes Global: The Partial Superpower*. Oxford: Oxford University Press.

———. 2015. "China's Soft Power Push." *Foreign Affairs* 99 (107): 99–107.

Shen, Gordon, and Victoria Y. Fan. 2014. "China's Provincial Diplomacy to Africa: Applications to Health Cooperation." *Contemporary Politics* (April): 1–27.

Shen, Xiaofang. 2015. "Private Chinese Investment in Africa: Myths and Realities." *Development Policy Review* 33 (1): 83–106.

Taylor, Ian. 1998. "China's Foreign Policy towards Africa in the 1990s." *The Journal of Modern African Studies* 36 (3): 443–60.

Thomas, Stafford. 2015. "Fake Goods Dumped in Africa Are Grave Threat." *DispatchLive*, July 22. https://www.dispatchlive.co.za/news/opinion/2015-07-22-fake-goods-dumped-in-africa-are-grave-threat/.

Thomson, Alex. 2010. *An Introduction to African Politics*. Third Edition. New York: Routledge.

Tomz, Michael, Jessica Weeks, and Keren Yarhi-Milo. 2017. "How and Why Does Public Opinion Affect Foreign Policy in Democracies?" Working Paper. https://web.stanford.edu/~tomz/working/TWY-PublicOpinion-2017-02.pdf.

Tseng, San-shiun. 2008. "The Republic of China's Foreign Policy towards Africa: The Case of ROC-RSA Relations." PhD Diss., University of the Witwatersrand.

Warmerdam, Ward, and Miene Pieter Van Dijk. 2013. "Chinese State-owned Enterprise Investments in Uganda: Findings from a Recent Survey of Chinese Firms in Kampala." *Journal of Chinese Political Science* 18 (3): 281–301.

Whitney, Christopher B., and David Shambaugh. 2009. "Soft Power in Asia: Results of a 2008 Multinational Survey of Public Opinion." *Brookings*. https://www.brookings.edu/wp-content/uploads/2012/04/0617_east_asia_report.pdf.

Xinhua. 2015. "Full Text: China's Second Africa Policy Paper." http://www.xinhuanet.com/english/2015-12/04/c_134886545.htm.

Yu, Hong. 2017. "Motivation behind China's 'One Belt, One Road' Initiatives and Establishment of the Asian Infrastructure Investment Bank." *Journal of Contemporary China* 26 (105): 353–68.

Yuan Sun, Irene, Kartik Jayaram, and Omid Kassiri. 2017. "Dance of the Lions and Dragons: How Are Africa and China Engaging, and How Will the Partnership Evolve?" https://www.mckinsey.com/~/media/McKinsey/Global Themes/Middle East and Africa/The closest look yet at Chinese economic engagement in Africa/Dance-of-the-lions-and-dragons.ashx.

Zhang, Denghua, and Graeme Smith. 2017. "China's Foreign Aid System: Structure, Agencies, and Identities." *Third World Quarterly* 6597 (June): 1–17.

Chapter 5

Chinese Economic Statecraft and the Gulf Cooperation Council

Jonathan Fulton

China's presence in the Gulf region has quietly intensified in recent years, and in the process, it has become the region's most important trade partner. Relations with the Gulf Cooperation Council (GCC) member states—Bahrain, Kuwait, Oman, Qatar, Saudi Arabia, and the United Arab Emirates (UAE)—have been especially robust; between 2000 and 2016, their trade with China increased from just under $10 billion to $114 billion. This expansion in trade relations has led to cooperation in diplomatic, political, and security realms as well. In a relatively short time, China has come to be an important regional actor, and as its regional interests intensify, the Gulf is coming to play a significant role in China's strategic calculus. As the Belt and Road Initiative (BRI) drives China's presence westward, cooperation with the GCC states will continue to grow.

This chapter begins with a brief description of the changes in China's economic statecraft as it has transitioned from a regional power to one with global interests. As China's relative power has increased, its willingness to take a more assertive role in the international system has become more evident. While this transition began late in President Hu Jintao's administration, President Xi's eloquence in articulating the China Dream and the introduction of the BRI early in his presidency have contributed to the linking of China's larger international presence with the Xi presidency. The next section discusses Chinese interests with the GCC member states. While the Arabian Peninsula is not formally a part of any of the BRI's economic corridors, this section demonstrates that China-GCC relations have followed the cooperation priorities of the BRI and contributed to a level of interdependence that is both multifaceted and dense. The third part of this chapter then looks at the features of the Gulf subsystem. While the GCC states enjoy a level of development and relative stability that are the envy of much of the Middle

East/North Africa (MENA) region, the Gulf as a subsystem is quite unstable, having suffered the Iran-Iraq War (1980–1988), Desert Storm (1991), and the Iraq War (2003–2011). Security agreements with the United States have provided a degree of stability for the GCC, which in turn has allowed China to enjoy the benefits of this American security umbrella in order to deepen its economic footprint in the region. The final section discusses how China has used a strategic hedging approach to maximize economic benefits with all states in the Gulf while developing stronger political relations across the region. This positions China to more effectively integrate different Gulf states into BRI projects as the initiative continues to develop.

CHINESE ECONOMIC STATECRAFT AND THE BRI

Economic statecraft has been defined as "the use of economic resources by political leaders to exert influence in pursuit of foreign policy objectives" (Reilly 2013, 2). Simply put, it is a matter of turning wealth into power. In a recent history of Chinese political and intellectual leaders since the first Opium War, Schell and Delury note that "a common chord rings through all their work—the abiding quest for *fuqiang*, 'wealth and power'" (Schell and Delury 2013, 5). Reform era policies have created wealth, and the BRI is designed to create power. As such, the BRI features centrally in China's economic statecraft in the Xi administration, and most likely will continue to do so long after. Zhang and Keith posit that the objectives of China's economic statecraft "include an explicit aim to sustain and project economic power in China's near- and far-abroad, covering all of the countries along the so-called One Belt, One Road, . . . and to resist Western dominance of the international institutions of global finance and commerce" (Zhang and Keith 2017, 186). They also stress that in pursuing this strategy, Beijing is not attempting to overturn the existing order, but rather to make adjustments to it, reflecting China's increase in relative power. This point is frequently emphasized by Chinese leaders, such as when Premier Li Keqiang discussed the Asian Infrastructure Investment Bank (AIIB) in an interview, insisting "China has no desire to create a new world order," and stated, "China wants to work with others to uphold the existing international financial system. [The AIIB] is intended to be a supplement to the current international system" (Barber, Anderlini, and Pilling 2015). This point is important; China has benefited tremendously from the existing international order, but it still has substantial development requirements domestically, with a gross domestic product per capita of just over $8,000 in 2016, compared with $57,000 in the United States (World Bank National Accounts Data). Given this stage in development, a more privileged position within the current system seems a more reasonable short-term goal than leadership in a China-centered order. Thus, until very recently, perceptions of China as a follower in the US-led order, with a limited capacity to affect change, were often used to explain Chinese foreign policy decisions.

That China could be considered as a realistic potential competitor to American global leadership reflects how dramatically perceptions of China's role in the international order have changed in a relatively short time. Less than twenty years ago, for example, a serious scholar of China could ask, "Does China Matter?" in a *Foreign Affairs* article, describing it as "a second-rank middle power . . . better understood as a theoretical power" (Segal 1999, 24). Even more recent, the US Deputy Secretary of State Robert Zoellick gave his famous "Whither China?" speech in 2005, in which he called on China to become a "responsible stakeholder" in the US-led international system, stating that China had "a responsibility to strengthen the international system that has enabled its success" (Zoellick 2005). Official attitudes in Washington and Beijing diverged on the PRC's role, with the United States describing China as a free-rider (Friedman 2014), while Chinese leaders countered that as a developing country, a focus on domestic development prevents a greater international role.

This was reinforced by China's approach to international politics for much of the period since 1978, articulated by Deng Xiaoping in his famous twenty-four-character dictum, *taoguang-yanghui*, or the hide-and-bide dictum: "Observe calmly; secure our position; cope with affairs calmly; hide our capacities and bide our time; be good at maintaining a low profile; and never claim leadership." Using this hide-and-bide approach allowed China to dramatically increase its state capacity and development, and in the process elevated China to the more privileged international role it enjoys today. Under President Xi, however, the hide-and-bide strategy has appeared less relevant, as Chinese leadership has appeared more confident in assuming a global leadership role. One telling example of this is Xi's speech at the World Economic Forum in Davos in January 2017, in which he offered an impassioned defense of globalization and articulated a Chinese vision for achieving growth and development (Jinping 2017). In contrast to the "America First" approach of the United States under President Trump, Xi's speech was widely viewed as evidence of a China more confident in an international leadership position; former Swedish Prime Minister Carl Bildt responded on Twitter, tweeting, "There is a vacuum when it comes to global economic leadership, and Xi Jinping is clearly aiming to fill it. With some success" (Barkin and Piper 2017).

Attributing this greater Chinese global role to Xi's leadership places too much emphasis on agency, however, ignoring the systemic factors contributing to this shift. China's "new assertiveness" has been a feature of the discourse on the PRC's foreign policy since the second term of Hu's administration (Swaine 2010; Yahuda 2013, 446–59; Johnston 2013, 7–48). President Xi has been highly effective in articulating this assertiveness, speaking about Chinese power in a way that its leaders have not since Mao. During a meeting on China's relations with its neighbors, Xi stated, "We must be more proactive in seeking achievements in the conduct of our peripheral diplomacy" (Lam 2015, 191). He used the phrase *fenfayouwei*, which translates as "be proactive in seeking achievements," and has since become a new paradigm for China's more assertive foreign policy (Yan 2014). This contributes to the linkage of Xi's leadership and a China more confident as a global power. Central to this has been his discussion of the China Dream: "In my opinion, the rejuvenation of the Chinese nation has been the greatest dream of the Chinese people since the advent of modern times" (Jinping 2014, 38). This China Dream narrative speaks in terms of a greater Chinese presence in world affairs; Xi cited a peaceful international environment, development, cooperation with other states, and win-win diplomacy as contributing factors, signaling that Chinese power is no longer focused on domestic development to the extent that it was in the hide-and-bide period.

The most important contributing factor to a greater Chinese global leadership claim is the BRI and the international institutions being developed to complement it, such as the AIIB and the Silk Road Fund. The BRI signals a transformational paradigm, reflecting what Rolland describes as "Beijing's newfound willingness to play a leading role in reshaping the world, starting with its extended periphery," which she sees as a part of an emerging "Sinocentric Eurasian order" (Rolland 2017, 3). While all serious analysis of the BRI puts China at the center of this initiative, Beijing emphasizes that it is an inclusive development initiative; Xi has stated that it "is not a tool to advance any geopolitical agenda, but a platform for practical cooperation" ("Xi Says Belt and Road Initiative Not Geopolitical Tool" 2017). Foreign Minister Wang Yi has also stressed the official cooperative, inclusive vision of the BRI, describing it as "not China's solo, but a symphony performed by all relevant countries" ("China's Belt and Road Initiatives Not Solo, but Symphony: FM" 2015). And all official discussion of the BRI emphasizes that it is an initiative rather than a strategy. The PRC's official statement explaining the goals of the BRI, "The Vision and Actions on Jointly Building Silk Road Economic Belt and 21st-Century Maritime Silk Road" (hereafter the Vision and Actions), was issued by the National Development and Reform Commission, the Ministry of Foreign Affairs, and the Ministry of Commerce. Shortly after the document was released in March 2015, the three ministries issued a statement stipulating that official English translations of BRI projects must use the word "initiative" (*chàng yì*), and avoid using the word "strategy" (Tao 2015). The distinction here is that an initiative in this usage indicates a call for action which provides a public good, while a strategy implies a plan that aims to achieve a security or trade advantage at the expense of a competing state. As the Vision and Actions (2015) document states, the BRI's focus is achieving "harmony, peace, and prosperity"; interpreted as a geopolitical strategy, it would be perceived by other states as an aggressive pursuit of geopolitical dominance.

For states in this emerging order, the substantial economic benefits associated with BRI participation have to be tempered with the possibility that Beijing can use this economic relationship as leverage in pursuing political and/or strategic goals. Feigenbaum has described five types of economic leverage that China utilizes as a means of achieving political ends with trade partners: passive, active, exclusionary, coercive, and latent. Passive refers to a relationship where China does not have to use its leverage to achieve desired goals; the economic interests of the other state ensure stable relations. Active leveraging, on the other hand, describes a situation where China takes a direct role in shaping the norms or parameters in its economic relations with another state. In this case, states that want to increase trade or investment with China would be compelled to provide support for the "one China" policy, for example, or to sever diplomatic relations with Taiwan. Exclusionary leverage is more forceful, preventing access to Chinese markets because of political conflict or disagreements, such as when China ended free trade negotiations with Norway after Liu Xiaobo was awarded the Nobel Peace Prize in 2010 (Jing 2017). Coercive leverage is more direct still, taking punitive actions against another state because of a political disagreement. When South Korea agreed to host the US Terminal High Altitude Area Defense missile system, the Chinese response was a boycott of South Korean companies selling consumer goods in China, and it banned Chinese travel agents from selling group tours to South Korea (Hancock and Wang 2017). Latent leverage, in Feigenbaum's (2017) description, is "the coercive cards it holds but chooses not to play." All of these types of leverage demonstrate the potential concerns that states could perceive in their economic relations with the PRC, especially those with substantial Chinese investment or trade dependency. Despite Beijing's insistence that the BRI is an inclusive, cooperative endeavor, strategic concerns will prevail for many of the participating states, and the economic pressure that China can apply is an important consideration.

For states in its immediate periphery, political considerations frequently feature in China's economic statecraft, such as with the South Korean boycott, or the banning of rare earth sales to Japan in 2010 (Bradsher 2010). In its relations with states in the Middle East, commercial interests rarely have an overt political consequence. Unlike its East Asian neighbors, in the Middle East there is relatively little in the way of historical baggage, no territorial disputes, and few issues that were one side would likely directly threaten the interests of the other. China is, therefore, able to practice a relatively benign form of economic diplomacy with its Gulf trading partners. Political and diplomatic tools are a means of facilitating an expansion of economic relations. China's commitment to the noninterference principle means that politics drives trade, with no expectation of trade influencing partner states' political system (Sun and Zoubir 2015, 907). This stands in contrast to the Washington Consensus, making China an attractive economic partner.

THE GULF COOPERATION COUNCIL AND THE BELT AND ROAD INITIATIVE

China's economic statecraft and its growing international presence are relevant to the GCC member states, as China's economic and political relations with each of them have increased substantially in recent years. The PRC has important long-standing trade interests with the GCC, and the emergence of the BRI has added a strategic element. Designed as a set of economic corridors linking China to different states and regions,[1] the BRI emphasizes five cooperation priorities: policy coordination, facilities connectivity, unimpeded trade, financial integration, and people-to-people bonds ("Vision and Actions" 2015). Until now, the Arabian Peninsula has not been included in any of these economic corridors, yet China's approach to developing relations with the GCC states indicates that they have been built upon these cooperation priorities. The peninsula is a crucial hub in the BRI, especially for the Maritime Silk Road Initiative component, connecting West Asia, Europe, and East Africa to points east. The initiative's success in linking Eurasian regions is therefore facilitated by a stable Gulf region, creating another rationale for greater Chinese engagement with the Gulf monarchies.

In terms of policy coordination, China-GCC leaders have used frequent state and official visits as opportunities to develop political, security, and economic cooperation. Top leadership from China as well as each of the GCC states makes frequent visits. Every GCC state except Oman has had a head of state visit China, and every Chinese president since Yang Shangkun has visited at least one GCC state. In recent years, the visits have intensified both in terms of frequency and outcomes, as deals worth tens of billions of dollars are signed. King Salman of Saudi Arabia paid a state visit to Beijing in March 2017, for example, and signed a series of bilateral deals totaling $65 billion (Blanchard 2017).

A common feature of the head of state visit with China is the upgrading of relations. This is a foreign policy tool unique to the PRC, which does not use alliances but instead has a hierarchy of diplomatic partnerships. The two highest levels are the comprehensive strategic cooperative partnership, which involves the full pursuit of cooperation and development, and the comprehensive strategic partnership, which involves close coordination on regional and international affairs ("Quick guide to China's diplomatic levels" 2016). Among the Gulf states, Saudi Arabia and Iran have reached the highest level of partnership, while Iraq, Qatar, and the UAE are the second level.

Increased policy coordination between China and the GCC states has been linked to the second cooperation priority, facilities connectivity, as the Gulf monarchies have embarked upon ambitious development plans. Saudi Vision 2030, the Abu Dhabi Economic Vision 2030, Qatar National Vision 2030, New Kuwait 2035, Bahrain's Economic Vision 2030, and Oman Vision 2040 are all national development projects within the GCC that will require significant infrastructure investment. Chinese firms are well-placed to win contracts for these projects as many have established a regional presence and have developed a reputation for delivering high-quality, low-cost, and on-time projects. In 2009, for example, the China Railway Construction Corporation won a contract to jointly build the Holy Shrines Metro with two Saudi firms. The purpose of this $1.8 billion light railway between Mecca and Medina is to transport pilgrims performing *hajj* (Karam 2009). The significance of this cannot be underestimated; its custodianship of the holiest sites in Islam is a fundamental legitimizing feature of Saudi rule, and to award this contract to a Chinese firm was a major development in Sino-Saudi relations. Other projects throughout the GCC have followed. In the UAE, a subsidiary of the China National Petroleum Company (CNPC) built a 404-km pipeline from the Habshan oilfield to the Indian Ocean port in Fujairah, allowing the UAE to bypass the Hormuz Straits in getting its crude to international markets ("Fujairah Established as a Fuel Storage Fulcrum" 2014). A consortium of five Chinese firms under the Jiangsu Provincial Overseas Cooperation and Investment Company announced in 2017 that they have invested $300 million to lease and develop a headquarters facility in Abu Dhabi's Khalifa Port Free Trade Zone (Crabtree 2017). Oman is the recipient of substantial Chinese infrastructure development investment, as Oman Wanfang, a consortium of firms from Ningxia province, have committed over $3 billion in developing the Duqm Free Zone project, with a projected $10.7 billion in future investments (Jabarkhyl 2017). Duqm, a village along Oman's south coast, will provide these Chinese firms with yet another Arabian Peninsula port that bypasses the Strait of Hormuz, securing trade routes should the Strait become compromised by GCC-Iranian hostilities. Qatar, with major construction projects in preparation for the 2022 FIFA World Cup, is another important market for Chinese firms, with $8 billion worth of contracts signed in 2014 alone (Hollingsworth 2017). Projects in Kuwait and Bahrain are also increasing, although not at the same level as with the other GCC states. Taken together, it demonstrates a strong linkage between the cooperation priority of facilities connectivity in China-GCC relations.

As for unimpeded trade, this provides the strongest evidence of the intensity of China-Gulf relations, as well as the rapid pace of development of these commercial ties. This can be attributed mostly to Gulf energy sales to China. In 2013 China became the world's largest importer of oil, a trend that looks set to continue despite efforts to diversify away from hydrocarbons (Chen 2013). At the same time, China's domestic production, while expected to increase, will not be able to meet its growing energy needs. This highlights the importance of Gulf trade for China's economic growth, which is a key pillar of its performance-based legitimacy model. Of China's main suppliers of energy imports, the Gulf is home to six of them, accounting for over 52 percent (US Energy Information Administration 2015).

Gulf-China trade is more than energy, however. Gulf states are also importing heavily from China. The UAE in particular presents an interesting case as the only GCC state with a significant trade imbalance that favors China.[2] For the UAE, trade with China is used as an important plank of its re-exporting economy, whereby its political stability, infrastructure, and business-friendly environment are used as a hub for trade throughout the MENA and East Africa. China has used the UAE extensively, with more than 230 Chinese MNCs and SOEs setting up regional headquarters in Dubai's Jebel Ali Free Zone (Scott 2015).

Financial integration is another cooperation priority that has seen substantial growth in recent years. Five of the six GCC members—Bahrain being the sole exception—were founding members of the AIIB.[3] The UAE has also partnered with China in its Silk Road Fund, with the Emirati sovereign wealth fund Mubadala partnering with two Chinese institutions, the China Development Bank Capital and the State Administration of Foreign Exchange, with a joint investment of $10 billion (Bouyamourn 2015). In August 2017, China and Saudi Arabia signed a Memorandum of Understanding to establish a similar joint investment fund with $20 billion in capital, with each side to contribute an even share ("Saudi Arabia Eyes Joint Investment Fund with China, with a Focus on Energy," 2017). Both the UAE and Qatar have signed currency swap agreements with China, the UAE for $5.4 billion ("China, UAE Renew 35 Billion Yuan Currency Swap Deal," 2015) and Qatar for $5.7 ("China Central Bank Signs $6 Billion Currency Swap with Qatar," 2014). These agreements allow trade and investment to be conducted in Chinese yuan, facilitating economic and financial cooperation. Saudi Arabia has also indicated an interest in using the yuan to finance projects related to Saudi Vision 2030 (Shamseddine and Paul 2017).

In terms of people-to-people bonds, this is the least developed cooperation priority for China with the GCC, but recent years have seen improvements with interactions focusing especially on religion, tourism, and education. Islam is the most important of these and was instrumental in building ties with Gulf leaders. During the 1980s, when China and Saudi Arabia had still not officially recognized each other, exchanges between high-ranking Saudi political and religious leaders and Chinese Muslim officials were a means of official communications and relationship building (Shichor 1989). The UAE and China have also used Islam to build ties, with the UAE's Khalifah bin Zayed Al Nahyan Foundation having funded the construction of the Sheikh Zayed Mosque in Wuhong, Ningxia province. Chinese tourism to the Gulf is focused mainly on the UAE, largely to Dubai but increasingly to Abu Dhabi as well. Lured by luxury shopping and its exemplary branding, Chinese visitors to Dubai have increased exponentially over the past five years and are projected to continue to do so at a tremendous rate. In 2010 there were 150,000 Chinese visitors to Dubai; by 2023 the UAE is expecting to host 545,000, who are projected to spend $781 million (Sahoo 2015). In terms of education and language training, China has opened Confucius Institutes in the UAE and Bahrain. Gulf states have also invested in similar projects in China. Oman established the Sultan Qaboos Chair of Arabic Language Studies at Peking University, and the UAE established the Sheikh Zayed Centre for Arabic Language and Islamic Studies at Beijing Foreign Studies University, which has paid political dividends, as many of China's ambassadors to Arab countries—eleven of twelve in 2012—were graduates from the department (Bardsley 2012).

Taken together, China-GCC relations clearly demonstrate a commitment to the BRI cooperation priorities, despite the current lack of an official BRI economic corridor on the Arabian Peninsula. Given the depth and breadth of these ties, the importance of Gulf energy exports to China, and the region's geographic centrality in the BRI, these relations will continue to intensify.

THE GULF SUBSYSTEM AS A REGIONAL SECURITY COMPLEX

Despite the GCC's importance to China, it presents serious political concerns. The Gulf is a volatile subsystem within an unstable MENA region. During the modern state period the three regional poles—Iran, Iraq, and the Gulf monarchies—have competed with and balanced against each other, resulting in three major wars in the Gulf since the Iranian Revolution in 1979. While the GCC states have enjoyed a high degree of stability relative to other MENA states, the potential for regional turbulence to spill over into their states is a constant concern.

The Gulf subsystem is best understood as a regional security complex, which Buzan defines as "a group of states whose primary security concerns link together sufficiently closely that their national securities cannot realistically be considered apart from one another" (Buzan 1983, 106). Until the end of the Cold War, the larger systemic competition between the United States and USSR largely drove regional political events, but in the post–Cold War period the region has operated—very uneasily—within the unipolar Pax Americana. In this order, the GCC states, with their defense cooperation agreements with the United States and dense participation in the liberal order, are status quo states, while Iran has consistently been a dissatisfied power, and Iraq was until it was dismantled in 2003. The US presence is perceived as the key to maintained stability of the status quo, or as the obstacle to a new, Iran-centered regional order.

This reliance on an external power to balance against larger, threatening regional powers has long been a feature of Arab Gulf monarchies' foreign policy. With relatively small populations and hostile neighbors, relationships first with the United Kingdom and later the United States have provided security for the GCC states. The GCC states have maximized the strategic advantages at their disposal: a geostrategic location and centrality in global energy markets make them important actors in the US-led order, and they have enhanced this with savvy political economic decisions, becoming active members in international organizations, significant sources of foreign direct investment, generous aid donors, and significant customers in arms markets. This combines to make regime stability within the GCC important for powerful states beyond the Gulf, and these relationships have been used to ensure that Iran and Iraq are unable to dominate the region.

Given their centrality in global energy markets, a key feature of Pax Americana, the continued stability of the Gulf monarchies of the GCC is in the interests of the United States. This has contributed to the intensity of GCC-US relations despite few shared values or norms that are often attributed to this type of alliance. It is largely a set of relations built upon shared security concerns for the region and the need for Gulf energy to fuel the US-led international order. American preponderance in the Gulf, therefore, is a strategic necessity, and it explains why the US regional policy since the Carter doctrine has been to ensure that no other outside power is able to dominate the region.

The current Gulf order is maintained by a US security architecture that features Defense Cooperation Agreements with Kuwait, Bahrain, Qatar, and the UAE, and a Facilities Access Agreement with Oman. The United States has bases or access to bases in each of these countries, and approximately 35,000 troops stationed in the Gulf. This security umbrella creates opportunities for other powers with interests in the Gulf to pursue stronger regional relationships without having to make provisions for securing their investments, assets, and citizens. This explains the strategy China has taken to develop relations with the GCC, while at the same time with Iran and Iraq. China has not had to balance with or against any regional actors, but instead has been able to pursue economic ties with everyone, benefiting from the status quo without the burden of maintaining it. Within the Gulf, therefore, the hide-and-bide dictum has dominated China's strategic approach. The question in the region is whether this will change as Chinese power and influence grow with the implementation of the BRI.

CHINA'S APPROACH IN THE GULF: HEDGING UNDER THE AMERICAN UMBRELLA

That China has taken advantage of this American security umbrella to bolster its position in the Gulf is not unique; all external powers have enjoyed the same opportunity (Sim and Fulton 2018). US preponderance in the Gulf has created an environment where the GCC states are able to participate in the liberal international order without a real threat to their security or sovereignty, allowing other states to pursue economic relations with them, without having to take on a larger role in providing security or protecting the shipping routes out of the Gulf. In China's case, this has led to complaints from Washington that it is freeriding on the regional security public good that the US provides. Not surprisingly, the view in China diverges from this US perception. Some in China argue that the US military presence in the Gulf is actually a destabilizing factor that has been detrimental to China's interests (Jin 2017, 42). Regional instability contributed to unprecedented oil price spikes after the 2003 war in Iraq, and as a major importer of Gulf energy, China was directly affected. Li Guofu of the China Institute of International Studies has countered, "the current turmoil in the Middle East is to a large extent due to the wrong policies by the West. Calling China a free rider under such a situation is bizarre and unacceptable" (Wu and Ye 2016). Wu Bingbing, from Peking University, has also responded to the free-rider characterization, drawing a distinction between Chinese and Western approaches to the Middle East, stating, "We focus on economy, trade and development, which helps these countries to solve domestic and regional problems on their own. But Western countries mainly care about political and security interests" (Wu and Ye 2016).

Despite this difference in perceptions on their respective approaches to the Gulf, a strategically competitive relationship between the United States and China is unlikely. Niblock for one sees nothing to be gained from China adopting a more assertive regional role, noting a limited capacity to project its power across the Indian Ocean as well as his assessment that the Gulf is not a core interest for China (2015, 16–18). Shichor also does not anticipate competition, describing a "relatively high convergence" of US and Chinese "attitudes, policies, and behavior on a variety of Middle East issues" (2016, 11). Furthermore, he does not believe that Chinese political influence in the Middle East is comparable with that of the United States. Taking a realpolitik view, he believes Chinese policy makers would prefer the United States to shoulder the political and military burdens in the region, saying, "given its core interests, Beijing prefers that the US not only maintain its deployment in the Middle East . . . but rather to incur as many penalties as possible" (Shichor 2016, 15). This view is not inconsistent with other analysts, with one stating, "But since China prefers that America bear the main cost of underwriting Saudi security, Chinese and American interests are convergent, not divergent" (Quilliam 2016, 157).

In developing its relations with the GCC states, it is more constructive to see the PRC's approach as strategic hedging rather than freeriding. Hedging is an approach common to second-tier powers that want to avoid antagonizing the dominant power, while at the same time expanding economic and military regional capabilities (Tessman 2012). This is an apt description of Chinese statecraft in the Gulf, as it has developed stronger ties with all regional actors under the relative stability of the US security umbrella. Goh defines strategic hedging as "a set of strategies aimed at avoiding (or planning for contingencies in) a situation in which states cannot decide upon more straightforward alternatives such as balancing, bandwagoning, or neutrality" (Goh 2005, 2). To balance against or bandwagon with any one regional actor would be detrimental to China's economic interests, and neutrality is inconsistent with China's expanding BRI ambitions. Hedging allows the PRC to continue building a significant regional presence at a lower cost than a more active military engagement.

China's approach to developing a Gulf presence also gives it an opportunity to play a unique diplomatic role in the region, as its strategic partnership approach to diplomacy provides leverage that the US alliance system does not. Alliances in the Gulf have exacerbated the hostility between the Iranian and GCC sides, leaving little diplomatic room for the United States to maneuver without alienating GCC allies or aggravating Iran. China's partnerships, on the other hand, allow it to build relationships with both sides, which could potentially allow China to play the role of mediator, evident when Foreign Minister Wang said, "China is friends with both Saudi Arabia and Iran. If there is a need, China is willing to play our necessary role" ("China Expresses Willingness to Mediate in Saudi/Iran Talks" 2017). With a focus on economic and diplomatic affairs, rather than a responsibility for military and security issues, China's role can contribute to a stable region, if it is able to navigate a very difficult political environment. Taken together, these hedging and partnership strategies have contributed to an increase in China's political influence in the Gulf, albeit one that does not yet match its economic influence. However, the dramatic increase in its regional economic role is providing China with significant political and diplomatic capital that will no doubt be useful as the BRI takes shape in the Gulf.

In terms of economic statecraft, China has thus far been able to enjoy the benefits of passive leverage with the GCC; the complementarity of strong trade relations has not translated into political pressure from either side. To be certain, there are areas where Gulf leaders might want to exert leverage of their own to achieve political outcomes, with Sino-Iranian ties being the most significant. China's BRI engagement with Iran in the China-Central West Asia Economic Corridor is increasing bilateral trade and investment; trade value between the two states has grown from $8.5 billion in 2005 to nearly $32 billion in 2016 (International Monetary Fund 2014). During a state visit to Tehran in January 2016, Presidents Xi and Rouhani agreed to increase trade to $600 billion over the next ten years, with President Rouhani declaring "a new chapter has begun in Tehran-Beijing relations" (Zhou 2016). The significance of this chapter became evident in September 2017, as China's state-owned CITIC investment firm provided Iranian banks a $10 billion line of credit to finance water, energy, and transport projects ("China Provides $10 Billion Credit Line to Iran" 2017). Given increased economic and political pressure from the US against Iran, this Chinese support for Iran signals an economic lifeline in the face of US sanctions. For the GCC, and especially Saudi Arabia, this strengthens their greatest regional threat, underscoring the GCC's concerns about the BRI's geostrategic implications (Cafiero and Wagner 2017). At the same time, the combined value of China-GCC trade, at $116 billion in 2016, greatly outweighs that of China's trade with Iran, at nearly $32 billion. Chinese interests on the Arabian side of the Gulf, as described above, are substantial, and give no indication of China abandoning the GCC in favor of Iran. Thus, the GCC's ability to or interest in using economic leverage against China to pursue political interests seems unproductive and unlikely. Given the lack of Chinese core interests in the Gulf, it is also unlikely that China would actively leverage against the GCC. Instead, the two sides will choose to continue diversifying engagement, focusing on strengthening economic relations.

CONCLUSION

In terms of its regional economic statecraft, China's approach to the GCC reflects a pragmatic, realistic, and ambitious assessment of its current capabilities relative to the United States. In the Gulf, the United States is still the preponderant military power, and no other state or coalition of states currently presents a realistic challenge to that status. However, through its strategic hedging approach to the region, China has built up its regional presence to a point where it has become the most important long-term economic partner for each of the Gulf states. Unless the Gulf order undergoes significant change, there is little reason for China to alter its approach to the GCC. Tremendous growth in economic relations throughout the Gulf will allow this passive leverage to pay increasing political and strategic dividends as the BRI takes shape, and if China-GCC relations continue to follow the cooperative priorities of the BRI, it stands to reason that political coordination through the Gulf development plans will lead to a greater convergence in interests, giving China a greater degree of influence in the region.

In the event that the Gulf order does undergo a transition, China has used this period of US preponderance to position itself as an important external power, regardless of the shape the emerging order takes. It has thus far successfully managed the difficult balance of developing and maintaining strong relationships with all of the Gulf states. That China has not taken a leadership role and has tended to stay behind the scenes in Gulf diplomacy is a strength; its offer to mediate between Saudi Arabia and Iran could not be realistically made by any other major power, and certainly not by the United States. Its comprehensive strategic partnerships with both Saudi Arabia and Iran, signed within days of each other, seem a blueprint to keep a foot planted squarely on both sides of the Gulf, intensifying relations and drawing both the GCC and Iran into deeper economic interdependence with China.

At the same time, it is not difficult to imagine a scenario where Beijing's passive economic leverage in the Gulf took a more active turn. Given its geostrategic importance, Gulf stability is a significant factor in the BRI's success. With the ever-present threat of US sanctions, the depth of Chinese investment in Iranian infrastructure will not be matched by any other state or collection of multinational corporations. This gives China economic leverage that it would no doubt exercise if its leaders felt Iranian aggression toward its Gulf neighbors threatened Chinese interests. This is true, to a much lesser extent, on the Arab side of the Gulf; Chinese investments and infrastructure development would seem to provide a latent economic leverage that could turn active in the unlikely event that any of the Gulf monarchies threatened to take action against Iran. As the most important external economic partner of the Gulf states, China has a level of diplomatic and political influence that has yet to be actively engaged. It will remain beneath the surface as long as the United States continues to accept the costs of Gulf leadership, but this lack of visibility should not be interpreted as a lack of influence.

NOTES

1. They are the New Eurasian Land Bridge, the China-Pakistan Economic Corridor, the China-Central West Asia Economic Corridor, China-Mongolia-Russia Economic Corridor, China-Indochina Peninsula Economic Corridor, and China-Myanmar-Bangladesh-India Economic Corridor.

2. Bahrain does as well, but at an amount insignificant compared with the others. The other four all export significantly more from China than they import.

3. Bahrain joined in 2017.

BIBLIOGRAPHY

Barber, Lionel, Jamil Anderlini, and David Pilling. 2015. "Interview: Li Keqiang on China's Challenges." *Financial Times*, April 15. https://www.ft.com/content/38307b3e-e28d-11e4-aa1d-00144feab7de.

Bardsley, Daniel. 2012. "China Honours Sheikh Zayed." *The National*, March 29. https://www.thenational.ae/uae/education/china-honours-sheikh-zayed-1.391682.

Barkin, Noah, and Elizabeth Piper. 2017. "In Davos, Xi Makes Case for Chinese Leadership Role." January 17. https://www.reuters.com/article/us-davos-meeting-china/in-davos-xi-makes-case-for-chinese-leadership-role-idUSKBN15118V.

Blanchard, Ben. 2017. "China, Saudi Arabia Eye $65 Billion in Deals as King Visits." *Reuters*, March 16. https://www.reuters.com/article/us-saudi-asia-china/china-saudi-arabia-eye-65-billion-in-deals-as-king-visits-idUSKBN16N0G9.

Bouyamourn, Adam. 2015. "UAE, China to Set Up $10bn Joint Strategic Investment Fund." *The National*, December 14. https://www.thenational.ae/business/uae-china-to-set-up-10bn-joint-strategic-investment-fund-1.105808.

Bradsher, Keith. 2010. "Amid Tension, China Blocks Vital Exports to Japan." *New York Times*, September 22. http://www.nytimes.com/2010/09/23/business/global/23rare.html.

Buzan, Barry. 1983. *People, States & Fear: The National Security Problem in International Relations*. Chapel Hill: The University of North Carolina Press.

Cafiero, Giorgio, and Daniel Wagner. 2017. "What the Gulf States Think of 'One Belt, One Road.'" *The Diplomat*, May 24. https://thediplomat.com/2017/05/what-the-gulf-states-think-of-one-belt-one-road/.

Chen, Jia. 2013. "China Is No. 1 Oil Importer." *China Daily*, October 18. http://usa.chinadaily.com.cn/business/2013-10/18/content_17041824.htm.

"China Central Bank Signs $6 Billion Currency Swap with Qatar." *Reuters*, November 3, 2014. http://www.reuters.com/article/china-economy-qatar/update-1-china-central-bank-signs-6-bln-currency-swap-with-qatar-idUSL4N0ST3LY20141103.

"China Expresses Willingness to Mediate in Saudi/Iran Talks." *Gulf Business*, March 9, 2017.

"China Provides $10 Billion Credit Line to Iran." *The Times of Israel*, September 16, 2017. https://www.timesofisrael.com/china-provides-10-billion-credit-line-to-iran/.

"China, UAE Renew 35 Billion Yuan Currency Swap Deal." *Reuters*, December 14, 2015. http://www.reuters.com/article/us-china-emirates-yuan/china-uae-renew-35-billion-yuan-currency-swap-deal-idUSKBN0TX0DE20151214.

"China's Belt and Road Initiatives Not Solo, but Symphony: FM." *Xinhua*, March 8, 2015.

Crabtree, Justina. 2017. "China's $300 Million Investment in Abu Dhabi Ports Is a 'Milestone.'" *CNBC*, July 31. https://www.cnbc.com/2017/07/31/china-300-million-investment-in-abu-dhabi-ports-is-a-milestone.html.

Feigenbaum, Evan. 2017. "Is Coercion the New Normal in China's Economic Statecraft?" *Marco Polo*, July 25. https://macropolo.org/coercion-new-normal-chinas-economic-statecraft/.

Friedman, Thomas L. 2014. "China as a Free Rider." *The New York Times*, August 9. https://www.nytimes.com/video/opinion/100000003047788/china-as-a-free-rider.html.

"Fujairah Established as a Fuel Storage Fulcrum." *The National*, March 14, 2014. https://www.thenational.ae/business/fujairah-established-as-fuel-storage-fulcrum-1.646469.

Goh, Evelyn. 2005. *Meeting the China Challenge: The United States in Southeast Asian Regional Security Strategies*. Washington, DC: East–West Center.

Hancock, Tom, and Wang Xueqiao. 2017. "South Korean Consumer Groups Bear Brunt of China's Thaad Ire." *Financial Times*, August 20. https://www.ft.com/content/f3c78afe-821d-11e7-94e2-c5b903247afd.

Hollingsworth, Julia. 2017. "Why Qatar Matters to China, In Spite of Gulf Isolation." *South China Morning Post*, June 7. http://www.scmp.com/news/china/diplomacy-defence/article/2097206/why-qatar-matters-china-spite-gulf-isolation.

International Monetary Fund. October 23, 2014. *Direction of Trade*. Ann Arbor, MI: Inter-university Consortium for Political and Social Research [distributor]. https://doi.org/10.3886/ICPSR07628.v2.

Jabarkhyl, Nawied. 2017. "Oman Counts on Chinese Billions to Build Desert Boomtown." *Reuters*, September 5. https://www.reuters.com/article/us-oman-china-investment/oman-counts-on-chinese-billions-to-build-desert-boomtown-idUSKCN1BG1WJ.

Jin, Lianxiang. 2017. "China's Role in the Middle East: Current Debates and Future Trends." *China Quarterly of International Strategic Studies* 3, no. 1: 39–55.

Jing, Meng. 2017. "China and Norway Resume Trade Talks, Ending Six-Year Diplomatic Freeze." *South China Morning Post*, April 8. http://www.scmp.com/news/china/diplomacy-defence/article/2086022/china-and-norway-resume-free-trade-negotiations-after.

Johnston, Alastair Iain. 2013. "How New and Assertive Is China's New Assertiveness?" *International Security* 37, no. 4: 7–48.

Karam, Souhail. 2009. "China Rail Cons Wins Part of $1.8 bln Saudi Deal." *Reuters*, March 4. http://uk.reuters.com/article/saudi-railway-chinarail/update-2-china-rail-cons-wins-part-of-1-8-bln-saudi-deal-idUKL454283820090304.

Lam, Willy Wo-Lap. 2015. *Chinese Politics in the Era of Xi Jinping: Renaissance, Reform, or Retrogression?* New York: Routledge.

Niblock, Tim. 2015. "Strategic Economic Relationships and Strategic Openings in the Gulf." In *The United States and the Gulf: Shifting Pressures, Strategies and Alignments*, edited by Steven W. Hook and Tim Niblock. Berlin: Gerlach Press.

"Quick Guide to China's Diplomatic Levels." *South China Morning Post*, January 20, 2016. http://www.scmp.com/news/china/diplomacy-defence/article/1903455/quick-guide-chinas-diplomatic-levels.

Quilliam, Neil. 2016. "China and the Gulf Co-operation Council: The Rebound Relationship." In *Toward Well-Oiled Relations? China's Presence in the Middle East Following the Arab Spring*, edited by Niv Horesh, 148–61. London: Palgrave Macmillan.

Reilly, James. 2013. *China's Economic Statecraft: Turning Wealth into Power*. Sydney: Lowy Institute for International Policy.

Rolland, Nadège. 2017. *China's Eurasian Century? Political and Strategic Implications of the Belt and Road Initiative*. Seattle: The National Bureau of Asian Research.

Sahoo, Sanandha. 2015. "Chinese Tourists to Stream into Dubai Over the Next Decade." *The National*, March 8. https://www.thenational.ae/business/travel-and-tourism/chinese-tourists-to-stream-into-dubai-over-the-next-decade-1.35363.

"Saudi Arabia Eyes Joint Investment Fund with China, with a Focus on Energy." *Al Bawaba*, August 23, 2017. https://www.albawaba.com/business/saudi-arabia-joint-investment-fund-with-china-1013606.

Schell, Orville, and John Delury. 2013. *Wealth and Power : China's Long March to the Twenty-First Century*. New York: Random House.

Scott, Emma. 2015. "China's 'One Belt, One Road' Strategy Meets the UAE's Look East Policy." *China Brief* 15, no. 11, May 29. https://jamestown.org/program/chinas-one-belt-one-road-strategy-meets-the-uaes-look-east-policy/.

Segal, Gerald. 1999. "Does China Matter?" *Foreign Affairs* 78 (5): 24–36.

Shichor, Yitzak. 1989. *East Wind Over Arabia: Origins and Implications of the Sino-Saudi Missile Deal*. Berkley: Berkley Center for Chinese Studies.

Shichor, Yitzhak. 2016. "Sino-American Crosscurrents in the Middle East: Perceptions and Realities." In *Toward Well-Oiled Relations? China's Presence in the Middle East Following the Arab Spring*, edited by Niv Horesh. London: Palgrave Macmillan.

Shamseddine, Reem, and Katie Paul. 2017. "Saudis May Seek Funding in Chinese Yuan." *Reuters*, August 24. https://www.reuters.com/article/us-saudi-china/saudis-may-seek-funding-in-chinese-yuan-idUSKCN1B413R.

Sim, Li-Chen, and Jonathan Fulton, eds. 2018. *External Powers and the Gulf Monarchies*. London: Routledge.

Sun, Degang, and Yahia H. Zoubir. 2015. "China's Economic Diplomacy towards the Arab Countries: Challenges Ahead?" *Journal of Contemporary China* 24 (95): 903–21.

Swaine, Michael. 2010. "Perceptions of an Assertive China." *China Leadership Monitor*, no. 32 May.

Tao, Xie. 2015. "Is China's 'Belt and Road a Strategy?" *The Diplomat*, December 16. http://thediplomat.com/2015/12/is-chinas-belt-and-road-a-strategy/.

Tessman, Brock. 2012. "System Structure and State Strategy: Adding Hedging to the Menu." *Security Studies* 21, no. 2 (April 1).

U.S. Energy Information Administration. 2015. *China Country Report*. May 14. https://www.eia.gov/beta/international/analysis.cfm?iso=CHN.

"Vision and Actions on Jointly Building Silk Road Economic Belt and 21st-Century Maritime Silk Road." *National Development and Reform Commission, Ministry of Foreign Affairs, and Ministry of Commerce of the People's Republic of China*, March 28, 2015. http://en.ndrc.gov.cn/newsrelease/201503/t20150330_669367.html.

World Bank National Accounts Data. https://data.worldbank.org/indicator/NY.GDP.PCAP.CD.

Wu, Xia, and Ye Shan. 2016. "China's 'Belt and Road' Initiative Boosts Mideast Development." *Xinhua*, January 19. http://www.xinhuanet.com/english/2016-01/19/c_135024451.htm.

Xi, Jinping. 2014. "Achieving Rejuvenation is the Dream of the Chinese People." *The Governance of China*. Beijing: Foreign Language Press, Co. Ltd.: 57–69.

Xi, Jinping. 2017. "Jointly Shoulder Responsibility of Our Times, Promote Global Growth." Keynote Speech by H. E. Xi Jinping President of the People's Republic of China at the Opening Session of the World Economic Forum Annual Meeting, Davos, January 17. http://www.china.org.cn/node_7247529/content_40569136.htm.

"Xi Says Belt and Road Initiative Not Geopolitical Tool." *Xinhua*, September 3, 2017. http://news.xinhuanet.com/english/2017-09/03/c_136579491.htm.

Yahuda, Michael. 2013. "China's New Assertiveness in the South China Sea." *Journal of Contemporary China* 22, no. 81: 446–59.

Yan, Xuetong. 2014. "From Keeping a Low Profile to Striving for Achievement." *The Chinese Journal of International Politics* 7, no. 2 (June).

Zhang, Xiaotong, and James Keith. 2017. "From Wealth to Power: China's New Economic Statecraft." *The Washington Quarterly* 40 (1): 185–203.

Zhou, Xin. 2016. "China, Iran Opens 'New Chapter' in Bilateral Ties as President Xi Jinping Visits Tehran." *South China Morning Post*, January 24. http://www.scmp.com/news/china/diplomacy-defence/article/1904328/china-iran-opens-new-chapter-bilateral-ties-president.

Zoellick, Robert. *Whither China: From Membership to Responsibility?* U.S. Department of State Archive. https://2001-2009.state.gov/s/d/former/zoellick/rem/53682.htm.

Chapter 6

Pulling the Region into Its Orbit?

China's Economic Statecraft in Latin America

Wei Liang

INTRODUCTION

After decades of low-level commercial interaction, China and Latin America significantly ramped up their economic relationship in the 2000s. China has become a top trading partner and an important destination for many Latin American/Caribbean (LAC) countries' exports. While not yet a main source of foreign direct investment overall, China has built a strong investment presence in South America, particularly in the natural resource and infrastructure sectors. There is a rich set of literature on the impact of China's economic engagement in the region, including an examination of the impacts of increased commodity concentration and neo-dependency as a result of China's strong demand for natural resources (Puyana and Constantino 2015), the importance of geopolitics (Piccone 2016), China's impact on Latin American economies and industrialization (Gallagher and Porzecanski 2010) and political institutions (Meyers and Wise 2016), the implications for US hegemony (Gallagher 2016), and China's projection of soft power (Ellis 2009). However, the domestic factors that have been attributed to the different policy responses to China's economic statecraft in these target states have largely been understudied.[1] Thus, this chapter is trying to reverse that research question in order to explore why China is more effective in using its economic power to pursue political and strategic goals in some LAC countries, but is less successful in others.

Economic statecraft can be broadly understood as state manipulation of international economic activities for strategic purposes (Baldwin 1985). Plenty of literature studied this subject and have identified a number of domestic and international variables to help examine the processes and outcomes of Chinese economic statecraft. Blanchard attributes success of economic statecraft to the target countries' level of stateness, which comprises three components: autonomy, capacity, and legitimacy (Blanchard and Ripsman 2008). Norris focuses on principle-agent problems by defining various business-government relations and conditions for the government to tightly control the actors (Norris 2018). The unique party-state system and state capitalism of China have made government planning and manipulation of Chinese firms, banks, and other players in international economic activities easier (Reilly 2013). The economic means that the government has widely adopted are mainly through trade, investment, foreign aid, and financial statecraft. These studies have greatly contributed to our understanding of China's motivation, process, and implementation of its economic statecraft. This chapter, however, will focus on the domestic economic and political conditions of the target states. It explores the question: What domestic economic and political conditions in the target country are more conducive/resistant to China's utilization of economic statecraft?

Latin America is a critical region for analyzing China's economic statecraft. Following the Monroe doctrine, Latin America has long been seen as part of the US sphere of influence. Due to Washington's overwhelming superiority in military and economic realms, the region has been considered the backbone of American hemispheric hegemony since World War II [27]. In contrast, China was a latecomer to this scene and only began to extensively engage the region at the beginning of the new millennium. Driven by the energy thirst resulting from its economic opening in the 1980s, Beijing has adopted a global strategy of securing energy and natural resources. Latin America is one of the main regions China has tried to secure its resource supply from. As one leading China specialist noted, "China historically has paid less attention to Latin America than to any other third world region" (Sutter 2008).

On the other hand, Latin American countries also take China's increasing engagement in the continent as a new leverage in dealing with the United States. Long, among some others, provided an excellent examination of how Latin American leaders were able to overcome power asymmetries with the United States to pursue their national interests by exploring the key moments in post–World War II inter-American relations (Long 2015). In this chapter I aim to further his argument by exploring the policy choices of Latin American countries in order to gain leverages when dealing with China.

With a wide range of countries in the region, it is difficult to present one overall regional assessment. Latin American countries' relationships with China vary widely; there is no single, coordinated regional response. China's growing economic engagement in the region, especially in the post-boom (post-2013) period, is driven primarily by Beijing's search for status and influence in the area. Within the context of their economic relationship with China, Carol Wise and Victoria Choon Ching divided the countries into three groups (Ramzy 2014), namely, the three most liberal and open economies in the region of LAC (Peru, Chile, and Costa Rica), resourceful countries like Brazil and Argentina, and the countries that also focus on manufacturing like Mexico. For the purpose of studying the effectiveness of China's economic statecraft I will focus on two largest economies and the most important political powers in the region: Brazil and Mexico. Both countries happened to be important target states (strategic partners) of China's economic statecraft in the region, albeit for different political and strategic goals. In the following section I will compare the different domestic political and economic conditions, interests, and institutions in these two countries to explain why China has made greater progress in projecting its economic power through trade and investment to pursue its political goals in Brazil, but has been less successful in Mexico. By examining domestic factors including different levels of trade dependence, proximity to the United States, existence of alternative market and source of capital, and a shared vision on global governance, I explain why China's economic statecraft is more successful in Brazil than in Mexico even though both countries have been identified by the Chinese government as strategic partners in Latin America.

This chapter proceeds in five parts. The following section sets a baseline for China-Latin America relations which traces the evolving cross-pacific economic exchange during the 2001–2013 boom and the post-boom new development. The third section examines the strategic goals of the Beijing government in Latin America. The next section compares the varied outcomes of China's economic statecraft in Mexico and Brazil and explores the domestic factors that have attributed to this outcome. Finally, the last section summarizes the findings and offers conclusions about the China's economic statecraft in LAC.

EVOLVING CHINA-LATIN AMERICA ECONOMIC RELATIONSHIPS: BOOM AND POST-BOOM PERIODS

China's trade with and investment in the region deepened at around the turn of the new century. China is now the second largest source of imports for Latin America and is its second largest export destination, in both cases directly behind the United States. This dramatic increase of China's demand for Latin American resources has been fueled by China's need to sustain its rapid industrialization and, in particular, export-oriented manufacturing (Ellis 2009). Ferchen further argues that it has corresponded with a change in

China's domestic development priority to switch from labor-intensive light and medium manufacturing toward capital-intensive, heavy industrial (over) production as a result of Chinese government's implementation of the post-2008 financial crisis stimulus package (Ferchen 2011).

In 2017, China-Latin America trade reached $266 billion (ECLAC 2018). Chinese president Xi Jinping made a commitment at the first China-Latin America forum hosted by Beijing in 2015 that between 2015 and 2019, China would invest $250 billion in direct investment in the region and about $500 billion in trade (ECLAC 2015). Similar to China's trade patterns with Africa, it is concentrated in a small number of countries and primarily follows the pattern of importing natural resources from LAC and exporting manufacturing products. In 2017, five products–soybeans, iron ore, copper ore, refined copper, and oil—made up 70 percent of the total value of exports from LAC. Barton and Rehner capture this new commercial relationship that is based on resource trade and features the pragmatic hybrid as China's "dragon doctrine" in Latin America (Barton and Rehner 2018).

THE BOOM (2001–2013)

Since joining the WTO in 2001, China has begun to integrate itself into the global economy. Following the East Asian export–driven development model, China began to develop itself as a global manufacturing powerhouse in order to take advantage of its population dividend and economy of scale. Consequently, China became a true global trader by importing raw materials, commodities, energy, and intermediate parts from the developing world and exporting the finished industrial goods to developed markets. The country's heightened demand for copper, crude oil, iron ore, and soybeans made Latin America a natural frontier for trade. Hence, it has done well with LAC countries possessing an abundance of these natural resources including Brazil, Argentina, Venezuela, Chile, and Peru. Commodity exports are a way for many LAC countries to (re)integrate into the global economy (Singh and Nem Singh 2014). Thanks to China's strong commodity demand, these Latin American countries were spared the worst of the 2008–2009 crisis. In fact, trade between the region and China multiplied twenty-two times between 2000 and 2013 (ECLAC 2013).

Before the burst of the commodity boom in 2013, China's investment projects were largely developed to support its trade relations with Latin America. Most Chinese companies invested in open commercial offices in Latin America to facilitate trade, some of which grew into small manufacturing units for assembling components imported from China. In the services sector, the only important investments were in finance, where the key objective is to finance trade operations with China. Even in the natural resources sector, many of the companies investing in mining and oil operations are large importers of these resources into China. In other words, China's economic influence over Latin America is conducted mostly through trade and not through direct investment (ECLAC 2018).

Direct foreign investment from China shows a strong degree of concentration, both in terms of sectors (with mining and fossil fuels represented at around 80 percent) and in terms of country destinations, with only three countries—Brazil, Peru, and Argentina—receiving 81 percent of said investment between 2005 and 2017 (ECLAC 2018). This reinforces the pattern of exchange of raw materials for manufactured goods that has characterized trade between the region and China.

POST-BOOM: 2013–PRESENT

The year 2013 represents a watershed moment in China-Latin America economic relations. Commodity prices worldwide plunged dramatically from 2013 to 2014 and China's economic growth has slowed to an average rate of 6–7 percent since 2013. The pass-through for LAC in terms of China's lower demand for lower-priced resources has been a slowing of growth to 1–2 percent on average since 2013 (Ramzy 2014). This is partly due to declining Chinese exports to developed markets and partly due to an intentional shift away from its previous export-oriented model to a more sustainable consumption and service-based development model. However, when the demand for commodities had slowed and prices plummeted, China continued and even further expanded its economic presence in the LAC region—especially through financial statecraft. This suggests that China has been pursuing more than just commercial interests from 2013 onward. The end of the commodity boom seems to provide an opportunity for China to revisit its economic engagement in the region and to make it more balanced and less controversial. Rather than solely using Latin America as a source of commodity imports, the Chinese government has applied its ever-increasing economic clout, utilizing trade, infrastructure investment, and aid to pursue its noneconomic goals.

During the post-boom period China's investment in the region is still highly concentrated in terms of host country selection. Though China invested $90 billion in Latin America between 2005 and 2016, it only accounts for approximately 5 percent of FDI inflow to the region during this period. Investment by Chinese companies in LAC in 2017 is estimated to be more than US$ 25 billion, equivalent to around 15 percent of total inflow to the region that year (ECLAC 2018). Brazil has received 55 percent of investments made by Chinese companies in the region since 2005, followed by Peru with 17 percent and Argentina with 9 percent. Thus, the top three recipient countries account for 81 percent of Chinese FDI inflows to the region (ECLAC 2018).

What has changed since 2013 is that Chinese companies have begun to invest in the manufacturing and agricultural sectors (Puyana and Constantino 2015). In January 2015, President Xi Jinping pledged $250 billion in Chinese investment in Latin America over the next ten years, some of which is expected to go into Brazil's recently proposed railroad that would link the Atlantic and Pacific Oceans via Peru. Chinese policy banks now provide more finance to Latin American governments each year than do the World Bank and Inter-American Development Bank (IDB) combined. The Chinese finance has functioned as a private sovereign debt market with some typical Chinese characteristics: focus on industry and infrastructure, large loans tied to purchase requirements of Chinese industrial goods, and natural resource purchase contracts which reduce repayment risk (Gallagher and Irwin 2015). China is less willing to operate at an economic loss just in order to bolster noneconomic ends in Latin America, which differs China's economic diplomacy strategy in LAC from that of its in Southeast Asia and Africa.

GAINING INFLUENCE AND STATUS THROUGH ECONOMIC STATECRAFT?

Chinese government prefers economic statecraft as it matches the global image China has long subscribed: China is going to rise peacefully and other countries will benefit from China's rise. Increasingly, China has employed its growing economic clout to pursue other objectives. As stated by David Baldwin, "economic measures are likely to exert more pressure than either diplomacy or propaganda, and are less likely to evoke a violent response than military instruments" (Baldwin 1985).

Compared to its neighborhood including Northeast and Southeast Asia, and its bilateral relationship with the major global powers including the United States, the EU, and Japan, China does not see Latin America as the most strategic region in relation to its core interests and key foreign policy objectives, which has been identified as regime stability, sovereignty and territorial integrity and development rights (Li 2017). Consequently Latin America attracted only about 13 percent of China's total FDI during the 2003–2016 period (about US$110 billion) compared to 70 percent directed elsewhere in Asia.

Where then does Latin America fit in the Chinese grand strategy and what are the geopolitical goals driving China's economic activities in this region of considerable interest to the United States? First and foremost is China's strategic interest in securing energy security and commodity supply to sustain its rapid economic growth. During the first decade of the twenty-first century, geopolitics did not seem to be the key driver for China's policy toward Latin America. Rather, Beijing was very cautious not to upset the United States by engaging the region economically. In the first Latin America policy white paper issued by the Chinese government in 2008, the focus was on energy security and the role that could be played by the LAC countries to help diversify China's energy supply (China-ECLAC Forum 2018). The "China fever" cooled down in 2013. With the burst of the commodity boom and the slowing down of the Chinese economy and its exports to the developed market, China reduced its commodity imports from LAC. However, to many people's surprise, China's engagement with the LAC continues to soar and China has even expanded its scope of engagement beyond commercial interest. China has maintained its presence in LAC's extractive sectors and Chinese investment and finance in LAC is still heavily focused on extraction. Mining, drilling, and refining accounts for over half of Chinese mergers and acquisitions in LAC, while coal, oil, and natural gas account for over half of public sector lending—a record US$17.2 billion in 2017 (Ray and Gallagher 2017).

The second strategic interest of China's economic statecraft in LAC is to integrate Latin America into its "Belt and Road Initiative." Under the new leadership of President Xi Jinping, China has adopted a more assertive foreign policy and gone through a major transformation to redefine its role in the developing world. In recent years, the Belt and Road Initiative (BRI), previously known as the "One Belt, One Road" (OBOR) strategy, has emerged as the cornerstone of Chinese foreign policy. According to the Chinese government, the twenty-first-century version of the Silk Road will take shape around a vast network of transportation, energy, and telecommunications infrastructure, linking Asia to Europe and Africa through Central and South Asia and accompanied by strengthened trade and investment and increased people-to-people exchanges (Xinhua 2015). Beijing sees physical infrastructure as a first step toward Eurasian integration, which will build economic corridors to enable greater integration and foster a vibrant "community of common destiny," a blueprint outlined by Chinese president Xi Jinping.

Consequently China has increasingly diversified its investment to other sectors, including finance, services, manufacturing, and, in particular, infrastructure. Between 2005 and 2016, China invested US$5.5 billion into ninety-one infrastructure projects in the region (Dussel-Peters 2017). Those projects include the region's most ambitious projects such as the development of a transcontinental railway linking Brazil's Atlantic coast to Peru's Pacific coast, the construction of the Two-Ocean Tunnel between Argentina and Chile, and the building of three nuclear plants in Argentina. Many of these new projects have not been completed yet, but they have reflected the diverse interest developed by Chinese state-owned enterprises in the region. Different from the previous focus on extractive diplomacy, this recent surge of infrastructure diplomacy has policy implications beyond commercial interest. It is an integral part of China's new global vision of connectivity and development, an alternative idea to complement and challenge existing international institutions. In a visit to Chile in May of 2013 the Chinese premier minister said, "The current industrial cooperation between China and Latin America arrives at the right moment, China has equipment manufacturing capacity and integrated technology with competitive prices, while Latin America has the demand for infrastructure expansion and industrial upgrading" (Elson 2014).

The third strategic interest of China's economic statecraft is to intensify its relationship with Latin America by institutionalizing the relations through both bilateralism and regional institutional building. China has not made much progress in this regard. So far China has only negotiated free trade agreements with three small and open economies in the region, which are Peru, Chile, and Costa Rica. Regionally, China has developed close economic ties with Community of Latin American and Caribbean States (CELAC) forum. The first meeting of China-CELAC forum in January 2015 aimed to double annual trade and significantly increase China's investment stock in the region. At the second China-CELAC forum held in January 2018, China's policy preference was no longer commercial interest, but instead the pursuit of strategic goals (Dussel-Peters 2017). It successfully persuaded a number of LAC countries to join the China-dominated Belt and Road Initiative (BRI). Before the forum was held, Chinese leaders had already endeavored to rephrase the Belt and Road discourse to include LAC. Now the new discourse describes LAC as a "natural extension" of the Maritime Silk Road and an "indispensable participant" of the BRI. This language was first used by President Xi Jinping during his meeting with Argentina's president Mauricio Macri on the sidelines of the 2017 Belt and Road Forum (Barrios 2018). The Declaration, signed during the Second China-CELAC Ministerial Forum in January 2018, presents the BRI as "a new platform for mutually beneficial cooperation" between China and Latin America, and affirms that the former "invites Latin American and Caribbean countries to join" (Dussel-Peters 2017). As of June 2018, four of the roughly seventy countries that have signed these agreements are located in the LAC region: Panama, Antigua and Barbuda, Trinidad and Tobago, and most recently, Bolivia. This new development is strategically critical as it is an important step to integrate LAC into China's global strategic vision.

The fourth strategic interest of China is the Taiwan issue—the core interest of Beijing government. In Latin America white papers issued by the Chinese government in 2008 (China–ECLAC Forum 2018) and 2016 (Ministry of

Foreign Affairs of the PRC 2016), Beijing emphasized the importance of "upholding the One-China principle" as the foundation for bilateral cooperation with LAC. We have witnessed the fiercest diplomatic contest between China and Taiwan in LAC; among the seventeen countries that still formally recognize Taiwan, nine of them are located in LAC.[2] This issue is more pressing now than ever, partly because China and Taiwan ended their tacit "diplomatic truce" (2008–2016) after pro-independence president Tsai Ing-wen came into power in 2016. The remaining group of eight Central American and Caribbean nations, plus Paraguay in South America, represents a large chunk of the only seventeen countries that presently recognize Taiwan. The conflict between Taiwan and China has indeed become more real, evidenced by China's shifting of focus from South America to Central America and the Caribbean. This diplomatic contest has influenced China's economic engagement with the region. China has been using economic incentives as sticks and/or carrots to bid for the nonrecognition of Taiwan (Urdinez et al. 2016). Countries that recognize Taiwan have found their access to the Chinese market restricted; none of the regional states that recognize Taiwan are on the list of the top thirteen destinations of Chinese lending (Li 2017). When Panama switched its diplomatic alignment from Taiwan to China in July 2017 and El Salvador in August 2018, Taiwan openly blamed China for its "checkbook diplomacy." From Beijing's point of view, considering its sheer size of economy and global status, it is not a difficult task to win this diplomatic battle if the United States doesn't support Taiwan by influencing their allies in Central America.[3] Therefore, Chinese diplomats consider this more so a battle between China and the United States than one with Taiwan.

The new development of US foreign policy under the Trump administration—including the decision to abandon the TPP agreement and the uncertainty associated with the new USMCA agreement—and the lack of US interest in multilateralism in general may prompt some Latin American countries to further "look east." The trade war between the United States and China as well as more protectionist policies toward countries including Canada, Japan, and most European nations will also help with the ongoing restructuring of China-Latin America relations. More LAC countries are considering China as an alternative market and source of capital to the United States. However, on the other hand, ongoing trade tensions with the United States will cause China's demand for commodities and resources to decline. China will then make more industrial and infrastructure investments in the LAC instead to take advantage of cheaper labor costs and to be close to new markets. Doing so will provide China a new opportunity to redefine its economic statecraft in the region, shifting away from "extractive diplomacy" to a more balanced and nuanced statecraft.

CASE STUDY: COMPARING CHINA'S ECONOMIC STATECRAFT TOWARD BRAZIL AND MEXICO

In order to provide in-depth examination on China's economic statecraft in Latin America and how the target countries responded, I chose Mexico and Brazil to conduct field research and used a process tracing approach. They have been chosen based on the case selection criteria including typical, diverse, influential, and most similar/different (Seawright 2016). First, they both are politically influential and economically powerful players in the region. Brazil and Mexico are the two largest economies in the region, one representing South America and the other one representing Central America geopolitically and geoeconomically. Second, China has adopted a distinctive diplomatic approach in LAC, by prioritizing its political and economic cooperation with a selective group of Latin American countries. As Table 6.1 shows, China has developed comprehensive strategic partnership agreements with seven countries in the region including Brazil, Mexico, Argentina, Venezuela, Peru, Chile, and Ecuador—the top rank in China's diplomatic partnership structure (Xinhua 2013). Among them, Brazil established this comprehensive strategic partnership in 2004, while the rest of the six countries established this priority partnership with China only in the last few years. It means that these seven countries have developed comprehensive cooperation with China in political, economic, trade, cultural, and military fields. Although the seven countries are all major petroleum and commodity producers and exporters in the region, it is evident that Brazil and Mexico have more diverse economy, and importing/exporting beyond commodity and natural resources and hence a better case to understand China's use of economic tools to achieve its noneconomic policy agenda. Chinese diplomats and MOFCOM (Ministry of Commerce) officials all confirmed that China considers Mexico and Brazil the two most important strategic and economic partners in LACs.[4]

It appears that China's economic diplomacy works more effectively with Brazil than Mexico. In the last two decades, Brazil has become China's most important ally in the region, standing side-by-side with China on a number of global fronts. On the other hand, Mexico continues to see China more as a competitor in global economy and rarely sides with China on foreign policy issues important to China. There are a number of critical domestic factors that account for these rather varied outcomes. In this section I will focus on the current level of trade dependence on Chinese market, proximity to the United States (both economically and politically), existence of alternative free trade agreements/investors to the target countries, and shared vision and interest on global governance, especially those toward multilateralism—toward the US influence in the global economic system.

Table 6.1 China's Diplomatic Partnership with Selected Countries in America

PRC	*Partners*	*Years of Establishment*	*Additional Information (Year and Name of Related Partnerships)*
LAC(8)	Brazil	1993	1993 strategic partnership, 2004 *comprehensive strategic partnership*
	USA	1997	1997 constructive strategic partnership; 2011 a cooperative partnership based on mutual respect and mutual benefit
	Venezuela	2001	2001 strategic partnership for common development; 2014 *comprehensive strategic partnership*
	Mexico	2003	1997 comprehensive partnership; 2003 strategic partnership of cooperation; 2013 *comprehensive strategic partnership*
	Argentina	2004	2001 comprehensive partnership; 2004 strategic partnership; 2014 comprehensive strategic partnership
	Canada	2005	1997 comprehensive partnership; 2005 strategic partnership
	Peru	2008	2004 comprehensive partnership; 2008 strategic partnership; 2013 *comprehensive strategic partnership*
	Chile	2012	2004 comprehensive partnership; 2012 strategic partnership; 2016 *comprehensive strategic partnership*
	Ecuador	2015	2015 strategic partnership; 2016 *comprehensive strategic partnership*

Source: Ministry of Foreign Affairs, China. Compiled by author.

First and foremost, China has more complementary trade relations with Brazil and more competitive relations with Mexico. It is noteworthy that China's trade penetration, especially its manufacturing exports into Brazil as well as its competition with Brazil in the United States and other third markets, has caused serious concerns in Brazil regarding "primarization" of the economy (Jenkins 2014). However, neoliberal economists would argue that this bilateral trade relationship has reflected the comparative advantage of the two countries and brought the benefit of trade to these two economies. While Brazil holds the largest trade surplus with China in the region, Mexico has a prolonged trade deficit with China. Mexico's trade deficit with China reached $67.4 billion in 2017 and accounted for roughly 77 percent of the region's total deficit with China. This reflects the fact that less than 2 percent of Mexico's exports, but 17 percent of its imports, were accounted for by China in 2014. As China's former consul general in Tijuana, Shoujian Gao, pointed out, the combination of economic competition with persisting social tensions constitutes a formidable challenge to efforts to build co-cooperation and understanding (Hearn 2012). Compared to the complementary trade relations between China and Brazil, there has been significant tension between China and other manufacturing-based economies such as Mexico. Competition from Chinese exports has undercut Mexico's primary comparative advantages: low labor costs and geographic proximity to the United States. China and Mexico not only share similar comparative advantages, but also similar export-driven investment policies. The "maquiladora" system of Mexico is similar to Chinese "special economic zones." Consequently, China has outcompeted Mexico in the US market for exports of industrial goods thus attracting a great amount of foreign investment in manufacturing away from Mexico. Mexico has suffered from its escalated trade deficit with China, as China exports large quantities of manufactured goods to Mexico as well as parts and intermediate goods to be processed in Mexico for export to the US market. In short, since the late 1990s, China has been "eating Mexico's lunch" (Rosen 2003). Meanwhile, as trade between China and Brazil expanded, China became Brazil's most important trade partner, outpacing traditional partners such as the United States and Europe. On the one hand, the trade relationship is imbalanced. In 2014 commodities (soybeans, minerals, and fuels) accounted for 85 percent of Brazilian exports to China (Albuquerque and Lima 2016). On the other hand, Brazil's economy grew 3.3 percent and poverty decreased from 13.6 percent in 2001 to 4.9 percent in 2013 during the decade of rapidly growing trade with China (Li 2017).

Second, while Brazil has received the largest portion of FDI from China, Mexico received much less Chinese FDI than Brazil, as shown in Figures 6.1 and 6.2, respectively. China invested $6.7 billion in Mexico during the period of 2003–2016, making Mexico only the fourth largest destination of Chinese FDI in the region (ECLAC 2018). Brazil drew about 56 percent of China's FDI in Latin America during 2003–2016, followed by Peru and Argentina. In 2017 alone Chia invested $24.7 billion in Brazil. Most Chinese investment in Brazil now has expanded from oil and gas extraction to electricity sector, financial service, telecommunication and manufacturing. This trend has continued in recent years, and from 2016 to 2017 China invested all its major non-resource projects in Brazil, as shown in Table 6.2. There are four major oil companies in China (CNPC, Sinopec, CNOOC, and Sinochem), all state-owned and all with significant investments in Latin America. Chinese oil companies have a presence in all of the Latin American countries that export oil and gas. Because Mexico has not fully opened its energy sector to foreign investment and China is a strong competitor in manufacturing, Chinese companies have not found many areas to invest in Mexico compared with Brazil.

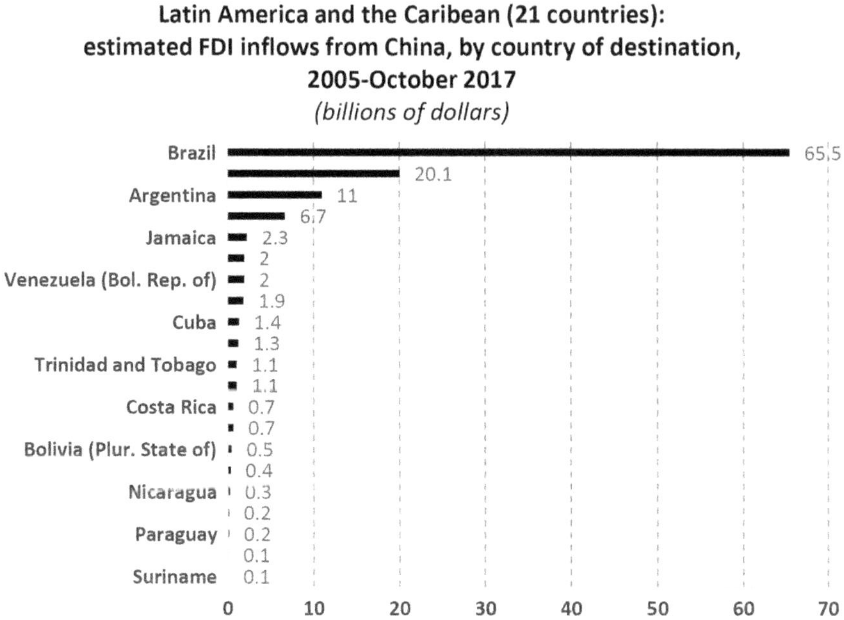

Figure 6.1 Latin America and the Caribbean (Twenty-one Countries): Estimated FDI Inflows from China, by Country of Destination, 2005–October 2017 (billions of dollars). *Source*: ECLAC. "Exploring new forms of cooperation between China and Latin America and the Caribbean," January 2018. https://repositorio.cepal.org/bitstream/handle/11362/43214/1/S1701249_en.pdf.

Third, Mexico and Brazil have carried out different domestic policies toward the United States and the subregional difference is noteworthy. For most countries in Central America and the Caribbean the United States is their most important trading partner and political ally. The strategic importance of Mexico is also mainly driven by its political and economic relations with the United States and its influence over the countries of Central America. Mexico's foreign policy and economic policy today have been shaped heavily by its geography. Its relationship with the United States is unique and unparalleled. Thus, Mexico prioritizes policies that help it liberalize its economy, deal with asymmetrical power and economic relations, and take advantage of its proximity with the United States while sovereignty-conscious South America, especially Brazil, appreciates more the principles emphasized by China in its usage of economic statecraft, such as mutual respect, non-interference, and protection of national sovereignty. During the Workers' Party's rule in Brazil, which started in 2003, the radical shift of Brazil toward a non-US-centered independent foreign policy as a result of regime change, not economics, is the major explanatory variable that drove the close relationship

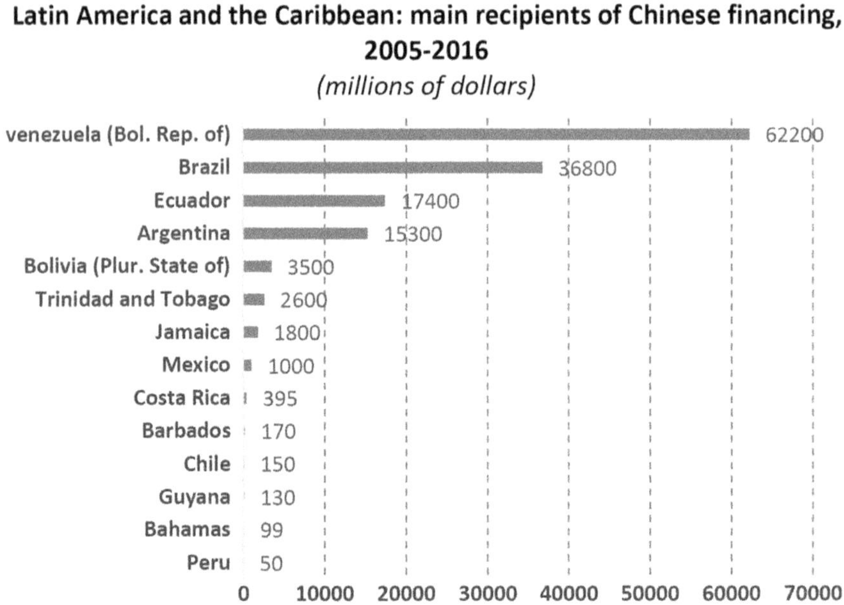

Figure 6.2 Latin America and the Caribbean: Main Recipients of Chinese Financing, 2005–2016 (millions of dollars). *Source*: ECLAC. "Exploring new forms of cooperation between China and Latin America and the Caribbean," January 2018. https://repositorio.cepal.org/bitstream/handle/11362/43214/1/S1701249_en.pdf.

between Brazil and China (Albuquerque and Lima 2016). The public opinion survey in Brazil empirically shows that the more Brazilians share the perception that the United States loses preeminence globally, the more they will be willing to accept China as a trustworthy partner (Urdinez and Rodrigues 2017). Keeping its economic and political independence from US influence and interference by diversifying its trade and source of capital from China seems to have been a welcome option. By contrast, public opinion in Mexico is less favorable about China and Chinese investment. The failure of the three major Chinese investment projects exemplifies this domestic tension. The first one was the Mexican government's unexpected cancellation of a China-led bid for a $3.7 billion bullet train project in 2014 which would have run 130 miles from Mexico City to Queretaro (Ramzy 2014). The second one was the construction of $180 million Dragon Mart in Cancun. The third troubled investment is the Chicoasen Power station project, which China's Sinohydro won the public bidding worth $400 million to construct a hydroelectric power station. All three projects were cancelled because one of the domestic opposition in Mexico. Dussel Peters attributed these investment obstacles to the lack of institutional expertise on China within the Mexican government, as

Table 6.2 China's Major Investment Projects in LAC in 2016–2017

	Corporation	*Assets Acquired (%)*	*Asset Location*	*Sector*	*Value (Millions of Dollars)*
2016	China Molybdenum Co., Ltd	Anglo American-niobium and phosphates	Brazil	Mining	1,500
	China Three Gorges Corporation	Duke Energy International, Brazil Ltda.	Brazil	Energy	1,200
	Hainan Airlines Co. Ltd.	Azul S.A. (23.7)	Brazil	Transport	450
January to November 2017	GIC Pte. Ltd (Singapore), Brookfield Infrastructure Partners LP (Canada), China Investment Corporation (China)	Nova Transportadora Do Sudeste SA (90)	Brazil	Energy	5,200
	State Grid Corporation of China	CPFL Energia SA (100)	Brazil	Energy	10,290
	State Power Investment Corporation	Sao Simao Hydroelectric Power Plant Brazil	Brazil	Energy	2,250
	CITIC Agricultural Industry Fund Management Co Ltd	Dow Agro Sciences Sementes & Biotenologia Brasil Ltda	Brazil	Chemicals	1,100

Source: ECLAC. "Exploring New Forms of Cooperation between China and Latin America and the Caribbean," January 2018. https://repositorio.cepal.org/bitstream/handle/11362/43214/1/S1701249_en.pdf.

well as the general public's anxiety about potential competition with China (Dussel-Peters 2016).

Fourth, Brazil shares the same principles as China on supporting a stronger role played by emerging economies in multilateralism and multipolarity. They both see multilateralism backed up by a multipolar system in the world as the most effective way to challenge US hegemony. Brazilian leaders, including former president Lula, echoed that a strategic relationship with Beijing would facilitate their cooperation in multilateralism (Hakim 2006). In the past decade, China and Brazil have worked closely and built coalitions in global trade negotiations including the WTO Doha Round Negotiation, IMF governance reform, global climate talks, and within the BRICS and G20 summits. Former Chinese president Hu Jintao stressed that "China forever stay on the side of developing countries" (Meyers and Wise 2016). This foreign policy goal of China has been endorsed by Brazil and other South American countries as well. Their shared vision of the ideal global system, common interest in counterbalancing US expansion in the Western hemisphere, and joint effort to build alternative institutions such as the BRICS New Development Bank have made Brazil China's most valuable global partner. Meanwhile, for Brazil China represents a valuable geopolitical counterweight to the United States. They both believe that a collective rise of developing countries and emerging economies more accurately reflects fundamental change in international politics. Brazil, as an emerging economy that has always placed great importance to its sovereignty and independence in its foreign policy, shares the similar vision of the new/better world order. Compared to Brazil, Mexico appears less interested in multilateralism and is less willing to build a coalition with China and other developing countries to confront the United States on the world stage.

Fifth, compared to Brazil, Mexico has enjoyed more (and better) alternative export market and source of investment. As a member of the NAFTA, Mexico enjoys privilege to enter into the North America market duty-free. Currently US market absorbs about 80 percent of Mexican exports. Because of its location and its NAFTA membership, many countries have chosen to invest in Mexico to take advantage of its cheap labors and the easy access to the US market. Besides its proximity to the United States, Mexico has successfully negotiated free trade agreements with Japan, the EU, and a large number of countries. Mexico is a key player in the Pacific alliance in the region and is also a member of the TPP11. With the exclusion of China from the TPP, increasing trade tensions between China and many developed countries, and the growing cost of labor in China, Mexico has become the new investment destination for the manufacturing sector, particularly for automobiles and auto parts. As a top recipient of FDI in Latin America, Mexico has access to international credit on favorable terms, which are very competitive to those offered by Chinese banks. In 2017 US foreign direct investment accounted for 46 percent of the total FDI inflow into Mexico while US investment only accounted for 22 percent of the total FDI inflow into Brazil. In contrast to Mexico, Brazil is struggling with economic slowdowns along with domestic political turmoil and institutional deficits. It has maintained relatively high tariffs and other trade protectionist measures. Trade relations with its Mercosur partners have not gone particularly well as the market is small. Thus, China assigns more importance to Brazil economically and politically.

By referring to the strategic interests outlined by the Chinese government in Latin America, it seems that Beijing's employment of economic means has achieved better results in Brazil than in Mexico. Brazil has become the largest supplier of energy, commodity, and agricultural products to Chinese market. This has matched China's strategic interest of energy and food security. Furthermore, Brazil has become one of the most important partners of China on global arena by building strong coalitions with China in global trade, financial and climate change governance. They have also coordinated policies in the G20 meetings. The creation of the BRICS and the New Development Bank has further promoted China's strategic interest in providing regional institutions to develop alternative mandates on development financing. Lastly, through its massive infrastructure investment in Brazil, China has successfully integrated Brazil into its Belt and Road Initiative. Compared to Mexico, it seems that China has been able to pursue more of its strategic interests by engaging Brazil economically.

CONCLUSION

Realists like John Mearsheimer and Stephen Walt have advocated for Washington to "preserve US dominance in the Western Hemisphere" (Mearsheimer and Walt 2016). Although more and more policy observers have warned that "Beijing is filling the void left by a diminished U.S. presence in the latter's own backyard" (Urdinez et al. 2016; Wiggel and Landivar 2019) the United States is and will continue to be the dominant power in the region and China has no intention to directly confront the United States and US core interests in the region.[5] Economically, the United States remains the largest market for the majority of Latin American exports. Latin America exported $406 billion in goods to the United States in 2017, with roughly 80 percent of that being manufactured products, and ran a $117 billion surplus with the northern power. In contrast, Latin America had a trade deficit of $67 billion with China, with around 90 percent of exports in raw materials. Commerce Secretary Wilbur Ross recently reminded the audience at the Summit of the Americas in Peru of this asymmetrical trade relation in April 2018, concluding that "the message is that Latin America is very important to the United States." His real message, however, is that "[the] U.S. is very important to Latin America." Beijing recognizes the geographic and geoeconomic realities of the Western Hemisphere and is aware of Washington's sensitivities to China's growing presence in LAC. While Beijing is keen to increase its role in the region economically and politically, it prefers to do so in a low-key and non-confrontational manner. Rather than targeting the whole region, China is only focusing on a small number of countries that present key strategic value to China. In fact, China is not seeking to target all thirty-four countries in the region, rather, it has selected seven "large and/or strategically important" countries, namely, Brazil, Mexico, Argentina, Venezuela, Peru, Chile, and Ecuador (Fan 2016). Chinese diplomats have repeatedly stated that China is "not directed at any third party and not at forming a bloc" (Xinhua 2018).

Given China's continued demand for energy, agricultural products, and commodities, as well as its quest for global markets for its manufacturing products in the midst of US-China trade war, it will continue to maintain strong economic engagements with Latin American countries. The analysis above shows that China's economic statecraft in Latin America has mixed effects on various countries in the region and poses challenges on both sides to sustain a win-win bilateral relationship in the midst of roiling geopolitics and the complexities of South-South cooperation. China's pursuit of strategic goals through economic means and the subsequent domestic logic of the receiving states explains the various responses of Latin American countries

Overall, Central American countries continue to be very dependent upon the US market for exports, and to a lesser extent, for investment and foreign aid. Due to their trade structures, Central American Countries have not significantly benefited from booming Chinese demand for primary products and instead have faced increased competition from Chinese products in third-country markets (like Mexico). Conversely, South American countries (like Brazil) have benefited from China's rapid economic growth and depend more heavily on Chinese markets for their exports and share some similar interests towards the United States.

By examining the varied outcome of China's economic statecraft in Mexico and Brazil, it appears that Latin America is the most challenging frontier for China. Compared to Asia and Africa, Latin America proves to be a more challenging region for China due to the lack of historical connection, cultural proximity, and mutual understanding on each other's political and social institutions. China began with a pragmatic expectation and so far has achieved very limited results. The success of China's economic statecraft is largely dependent on the domestic economic and political conditions of the target state, not necessarily correlates with the scope and strategies of the China's economic inducement. Economic statecraft can take many forms.

Some of the economic statecraft tools, such as sanctions and economic pressures, have been rarely used by China as it does not have the unrivaled political and economic power to make it work effectively. Instead, China has more frequently used economic inducement, through trade, investment, and development financing to ensure its own economic (energy, commodity) security, expand its international influence (mostly vis-à-vis Taiwan in LAC), and work with other like-minded developing countries to challenge the US dominance in the region and in multilateral institutions. In the future, the economic and political divide in Latin America—between Central and South America—will continue to have fundamental implications in US–China competition for effective economic statecraft in the region.

NOTES

1. There are important exceptions, including Gonzalez-Vicente, R. (2012). Mapping Chinese mining investment in Latin America: Politics or market? *The China Quarterly*, *209*, 35–58; Urdinez, F., Mouron, F., Schenoni, L. L., & de Oliveira, A. J. (2016). Chinese economic statecraft and US hegemony in Latin America: An empirical analysis, 2003–2014. *Latin American Politics and Society*, *58*(4), 3–30; Gallagher, K. P., & Irwin, A. (2015). China's economic statecraft in Latin America: Evidence from China's policy banks. *Pacific Affairs*, *88*(1), 99–121.
2. The nine countries are: Belize, Haiti, Nicaragua, St. Kitts and Nevis, St. Vincent & the Grenadines, the Dominican Republic, Guatemala, Paraguay, Honduras, and Saint Lucia.
3. Interviews with government officials from Ministry of Foreign Affairs, May 2018.
4. Interviews with government officials from Ministry of Foreign Affairs and Ministry of Commerce, June 2016.
5. Interviews with government officials in Ecuador and Brazil, July 2018.

BIBLIOGRAPHY

Albuquerque, Jose Augusto Guilhon, and Luís Afonso Fernandes Lima. "Chinese Investment in Brazil: Can It Match the Relevance of Bilateral Trade?" *Asian Perspective* 40 (2016): 579–601.

Baldwin, David Allen. *Economic Statecraft*, revised edition. Princeton, NJ: Princeton University Press, 1985.

Barrios, Ricardo. "China's Latin American Belt and Road Chimera." *News Lens*, July 14, 2018. https://international.thenewslens.com/article/99609.

Barton, Jonathan, and Johannes Rehner. "Neostructuralism through Strategic Transaction: The Geopolinomics of China's Dragon Doctrine for Latin America." *Political Geography* 65 (2018): 77–87.

Blanchard, Jean-Marc F., and Norrin M. Ripsman. "A Political Theory of Economic Statecraft." *Foreign Policy Analysis* 4 (4) (2008): 371–98.

China-ECLAC Forum. "The Declaration of the Second China–CELAC Ministerial Forum." January 2018. http://www.chinacelacforum.org/eng/.

Dussel Peters, Enrique. "Chinese Investment in Mexico: The Contemporary Context and Challenges." *Asian Perspective* 40 (2016): 627–52.

Dussel Peters, Enrique (ed.). "América Latina y el Caribe y China: Economía, Comercio e_Inversión." *Enrique Dussel Peters* website, 2017. www.redalcchina.org/v21/images/docs/RedALCChina-2017-economia.pdf. Accessed March 15, 2018.

ECLAC (Economic Commission for Latin America and the Caribbean). "Promoción del comercio y la inversion con China: desafíos y oportunidades en la experiencia de las cámaras empresariales latinoamericanas." 2013. https://www.cepal.org/es/publicaciones/3204-promocion-comercio-la-inversion-china-desafios-oportunidades-la-experiencia.

ECLAC. "Latin America and Caribbean with China: Towards a New Era of Economic Cooperation." 2015. https://www.cepal.org/en/publications/38197-latin-america-and-caribbean-and-china-towards-new-era-economic-cooperation.

ECLAC. "Exploring New Forms of Cooperation between China and Latin America and the Caribbean." 2018. https://repositorio.cepal.org/bitstream/handle/11362/43214/1/S1701249_en.pdf.

Ellis, R. Evan. *China in Latin America: The What's and Wherefores*. Boulder, CO: Lynne Rienner Press, 2009.

Elson, Anthony. "Dragons among the Iguanas." *Finance & Development International Monetary Fund* 51 (4) (December 2014). http://www.imf.org/external/pubs/ft/fandd/2014/12/elson.htm.

Fan, Hesheng. "China's Foreign Policy Logic towards Latin America." *People's Forum*, June 16, 2016. http://www.cssn.cn/zzx/gjzzx_zzx/201606/t20160616_3073037.shtml.

Ferchen, Matt. "China–Latin America Relations: Long-term Boon or Short-term Boom?" *The Chinese Journal of International Politics* 4 (1) (2011): 55–86.

Gallagher, Kevin P. *The China Triangle: Latin America's China Boom and the Fate of the Washington Consensus*. Oxford: Oxford University Press, 2016.

Gallagher, Kevin P., and Amos Irwin. "China's Economic Statecraft in Latin America: Evidence from China's Policy Banks." *The Pacific Review* 88 (1) (2015): 99–121.

Gallagher, Kevin P., and Roberto Porzecanski. *The Dragon in the Room: China and the Future of Latin American Industrialization*. Palo Alto, CA: Stanford University Press, 2010.

Gonzalez-Vicente, Ruben. "Mapping Chinese Mining Investment in Latin America: Politics or Market?" *The China Quarterly* 209 (2012): 5–58.

Hakim, Peter. "Is Washington Losing Latin America?" *Foreign Affairs* 85 (1) (2006): 39–53.

Hearn, Adrian H. "Harnessing the Dragon: Overseas Chinese Entrepreneurs in Mexico and Cuba." *The China Quarterly* 209 (March 2012): 111–33.

Jenkins, Rhys. "Chinese Competition and Brazilian Exports of Manufactures." *Oxford Development Studies* 42 (3) (2014): 395–418.

Li, Mingjiang. *China's Economic Statecraft: Co-optation, Cooperation and Coercion.* Singapore: World Scientific, 2017.

Long, Tom. *Latin America Confronts the United States: Asymmetry and Influence.* Cambridge: Cambridge University Press, 2015.

Mearsheimer, John, and Stephen Walt. "The Case for Offshore Balancing: A Superior US Grand Strategy." *Foreign Affairs* 95 (4) (2016): 70–83.

Ministry of Foreign Affairs of the People's Republic of China. "China's Policy Paper on Latin America and the Caribbean." 2016.

Myers, Margaret, and Carol Wise (eds.). *The Political Economy of China–Latin America Relations in the New Millennium.* New York: Routledge, 2016.

Norris, William J. *Chinese Economic Statecraft: Commercial Actors, Grand Strategy, and State Control.* Ithaca, NY: Cornell University Press, 2018.

Piccone, Ted. "The Geopolitics of China's Rise in Latin America." *Brookings*, Geoeconomics and Global Issues No. 2, November 2016. https://www.brookings.edu/wp-content/uploads/2016/11/the-geopolitics-of-chinas-rise-in-latin-america_ted-piccone.pdf.

Puyana, Alicia, and Agostina Costantino. "Chinese Land Grabbing in Argentina and Colombia." *Latin American Perspectives* 42 (6) (2015): 105–19.

Ramzy, Austin. "Dismay From China After Mexico Cancels High-Speed Rail Bid." *New York Times*, November 10, 2014. http://sinosphere.blogs.nytimes.com/2014/11/10/dismay-from-china-after-mexico-cancels-high-speed-rail-bid/.

Ray, Rebecca, and Kevin P. Gallagher. "China–Latin America Economic Bulletin 2017 Edition." Boston University Global Economic Governance Imitative Working Paper, 2017. https://www.bu.edu/pardeeschool/files/2014/11/Economic-Bulletin.16-17-Bulletin.Draft.pdf.

Reilly, James C. *China's Economic Statecraft: Turning Wealth Into Power.* Sydney: Lowy Institute Analyses, 2013.

Rosen, Daniel H. "How China Is Eating Mexico's Lunch." *The International Economy* 17 (2) (Spring 2003): 22–25.

Seawright, Jason. *Multi-Method Social Science: Combining Qualitative and Quantitative Tools.* Cambridge: Cambridge University Press, 2016.

Singh, Jewellord, and Tolentino Nem Singh. "Towards Post-Neoliberal Resource Politics?" *New Political Economy* 19 (3) (2014): 329–58.

Sutter, Robert G. *Chinese Foreign Relations: Power and Policy Since the Cold War.* Lanham, MD: Rowman & Littlefield, 2008.

Urdinez, Francisco, and Pietro Rodrigues. "Trapped in Proto-Bipolarism? Brazilian Perceptions of an Emerging Chinese-American Rivalry." *Rising Powers Quarterly* 1 (2) (2017): 105–23.

Urdinez, Francisco, Fernando Mouron, Louis L. Schenoni, and Amâncio J. de Oliveira. "Chinese Economic Statecraft and US hegemony in Latin America 2003–2014: An Empirical Analysis." *Latin America Politics and Society* 58 (4) (2016): 3–30.

Wigell, Mikael, and Ana Soliz Landivar. "China's Economic Statecraft in Latin America: Geostrategic Implications for the United States." Forthcoming in M. Wigell, S. Scholvin, and M. Aaltola (eds.). *Geo-Economics and Power Politics*

in the 21st Century: The Revival of Economic Statecraft. London: Routledge, 2019.
Xinhua News Agency. "China, Mexico Enter Comprehensive Strategic Partnership." June 5, 2013. http://english.cpc.people.com.cn/206972/206976/8272224.html.
Xinhua News Agency. "Full Text: Vision and Actions on Jointly Building Silk Road Economic Belt and the 21st-century Maritime Silk Road." March 28, 2015. http://news.xinhuanet.com/english/china/2015-03/28/c_134105858.htm.
Xinhua News Agency. "Ministry of Foreign Affairs: China Is Not Directing at Any Third Party in Latin America." January 24, 2018. http://www.xinhuanet.com/2018-01/24/c_1122310165.htm.

Chapter 7

Blackening Skies for Chinese Investment in the EU?

Bas Hooijmaaijers[1]

INTRODUCTION: ECONOMIC STATECRAFT AND COFDI IN THE EU

In September 2017 the European Commission proposed a Regulation establishing a framework for screening of foreign direct investment (FDI) into the European Union (EU) (European Commission, 2017ab).[2] The proposal followed a move by Germany, France, and Italy that earlier that year sent a letter to the European Commission arguing that EU member states "should have more scope to investigate individual takeovers and, where applicable, block them" (Euractiv, 2017a). The recent development of increased Chinese investment in Europe with Chinese firms acquiring assets in strategic EU sectors (see also Rabe and Gippner, 2017)—with, for instance, Chinese home appliance manufacturer Midea's billion-euro acquisition of the German high-tech robotics firm KUKA being a critical case—led to European countries seeking stronger veto on foreign takeovers.[3,4] The three EU member states wanted a legal basis to block state-backed moves on strategic industries.

This chapter focuses on the link between economic statecraft and Chinese outward foreign direct investment (COFDI). The leading questions are how does China use OFDI as a tool of economic statecraft? And how does the fact that OFDI is a tool of economic statecraft influence the reception of Chinese investment in European host countries? It also analyzes the conditions in the host country under which economic statecraft facilitates or complicates the completion of a deal, making an important theoretical contribution to the Chinese economic statecraft literature. It particularly does so for two cases: KUKA and Aixtron. The two cases were selected because they bring to the attention the challenges that Chinese firms face when investing in the EU due to their inseparable or suspected connections with the Chinese party-state.

This is of particular importance due to KUKA's investor Midea being "cited to be a private enterprise" (Rabe and Gippner, 2017: 470), whereas Aixtron's investor Fujian Grand Chip Investment Fund LP (FGC) has state links (see *New York Times*, 2016). To support our analysis we will rely on multiple sources of data, including European Commission documents, newspaper articles, press statements from involved firms, a handful semi-structured interviews, and secondary literature.

This chapter will proceed in the following order: The next section is dedicated to the theoretical framework, before proceeding through the two case studies to analyze how conditions in the host country can help or hinder the success of Chinese economic statecraft. In the subsequent section, this chapter examines the policy implications, including the tightening of the screening regime for investment in the EU and the progress of the China-EU Bilateral Investment Treaty (BIT) negotiations. The concluding section summarizes the main findings of this chapter and expounds their relevance.

THEORETICAL FRAMEWORK: ECONOMIC STATECRAFT

The Various Tools of Economic Statecraft and How OFDI Fits Into This

Recently, Chinese economic statecraft has drawn increased academic attention (see Norris, 2016; Blackwill and Harris, 2016; Zhang and Keith, 2017; Reilly, 2017; Li, 2017). Economic statecraft can be defined as the use of economic means to pursue foreign policy goals (Baldwin, 1985). Or, as phrased by Norris, economic statecraft can be understood as "state manipulation of international economic activities for strategic purposes" (Norris, 2016: 4). In order to do this effectively, Norris argues, it is critical—yet often overlooked—that states must be able to control the behavior of commercial actors conducting the vast majority of international economic activity (Norris, 2016). State control is likely to be determined by so-called state unity. In the Chinese context this is of particular importance, because whether Chinese businesses are state-owned enterprises (SOEs) or private firms, in reality there is virtually always some (suspected) government link.

Manipulation may occur through a wide variety of state policy tools including subsidies, tariffs, taxation, investment guarantees, trade agreements, dumping and currency manipulation (Baldwin, 1985; Blanchard, Mansfield, and Ripsman, 2000; Blanchard and Ripsman, 2013). Traditionally, economic statecraft involves a government's use of economic instruments in order to influence the behavior of another country, with these economic instruments including economic sanctions and economic inducements (also known as economic incentives), with the former sometimes being referred to as negative sanctions, and the latter as positive sanctions (Baldwin, 1985; Blanchard, Mansfield, and Ripsman, 2000; Blanchard and Ripsman, 2013).

China is among the world's largest traders and among the largest hoarders of foreign exchange reserves. Moreover, it is an increasingly important source of FDI, meaning that Beijing has the necessary leverage and tools to use economic statecraft as part of its foreign policy (Pacheco Pardo, 2018). Moreover, Chinese economic inducements in the form of the availability of capital to fund infrastructure building supportive of the Belt and Road Initiative's connectivity goals in five areas being policy communication, facilities and infrastructure, unimpeded trade, people-to-people bonds and financial integration, is a key feature of China's economic statecraft, including providing funding for European projects still afflicted by capital shortages (Pacheco Pardo, 2018). As argued by Reilly, China's economic statecraft in Europe relies upon three distinct strategies: specific and diffuse reciprocity, as well as strategic engagement, with each strategy being designed to "advance a specific type of policy objective" (Reilly, 2017: 173). More general, extant literature suggests that the People's Republic of China (PRC) has keenly used economic statecraft in various parts of the world to pursue its foreign policy goals, particularly economic inducements (Pacheco Pardo, 2018; see also this edited volume).

Even though OFDI traditionally is not considered as a tool of economic statecraft, Meunier points out various reasons emphasizing that due to the way COFDI is executed, it should be analyzed as a tool of economic statecraft: First, via its "going global" (走出去) policy COFDI is an explicit policy goal of Beijing that can manipulate it as a way to achieve political goals; second, a substantial part of COFDI is realized by SOEs that "are more prone" to connect economic goals to political goals than privately owned enterprises, and third, there is the precedent of an opaque mix of foreign aid and investment in other parts of the world to gain support for Beijing's positions in multilateral fora (Meunier, 2014a: 146). China has a strategic understanding of how to support its economy and how to support specific industries. Companies are not acting independent, but they have the backup from the government. The Chinese government giving fundamental guidance is critical, for instance when it comes to investment, because they can see the future, and indicate that this is where the country wants to be strong in the future, so it supports the strategic aim. Beijing wants to have at least one Chinese company that can compete with international ones in every important field. This chapter touches on an important but under-investigated dimension of China's economic statecraft. Current research, such as Norris (Norris, 2016), focuses on the principal-agency problem to explain the success and failure of China's economic statecraft strategies. This chapter brings to the attention the challenges that Chinese businesses face when investing in the EU due to their inseparable or suspected connections with the Chinese party-state. In these cases, the (suspected) state-firm unity may result in the failure of the investment effort or may lead to a call for measures.

Chinese State-Owned Enterprises and Privately Owned Enterprises

Although SOEs account for a substantial part of COFDI in Europe, privately owned enterprises (POEs) have recently become an increasingly important COFDI actor (see Amighini, Rabellotti, and Sanfilippo, 2013; Hanemann and Huotari, 2016; Meunier, Burgoon, and Jacoby, 2014). However, various remarks should be made regarding Chinese SOEs and POEs. First, it will be difficult to argue that all Chinese SOEs are the same or behave in the same way. There are SOEs at the central level as well as at the provincial and local level. Most SOE investment now is from local ones rather than central ones. Moreover, in the late 1990s and early 2000s, Chinese businesses, including many in the manufacturing sector, were partially privatized, however they still retain strong links to the Chinese government (Garcia-Herrero and Xu, 2017). Milhaupt and Zheng point out that 5 percent of Chinese private companies are under Communist Party of China (CPC) members' direct control (Milhaupt and Zheng, 2015), and "even non-party entrepreneurs are also likely to pursue political resources and sometimes recruit CPC members or those people with relationships with government, in order to improve their chances of accessing scarce resources" (Garcia-Herrero and Xu, 2017: 10–11). Moreover, or in contrast, Zhao demonstrated for a number of Chinese SOEs that they make investment decisions without government influence (Zhao, 2015). Overall, in China, it is hard to specify with any precision which firms are "private" and which companies are "SOEs" (Buckley et al., 2018). Due to the similarities between SOEs and some special private companies, Milhaupt and Zheng argue that "drawing a stark distinction between SOEs and privately owned enterprises (POEs) misperceives the reality of China's institutional environment and its impact on the formation and operation of large enterprises of all types" (Milhaupt and Zheng, 2015: 665). In addition, these scholars argue that because of the PRC's institutional environment, big, successful businesses—regardless of ownership—"exhibit substantial similarities" in areas commonly thought to differentiate SOEs from their private counterparts, including market dominance, proximity to state power, receipt of state subsidies and execution of the state's policy objectives (Milhaupt and Zheng, 2015: 665).

To some degree, private firms are also connected to the Chinese government, for instance because they need to have permission to go abroad. Though it is also worth mentioning that one of the reasons for the recent

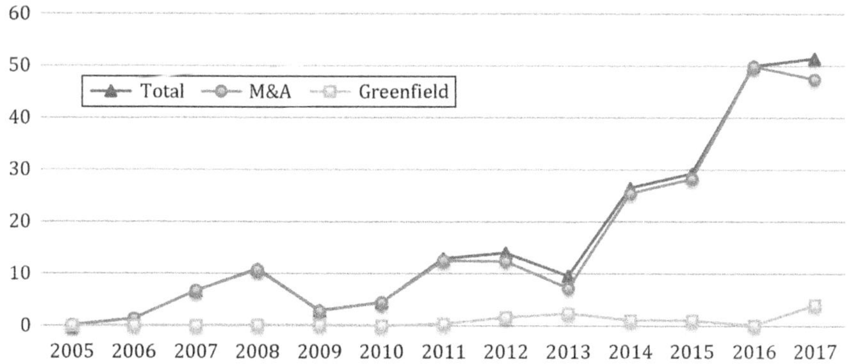

Figure 7.1 Chinese investment in the EU28, 2005–2017 (quantity in billions USD). *Source*: China Global Investment Tracker (CGIT). (The deals described in the CGIT are worth $100 million or more)

massive explosion of investment (see also Figure 7.1) was that these permissions and regulations were changed, which made it much easier for small and private companies to invest overseas. The degree that they did so led to a regulatory rethink in 2017 and bans on certain types of investments (see *Bloomberg*, 2017). This shows that the Chinese state is setting the overall agenda, but not least when it loosens its control, other actors might go off and pursue their own interests.

How OFDI in Europe Can Be Used to Achieve the Chinese State's Long-Term Goals

One worrisome political implication of COFDI in Europe is "its potential to be used by China as a tool for economic statecraft in order to achieve foreign policy goals" (Meunier, 2014a: 146). Chinese firms have various commercial motives for investing in Europe including acquiring technology, learning know-how, building brands, servicing Chinese firms abroad, and circumventing trade barriers (Knapp and Meunier, 2012; Meunier, Burgoon, and Jacoby, 2014). However, another driver of COFDI is China's "going global" policy (Shen and Mantzopoulos, 2013; Wang, 2014; Zhu, 2018). The Chinese government encourages and facilitates its firms to go abroad, which is reflected in the fact that the policy is referred to in various recent Five-Year Plans (for more on the politico economy of COFDI, see also Blanchard, 2011). On a similar note, in 2015 China launched an initiative to significantly upgrade its industry, which was called "Made in China 2025" (中国制造2025). Made in China 2025, also known under its abbreviation MIC2025, is Beijing's industrial policy that aims to make China move higher up the global value chain, because currently China is still at the lower end of this chain (Li, 2017).

The initiative's ambition is not simply to move up the global value chain, but to control technologies that make this shift possible. This means that for instance high-end technology should now be produced in China as well. However, since often China does not possess this kind of high-end technology (yet), a way to acquire this is through foreign acquisitions. Made in China 2025 is Beijing's overall objective, and it was this that has led to changes in the outward investment regulations and regime. Because of China's "going global" policy, its MIC2025 strategy, as well as the various SOEs realizing these policies (or a suspected state-firm link in case it concerns Chinese private businesses), COFDI can be considered a substantial part of China's economic statecraft, because it can be used as a means to achieve political goals (Meunier, 2014a). Or per Rabe and Gippner, "it is the Chinese ability to develop international investment strategies aiming to turn China into an industrial superpower that drive the fear that investment projects would follow a hidden agenda leading to disadvantages for Europe in the long term" (Rabe and Gippner, 2017: 481).

Conditions in the Host Country: Recipe for Success or Failure?

As pointed out by Blanchard and Ripsman, the hallmark of economic statecraft seems to be its inconsistent results due to high-profile applications having shown varying degrees of success (Blanchard and Ripsman, 2013). On a similar note, this special issue also shows the rising influence, but mixed results of China's economic statecraft. The mixed results of economic statecraft raise important questions including under what conditions it can be successful. Consequently, this section focuses on how conditions in the host country can help or hinder the success of Chinese economic statecraft. Apart from economic mechanisms, political mechanisms may play a role (Meunier, 2014b). This includes lessened political resistance and several tools such as investment promotion, simplified investment processes, and various financial and operational incentives, as well as golden visa programs. Beijing has made use of Europe's financial security needs following the severe credit crunch suffered due to the Global Financial Crisis (GFC) and subsequent Eurozone Sovereign Debt Crisis (ESDC) to influence the policies of countries across the continent and the EU (Pacheco Pardo, 2018). The wider geographic division between COFDI in Europe has triggered competition between the EU member states for Chinese investment (Hanemann and Huotari, 2016). COFDI in Southern Europe predominantly focuses on "government-initiated privatisations" to gain a foothold in the economy; in need for cash and in the aftermath of the global financial crisis, Southern European governments welcome FDI (Rasmussen Global, 2017: 3). Moreover, the Central and Eastern European Countries (CEECs) provide a home for COFDI, and the CEECs generally hold a more positive stance vis-à-vis COFDI. China cooperates with the CEECs and other Balkan states that are not EU members in the 16+1 framework.[5]

It is however critical to point out that inward FDI flows are not equally welcomed by the countries receiving investments, and often encounter strong political opposition (Tingley et al., 2015). As a non-EU example, Tingley et al. found that American political actors are more likely to protest Chinese inward merger and acquisition (M&A) investments in security sensitive industries, economically distressed industries, and sectors in which US companies faced restrictions in China's M&A markets (Tingley et al., 2015: 53). A change in government may also shape the conditions for COFDI in Europe, as the China General Nuclear Corporation (CGN) investment in Hinkley Point C illustrated. When British prime minister David Cameron left the government, new prime minister Theresa May immediately put CGN's investment into question due to national security considerations. Following the introduction of a new legal framework that gave the UK government veto right on FDI in critical infrastructure, May eventually gave the green light (Rabe and Gippner, 2017).

There is also a role for the private sector. For instance in Germany, efforts to attract Chinese investment are generally driven by the private sector, because firms do not only attract capital but also seek better market access in China (Rasmussen Global, 2017: 3). However, this may create tensions with governments that have increasingly become reluctant to approve Chinese acquisitions affecting strategic sectors (Rasmussen Global, 2017: 3). Thus, another condition in the host country that can help or hinder the success of Chinese economic statecraft is the presence of a legal basis to block an acquisition, for instance in a strategic sector or on national security grounds. Thus far, several relatively open European societies frequently lacked a legal basis or screening mechanism to block certain investments.

In sum, various conditions in the host country can help or hinder the success of Chinese economic statecraft, including a country's financial security needs, the health of its economy, its technological advancement, the sector in which the investment is taking place, screening mechanisms that may provide legal grounds for blocking, investment promotion tools, the geopolitical aspirations of the host country, or the efforts of the private sector to attract investment.

THE RECENT SURGE OF COFDI IN THE EU

Over the past years, the COFDI in Europe has increased rapidly, as can be seen in Figure 7.1 (see also Casaburi, 2017; Clegg and Voss, 2016; Hanemann and Huotari, 2015, 2018; Le Corre and Sepulchre, 2016; Meunier, 2014ab).

Regarding the recent surge of COFDI in the EU several remarks should be made. A very limited amount of the current COFDI in the EU is greenfield investment; by contrast, even though COFDI in the EU significantly outnumbers EU investment in China, EU greenfield investment in the PRC is much higher than vice versa (Rhodium Group, 2017). Moreover, mega deals like the 2017 Logicor deal in the UK, or the 2016 KUKA deal in Germany may have a significant influence on one-year data. On a related note, if for some reasons a mega deal gets (slightly) delayed, or is concluded in the subsequent year this also may substantially affect one-year data. Therefore, it is worthwhile looking at the bigger trends. Moreover, it is critical to distinguish between FDI stocks and flows when summarizing the recent surge of COFDI in the EU. Although over the past years COFDI in Europe has increased rapidly, China's investment stock in many EU countries—although increasing—remains relatively low compared to other (older) investors, with for instance the United States being a much bigger foreign investor in the EU. Half of the known COFDI total is concentrated in Europe's five largest economies, and has clustered in a few key industries (*Bloomberg*, 2018). Energy makes up a substantial chunk of Chinese investment in Europe; however, it also targets high-end technology and infrastructure sectors.

Moreover, with the growing Chinese investment in the EU the imbalances between both parties have increased as well (Hanemann and Huotari, 2017). Besides a massive trade deficit between both parties, imbalances include COFDI in the EU that for instance in the year 2016 was approximately four times as high as the investment of the EU in China, as well as the continuing lack of reciprocity. While European sectors such as banking, automotive, robotics, strategic services, and legal services are open for Chinese investors, these sectors remain restricted for European foreign investors in the PRC (European Union Chamber of Commerce in China, 2017).

CASE STUDIES

This section will be dedicated to the two case studies. The discussion of the cases will be followed by an analysis of the conditions under which Chinese economic statecraft facilitated or complicated the completion of the acquisition.

The KUKA Case: A Chinese Household Appliance Maker Acquiring Germany's Industry 4.0 Flagship

KUKA is a German world leading manufacturer of industrial robots and supplier of intelligent automation solutions. The successful high-tech robotics firm attracted the interest of Chinese investors, and in August 2015 Midea—a Chinese household appliance maker—acquired 5.4 percent of the KUKA stock. In the light of China's "Made in 2025" policy, automation as well as robotics have become high priority sectors, because the PRC seeks to move up the global value chain. Midea's investment in KUKA continued in 2016, as in February of that year it raised its stake to 10.2 percent, hence making Midea the second-largest shareholder after Voith, a German industrial group that held 25.1 percent of the KUKA shares (*Reuters*, 2016a). While increasing its share at the same time it stated that it wanted to further increase its stocks in the robotics firm. Correspondingly, in mid-May 2016, the Midea Group made an offer of €115 per share, making the robotics firm value around 4.5 billion euro. This seemed to be a hefty premium because the share price on closing of the stock market on the day before the bid was made was only 84.41 euro (*Reuters*, 2016b). Moreover, compared to the stock prices early February it was a 60 percent premium (*Financial Times*, 2016a). At the time of the bid Midea just owned 13 percent of the KUKA shares, but because it expressed its ambition of a stake greater than 30 percent, the company was obliged under German law to make an offer for the remainder of the shares (*Financial Times*, 2016a; *Wall Street Journal*, 2016a).

Despite the words of Midea's executives that they "would like to have a meaningful stake in KUKA above 30 per cent and have no intention of concluding a domination agreement or delisting the company" (South China Morning Post, 2016a), the company's KUKA offer sparked controversy in Germany including fears that crucial technologies were falling into foreign hands, while at the same time China prevents German and other foreign firms from taking over their Chinese counterparts. This lack of reciprocity is undeniably a continuing issue in the Sino-European bilateral relations (Farnell and Crookes, 2016; Hanemann and Huotari, 2018). Concerns were expressed that Germany's Industry 4.0, which is considered as the future of German industry because it seeks automation and data exchange in manufacturing technologies, would be harmed by this Chinese takeover, because KUKA could indeed be considered one of the leading businesses pushing this innovation.

Markus Ferber, a member of the European Parliament (MEP) for the German Christian Social Union party for instance said "We really need to think about whether we want to give such a key enterprise to the Chinese, or try to keep it in European hands" (*Financial Times*, 2016b). German chancellor Angela Merkel addressed the issue of reciprocity and imbalance in the Sino-German relations during her visit to Beijing, where she stated: "We expect reciprocity on the Chinese side too" (*Financial Times*, 2016b). Sigmar Gabriel, at that time Germany's vice chancellor and economy minister in particular was very vocal on this issue, as he wrote in a guest article for WirtschaftsWoche: "Should it remain the case that government agencies are only allowed to conduct preliminary investigations into investment in areas deemed relevant for security and defense?" He added, "we need to clarify whether we should not create the option to assess the interests of investors against the EU's industrial interests for sectors that can be of existential significance for the strategic future of the European economy" (*Reuters*, 2016d; Wirtschafswoche, 2016).

Rather than a Chinese takeover, various politicians preferred a European acquisition of KUKA, and suggested a consortium of European technology companies or other main shareholders to come up with an alternative bid. KUKA's largest shareholders at that time included the Voith Group, which owned 25.1 percent of the shares, and German billionaire Friedhelm Loh who owned 10 percent. However, as was also pointed out by Rabe and Gippner, Midea's high offer made it impossible for European firms to compete, and a perception of being unable to avoid deals that are not uniquely welcome sparked the debate to regulate investments on both national and supranational levels (Rabe and Gippner, 2017). European businesses felt KUKA simply was not worth that price. Moreover, the German government made a move to cap Midea's share in KUKA at 49 percent, thus preventing it from obtaining a majority share in the robotics firm (*Reuters*, 2016f).

Allegedly driven by the ongoing concerns on crucial technology falling in Chinese hands, on June 28, 2016, KUKA and Midea announced that both parties entered into an investment agreement. The investment agreement is "a legally binding contract governed by German law, which contains profound and long-term obligations and declarations" of the MECCA International (BVI) Limited, a 100 percent subsidiary of Midea Group Co., Ltd. (KUKA, 2016a). Additionally, the agreement included that MECCA and Midea have committed not to initiate any corporate reorganizations of KUKA Group, and declared not to purpose to enter into any domination agreement or to cause a delisting of KUKA. Both parties agreed that the investment agreement has a fixed term of 7.5 years, meaning that the agreement will expire by the end of 2023. Additionally, in a separate statement KUKA announced that both its management and supervisory boards recommended the Midea offer and considered the offer of €115 per share as "fair," with KUKA's Chief Executive Till Reuter stating, "Together with Midea we will be able to translate our strategy even better. At the same time we will remain a German company" (*Reuters*, 2016c).

On August 8, Midea announced it possessed 94.55 percent of the KUKA shares, and mid-August, Berlin approved Midea's acquisition of KUKA, as a spokesman of the German Economics Ministry stated that an initial examination on the case had shown no evidence that the acquisition would threaten "the security and the public order of Germany," adding that "the ministry can only launch a formal inquiry against the sale if crucial German interests such as telecommunications or water and power safety are affected" (Deutsche Welle, 2016). The approval of the deal by the German ministry showed that the plan of the government to cap Midea's stock at 49 percent did not work out (*Reuters*, 2016f).

Following the trend of increasing COFDI, in mid-October Welt am Sonntag reported that the German Economy Ministry wants to protect "high tech companies in Germany from unwanted takeovers," particularly from state-owned and partly state-owned companies in non-EU countries (*Reuters*, 2016e). Deputy Economy Minister Matthias Machnig had indeed sent to members of the German government a working paper containing six key points for reviewing investment at the EU level, which foresaw wide-reaching rights for both the EU and its member states to prevent company takeovers by investors from non-EU countries (*Reuters*, 2016e).

Besides the German authorities, the US authorities launched an examination on the deal. Because KUKA has US subsidiaries, the US authorities were qualified to do so. On December 15, 2016, KUKA announced the sale of its unit KUKA Systems Aerospace North America to the US automation company Advanced Integration Technology Inc. The decision to sell this section was related to open regulatory approvals in the United States, because the sale can be regarded as "an important step" to fulfill security-relevant requirements of the US authorities Committee on Foreign Investment in the United States (CFIUS) and Directorate of Defense Trade Controls (DDTC), as at the time both authorities were reviewing the takeover offer from MECCA/Midea for KUKA, focusing on the firm's "activities in military and security-relevant areas" in the United States (KUKA, 2016b). KUKA's US subsidiary was International Traffic in Arms Regulations (ITAR) registered, however following sanctions imposed on China after the Tiananmen crackdown Chinese ownership of ITAR-registered firms is banned. Eventually late December KUKA announced that the US government, CFIUS, and DDTC had cleared the take-over of KUKA by MECCA International (BVI) Limited, a 100 percent subsidiary of the Midea Group (KUKA, 2016c). As pointed out by Rabe and Gippner, the deal also had a symbolic character in the PRC, because the acquisition was seen by some of their interviewees as a "victory" and a huge success in the country's economic development, whereas others found the acquisition "incredible" due to KUKA's and the German industry's high technological development (Rabe and Gippner, 2016: 476)

Case Analysis

One of this case's most fundamental questions is why does a household appliance manufacturer acquire a high-tech robotics firm? Chinese prime minister Li Keqiang and Midea vice president Andy Gu "emphasized that

Midea were a private company" (Rabe and Gippner, 2017: 476); however, other parties argue that "in China nothing is private" (Interview senior EU business representative, 12 June 2017). The analytical point is the following: China has a strategic understanding about how to support its economy and how to support specific industries. In China it is the government that gives fundamental guidance when it comes to manufacturing industries.[6] Moreover, it is quite common for a Chinese firm to do something completely different compared to its core business when money can be made, which means that companies may not only invest in the products they already produce. It was a clever decision from Midea, because the robotics industry is a field with enormous potential. Its strategic importance is clear, and in the short-term around 50 percent of the market for this type of robotics will be in China. The Chinese government giving fundamental guidance is critical. They can see the future, and indicate that this is where the country wants to be strong in the future, so it supports the strategic aim. Support may also come from the process of approval to set up construction and start production. With the right support firms can be quicker than others. Indeed, the interplay between politics and economics occurs elsewhere as well, however in China it differs when it comes to for instance volume and type of support. So Midea's acquisition of KUKA should be understood in the context of China's Made in China 2025 strategy, which focuses on moving up the global value chain and control technologies that make this shift possible. This means that for Germany, China has evolved from an economic partner to a serious global competitor, because both parties have similar ambitions and initiatives. As reported by the South China Morning Post, early July 2016 KUKA announced a venture with Chongqing-based Changan Industry (Group) Co., a wholly owned subsidiary of China South Industries Group Corp, one of China's largest state-owned military enterprises to set up a business to help Chinese manufacturers automate their operations (South China Morning Post, 2016b). Per Wang Cairong, secretary general of the China Artificial Intelligence Robot Industry Alliance, "Midea's strategy is to be the Chinese leader in robotics and automation," adding that "[The] Chinese government needs and encourages new 'heavyweight' companies in this sector" (South China Morning Post, 2016b).

How did the conditions in Germany help or hinder the success of Chinese economic statecraft in the KUKA case? Per Freshfields, the law firm that advised Midea on the deal, "Political friction between the two countries was the deal's main obstacle, with the potential to spark significant anger among German investors and government officials," also stating that "The potential involvement of some Chinese government programmes in these acquisitions, particularly those of hi-tech companies, has generated criticism and calls for China to provide greater market access to German investors," adding that "Opposition from Kuka's management and supervisory board, as well as shareholders and politicians, could have scuppered the deal entirely" (Freshfields, 2018). This is somewhat in line with Tingley et al.'s findings that political actors are more likely to protest Chinese investments in security sensitive industries and sectors in which firms face restrictions in China (see Tingley et al., 2015). Thus, Midea built up its ownership in KUKA step by step, and a dialogue between both firms eventually led to an investment agreement that overcame opposition from various parties including KUKA's management and supervisory board, certain shareholders and German politicians (see KUKA, 2016a; Freshfields, 2018). Eventually, Midea acquired a high-tech robotics firm, KUKA's shareholders benefited from the hefty premium of €115, a share that Midea was willing to pay, and KUKA itself remained independent and gained market access in China. Or, per KUKA's Chief Executive Till Reuter, "Together with Midea we will be able to translate our strategy even better. At the same time we will remain a German company" (*Reuters*, 2016c).

There is a critical role for law and regulations as well. To finalize the deal, KUKA's US subsidiary had to be divested, because Chinese ownership of ITAR-registered firms is prohibited. Moreover, already in mid-August Berlin approved Midea's acquisition of KUKA, as a spokesman of the German Economics Ministry stated that an initial examination on the case had shown no evidence that the acquisition would be a threat to "the security and the public order of Germany," adding that "the ministry can only launch a formal inquiry against the sale if crucial German interests such as telecommunications or water and power safety are affected" (Deutsche Welle, 2016). This means that in this case there was no legal basis to block the deal even if Berlin would have wanted to.

The Aixtron Case: Opaque Links and a Failed Acquisition

Aixtron is a German semiconductor firm that produces cutting-edge technologies. After various successful years the chip manufacturing systems producer suffered losses since 2012. The company was facing a slowdown in demand in 2015 when San'an Optoelectronics made a last-minute order cancellation, making that its share prices significantly dropped. In the aftermath of this event, in May 2016, the Fujian Grand Chip Investment Fund LP (FGC) offered up to €676 million for the financially troubled company, an offer that according to Aixtron Chief Executive Martin Goetzeler was appreciated, as he stated that "the executive and supervisory boards welcome the offer. It comes at the right time" (Handelsblatt, 2016a). FGC's offer of €6 per share was more than 25 percent higher than Aixtron's closing price at the end of the week prior to the bid, which was already up due to the takeover speculation

(Handelsblatt, 2016a). Put differently, it reflected a 50.7 percent premium to the three-month volume-weighted average stock price prior to announcement of the offer (Aixtron, 2016a).

However, not everyone seemed to be pleased with the bid, given the move of the German government that despite its initial approval of the sale early September 2016, withdrew the clearance certificate for FGC around six weeks later, and announced a reopening of review proceedings in connection with the acquisition offer by Grand Chip Investment GmbH (Aixtron, 2016b). Berlin's move to reopen the review of the Chinese acquisition of Aixtron allegedly followed security concerns that were raised about the bid. Then German deputy economics minister Matthias Machnig, said this move followed the receiving of "previously unknown security-related information" (*Financial Times*, 2016c). According to Handelsblatt, US intelligences services were behind this sudden decision by the German authorities. Because Aixtron's manufacturing technology also has military applications, the United States was concerned that China might use Aixtron's gear to produce electronic chips for its nuclear program (Handelsblatt, 2016b). In this light it is important to take into account that the technology that Aixtron produces can have military applications in both satellite communications and radar, and that Aixtron's customer Northrop Grumman is a major US defense contractor (*Bloomberg*, 2016a).

Apart from the alleged security concerns on the deal, in various commentaries then German vice chancellor and economy minister Sigmar Gabriel, a member of the German Social Democratic Party of Germany (SPD), expressed his displeasure with the current state of affairs of COFDI in Germany: "It's not on that Germany sacrifices its companies on the altar of free markets, while at the same time our own companies have huge problems investing in China" (Politico, 2016). In a contribution on the matter to Die Welt he stated something similar: "If you want to invest in other parts of the world, you can't block those countries from investing in your own" (Die Welt, 2016).

Gabriel's view seemed to be supported by EU Digital Economy Commissioner Guenther Oettinger, a member of the German Christian Democratic Union (CDU), who commented on the issue of reciprocity: "It's absolutely right to initiate this debate at the European level. Everybody has to play by the same rules. Clearly, there are many countries, including big ones such as China, that make market access or corporate takeovers difficult or effectively impossible" (*Bloomberg*, 2016b).

Besides the lack of reciprocity there were other issues with COFDI in Europe. As was reported by the *New York Times*, conflicting interests may lurk behind Chinese investment deals, as San'an—the firm that cancelled at the last minute an Aixtron order late 2015—has various connections to

FGC—the company that made an Aixtron offer in 2016—including a common investor and existing financial relationships (*New York Times*, 2016). Moreover, even though it remains unclear whether both firms coordinated their actions in any way, ultimately both San'an and FGC are recipients of Chinese government funds assigned to help China build out its semiconductor capabilities (*New York Times*, 2016).

The German national security concerns were echoed by the US authorities, which resulted in a ban on the acquisition by then US president Barack Obama as he followed the advice of CFIUS. Despite Aixtron's headquarters being based in Germany, under American law US officials were allowed to block the purchase of Aixtron's US subsidiary Aixtron Inc. The US Treasury Department stated "The national security risk posed by the transaction relates, among other things, to the military applications of the overall technical body of knowledge and experience of Aixtron" (*Bloomberg*, 2016b). Obama's ban was a rare move, because it was only the third time in twenty-five years that a US president had blocked an international acquisition because of national security concerns.

Despite the fact that the ban only counted for the United States because its jurisdiction is limited to its national territory, a statement from FGC said that this block meant the takeover offer was not fulfilled and caused the deal to collapse. Following the fall through of the deal, a spokeswoman for Germany's economy ministry stated this meant that Berlin would "no longer continue to review the case" (*Wall Street Journal*, 2016b).

Case Analysis

How did conditions in the host country help or hinder the success of Chinese economic statecraft in the Aixtron case? Concerning private party support, Aixtron was seeking to attract capital. For the financially troubled company the offer meant support for its research and development activities, and it improved the firm's ability to compete and grow in China (see Aixtron, 2016a). Or per the firm's leaders, "The executive and supervisory boards welcome the offer. It comes at the right time" (Handelsblatt, 2016a). For Aixtron's shareholders, FGC's offer meant they could benefit from a hefty premium for their share in the company (see also Handelsblatt, 2016a; Aixtron, 2016a). Similar to the KUKA case, the Chinese offer was that high that it made it virtually impossible for European firms to compete with it.

National security concerns as well as the sector the firms were operating in shaped the conditions that hindered the success of Chinese economic statecraft in the Aixtron case. Berlin withdrew the clearance certificate for the deal that it had issued six weeks earlier, based on previously unknown security-related information. For Aixtron's US subsidiaries, national security risks resulted in a ban on the acquisition by then US president Barack Obama as he followed the advice of CFIUS. This is rather in line with Tingley et al.'s findings that political actors are more likely to protest Chinese investments in security sensitive industries and sectors in which—in this case European—firms face restrictions in China (see Tingley et al., 2015). Moreover, concerns were raised on the origin of money supporting Chinese bids, with in this case being opaque links between the Chinese customer, the Chinese buyer and the Chinese government (*New York Times*, 2016). Following the withdrawal of the offer by FGC, the German authorities decided to no longer continue to review the case, which means that formally we do not know the outcome of the investigation on national security concerns that was conducted by Berlin. For the Chinese investors it showed that even though *ex ante* there seemed to be no issues, this may change and previous approvals can indeed be withdrawn.

POLICY IMPLICATIONS

When it comes to the link between economic statecraft and COFDI, one key point is the basic and fundamental suspicion of Chinese motives and goals that exists in parts of the EU, and has got stronger in recent years. Even if you are a private company with no direct state links, you might still be assumed to be part of this state project. Chinese firms face challenges when investing in Europe, because of their inseparable or suspected connections with the Chinese party-state. The issue, and the EU concerns, is not so much with COFDI as such, but with the Chinese controlling tech companies and the potential of being able to control the whole value chain through these firms. In both the KUKA and Aixtron cases we saw Chinese investors that were willing to pay hefty premiums for the firms' shares; however, this may lead to uncertainty about the real motives of the Chinese investors; was there a political decision to complete the acquisition no matter what? (see Meunier, 2014a). Still, it should be noted that despite Midea indeed having paid a hefty premium, this is not unique. It could possibly be more common in software and less common in hardware, but paying a hefty premium in order to secure an acquisition does occur more frequently.

The increasing presence of (suspected) state-sponsored companies is a relatively new situation for the EU. It is limited by its institutions and by its beliefs in free market and free capital flows. By contrast, the Chinese side is more able to play the long-term game, especially because it is a one-party state. To deal with this situation, action has to come from the EU member states. However, there are diverging opinions among them. A senior EU business representative illustrated the current situation with an American football analogy:

> China wants to gain yards, market space, until you cross the line. So you have to push back. However, the EU has 28 players on the field, with no coach. This means that if we do not have our defense lines intact we cannot blame them to score. (Interview senior EU business representative, 12 June 2017)

The various Chinese acquisitions led to European countries seeking stronger veto authority over Chinese takeovers, as Germany, France, and Italy wanted a legal basis to block state-backed moves on strategic industries.[7] Early 2017 they sent a letter to the European Commission arguing that EU member states "should have more scope to investigate individual takeovers and, where applicable, block them" (Euractiv, 2017a). With this letter addressed to EU Trade Commissioner Cecilia Malmström, the three countries were seeking to open up a debate on the issue, because they wanted to create a legal basis for the member states to be able to "intervene in direct investments which are state-controlled," hence calling for "more scope to investigate individual takeovers and, where applicable, block them," which is driven by recent deals that were "unfair…because they rely on state funds or are aimed at buying up important technologies" (*Financial Times*, 2017a). German officials wanted to substantially increase their powers, making it possible to red-flag any acquisition that appears to be "dictated by Chinese state industrial policy" or is "designed to enable technology transfers" (*Financial Times*, 2017a). Imposing such new rules may prove to be challenging, because agreement at EU level needs to be reached.

Media reports late May 2017 showed that despite pressure exerted by Germany, France, and Italy, the EU member states disagree on whether it is appropriate to establish a EU mechanism to protect strategic sectors against foreign acquisitions, with opposition expected to come from countries that are keen on attracting FDI and with better ties with the PRC, including Greece, Portugal, and Slovakia (Euractiv, 2017b). In this light it is also worth mentioning the 16+1 initiative, and its (potential) political implications. The initiative, which is related to China's Belt and Road Initiative, makes these countries potentially more reliant on the PRC. As pointed out by Meunier, the PRC has a "pattern" of having used "a blurred blend of foreign aid and investment" in other parts of the world, to ensure support for its positions in international fora (Meunier, 2014a: 146). Logically, this also may affect EU unity.[8] As stated by Sigmar Gabriel, "If we do not succeed for example in developing a single strategy towards China, then China will succeed in dividing Europe" (*Financial Times*, 2017c). A senior EU business representative stated: "China is slicing and dicing Europe" (Interview senior EU business representative, 12 June 2017). Though there are critical voices as well among the CEECs, with Poland for instance that has been quite critical about 16+1, because they were not gaining anything. Thus far, 16+1 has not been that successful, because 95 percent of the cooperation projects only reached the level of memorandum of understanding, leading to the CEECs getting more impatient. Still, it illustrates the (perceived) challenges that Europe is facing concerning COFDI and a China policy more general.

In September 2017, the Commission proposed a framework for screening of foreign direct investments (European Commission, 2017ab):

- A European framework for screening of foreign direct investments by the EU member states on grounds of security or public order.
- A cooperation mechanism between member states and the European Commission.
- European Commission screening on grounds of security or public order for cases in which foreign direct investment in member states may affect projects or programs of Union interest.

Per the European Commission: "Acquisitions by foreign state-owned or controlled companies in these strategic areas may allow third countries to use these assets not only to the detriment of the EU's technological edge, but also to put our security or public order at risk" (European Commission, 2017b). In screening FDI on the grounds of security or public order, the EU member states and the European Commission may consider the potential effects on critical infrastructure and critical technology (European Commission, 2017a).[9,10] The listing of areas and keeping the categories wide was a deliberate move to make sure there is some space for maneuver. Eventually, on November 20 the European Parliament, the Council, and the European Commission reached a political agreement on an EU framework for FDI screening.

However, the member states keep the last word in any investment screening (European Commission, 2017b).[11] Though as former Danish prime minister and former secretary general of NATO Anders Fogh Rasmussen emphasized, "A Europe-wide early warning system will not make up for the lack of national screening rules in 15 EU states. The measures are discretionary and far less stringent than those we see in any other G7 nation" (*Financial Times*, 2017b). Moreover, worth emphasizing is that none of the national screening mechanisms that currently are in place scrutinize "whether FDI from private or public sources may benefit from foreign-state funding for the implementation of national industrial policy goals" (Grieger, 2017: 2).

Because the Commission proposal follows the so-called ordinary legislative procedure, this means that it needs the approval of the European

Parliament, and the EU Member States in the Council, so even when it will be adopted it will take time before it will come into force. However, not only the European concerns are influencing COFDI in Europe. Chinese domestic policy changes play a role as well. While in 2016 there was a massive surge in Chinese foreign acquisitions, this seemed to have changed to some degree because Beijing has imposed capital control measures, which slowed down the foreign buying spree; "Cooling off the buying frenzy" has become China's policy priority, and a decrease in outbound M&A activity should contribute to stem capital flight as well as stabilize the PRC's battered currency (*Bloomberg*, 2017).[12] Recently, another shift became visible, as China has lately remained silent about Made in China 2025. As good as Beijing usually is in marketing its policies, for instance with the Belt and Road Initiative, Made in China 2025 was "bad" in a way that it raised awareness about what is going on. Europe (and the West) became more conscious about China's aim. Beijing wants to have at least one Chinese company that can compete with international ones in every important field.

Chinese SOEs are a critical point in the Sino-European talks on a BIT that have been ongoing for several years. As emphasized by Garcia-Herrero and Xu, when evaluating the undue advantage enjoyed by Chinese firms, preferential market access in the PRC rather than ownership of SOEs should be the key factor, since private firms with ties to the Chinese government might also benefit from this (Garcia-Herrero and Xu, 2017). In addition, they argue that creating barriers to prevent Chinese firms acquiring European assets will not solve the problem, but rather equal market access in the PRC is a much better goal to pursue to reduce "the seemingly unlimited resources" that Chinese SOEs seem to have to compete overseas (Garcia-Herrero and Xu, 2017: 1).

CONCLUSION

This chapter focused on the link between economic statecraft and COFDI. The leading questions were how does China use OFDI as a tool of economic statecraft? And how does the fact that OFDI is a tool of economic statecraft influence the reception of Chinese investment in European host countries? It analyzed the conditions under which economic statecraft facilitates or complicates the completion of an acquisition. It particularly did so for two case studies: the KUKA and Aixtron cases. Both cases illustrated the challenges that Chinese firms face when investing in the EU, because of their inseparable or suspected connections with the Chinese party-state, making an important theoretical contribution to the Chinese economic statecraft literature.

It showed the rising influence, but mixed results of China's economic statecraft. The KUKA and Aixtron cases that were discussed above support this point, because they were part of a group of similar cases that worked as an eye-opener. Following the increasing Chinese direct investment in critical EU sectors for instance driven by Beijing's industrial policy MIC 2025, in September 2017 the European Commission proposed a framework for screening of FDI, and on November 20 the European Parliament, the Council, and the European Commission reached a political agreement on an EU framework for FDI screening. There are various implications of the case analyses for the future of COFDI as a tool of China's economic statecraft and the conditions in the host country. As pointed out by Derek Scissors, "The money will flow to where it is most welcome. Until a European review mechanism is put in . . . Europe is likely to win the lion's share of Chinese investment" (*Bloomberg*, 2018). Moreover, he stated that "a move in Europe to regulate Chinese investment" could be expected; however, for the time being it is "the number one destination" (*Bloomberg*, 2018). Chinese investment in the EU has become even more important in the Trump era, due to COFDI in the United States having decreased dramatically. From a European perspective, the lack of reciprocity and the quest for market access continue to be important issues in the Sino-European bilateral investment relationship. COFDI in Europe is not always welcomed, as was illustrated by the German, French, Italian joint initiative to intervene in state-controlled FDI. However, the EU member states, stakeholders, as well as academia are divided in their views on the FDI screening proposal (Grieger, 2018). Not surprisingly, this limits Europe in its efforts to respond to COFDI as a part of Chinese economic statecraft. Be that as it may, the interplay between politics and economics on various levels is critical for a better understanding of the Sino-European bilateral investment relations. The contemporary issues with COFDI in Europe also fit in the context of the rise of China and the EU's challenge to deal with this emergence (see Keukeleire and Hooijmaaijers, 2014).

NOTES

1. The author would like to thank the editors, the anonymous JCPS reviewers, and Professor Jean-Marc F. Blanchard for their comments and support.

2. A regulation is a binding legislative act and must be applied in its entirety across the EU.

3. Other, similar high-profile cases in Europe around that time included Hinkley Point C, Syngenta, Osram Licht, and Aixtron.

4. The development of COFDI in Germany illustrates the suddenness of Chinese investment in Europe, as it grew from €1.2 billion in 2015 to €11 billion in 2016.

5. The eleven EU Member States and five Balkan countries that participate in the 16+1 framework include Albania, Bosnia and Herzegovina, Bulgaria, Croatia, the Czech Republic, Estonia, Hungary, Latvia, Lithuania, Macedonia, Montenegro, Poland, Romania, Serbia, Slovakia, and Slovenia.

6. By contrast, in Germany, this is more bottom-up, businesses are in the driver's seat. Enterprises are in the lead and the government focuses on facilitating the process of innovation and technological development.

7. When it comes to undertaking any action concerning this issue, the initiative has to come from the EU member states. This also has a political dimension, because *de facto* it is most likely that it has to come from the Big Three.

8. Two examples illustrate this point: in June 2017, Greece blocked an EU statement at the United Nations Human Rights Council criticizing China's human rights record; Moreover, Hungary has "repeatedly blocked" EU statements criticizing the PRC's human rights record (*Reuters*, 2017).

9. The full list as proposed by the Commission includes critical infrastructure, including energy, transport, communications, data storage, space or financial infrastructure, as well as sensitive facilities; critical technologies, including artificial intelligence, robotics, semiconductors, technologies with potential dual-use applications, cyber security, space or nuclear technology; the security of supply of critical inputs; or access to sensitive information or the ability to control sensitive information (European Commission, 2017a).

10. Worth noting is that the proposal is focused on security interests and was not launched to tackle the reciprocity issue (Hanemann and Huotari, 2018).

11. Currently twelve of the twenty-eight EU member states have a national review mechanism in place including Austria, Denmark, Germany, Finland, France, Latvia, Lithuania, Italy, Poland, Portugal, Spain, and the UK.

12. Besides these matters the case studies revealed uncertainty for Chinese investors in Europe, because we have seen cases including the Aixtron case where *ex ante* there were no issues; however, in a later stage approvals were withdrawn. Also, in December 2016 Sanan Optoelectronics and GSR Go Scale Capital Advisors stopped pursuing a bid for the whole acquisition of lighting group Osram Licht, because of signs of increasing political opposition to Chinese takeovers of German firms, reflecting a perception that "resistance from labour representatives and from politicians has left an impression on the Chinese" (*Reuters*, 2016g).

BIBLIOGRAPHY

Aixtron. 2016a. GCI to Launch Offer for AIXTRON SE. May 23. Access @ https://www.aixtron.com/en/investors/GCI%20to%20launch%20offer%20for%20AIXTRON%20SE_n929.

Aixtron. 2016b. AIXTRON SE: Withdrawal of Clearance Certificate and Reopening of Review Proceedings by the Ministry of Economics Pertaining to the Takeover by Grand Chip Investment GmbH. October 24. Access @ https://www.aixtron.com/

en/press/press-releases/detail/aixtron-se-widerruf-der-unbedenklichkeitsbescheini gung-und-wiederaufnahme-des-pruefverfahrens-durch-das-bundeswirtschaftsmini sterium-im-rahmen-der-uebernahme-durch-die-grand-chip-investment-gmbh/.

Amighini, Alessia, Roberta Rabellotti, and Marco Sanfilippo. 2013. "Do Chinese State-owned and Private Enterprises Differ in their Internationalization Strategies?" *China Economic Review* 27:312–325.

Baldwin, David A. 1985. *Economic Statecraft*. Princeton, NJ: Princeton University Press.

Blackwill, Robert D., and Jennifer M. Harris. 2016. *War by Other Means: Geoeconomics and Statecraft*. Cambrige, US: Harvard University Press.

Blanchard, Jean-Marc F. 2011. "Chinese MNCs as China's New Long March: A Review and Critique of the Western Literature." *Journal of Chinese Political Science* 16 (1):91–108.

Blanchard, Jean-Marc F., and Norrin M. Ripsman. 2013. *Economic Statecraft and Foreign Policy: Sanctions, Incentives and Target State Calculations*. Abingdon: Routledge.

Blanchard, Jean-Marc F., Edward D. Mansfield, and Norrin M. Ripsman, eds. 2000. *Power and the Purse: Economic Statecraft, Interdependence and National Security*. Oxon: Frank Cass & Co.

Bloomberg. 2016a. German Push Grows for Chinese Investment Curbs as Aixtron Probed. October 24. Access @ https://www.bloomberg.com/news/articles/2016-10-23/german-momentum-grows-for-curbs-on-chinese-overseas-investment.

Bloomberg. 2016b. Obama Blocks Chinese Takeover of Aixtron as U.S. Security Risk. December 3. Access @ https://www.bloomberg.com/news/articles/2016-12-02/obama-blocks-chinese-takeover-of-aixtron-as-u-s-security-risk.

Bloomberg. 2017. China's $246 Billion Foreign Buying Spree Is Unraveling. May 11. Access @ https://www.bloomberg.com/news/articles/2017-05-10/china-s-246-bi llion-takeover-spree-is-crumbling-as-sellers-balk.

Bloomberg. 2018. How China Is Buying Its Way Into Europe. April 23. Access @ https://www.bloomberg.com/graphics/2018-china-business-in-europe.

Buckley, Peter J., Jeremy Clegg, Hinrich Voss, Adam R. Cross, Xin Liu, and Ping Zheng. 2018. "A Retrospective and Agenda for Future Research on Chinese Outward Foreign Direct Investment." *Journal of International Business Studies* 49 (1):4–23.

Casaburi, Ivana. 2017. *Chinese Investment Trends in Europe – 2016–17 Report*. ESADE China Europe Club.

China Global Investment Tracker. 2018. Data Compiled by The American Enterprise Institute and The Heritage Foundation. Access @ http://www.aei.org/china-globa l-investment-tracker/.

Clegg, Jeremy, and Hinrich Voss. 2016. "The New Two-way Street of Chinese Direct Investment in the European Union." *China-EU Law Journal* 5 (1):79–100.

Deutsche Welle. 2016. Berlin Approves Kuka Sale to Midea. August 17. Access @ http://www.dw.com/en/berlin-approves-kuka-sale-to-midea/a-19479483.

Die Welt. 2016. Gabriel wirft China Foulspiel bei Übernahmen vor. October 29. Access @ https://www.welt.de/wirtschaft/article159131595/Gabriel-wirft-China-Foulspiel-bei-Uebernahmen-vor.html.

Euractiv. 2017a. Commission Says Proposal to Block Chinese Takeovers is 'Worth Discussing'. February 16. Access @ https://www.euractiv.com/section/trade-society/news/commission-says-proposal-to-block-chinese-takeovers-is-worth-discussing/.

Euractiv. 2017b. Proposal to Block Chinese Foreign Investment Faces Uncertain Future. May 30. Access @ https://www.euractiv.com/section/economy-jobs/news/tuesday-story-for-eu-chinaproposal-to-block-chinese-foreign-investment-faces-uncertain-future/.

European Commission. 2017a. *Proposal for a Regulation of the European Parliament and of the Council Establishing a Framework for Screening of Foreign Direct Investments into the European Union*. Brussels: {SWD(2017) 297 final}, September 13.

European Commission. 2017b. State of the Union 2017 – Trade Package: European Commission Proposes Framework for Screening of Foreign Direct Investments. September 14. Access @ http://europa.eu/rapid/press-release_IP-17-3183_en.htm.

European Union Chamber of Commerce in China. 2017. European Business in China Position Paper 2017/2018.

Farnell, John, and Paul Irwin Crookes. 2016. *The Politics of EU-China Economic Relations. An Uneasy Partnership*. Basingstoke: Palgrave Macmillan.

Financial Times. 2016a. China's Midea Makes Offer for German Robotics Group Kuka. May 19. Access @ https://www.ft.com/content/90f9f7ae-1cd4-11e6-b286-cddde55ca122.

Financial Times. 2016b. Berlin and Brussels Wary of Chinese Robotics Bid. June 14. Access @ https://www.ft.com/content/acbda1cc-3186-11e6-bda0-04585c31b153.

Financial Times. 2016c. Germany Withdraws Approval for Chinese Takeover of Tech Group. Berlin Reopens Probe into Aixtron Deal Amid Protectionist Backlash against China. October 24. Access @ https://www.ft.com/content/f1b3e52e-99b0-11e6-8f9b-70e3cabccfae.

Financial Times. 2017a. EU Capitals Seek Stronger Right of Veto on Chinese Takeovers. Berlin, Paris and Rome Want Legal Basis to Block State-backed Moves on Key Industries. February 15. Access @ https://www.ft.com/content/8c4a2f70-f2d1-11e6-95ee-f14e55513608.

Financial Times. 2017b. China's Investment in Europe Offers Opportunities – and Threats. November. Access @ https://www.ft.com/content/9e7428cc-c963-11e7-8536-d321d0d897a3.

Financial Times. 2017c. Brussels Rattled as China Reaches Out to Eastern Europe. November 27. Access @ https://www.ft.com/content/16abbf2a-cf9b-11e7-9dbb-291a884dd8c6.

Freshfields. 2018. A Blueprint for Chinese Outbound Investment. Access @ https://www.freshfields.com/en-us/what-we-do/case-studies/midea-kuka-case-study/.

Garcia-Herrero, Alicia, and Jianwei Xu. 2017. How to Handle State-owned Enterprises in EU-China Investment Talks. June 19, 2017. Bruegel Policy contribution 18.

Grieger, Gisela. 2017. *Foreign Direct Investment Screening. A Debate in Light of China-EU FDI Flows*. Brussels European Parliamentary Research Service.

Grieger, Gisela. 2018. *EU Framework for FDI Screening*. Legislative briefing, January 2018. PE 614.667. Brussels: European Parliamentary Research Service.

Handelsblatt. 2016a. Chinese Firm Bids €676 Million for Aixtron. 24 May. Access @ https://global.handelsblatt.com/companies-markets/at-aixtron-chips-are-up-with-chinese-bid-525000.

Handelsblatt. 2016b. U.S. Said to Intervene in Aixtron Deal. October 26. Access @ https://global.handelsblatt.com/politics/uncle-sam-intervened-in-aixtron-deal-630912.

Hanemann, Thilo, and Mikko Huotari. 2015. *Preparing for a New Eara of Chinese Capital. Chinese FDI in Europe and Germany*. Berlin: Mercator Institute for China Studies and Rhodium Group.

Hanemann, Thilo, and Mikko Huotari. 2016. *A New Record Year for Chinese Outbound Investment in Europe*. Berlin: Mercator Institute for China Studies and Rhodium Group.

Hanemann, Thilo, and Mikko Huotari. 2017. *Record Flows and Growing Imbalances. Chinese Investment in Europe in 2016*. Berlin: Mercator Institute for China Studies and Rhodium Group.

Hanemann, Thilo, and Mikko Huotari. 2018. *EU-China FDI: Working towards Reciprocity in Investment Relations with China*. Berlin: Rhodium Group (RHG) and the Mercator Institute for China Studies (MERICS).

Interview senior EU business representative, Beijing June 12, 2017.

Keukeleire, Stephan, and Bas Hooijmaaijers. 2014. "The BRICS and other Emerging Power Alliances and Multilateral Organisations in the Asia-Pacific and the Global South: Challenges for the European Union and its View on Multilateralism." *Journal of Common Market Studies* 52 (3):582–599.

Knapp, Justin, and Sophie Meunier. 2012. Coming to America: Top Ten Factors Driving Chinese Foreign Direct Investment. *The Huffington Post*, July 31.

KUKA. 2016a. Tender Offer Midea Group: Investor Agreement. 28 June. Access @ https://www.kuka.com/en-de/press/news/2016/06/tender-offer-midea-group-investor-agreement.

KUKA. 2016b. KUKA Sells Systems U.S. Aviation Section to Advanced Integration Technology Inc. December 15. Access @ https://www.kuka.com/-/media/kuka-corporate/documents/press/news/2016/12/press-release15122016.pdf.

KUKA. 2016c. US Government Authorities Grant Clearances for Take-over of KUKA by Midea. December 30. Access @ https://www.kuka.com/en-de/press/news/2016/12/clearances-for-take-over-of-kuka-by-midea.

Le Corre, Philippe, and Alain Sepulchre. 2016. *China's Offensive in Europe*. New York: Brookings Institution Press.

Li, Ling. 2017. "China's Manufacturing Locus in 2025: With a Comparison of "Made-in-China 2025" and "Industry 4.0"." *Technological Forecasting & Social Change* 135:66–74.

Li, Mingjiang, ed. 2017. *China's Economic Statecraft: Co-optation, Cooperation and Coercion*. New Jersey: World Scientific.

Meunier, Sophie. 2014a. "A Faustian Bargain or Just a Good Bargain? Chinese Foreign Direct Investment and Politics in Europe." *Asia Europe Journal* 12 (1):143–158.

Meunier, Sophie. 2014b. "'Beggars Can't be Choosers': The European Crisis and Chinese Direct Investment in the European Union." *Journal of European Integration* 36 (3):283–302.

Meunier, Sophie, Brian Burgoon, and Wade Jacoby. 2014. "The Politics of Hosting Chinese Investment in Europe–An Introduction." *Asia Europe Journal* 12 (1–2):109–126.

Milhaupt, Curtis J., and Wentong Zeng. 2015. "Beyond Ownership: State Capitalism and the Chinese Firm." *Georgetown Law Journal* 103 (3):665–722.

New York Times. 2016. Rush of Chinese Investment in Europe's High-Tech Firms Is Raising Eyebrows. September 18. Access @ https://cn.nytimes.com/business/20160918/china-germany-takeover-merger-technology/en-us/.

Norris, William J. 2016. *Chinese Economic Statecraft: Commercial Actors, Grand Strategy, and State Control*. Ithaca: Cornell University Press.

Pacheco Pardo, Ramon. 2018. "Europe's Financial Security and Chinese Economic Statecraft: The Case of the Belt and Road Initiative." *Asia Europe Journal* 16 (3):237–250.

Politico. 2016. Sigmar Gabriel's Mission to Halt China's Investment Spree. German Vice Chancellor Heads to Beijing with a Tough Message on Trade. November 1. Access @http://www.politico.eu/article/sigmar-gabriels-mission-to-halt-chinas-investment-spree/.

Rabe, Wiebke, and Olivia Gippner. 2017. "Perceptions of China's Outward Foreign Direct Investment in European Critical Infrastructure and Strategic Industries." *International Politics* 54 (4):468–486.

Rasmussen Global. 2017. Foreign Investment Screening and the China Factor. New Protectionism or New European Standards? November 16. Access @ https://rasmussenglobal.com/wp-content/uploads/2017/11/INVESTMENT_REPORT_RG_Memo_Nov_16.pdf

Reilly, James. 2017. "China's economic statecraft in Europe." *Asia Europe Journal* 15 (2):173–185.

Reuters. 2016a. China's Midea Raises Stake in Germany's Kuka to 10.2 pct. February 4. Access @ http://www.reuters.com/article/kuka-ma-midea-group-idUSL8N15J4MB.

Reuters. 2016b. China's Midea Makes $5-billion Bid for German Robot Maker Kuka. May 18. Access @ http://www.reuters.com/article/us-kuka-m-a-midea-group-idUSKCN0Y90DB.

Reuters. 2016c. Kuka and Midea Sign Investment Agreement. June 28. Access @ http://www.reuters.com/article/us-kuka-m-a-midea-group-idUSKCN0ZE2DU.

Reuters. 2016d. Germany's Gabriel Seeks EU Rule to Block Foreign Takeover of Key Technologies. June 9. Access @ http://www.reuters.com/article/us-kuka-m-a-mideagroup-germany-idUSKCN0YV147.

Reuters. 2016e. Germany Considers Protecting Firms from Foreign Takeovers: Newspaper. October 16. Access @ http://www.reuters.com/article/us-germany-mergers-economy-ministry-idUSKBN12G06Q.

Reuters. 2016f. UPDATE 1-German Ministry to Clear Takeover of Kuka by China's Midea. August 17. Access @ http://www.reuters.com/article/kuka-midea-group-ministry-idUSL8N1AY16H.

Reuters. 2016g. Chinese Bidders Walk Away from Osram Takeover: Sources. December 13. Access @ http://www.reuters.com/article/us-osram-licht-m-a-china-idUSKBN1421RR.

Reuters. 2017. Greece Blocks EU Statement on China Human Rights at U.N. June 18. Access @ https://www.reuters.com/article/us-eu-un-rights/greece-blocks-eu-statement-on-china-human-rights-at-u-n-idUSKBN1990FP.

Rhodium Group. 2017. EU-China FDI Monitor 3Q 2017 Update: Public Version. Access @ http://trade.ec.europa.eu/doclib/docs/2018/january/tradoc_156572.pdf.

Shen, Raphael, and Victoria Mantzopoulos. 2013. "China's "Going Out" Policy: Inception, Evolution, Implication." *Journal of Business and Behavioral Sciences* 25 (2):121–136.

South China Morning Post. 2016a. China's Midea Group Bids for Greater Ownership of Robot Maker KUKA; German Company's Shares Surge. May 18. Access @ http://www.scmp.com/business/companies/article/1946774/chinas-midea-group-bids-greater-ownership-robot-maker-kuka-german.

South China Morning Post. 2016b. Revealed: The 10 Billion Yuan Masterplan to Turn Midea into China's Robot Powerhouse China's Largest Maker of Home Appliances Wants to take the Next Step in Manufacturing: Build Robots. August 11. Access @ https://www.scmp.com/tech/china-tech/article/2002361/midea-spends-10-billion-yuan-make-robots.

Tingley, Dustin, Christopher Xu, Adam Chilton, and Helen V. Milner. 2015. "The Political Economy of Inward FDI: Opposition to Chinese Mergers and Acquisitions." *The Chinese Journal of International Politics* 8 (1):27–57.

Wall Street Journal. 2016a. China's Midea Offers $5 Billion for German Robot Maker Kuka; Bid Aims to Help Satisfy Beijing's Ambitions to Become High-end Manufacturing Power. May 18. Access @ https://www.wsj.com/articles/chinas-midea-group-announces-bid-for-germanys-kuka-1463556160.

Wall Street Journal. 2016b. Chinese Takeover of Aixtron Collapses After U.S. Ban; President Barack Obama Blocked Offer for Semiconductor Firm on National-security Grounds. December 8. Access @ https://www.wsj.com/articles/chinese-takeover-of-aixtron-collapses-after-u-s-ban-1481203244.

Wang, Huiyao. 2014. "Ten Chinese Going Global Models: Emerging Patterns and Analysis." *The European Journal of Finance* 20 (7–9):625–636.

Wirtschaftswoche. 2016. Kuka-Übernahme durch Chinesen: Gabriel will Abwandern. June 9. Access @ http://www.wiwo.de/impressum/nutzungshinweise/blocker/?callback=%2Funternehmen%2Findustrie%2Fkuka-uebernahme-durch-chinesen-sigmar-gabriel-will-abwandern-von-schluesseltechnologien-per-eu-schutzklausel-verhindern%2F13710652.html.

Zhang, Xiaotong, and James Keith. 2017. "From Wealth to Power: China's New Economic Statecraft." *Washington Quarterly* 40 (1):185–203.

Zhao, Hongtu. 2015. "The Myth of China's Overseas Energy Investment." *East Asia Forum Quarterly,* March 4.

Zhu, Zhiqun. 2018. "Going Global 2.0: China's Growing Investment in the West and Its Impact." *Asian Perspective* 42 (2):159–182.

Chapter 8

Nuclear Infrastructure Investment

China's New Tool of Economic Statecraft?

Biao Zhang[1]

In recent years China has invested in many overseas nuclear projects. China General Nuclear Power Group (CGN), one of the three largest state-owned nuclear companies, has committed to finance 33.5 percent of the construction cost of the British Hinkley Point C (HPC) project.[2] CGN is also negotiating with Romania about financing the construction of two CANDU units in the Cernavoda project (worth $7.7 billion) and is currently preparing to bid for the Czech Dukovany and Temelin projects (worth $15 billion). China National Nuclear Corporation (CNNC), another nuclear company of the "big three," has signed a contract with Argentina which commits it to finance 85 percent of the Atucha project worth $15 billion (WNN 2017).

A "strategic reading" may see these investments as a strategy that seeks to achieve leverage over key countries. Matthew Cottee (2017) suggests that China is providing finance, technology, and expertise to other countries in order to strengthen relations with them; China's nuclear infrastructure investments are "geopolitically motivated investment[s]."[3] Richard Turcsanyi (2017, 714) reports that many experts based in the Central and Eastern European region view China's intention to build a Czech nuclear plant "as a logical step in its strategy to build up its presence." For these scholars and observers, China is investing in political influence (Meunier 2014). China is trying to gain political influence by providing finance and technology to the target countries and satisfying their infrastructure development needs, in the same way as Russia and France have done previously.[4]

My aim in this chapter is to examine whether nuclear infrastructure investment has indeed become China's new tool of economic statecraft. While the literature on China's economic statecraft has said much on how government uses a variety of means to advance its political purposes, few contributions appear to have examined China's investment in nuclear infrastructure (except Thomas 2016; see more generally Blackwill and Harris 2016, Ch.4; Bräutigam and Tang 2012; Drezner 2017; Lai 2017; Norris 2016; Reilly 2012; Zhang and Keith 2017). The central questions are: First, is China using nuclear infrastructure investment to induce the target countries to change their policies; and second, do the target countries change their policies in order to attract Chinese nuclear investment?

To answer both questions, I examine China's investment in the United Kingdom (UK) and the Czech Republic. I focus on these two examples because they are widely considered to be more strategically motivated than other possible examples. Both the UK and Czech Republic were keen to attract investment into their nuclear infrastructure.[5] Second, both countries changed their stances toward the Dalai Lama; only months after they announced that would refuse to meet the Dalai Lama and would respect China's territorial integrity, China's state-owned nuclear companies agreed to invest in the UK's Hinkley Point C project and declared their interest in bidding for the Czech Dukovany and Temelin projects. Third, after distancing themselves from the Dalai Lama, both countries received state visit from the Chinese president and their bilateral ties with China were elevated to the level of a strategic partnership. During these state visits, China's state-owned nuclear companies also signed deals and expressed their interest in participating in the nuclear projects.

In examining the two cases, I suggest that there are three commonalities which conjoin the two cases. First, the target countries did not change their policies with the particular purpose of attracting Chinese *nuclear* investment. The UK and Czech governments did not abandon the Dalai Lama for Chinese *nuclear* infrastructure investment. This might have been conceivable in other investment contexts (e.g., high-speed railway) but not in the nuclear sector. Although both governments are keen to attract investment in nuclear infrastructure, it is clear that China is not their first choice. Rather, China's nuclear companies usually "enter into the scene" (invest in and bid for their projects only) because of some negative reasons—for example, the old partners pulled out and European and Russian utilities are unwilling to be involved in (Point A).

Second, China's state-owned nuclear companies played a bigger role than the government in the early stage of making decisions. For instance, their decisions to enter into negotiation could even precede significant improvement in political relations: the Chinese nuclear companies agreed to "participate" (i.e., invest) in the HPC project before the British government declared that it would avoid meeting the Dalai Lama (Point B). They did so for commercial interest, that is, investment in exchange for the possibility of using Hualong One technology in the UK and Czech (Point C). In most instances, the government helped to conclude, rather than initiate, preexistent agreements and negotiations.

Third, the Chinese government provided political and financial support to the nuclear companies only after the UK and Czech announced their policy to avoid meeting the Dalai Lama. It is also noticeable that when the Chinese government provided support to the deal, the government focused on the question of whether the Chinese nuclear companies would be given the opportunity to build a nuclear plant and deploy their indigenously designed Hualong One reactor (Point D).

In the ensuing discussion, I first examine China's investment in the UK and then proceed to the Czech projects. In the final section, I demonstrate how an examination of China's involvement in nuclear projects can make two contributions to the literature on China's economic statecraft. First, I suggest that China's nuclear infrastructural investments lack the strategic intent that is frequently ascribed to them. Rather, in China's nuclear infrastructure investment, the commercial actor and economic motivation plays an important role (Points A, B, and C). Second, China's nuclear infrastructure investment always tends to be politicized. While the government will provide political and financial support after the target countries change their positions toward the Dalai Lama, it is also keen to see that in exchange for its investment China's nuclear companies could have a chance to build Hualong One abroad (Point D).

CHINA'S ECONOMIC STATECRAFT IN THE UK? THE CHINESE INVESTMENT IN THE HINKLEY POINT C PROJECT

In this section I examine China's nuclear infrastructure investment in the UK. In the first subsection, I show that the "strategic account" of China's investment in the HPC project tends to overemphasize the strategic dimensions of the deal and considerably attenuates the role of China's nuclear companies. In the second subsection, I then proceed to demonstrate that the Chinese government provides political support to the project subsequent to the change within the British government's stance toward the Dalai Lama—but the Chinese government tends to focus on the likelihood that the indigenously designed Hualong reactor would be successfully deployed.

China-UK Relations, the Dalai Lama, and the Hinkley Point C

The strategic account of how China's investment came into the HPC project would suggest that the Conservative-Liberal Democrat coalition government (2010–2015) sought to attract foreign (especially Chinese) investment in British infrastructure. However, the prospect that this funding would be provided by China was substantially complicated in early 2012, when the then prime minister David Cameron and his deputy Nick Clegg announced in early 2012 that they planned to meet the Dalai Lama in London. This arrangement enraged the Chinese government (BBC 2012; FM 2012). After this meeting took place, China barred UK leaders from its territory, cancelled a leader's visit to the UK and suspended all bilateral dialogues and meetings.

The account then proceeds to reiterate the British government's concern that this could potentially jeopardize billions of pounds of Chinese investment from China. For instance, *The Telegraph* (2013) reported, the fear that the frosty relations with China could endanger "large infrastructure projects such as HS2 rail network and the government's nuclear investment program missing out on billions of pounds." In May 2013, Cameron openly addressed these concerns when giving a speech in which he reiterated Britain's respect for Chinese sovereignty. After this statement, China-UK relations reverted to their previous state. During George Osborne's October 2013 visit to China—the first visit by one of Britain's leading politicians after David Cameron's meeting with the Dalai Lama in 2012—both CGN and CNNC signed letters of intent that signaled their interest in financing 40 percent of the HPC's project (EDF 2013). During Xi's 2015 state visit to the UK, a CGN-led consortium (including CNNC) signed an investment agreement with Électricité de France (EDF), which committed the CGN-led consortium to finance 33.5 percent of the HPC project. EDF and the British government approved this deal in 2016.

According to this account, the British government eventually "lost and won China back" (*Financial Times* 2015). The British government changed its position toward the Dalai Lama because it feared that this would jeopardize Chinese investment. From an alternative perspective, China can be viewed as using economic pressure (cancelation of nuclear investment) to keep the British government from the Dalai Lama. If this was the case, then China was exercising "unilateral sanction" (Reilly 2012, 126).[6]

But was the British government pressed to change its position toward the Dalai Lama in exchange for Chinese investment into its nuclear infrastructure? The answer is far from straightforward. First, the coalition government did not intend to attract Chinese investment into its *nuclear* infrastructure in the first place. The British government promoted the HPC project as a key part of its strategy to secure energy supply and combat climate change: the project was on the top of the national infrastructure list and was considered as a "testing case" (or template) for later nuclear projects (Gov UK 2011). However, the original plan was that EDF would work with Centrica (a British energy company) to finance the project. Unfortunately, Centrica pulled out of the HPC project in February 2013, citing uncertainty in return and an extended construction schedule as a justification (BBC 2013a). The withdrawal of Centrica, in addition to the level of EDF debt, resulted in both the British government and EDF requesting help from the Chinese companies.

Second, the Dalai Lala incident did *not* impact the Chinese nuclear companies' interest in investing in the HPC projects. When Centrica pulled out in February 2013, the Chinese companies agreed to assume Centrica's place and entered into negotiation with the EDF about the HPC project (CGN 2016a). According to CGN (2016a), CGN and EDF reached "initial agreement [to participate in the HPC project]" on March 18, with GGN then sending a letter of intent to EDF—this was two months in advance of Cameron's speech. The commitment of China's state-owned company therefore preceded Cameron's clarification of the British government's stance upon the Dalai Lama. As Kerry Brown (2015, 43) observes, Chinese investment into the UK was not affected after the Dalai Lama controversy. In addition, CGN reached a more detailed agreement with EDF (albeit which still operated at the level of principle) in June 2013 which committed them to invest billions of pounds into the project in exchange for Hualong One—this was only one month after Cameron's statement (CGN 2016a).

Third, Chinese nuclear companies were interested in the project because they wished to exchange investment for the possibility of deploying China's indigenously designed Hualong One reactor.

Thus, the Chinese investment in the HPC project was from the outset a decision that was made by the Chinese nuclear companies to seize the opportunity, having been made at a time when China-UK relations were frozen.

The Chinese Government's Position

The Chinese government played two roles in the HPC project. First, the government provided political and financial support to the deal—after the British counterpart pledged respect for sovereignty. After Cameron's statement in May, the Chinese government soon allowed the British politicians to visit China. In September, Ed Davey, the then minister for the Department of Environment and Climate Change (DECC), was granted a ten-day visa to visit China during which he met his Chinese counterparts and visited several state-owned nuclear energy companies, including CGN and CNNC. One month later, George Osborne, the then chancellor, visited China in October 2013 during which the two sides signed a MoU on *Enhancing Cooperation in the Field of Civil Nuclear Energy*. The MoU, which aimed to establish the basis for a China-UK intergovernmental nuclear cooperation agreement (NCA), expressed the two governments' "willingness to foster increased cooperation in their respective domestic markets" (Gov UK 2013a, 1; see also, Mofcom 2013).

Eight months later, Li visited the UK and the two governments signed an NCA before issuing a *Joint Statement between the Government of the UK and*

PRC on Civil Nuclear Energy Cooperation—this declared the intention of the Chinese companies to invest and participate in the construction of the nuclear plant in Hinkley Point C (Gov UK 2014b). During Xi's September 2015 state visit to the UK, he presided over the signing of the final investment agreement between CGN and EDF; the two countries also issued *UK-China Joint Statement 2015*, which declared a joint commitment to "a global comprehensive strategic partnership for the 21st century" and that "both sides welcome the commercial agreement on HPC" (Gov UK 2015a).

Second, when the Chinese government provided support to the deal, it also focused on the question of whether the Chinese nuclear companies would be given the opportunity to build a nuclear plant and deploy their indigenously designed Hualong One reactor. This concern with export success was reflected in all the MoUs and statements—the Chinese government seems to have continually sought to enlist the British government's formal commitment to the CGN-led project. For instance, the 2013 MoU stated that the UK government "actively supports and welcomes Chinese enterprises, with their expertise and technologies, into the UK civil nuclear energy market" (UK Gov 2013a). Li reportedly "pushed for breakthroughs" during his December 2013 meeting with Cameron and expressed his desire for his country to both participate and also purchase equities and stocks in UK nuclear power projects (BBC 2013b).

During Li's 2014 visit to the UK, the two governments also published a *China-UK Joint Statement* which functioned alongside the joint NCA statement and reiterated the commitment of both sides to work together to ensure the complete success of Hinkley Point (Gov UK 2014a). The *UK-China Joint Statement 2015* further reiterated the consensus which supported the Chinese-led project and envisaged the progressive expansion of the Chinese role within civil nuclear energy projects. The *UK-China Statement of Cooperation in the Field of Civil Nuclear Energy 2015*, which was issued during Xi's state visit, stated that both parties were committed to a Chinese-led project at Bradwell B (Gov UK 2015b, 2–3). Each of the preceding points serves to further suggests that China's nuclear infrastructure investment in the UK is less strategic than it is usually understood to be.

CHINA'S ECONOMIC STATECRAFT IN CZECH? THE CHINESE INTENT TO BID FOR TEMELIN AND DUKOVANY PROJECTS

In this section I examine China's declared interest in bidding for the Dukovany and Temelin projects in the Czech Republic. In the first subsection I seek to demonstrate that China's project of bidding for Czech's nuclear projects (probably based on Hualong One) is far less strategic than is usually understood. In the second sub-section, I show that the Chinese government's commitment of political support is underpinned by commercial motivations.

China-Czech Relations, the Dalai Lama, and the Nuclear New-Builds

The strategic narrative may suggest that a state-owned nuclear company's bidding for two nuclear projects in the Czech Republic serves to further illustrate how the government uses nuclear infrastructural investment to consolidate China-Czech relations and isolate the Dalai Lama in the region (Turcsanyi 2017, 714).

The Social Democratic government wanted to attract investment into the country and develop infrastructure. President Melos Zeman and Prime Minister Bohuslav Sobotka abandoned the previous approach of criticizing China's human rights record, and instead sought to improve China-Czech relations (Furst 2018).[7] Zeman held his first meeting with Xi in Sochi in February 2014. During the course of this meeting, Zeman stated that his government would change its past policy and respect China's sovereignty (*People's Daily* 2014). Only five months after Zeman's first meeting with Xi, China's Vice Premier Zhang Gaoli informed the Czech government that Chinese nuclear companies were interested in bidding for the Czech Republic's Temelin and Dukovany projects (*Xinhua* 2014c). In August 2014, the Czech Minister of Trade also confirmed that CGN would submit bids for the new-builds (*Global Times* 2014).

Zeman undertook several visits to China later.[8] During a state visit to China in October 2014, for instance, Zeman stated explicitly that the Czech government would recognize Tibet as an integral part of China, "firmly support[s]" China's stance on "Tibet-related and other issues," and determine to "safeguard and develop the friendly cooperative relations with China" (FM 2014). During this visit, Zeman also raised the prospect of nuclear infrastructure investment from China, and expressed to the Chinese part the "Czech government's interest in [bringing the Chinese] investments into the upgrade of nuclear power plants" (CEZ 2014).

In return for the expressions of support by Czech leaders, Xi made a state visit to the country. This was the first-ever state visit by a Chinese president since bilateral diplomatic relations had been established, and it was the first-ever state visit a Chinese president had made to a CEEC country. During this visit, the two governments issued a joint statement in which they agreed to enhance "productivity cooperation in [. . .] nuclear energy" and set up a "strategic partnership" (*Xinhua* 2016a). CGN announced that the Chinese company was keen to support the country's new national energy strategy (which afforded nuclear infrastructure a central role) and committed it to actively participate in the construction and development of new nuclear projects at Dukovany and Temelin (CGN 2016b). CGN signed a MoU with České Energetické Závody (CEZ) on the Comprehensive Collaboration in nuclear energy with the intention of establishing long-term collaboration (*China Daily* 2016; CGN 2016b). These are designed for integrating local firms into the supply chain, and preparing the way for Czech companies to participate in the NPP (WNN 2016).

The "strategic account" might suggest that the Czech leaders' pro-China policy increased their chances of receiving a bid from China's nuclear company that would result in billions of dollars being invested into the project. This raises the question of whether China was using its nuclear investment to reward the Czech Republic for changing its stance upon the Dalai Lama.

The answers here are again complicated. First, the Czech leadership did seek to adopt a pro-mainland China policy with the intention of attracting Chinese investment into the country. However, with regard to the nuclear sector, it remains unclear if the Czech government actively sought Chinese investment and technology. In common with the HPC project, the Czech government pushed for the nuclear new-builds—it was originally envisaged that CEZ might select a Rosatom-led consortium or Westinghouse to build the project. In 2009, CEZ launched a tender for a plan to expand the Temelin nuclear plant. The tender called for the selection of a reactor supplier/design who would be tasked with building two units (3 and 4) at Temelin before the end of 2013. The tender attracted bids from three candidates. Areva made a bid based on its EPR but was disqualified; a Rosatom-led consortium and Westinghouse, who based their bids on MIR1200 and AP1000, were the remaining competitors. Rosatom and Westinghouse competed with such ferocity that the American and Russian governments intervened in what had become a Cold War (*The Economist* 2014). After being subject to sustained political pressure, CEZ cancelled the tender in 2014, while citing market price as its key justification.

Second, CGN expressed interest in bidding for the Czech nuclear projects so quickly (only several months after the Sochi meeting between Zeman and Xi) because CEZ cancelled its tender in April 2014 and it was expected that CEZ would introduce another tender towards the end of the year. This explained why CGN registered its interest to bid for the projects so quickly.

Third, like the HPC case, CGN's bid for the Czech projects was part of a broader strategy that sought to promote Hualong One. CGN aimed to promote its own nuclear technology in exchange for investment: CGN would probably bid for the project upon the basis of Hualong One; CGN's strategy to promote Hualong One was usually "investment + Hualong One." As the CEO of CGN stated, "We look forward to working with local players across the industry supply chain to promote the application of Hualong 1 Technology to achieve mutual success while contributing to the local economy" (CGN 2016b). Thus, for CGN, bidding for the nuclear projects in Czech was driven by commercial considerations.

To sum up, China's intent to bid for the nuclear projects in Czech—to "actively participate in the development and construction of new nuclear projects at Dukovany and Temelin"—and the MoUs signed during Xi's state visit do not indicate a strategic motivation behind these activities.

The Chinese Government's Role

In the Czech case, the Chinese government played two roles. First, the government pledged financial and political support. For instance, in his October 2014 state visit to China, Sobotka held a meeting with Li. During the meeting, Li stated that "the Chinese government encouraged nuclear companies to actively participate in Czech's projects" (Xinhua 2014a).

Second, the Chinese leaders and officials did express to the Czechian counterpart their interest in making nuclear infrastructure investment many times, but reasons cited for their interest was the advancement of Chinese nuclear technology and equipment. In his October 2014 meeting with Zeman, Li advocated that "Chinese nuclear tech and equipment is safe, economic, and internationally competitive, and willing to actively participate in the construction of NPP" (Xinhua 2014a). During a meeting with Sobotka in a December 2014 "16+1" summit, Li also urged that both sides should "strengthen cooperation in nuclear energy, finance and aviation" (Xinhua 2014b). Li reiterated in his meeting with Sobotka that China's nuclear technology and equipment were "safe and inexpensive, which has made them competitive globally" (Xinhua 2015b). In his meeting with Zeman, Xi called on the two countries to "conduct cooperation" in "nuclear power and infrastructure" (Xinhua 2015a; *China Daily* 2015). In his article published in *Pravo Daily*, Xi declared that "more than 30 years of reform and opening-up has sharpened China's competitive edge in terms of capital, technology and equipment, especially in [. . .] nuclear plant construction" (*China Daily* 2015).

CONCLUSION

The discussion of China's investment in the Czech Republic and the UK has served to highlight the following shared features. First, in both instances, the recipient government is keen to attract general infrastructural investment but is not particularly keen on Chinese investment *in the nuclear sector*. Ultimately it was Centrica's withdrawal from the HPC project that opened up an opportunity for China's participation and the cancellation of the tender in the Czech Republic made it possible for China to express an interest. In both cases, Chinese investment and technology was not a first choice. This perhaps reflects the fact that nuclear infrastructure is one of the most security-sensitive sectors that the UK and Czech governments are reluctant to open to China.

Second, in both cases, the Chinese nuclear companies are keen to participate in the projects on the basis of a clear business rationale (investment in exchange for Hualong One technology). In the British case, the Chinese nuclear companies have even overridden the protests of the Ministry of Foreign Affairs. For these actors, economic incentives are clearly foregrounded and privileged.

Third, after changing their position toward the Dalai Lama, UK and Czech received the Chinese leader and sought to elevate bilateral relations to the status of a strategic partnership. This politicization of nuclear issue has however been accompanied by a clear desire to ensure the increased use of Chinese nuclear technology. The priorities of the Chinese government and nuclear companies therefore jointly converge on the marketing of Chinese reactor Hualong One.

These findings can make several contributions to the study on China's economic statecraft. First, China's nuclear infrastructural investments lack the strategic intent that is frequently ascribed to them. Rather, in China's nuclear infrastructure investment, the commercial actor and economic motivation play an important role. This supports the "development model" view that in studying China's "economic statecraft" one cannot separate economic motivations from political ones—or rather, China's economic statecraft may be driven more by economic considerations than by political ones (Bräutigam and Tang 2012). In the case of investment in nuclear infrastructure, it seems that China's investments are driven heavily by the hope that investment can secure a chance for using China's Hualong One. This also supports Norris' (2016) view that in studying China's economic statecraft, the government and the commercial actor are not always in agreement.

Second, China's nuclear infrastructure investment always tends to be politicized. But while the Chinese government provides political support to the project subsequent to the change within the British government's stance toward the Dalai Lama, the focus tends to be on the likelihood that the indigenously designed Hualong reactor would be successfully deployed.

NOTES

1. I thank Ben Boulton, Nele Noesselt, Yi Edward Yang, and the participants in the 2017 annual meeting of the Association of Chinese Political Studies at Nankai University.

2. CGN is eventually leading a Chinese consortium composed of CGN and CNNC. Further, HPC's construction cost was estimated at $24 billion in 2016. An extra 2 billion was added to the cost in 2017 (BBC 2017).

3. Cottee does, however, recognize that these investments are also business motivated.

4. Nuclear experts have long recognized that the provision of finance, technology, and material to a country that seeks to develop nuclear energy is an act of statecraft (Fuhrmann 2009). For insight into the Russian example, see Saha (2017).

5. The British government had made its preference for private sector funding but had, in the case of the Hinkley Point C project, instead been forced, in 2015, to provide an infrastructural guarantee of £2 billion. The Czech government's reluctance to provide similar financial support resulted in the cancellation of the 2014 tender for the Temelin project (see below).

6. Reilly (2012, 126) correctly observes that China froze an order to purchase 150 planes from Airbus after a meeting between the Dalai Lama and the then French president Nicholas Sarkozy. However, his 2017 study does not examine if China cancelled UK-based orders or investment plans in response to the actions of the UK government (Reilly 2017).

7. In the Czech political system, it is usually the prime minister rather than the president who makes foreign policy decisions. However, Zeman's pro-China policy, and his personal relations with Chinese leaders, are so high profile that makes his role prominent.

8. Two visits are notable. One is his state visit to China in October 2014. The other is a visit to Beijing for attending the military parade commemorations marking the 70th anniversary of the victory of the Chinese Peoples' War of Resistance Against Japanese Aggression (1937–1945). As the only EU leader attending this event (Western leaders were avoiding this event on the suspicion that it was orchestrated to provoke anti-Japanese sentiment), Zeman demonstrated support of the Chinese government (*China Daily* 2015).

BIBLIOGRAPHY

Alves, A. C. 2013. "Chinese Economic Statecraft: A Comparative Study of China's Oil-backed Loans in Angola and Brazil." *Journal of Current Chinese Affairs* 42 (1): 99–130.

Baldwin, David. 1985. *Economic Statecraft*. Princeton, NJ: Princeton University Press.

BBC. 2012. "David Cameron's Dalai Lama Meeting Sparks Chinese Protest." http://www.bbc.com/news/uk-politics-18084223.

———. 2013a. "Centrica Pulled Out of New UK Nuclear Projects." http://www.bbc.com/news/business-21319031.

———. 2013b. "David Cameron Promises China 'Growth Partnership'." http://www.bbc.com/news/uk-25176613.

———. 2017. "Hinkley Point: EDF Adds £1.5bn to Nuclear Plant Cost." http://www.bbc.com/news/business-40479053.

Blackwill, Robert D., and Harris, Jennifer M. 2016. *War by Other Means*. Cambridge, MA: Harvard University Press.

Bräutigam, Debora, and Tang, X. 2012. "Economic Statecraft in China's New Overseas Special Economic Zones: Soft Power, Business or Resource Security?" *International Affairs* 88 (4): 799–816.

Brown, Kerry. 2015. *Erase and Rewind*. Sydney: Australia–China Relations Institute.

CEZ. 2014. "President Zeman to Negotiate Nuclear Investments in China." https://www.cez.cz/en/cez-group/media/macroeconomic-news/3706.html.

CGN. 2016a. 英国政府批准中广核参与新建核电项目,中广核成功挺入英伦 (The British government approved CGN to participate in the new nuclear power project, CGN successfully entered the UK market). http://www.cgnpc.com.cn/n471046/n471126/n471156/c1310636/content.html.

———. 2016b. "CGN and CEZ Collaborate on Renewable and Nuclear Energy in the Czech Republic." http://en.cgnpc.com.cn/n1305393/n1305428/c1295759/content.html.

———. 2016c. "He Yu: CGN Intends to Participate in the Construction of the Czech Nuclear Power Project." http://en.cgnpc.com.cn/n1305391/n1305404/c1298100/content.html.

China Daily. 2014. 捷克称中资有意投标核电站. http://www.chinadaily.com.cn/hqgj/jryw/2014-09-01/content_12298035.html.

———. 2016a. "Beijing and Prague Form New Key Link." http://www.chinadaily.com.cn/world/2016xivisitczech/2016-03/29/content_24171036.htm.

———. 2016b. "Deals Lay Foundation for Sino-Czech Ties." http://europe.chinadaily.com.cn/epaper/2016-04/01/content_24224808.htm.

———. 2017. "Czech President Praises Initiative." http://www.chinadaily.com.cn/world/2017-05/10/content_29275477.htm.

Cottee, Matthew. 2017. "China's Nuclear Export Ambitions Run into Friction." *Financial Times*, https://www.ft.com/content/84c25750-75da-11e7-90c0-90a9d1bc9691.

Drezner, Denial. 2017. "Perception, Misperception, and Sensitivity: Chinese Economic Power and Preferences after the 2008 Financial Crisis." In *Strategic Adjustment and the Rise of China: Power and Politics in East Asia*, edited by Robert Ross, 69–99. Ithaca, NY: Cornell University Press.

EDF. 2013. "Agreement Reached on Commercial Terms for the Planned HPC Nuclear Power Station." https://www.edfenergy.com/media-centre/news-releases/agreement-reached-commercial-terms-planned-hinkley-point-c-nuclear-power.

FM. 2012. 2012年5月15日外交部发言人洪磊举行例行记者会. http://www.fmprc.gov.cn/ce/cegr/chn/ztlm/lxjzzdh/t931997.htm.

———. 2014. "Xi Jinping Holds Talks with President Milos Zeman of the Czech Republic." http://www.fmprc.gov.cn/mfa_eng/zxxx_662805/t1205146.shtml.

———. 2015a. "The Suzhou Guidelines for Cooperation between China and Central and Eastern European Countries." http://www.fmprc.gov.cn/mfa_eng/zxxx_662805/t1318039.shtml.

———. 2015b. "Xi Jinping Meets with Prime Minister Bohuslav Sobotka of the Czech Republic." http://www.fmprc.gov.cn/mfa_eng/zxxx_662805/t1320015.shtml.

Furst, Rudolf. 2018. "Czechia's Relations with China: On a Long Road toward a Real Strategic Partnership? *Rudolf*." In *China's Relations with Central and Eastern Europe: From Old Comrades to New Partners*, edited by Weiqing Song, 199–218. London: Routledge.

Global Times. 2014. 捷克称中资有意投标核电站. http://world.huanqiu.com/exclusive/2014-09/5123371.html.

Gov UK. 2011. "National Infrastructure Plan 2011." https://www.gov.uk/government/publications/national-infrastructure-plan-november-2011.

———. 2013a. "MoU between the Governments of the UK and PRC on Enhancing Cooperation in the Field of Civil Nuclear Energy." https://www.gov.uk/government/uploads/system/uploads/attachment_data/file/251211/signed__MOU_EN_130924_UKSIDE.pdf.

———. 2013b. "Government Gives Go Ahead Given for China to Take Stake in British Nuclear Power." https://www.gov.uk/government/news/go-ahead-given-for-china-to-take-stake-in-british-nuclear-power.

———. 2014a. "Joint Statement from Government of the People's Republic of China and Government of the United Kingdom of Great Britain and Northern Ireland." https://www.gov.uk/government/news/joint-statement-from-government-of-the-peoples-republic-of-china-government-of-the-united-kingdom-of-great-britain-and-northern-ireland.

———. 2014b. "Joint Statement between the Government of the UK of Great Britain and Northern Ireland and the Government of the PRC on Civil Nuclear Energy Cooperation." https://www.gov.uk/government/uploads/system/uploads/attachment_data/file/327758/uk_china_joint_statement_civil_nuclear_energy_co_operation.pdf.

———. 2015a. "UK–China Joint Statement 2015." https://www.gov.uk/government/news/uk-china-joint-statement-2015.

———. 2015b. "UK–China Statement of Cooperation in the Field of Civil Nuclear Energy 2015." https://www.gov.uk/government/uploads/system/uploads/attachment_data/file/470590/Statement_of_cooperation_field_civil_nuclear_energy.pdf.

———. 2015c. "Joint Press Conference: David Cameron and Xi Jinping." https://www.gov.uk/government/speeches/joint-press-conference-david-cameron-and-president-xi-jinping.

Lai, Christine. 2017. "Acting One Way and Talking Another: China's Coercive Economic Diplomacy in East Asia and Beyond." *The Pacific Review* 31 (2): 169–87.

Li, Keqiang. 2013. "Chinese Premier Li Keqiang Emphasized the Need to Promote Sound and Steady Development of China-UK Relations." http://www.chinese-embassy.org.uk/eng/HotTopics/davidcameron/t1108772.htm.

Meunier, S. 2014. "A Faustian Bargain or Just a Good Bargain? Chinese Foreign Direct Investment and Politics in Europe." *Asia Europe Journal* 12 (1–2): 143–58.

Norris, William. 2016. *Chinese Economic Statecraft: Commercial Actors, Grand Strategy, and State Control*. Ithaca, NY: Cornell University Press.

People's Daily. 2014. 习近平会见捷克总统泽曼. http://politics.people.com.cn/n/2014/0208/c1024-24294692.html.

Reilly, James. 2012. "China's Unilteral Sanction." *The Washington Quarterly* 35 (4): 121–33.

———. 2017. "China's Economic Statecraft in Europe." *Asia Europe Journal* 15 (2): 173–85.

Saha, N. 2017. "Russia's Nuclear Diplomacy How Washington Should Respond." *Foreign Affairs*. https://www.foreignaffairs.com/articles/russian-federation/2017-04-02/russia-s-nuclear-diplomacy.

The Economist. 2014. "Czech Pull Plug on Nuclear Expansion." https://www.economist.com/eastern-approaches/2014/04/16/czechs-pull-plug-on-nuclear-expansion.

The Financial Times. 2015. "How David Cameron Lost, and then Won, China." https://www.ft.com/content/98c6f8f0-c8df-11e4-bc64-00144feab7de.

The Telegraph. 2013. "David Cameron's Rift with China Could Cost UK billions." https://www.telegraph.co.uk/news/politics/david-cameron/10040319/David-Camerons-rift-with-China-could-cost-UK-billions.html.

Thomas, Stephen. 2017. "China's Nuclear Export Drive: Trojan Horse or Marshall Plan?" *Energy Policy* 101: 683–91.

Turcsanyi, Richard. 2017. "Central European Attitudes towards Chinese Energy Investments: The Cases of Poland, Slovakia, and the Czech Republic." *Energy Policy* 101: 711–22.

WNN. 2016. "CGN Boosts Cooperation with Czech Firms." http://www.world-nuclear-news.org/C-CGN-boosts-cooperation-with-Czech-firms-3103166.html.

———. 2017. "China, Argentina Sign Contract for Two Reactors." http://www.world-nuclear-news.org/NN-Argentina-and-China-sign-contract-for-two-reactors-1805175.html.

Xinhua (News Agency). 2014a. 李克强会见捷克总统泽曼:鼓励中方企业参与捷克核电设施扩建改造. http://politics.people.com.cn/n/2014/1027/c1024-25917942.html.

———. 2014b. 李克强会见捷克总理索博特卡. http://news.xinhuanet.com/world/2014-12/16/c_1113667528.htm.

———. 2014c. "Zhang Gaoli Visited Romania." http://news.xinhuanet.com/world/2014-09/26/c_1112643098.htm.

———. 2015a. "China, Czech Republic Vow to Strengthen Relations." http://news.xinhuanet.com/english/2015-09/04/c_134590243.htm.

———. 2015b. "China, Czech Pledge Closer Nuclear Power, Finance Cooperation." http://news.xinhuanet.com/english/2015-11/27/c_134862920.htm.

———. 2016a. "China, Czech Republic Set up Strategic Partnership." http://news.xinhuanet.com/english/2016-03/30/c_135234520.htm.

———. 2016b. "China–Czech Joint Statement." http://news.xinhuanet.com/politics/2016-03/29/c_1118480426.htm.

———. 2016c. "'Time to Renew and Energize China–Czech Ties': China's Xi's Signed Article on Czech's Newspaper." http://news.xinhuanet.com/english/2016-03/26/c_135225969.htm.

Zhang, Xiaotong, and Keith, James. 2017. "From Wealth to Power: China's New Economic Statecraft." *The Washington Quarterly* 40 (1): 185–203.

Part III

CHINA'S ECONOMIC STATECRAFT

CREATING AND SHAPING INTERNATIONAL INSTITUTIONS

Chapter 9

Expanding Normative Power in Financial Governance through Economic Statecraft?

The Case of the AIIB

Zhongzhou Peng and Sow Keat Tok[1]

In October 2013, the Asian Infrastructure Investment Bank (AIIB) was unveiled by Chinese president Xi Jinping and premier Li Keqiang during their respective visits to Southeast Asia. The objective of this bank, as claimed by the initiators, is to provide support to Asian infrastructure construction (*China Daily* 2013). According to an oft-cited study by the Asian Development Bank (ADB) in 2009, the Asia region needs $8 trillion to develop its infrastructure between 2010 and 2020, 68 percent of which would be for new capacity. As for how it is spent, 51 percent would be for electricity, 29 percent for roads, and 13 percent for telecommunications (Bhattacharyay 2010). Compared to the astronomical amount of need, the World Bank (WB) and the ADB only provide about 20 billion US dollars each year in the Asia region (Renard 2015, 2). The AIIB, with an authorized capital of $100 billion, seeks to contribute to this specific area.

The influence of this bank was expected to be rather limited, since the United States and Japan rejected this initiative at the early stage of its formation (*New York Times* 2014). Considering the enormous influence wielded by the United States and Japan in financial governance, both globally and in the Asian region, it was a general assumption that "the AIIB would start out as a modest venture involving mainly Asian and Middle Eastern countries" (Wihtol 2015, 7).

However, on March 12, 2015, the United Kingdom (UK) announced its intention to join the AIIB, shifting the situation drastically (the United Kingdom 2015). Although the UK was not the first European country to make this decision (Luxembourg joined a few days ahead of the UK) its political and financial clout triggered a scramble for founding membership in the AIIB. In a span of days, a group of Western governments including France, Germany, and Australia, announced their intentions to join the AIIB. By the time of the signing ceremony of the Articles of Agreement (AOA) held in Beijing on June 29, 2015, the AIIB had become a significant multilateral financial institution involving fifty-seven Prospective Founding Members (PFMs). After the AOA had been signed by all fifty-seven PFMs between June 29, 2015, and December 31, 2015, the AIIB opened for business on January 16, 2016. Jin Liqun, former ranking vice president of the Asian Development Bank (ADB) was elected as the first president of the AIIB.

The establishment of the AIIB, especially the agreement with major European states who have been the close allies of the United States, was regarded as a diplomatic triumph for Beijing over Washington. Quite a few articles put their focus on how Jin Liqun, the leader of Chinese negotiating team, used the economic interest to gain support from the allies of the United States (*Financial Times* 2015b). Some others suggest that the AIIB will become a great challenge to existing US-led financial institutions, especially the WB, the ADB, and even the IMF (The Economist 2015a, 2015b).

This chapter seeks to analyze the normative implications of the AIIB rather than its diplomatic influence. Through the lens of normative power concept, this chapter argues that the AIIB contributes to enhancing China's normative power in financial governance since it is both a successor of Chinese norms in the financial governance area and a broader platform of Chinese normative projection. Therefore, the AIIB represents a case of Chinese economic statecraft in terms of advancing its normative influence in global financial governance. However, while the AIIB may serve as a new vehicle for Chinese normative diffusion, the inclusion of developed Western economies, the interactions with other institutions, and the internal governance structure might also challenge and shape China's normative approach in global financial governance.

STUDYING CHINESE ECONOMIC STATECRAFT THROUGH THE CONCEPTUAL FRAMEWORK OF NORMATIVE POWER

By 2014, China had the world's second largest nominal GDP, exceeding 60 trillion RMB or 10 trillion USD (National Bureau of Statistics 2015). The rise of China's economic capacity allows for the purposeful application of capital to pursue power in global affairs, a process otherwise known as "economic statecraft" (Norris 2016, 3). This chapter contributes to the study of Chinese economic statecraft by exploring its effectiveness in shaping the normative structure of global financial governance. Indeed, China's increasing economic strength has stimulated renewed interests in promoting its norms of financial governance. In addition, the increasing clout in international political economy has given China new appeal regarding international institutions and governance regimes. What, then, are the economic tools utilized by China to spread these norms in global financial governance? And what is the influence of Chinese economic statecraft to its normative power in this governance area?

"Normative power," a phrase coined by Ian Manners, was used as to describe a European Union that "evolved" into a form of governance that "transcends Westphalian norms" (Manners 2002, 240). Specifically, Manners argues that the EU embraces norms, such as human rights, democracy, and rule of law, and puts these norms at the center of its relations with member states (Manners 2002, 241). In addition, the EU has been diffusing these norms to other countries and regions through economic and political interaction. Moreover, the EU aims to change the regimes in other countries through its normative diffusion. Building upon these characters of the EU's foreign policy, Manners (2002, 239) defines the EU as a normative power with "the ability to shape conceptions of 'normal' in international relations."

Since its inception, normative power literature has become an influential branch among the discussions of the EU's external behavior. Throughout the debates on the concept of normative power, one of the core research agendas is the criteria by which an international actor needs qualifies as a normative power. Manners defines the EU as a normative power because of its internal implementation of the norms and its policy of diffusing these norms into other countries and regions (Manners 2002, 238–45). However, for an international actor to gain normative power, self-representation alone is not enough. Even if there are modifications of policies among its partners, it is possible that political and economic interests motivate these actions rather than true belief in the norms and regimes. Indeed, as some scholars point out, the reactions of other countries can be "half-compliance" or "fake compliance" if they do not accept the normative component of the EU's policy (Noutcheva 2009). Thus, it is as important that the alleged normative power can convince its partners to accept the normative principles and to transform their policies to consist with them.

In this regard, external perceptions of the EU's partners are considered by some scholars as essential for the evaluation of EU foreign policy (Lucarelli 2007). Based on this discussion, Kavalski (2013) argues that external perception is another essential criterion of normative power qualification. He argues that since normative power emerges from the interaction with the others, recognition by contextual counterparts is also crucial for an international actor to qualify as a normative power. As he states, "normative power emerges in relation to the inter-subjective environment to which its agency is applied" (Kavalski 2013, 250; emphasis in original). Zupančič and Hribernik (2013) agree with Kavalski's argument, contending that "normative power is more than a rather vague notion that someone is 'doing good.' This 'good' should also be recognized and, consequently, accepted as 'good' by the other" (Zupančič and Hribernik 2013, 111). Lucarelli also argues that the role of the EU "[is] determined by both an actor's own conceptions about appropriate behavior and by the expectations of other actors" (Lucarelli 2007, 257). Hence, the feedback from relevant contextual actors is another determinant of the EU's political identity.

In summation, existing literature sets three criteria for an international actor to meet to qualify as a normative power: internal norm construction, the diplomatic capacity of normative diffusion, and external perceptions of normative power. However, current literature more or less presumes that the EU is the exclusive normative power in international relations. This assumption does not accord much attention to the fact that other international actors also have their series of norms to guide their foreign policy. In addition, some of these actors may also be successful during their normative diffusion. This chapter resonates with the argument made by Larsen (2014) that normative power scholarship needs to take into account other potential normative actors in international relations. In global financial governance, China is perceived as an emerging normative actor. Examining the correlation between the establishment of the AIIB and the emerging normative power of China in international financial governance will give some insights into the changing contours of international political economy following China's emergence as the world's second largest economy.

This chapter suggests that the AIIB is a case of China utilizing economic statecraft to advance its normative power in financial governance. Because of its predominant role in the AIIB, China can considerably define the policy framework of the Bank, which makes it an important vehicle to carry Chinese norms. Meanwhile, through the programs of the AIIB, China is able to increase its normative influence in the Asian region and across the globe. Using the conceptual framework of normative power, the following sections of this chapter will analyze the linkage between the AIIB and China's normative power in international financial governance.

THE AIIB AND CHINESE NORMATIVE POWER IN INTERNATIONAL FINANCIAL GOVERNANCE

The AIIB Consists of Chinese Norms regarding International Financial Governance

The establishment of the AIIB is a milestone in China's financial policy. Together with the New Development Bank (NDB, commonly known as the

"BRICs Bank"), they are both new multilateral financial institutions in which China is the major shareholder. Compared to the NDB, whose capital is evenly held by Brazil, Russia, India, South Africa, and China (NDB 2014), the AIIB relies more on China's capital contribution. According to the AOA, China holds more than 30 percent of the AIIB's capital. This proportion is significantly larger than any other member of the bank. As a result, China has the leading position in the policy making of the AIIB, and thus, it can implement its norms of external assistance into the programs of the bank. Meanwhile, the entrance of other member states may be taken as implicit endorsement of China's principles in foreign aid and investment. Therefore, the operation of the AIIB will enhance the Chinese normative influence in both the recipient countries and the AIIB's member states.

Foreign aid programs have been the major vehicles for China's normative diffusion. According to public information, AIIB policies have inherited China's traditional principles of external assistance. Then premier Zhou Enlai defined "equity and mutual benefit" and "never poses conditions" as the key norms of Chinese foreign aid policy to African countries in the 1960s (Zhou 1964). Chinese official documents still echo his words. Beginning in 2011, the Chinese government has published a series of white papers to review its foreign aid policy. All these annual reports begin with the declaration that Chinese foreign aid is based on norms including equality, mutual benefit, and the concept of "no strings attached."

When providing foreign assistance, China adheres to the principles of non-imposition of political conditions, noninterference with the internal affairs of the recipient countries, and fully respecting recipient countries' rights to independently choosing their own paths and models of development. The basic principles China upholds in providing foreign assistance are mutual respect, equality, keeping promises, mutual benefits, and win-win conditions (State Council 2014).

The fact that Zhou's principles of "mutual benefit," "no strings attached," and "non-interference" are all repeated in this report indicates that these normative approaches remain to be the guidelines of China's foreign aid and investment. China adheres to the belief that the political system is the internal business of each state. Thus, no country has the right to interfere or to decide the regime of another one. This position formulates China's interpretation of unconditionality in foreign aid programs. As China's special envoy for Africa, Liu Guijin, outlines, "We don't attach political conditions. We have to realize the political and economic environments are not ideal. But we don't have to wait for everything to be satisfactory or human rights to be perfect" (*Financial Times* 2008).

This principle is also manifested in the policy framework of the AIIB. Chinese leaders and officials have expressed clearly that the AIIB does not impose political conditions on its investment (*Reuters* 2015). In addition, there is no mention of political requirements among the operating principles in the AOA. Article 13 of the AOA states that "the Bank shall ensure that each of its operations complies with the Bank's operational and financial policies, including without limitation, policies addressing environmental and social impacts" (AIIB 2015a). Since the AOA has been agreed upon and signed by all fifty-seven PFMs (AIIB 2015c), China has not only introduced its norm of unconditionality into the AIIB, but also successfully gained endorsement for this norm from all the bank's member states.

In addition, the AIIB's preference for infrastructure construction is also in line with China's foreign aid and investment policy. Drawing on its own experience, especially the reform and opening-up policy, China holds the idea that for developing countries to increase its national power, the focus should be economic development. In addition, to accelerate economic development, infrastructure building is the foundation. Guided by this principle, a large proportion of China's foreign aid is devoted to infrastructure construction. According to the State Council, 44.8 percent of aid was used for economic infrastructure, while 27.6 percent was used for social and public infrastructure during 2010–2012 (State Council 2014). These infrastructure programs include the construction of hospitals, schools, water supply, public facilities, transport and communications, broadcasting and telecommunications, and power supply. China has also helped the construction of over seventy transport projects, including roads, bridges, airports, and ports. In Africa alone China has built 2,233 km of railroads and 3,391 km of highways (State Council 2014). It is clear that AIIB's programs share this preference for infrastructure construction. As the first article of the AOA clearly announces, "the purpose of the Bank shall be to foster sustainable economic development, create wealth and improve infrastructure connectivity in Asia by investing in infrastructure and other productive sectors" (AIIB 2015a).

The first series of projects of the AIIB goes on to show that infrastructure building is the major target of this bank. In 2016, the AIIB approved 1.73 billion USD in financing nine projects in the first year of its operation: the national motorway project in Pakistan; the Dushanbe-Uzbekistan Border Road Improvement project in Tajikistan; the distribution system upgrade and expansion project in Bangladesh; the national slum upgrading project in Indonesia; hydro power extension project in Pakistan; Myingyan power plant project in Myanmar; railway system preparation project in Oman; Duqm port commercial terminal project in Oman; and Trans Anatolian Natural Gas Pipeline Project in Azerbaijan (AIIB 2017). These projects aim to increase the transportation ability, electric supply, and urban infrastructure in Asian developing countries. Similarly, the fifteen approved projects in 2017 are devoted to the energy, telecommunication, and transportation sectors (AIIB n.d.).

Meanwhile, the official documents of these projects reveal that the recipient countries also recognize that infrastructure building is essential for them to achieve economic growth. For instance, Pakistan government states that the national motorway project fosters road connectivity, which is "essential for economic development and poverty reduction" (AIIB 2016b, 3). Similarly, Bangladesh government has identified electricity supply as "a major constraint on GDP growth, and overall economic development" (AIIB 2016c, 1). These official statements are in line with Chinese norms of infrastructure construction. None of these projects contain political conditions whatsoever. These projects manifest the AIIB's commitment to foster infrastructure construction; it is not just rhetoric. The AIIB has already put effort to increase infrastructure building in the Asian region.

However, although the AIIB may well be understood as a platform for China to enhance the influence of its norms regarding financial governance, the structure of this institution—as well as the interactions between China and other member states—potentiate challenges to China's cultivation of its normative influence. To start with, it is undoubtedly a significant achievement for China to persuade a group of major European countries including Britain, German, and France to join the AIIB. Their decisions to become PFMs indicate that they, unlike the United States, do not oppose the norms and structures proposed by China. However, this does not mean that China has successfully persuaded these Western countries to accept its norms of financial governance without reservations. When analyzing the motivations of Britain, German, and other European countries to join the AIIB, reports often note that the nations have been driven primarily by political and economic interests. For instance, Germany and France aim at the contracts of construction projects they can get from the AIIB; Britain seeks to host the AIIB's European base so it can expand its financial influence (The Diplomat 2015). There is hardly any proof that their membership means that they have accepted Chinese way of foreign aid and investment. In contrast, some countries, including Britain and Australia, have suggested that they aim to improve the governance structure of the AIIB, so that it will be more integrated with international regime (the United Kingdom 2015; *Guardian* 2015b). As a result, even though the AIIB has successfully gained support from European countries, it does not mean that Chinese norms have been diffused and accepted by these states. China's financial policy may face considerable internal questioning and challenge during the operation of the AIIB.

Moreover, the AIIB aims to establish broader cooperation among regional financial institutions in infrastructure construction area. Up until now, China has declared that the AIIB seeks to enhance the relationships with the ADB, the African Development Bank, the Inter-American Development Bank, the West African Development Bank, and the Caribbean Development Bank to channel more capital into the fields of infrastructure, environmental protection, education, and health care in developing countries. However, if the AIIB seeks to establish cooperation with WB, ADB, and other institutions, it has to adopt the norms of environment protection, good governance, and social security in its policy framework. Indeed, China has altered its position on these matters in response to the challenges. For instance, China's recent Foreign Aid White Paper has included environmental protection as a part of China's goals and achievements in this field (State Council 2014). The AIIB has also listed environmental protection and urban development as its areas of engagement. It has also produced an Environmental and Social Framework to regulate its operation, which has recently been approved by the Board of Directors (AIIB 2016a). It is thus interesting to observe how far will the AIIB move beyond the traditional "economic centralism" in China's foreign aid policy and be more integrated into international aid structure.

To sum up, since Chinese norms of financial governance underpin the setup of the AIIB and its policy, the AIIB provides a more direct channel for China to present its norms of financial governance to its Western partners and to increase the influence of its normative power. However, during the internal bargaining and external interactions, China may review and reassess its norms of foreign aid and foreign investment through workings within the AIIB.

The AIIB is a Litmus Test of China's Position in the Reform of Global Financial Governance

Aside from the norms of foreign aid and foreign investment, the AIIB is also a manifestation of China's normative appeals regarding the financial governance structure. In recent years, China has been actively promoting the reform of governance structure in major multilateral financial institutions. In Chinese rhetoric, the aim is to establish a fair governance structure in multilateral organizations (Lu 2011, 89). The key point of this reform is the redistribution of voting rights. China has been suggesting that the current apportionment of voting rights shares to emerging economies in the WB and IMF does not correspond to their actual economic status. For instance, before 2010, China had only 2.8 percent and 5.5 percent voting right in WB and ADB, respectively, and is ranked only 6th in terms of voting rights in International Monetary Fund (IMF). On the other hand, Japan and the United States had a combined 23.6 percent and 26 percent in WB and ADB, respectively. They also have the two largest shares of voting rights in the IMF: the United States has 17 percent and Japan has 6 percent. The unbalanced distribution of voting rights is also substantial between developed countries and developing countries. Before 2008, the G7 countries had a combined

41.2 percent voting rights in the IMF, while Brazil, Russia, India, China, and South Africa (BRICS) together have only 14.2 percent (Chen and Tan 2013). China argues that the developing countries, especially emerging economies, such as the BRICS, have less proportion of voting rights than their economic weight in the world economy (Cui and Chang 2013, 25). In contrast, although the economic clout of developed countries is diminishing, they still have an enormous share of voting rights so that they can control the policies of the organizations. The voting right distribution should be reformed to fit the new structure of the global economy.

Aside from the unbalance distribution of voting rights, China has also been criticizing the United States's unilateral veto power in the IMF. In the IMF's governance structure, major decisions need 85 percent of votes to get passed. Since the US share of voting rights is more than 16 percent, it effectively holds veto power on major policy decisions. China argues that this unilateral veto power makes IMF a tool of the United States to execute its policies and suggests that it is not "fair" to other countries (Lu 2011).

China has been actively promoting its understanding of a "fair governance structure" in international financial institutions in recent years. The strategy of China is to establish a coalition of emerging economies and developing countries to push forward the reform in the IMF and WB. The major partners of China in this issue are Russia, Brazil, and India. Together with South Africa, they are called the "BRICS" group. In September 2009, China, Russia, Brazil, and India jointly announced that IMF should transfer 7 percent of the voting rights from developed countries to developing countries (BRICS 2009). China also suggests that the management level of IMF should have more representatives from developing countries (Cui and Chang 2013, 24).

The effort of China and other developing countries has resulted in limited reforms in existing institutions. In 2010, the WB presented a new distribution of voting rights. Under this new framework, the developed countries will transfer 3.13 percent of voting rights to developing countries. Mean while, China's voting rights have increased from 2.77 to 4.42 percent, which makes it the third biggest shareholder in WB. On the other hand, IMF also made a decision to reform its governance structure in 2009. The reform plan increases the weight of GDP, which is beneficial to emerging economies and developing countries. With this decision, the voting rights of China, Brazil, and India will increase from 3, 1.7, and 1.9 percent to 6, 2.3, and 2.6 percent, respectively (G20 2009).

Despite the progress mentioned above, there is still room for Chinese appeals. Although the reform plans of the IMF have given China the largest increase of voting rights and provided the emerging economies more power in the governance structure, the United States still controls the veto power in the IMF. Meanwhile, China has not been able to increase its share of voting rights in the ADB. Until December 2016, China's voting right was only 6.4 percent (ADB n.d.) Even though China has been actively promoting its blueprint of financial governance, it has not yet become influential enough to shape existing institutions through internal mechanisms with the United States and Japan in dominant positions in the current regime structure.

In this light, the AIIB, as a Chinese initiative, serves as a vehicle of China to manifest its illustration of an ideal financial governance structure. The first characteristic of the AIIB is its lean management arrangement. A week after the AIIB was inaugurated, Jin Liqun stated at the World Economic Forum that the bank will be "lean, clean and green." In terms of the "lean" commitment, the AIIB maintains a small number of employees in its early stages of operation. It began with an initial staffing level of 50, and increased its workforce to a number between 100 and 150 in the first year (*Wall Street Journal* 2015). The AIIB also abandons a resident board of directors; instead the board of directors shall "function on a non-resident basis" and "meet as often as the business of the Bank may require, periodically throughout the year" (AIIB 2015a, Article 27.1). Compared with the World Bank, which has over 12,000 staff and consultants, and the ADB, which has 3,000 employees, the AIIB's workforce is significantly smaller in scale. More importantly, operating without a resident board of directors should save the bank money and friction in decision making. The resident board costs the World Bank some $70 million annually and there have been complaints that "there was often a certain tension between the management and the board members whose resident staff wanted to find out about projects at an early stage" (*Wall Street Journal* 2015). These arrangements reflect that the AIIB represents a more efficient management structure which China has attempted repeatedly to introduce to international institutions.

Meanwhile, the AIIB carries another essential Chinese norm regarding financial governance: a supposedly fairer distribution of voting rights. According to the final text of the AOA, the voting rights of AIIB are divided into two parts: Asian countries and regions have 70–75 percent of voting rights, and the countries and regions outside Asia have 25–30 percent. The voting rights of individual countries consist of three parts: its share of the capital, basic voting rights, and 600 votes of PFM. In particular, the share of the capital is calculated according to the weighted average of GDP (60 percent market exchange rate and 40 percent purchasing power parity). The basic voting rights constitute 12 percent of the total voting rights and are divided evenly among all the members (AIIB 2015a). It is noteworthy that the basic voting rights and PFM votes have a 15 percent proportion in the total voting rights. In contrast, the IMF counts the basic voting rights as only 5.5 percent of the total voting rights. As a result of this complex formula, Asian developing countries, excluding China, have a combined 30 percent voting power in the bank. In comparison, European developed countries together have around 20 percent votes (AIIB 2015a). This distribution ensures that Asian developing countries can have considerably larger influence in the institution than what they have in the WB and the ADB. In addition, the Board of Directors incorporates twelve representatives from twelve different countries from Asia, Europe, South America, and Oceania (AIIB 2015b). These settings in the AIIB's governance structure can be regarded as an improvement of fairness among members, since they increase the basic votes and the decision power of the smallest members quite significantly.

However, according to the calculation of capital shares, China has 26.06 percent of total voting rights in the AIIB. The AOA has stated that the Board of Directors needs 75 percent of total voting power of the members to "take decisions on major operational and financial policies and on delegation of authority to the President under Bank policies" (AIIB 2015a, Article 26). This means that China has the single unilateral veto power in the bank's major policy making, just like what the United States has in the IMF. Although Beijing suggests that the successive entrance of new members will dilute China's voting power in the institution and that China will not use its veto power (*China Daily* 2016), it still needs a large economy such as Japan to reduce China's share of voting rights to less than 25 percent. The gap between China's normative appeal of governance structure and the actual setting of the AIIB indicates that the Bank is not only a larger platform for China to diffuse its norms, but also a dilemma China is facing: it either abandons its veto power and undertakes the risk of losing control of the AIIB's decision-making process, or it obtains veto power which will undermine its normative approach in financial governance. After the AIIB commenced its operation in 2016, the decision-making process of the AIIB's investment programs will continue to demonstrate the extent to which China will balance its normative principles and practical interests.

Will the AIIB Improve External Perceptions of China's Normative Power?

The prior sections of this chapter have discussed the AIIB's impact on the normative aspects of China's foreign financial policy. However, as the debate of normative power concept has revealed, having a normative approach is not enough for an international actor to become a normative power (Kavalski 2013). The perceptions, as well as the level of acceptance, are also essential factors that determine whether an actor has normative influence. Judging from this assumption, the analysis of the AIIB's influence should also encompass its effect on the views of other countries regarding China's normative power. In this regard, China's image is controversial. On the one hand, there is proof that China's understanding of foreign aid, and good governance is acquiring more support in the African region. On the other hand, in recent years, China's foreign aid policy has been a major target of Western criticism for its disregard of social development and environmental protection. In this sense, the AIIB underpins the shaping of the external perceptions of the normative power of China in financial governance area. Since the AIIB had become a multilateral institution with more than fifty members, it significantly increases the interactions among China, Western developed countries, and emerging economies. Through the cooperation with developed countries, the operation of the AIIB takes into account the social and environmental policies. Thus, this institution gives China a chance to improve its image among Western countries and expand its normative influence among developing countries.

African countries, as the direct recipients of China's aid, tend to have positive feedback for China's financial policy, and they have been adopting the Chinese way of state governance. Since the end of the Cold War, Africa's perception of China has developed from that of an ally against colonialism to that of a reliable economic partner. Chinese aid—especially its infrastructure construction programs—has made African countries recognize that China's policy brings actual benefit to them. In addition, African leaders repeatedly showed the public appreciation of China's norm of unconditionality. They are comfortable that there are no benchmarks and preconditions, no environmental impact assessments to hinder the negotiations (Bräutigam 2011a). Moreover, China is also perceived as an alternative model of development to African countries. As a Nigeria diplomat states:

> China has become . . . a good model for Nigeria in its quest for an authentic and stable development ideology . . . China [is] a lesson to Nigeria on the enormous good that a focused and patriotic leadership can do to realize the dreams of prosperity and security for the citizens. (Manji and Marks 2007)

Aside from African political elites, African civil society also has a positive perception of China's existence. In a study of the African perceptions of China, Keuleers (2015, 812) finds out that 36 percent of respondents indicated that China "helps a lot" and an additional 30.5 perhaps said China "helps somewhat." As a result, two-thirds of respondents hold a positive or very positive view regarding China's role in the African region. In another survey which covered 250 students and university staff from 9 African countries, the result shows that the majority of the respondents (74 percent) believe that China's way of development is a positive model for their country. Overall, half of the respondents think that China's policy is more beneficial to African than Western policy and only 20 percent of the respondents agree that China is practicing neocolonialism to Africa (Sautman and Yan 2009). In addition, more than half of them (60 percent) think that China's policy of noninterference is a good thing. Similarly, in BBC's annual poll of global perceptions, the most favorable views of China are found in Africa where no surveyed country has less than 65 percent of positive views (BBC 2015, 37).

In contrast to the overall positive image of China among African countries, Western developed states including European countries and the United States regarded China as a negative normative power in Africa. The conventional Western aid programs not only provide financial assistance, but also impose social and political requirements to the recipient countries. For instance, the EU includes a human rights clause in its aid agreement with African, Caribbean, and Pacific countries. With this clause, the EU has the right to withdraw or suspend its aid if there is human right violation in the recipient countries (Cotonou Agreement 2010, Article 8). Chinese aid programs focus on infrastructure alone. This approach is considered to be "far simpler and does not overstretch the weak capacity of many African governments faced with multiple meetings, quarterly reports, workshops, and so on" (Bräutigam 2011b, 761). Another criticism targets the unconditionality and noninterference principles in Chinese aid programs, especially those targeting African countries (Bräutigam 2011a). The focus is China's omission of social, environmental, and governance standards applied by the West. For instance, the president of the European Investment Bank accused the Chinese of "unscrupulous" behavior (Condon 2012, 16). The nongovernmental organization Human Rights Watch presents a popular critic that "China's growing foreign aid program creates new options for dictators who were previously dependent on those who insisted on human rights progress" (Leonard 2008). To sum up, the West has been describing China's approach in Africa as unethical and perceiving China as a negative normative power in this region.

Focusing solely on the external perceptions of China's partners of its foreign aid programs, China's norms appear widely accepted by the target countries of its financial policy. Indeed, African countries find China a more amicable collaboration partner and thus receptive to China's principles, given their common experience as victims of colonialism, and identify each other as peers in the developing South. China's norms, when compared to most Western paradigms, better meet the developmental needs of African countries. China's principles of equality and noninterference have, by and large, differentiated themselves from the Western approach which is considered by some Asian and African countries to be a new form of colonialism (Larsen 2014).

However, the fact that China is perceived as a negative normative power by Western observers sheds light on the relationship between Chinese norms and the international normative structure. It illustrates that although China's normative clout is expanding globally, it is still viewed by most of the Western observers as a country in which democracy and human rights conditions are below the international standard (Zhang 2011, 241). As a result, China is still regarded as the "other" in international normative structure. This analysis illustrates that there is a lack of interaction and integration between China's norms and the international normative structure. China has been playing its own game with its own rules. In addition, Western countries are becoming more and more frustrated, because they think that China is compromising their efforts to promote their norms.

This skepticism manifested in some initial responses toward the AIIB among developed countries. Since the AIIB's normative guidelines are distinct from existing policies of external assistance, there are concerns that the AIIB lacks transparency and accountability. This has been the major argument of the United States and Japan to oppose the formulation of the AIIB. Japan's finance minister Taro Aso stated that Japan will "consider" joining the AIIB if "it proves to be a credible institution complying with generally accepted governance and environmental standards." Taro Aso states that the AIIB has to "ensure debt sustainability, taking into account its impact on environment and society" (Japan Times 2015). The White House National Security Council, in a statement to *The Guardian* (2015a), makes this declaration:

> Our position on the AIIB remains clear and consistent. . . . Based on many discussions, we have concerns about whether the AIIB will meet these high standards, particularly related to governance, and environmental and social safeguards. . . . The international community has a stake in seeing the AIIB complement the existing architecture, and to work effectively alongside the World Bank and Asian Development Bank.

Despite these concerns and doubts regarding the AIIB, the establishment of this bank has resulted in substantial changes in the perceptions of China's involvement in financial governance. To start with, compared to the WB and IMF, the AIIB is a new institution serving a different goal: infrastructure construction. Compared to the enormous need of funding for infrastructure construction in the Asian region, what each institution can provide is far from sufficient. Since the WB and the ADB are both focusing on reducing poverty (Wan 2016, 48), the formation of the AIIB is rather a complement to the existing institutions than a direct challenge (People's Daily Online 2014). In 2016, six of the nine projects of the AIIB were co-financed with ADB, World Bank, and European Bank for Reconstruction and Development (EBRD). In 2017, eleven of the seventeen projects approved by the AIIB had ADB, WB, or European Investment Bank (EIB) as the co-financer (AIIB n.d.). The cooperation between the AIIB and other Multilateral Development Banks (MDBs) illustrates that this Chinese initiative has begun contributing to the promotion of development in the Asian Region. In addition, many existing institutions welcome the AIIB—along with the Chinese norm of infrastructure construction.

The president of the WB, Jim Yong Kim, the head of IMF, Christine Lagarde, and the president of the ADB Takehiko Nakao have expressed their support of the AIIB. The United Nations (2015, 73) has addressed the launch of AIIB as "scaling up financing for sustainable development" for the concern of Global Economic Governance. These statements prove that there is sufficient space for the AIIB to cooperate with existing international governance structure rather than to challenge or replace it. Moreover, the AIIB (2016a) has introduced the Environmental and Social Framework. This framework, operationalized in February of 2016, aims to provide "a mechanism for addressing environmental and social risks and impacts in Project identification, preparation and implementation" to "ensure the environmental and social soundness and sustainability of Projects" (Article 5). The framework also makes clear reference to the idea of sustainable development, including economic, social, and environmental aspects (Article 8). The inclusion of the Environmental and Social Framework implies that China is willing to apply international standards to the AIIB's operation. As Jin Liqun underlines, the AIIB adheres to the highest standards of existing financial institutions (*Xinhua* 2016). Since the ADB, EBRD, EIB, and World Bank have attached considerable importance to environmental protection and social security, adopting this framework helps to bridge the gap between China's norms and western norms regarding external assistance, thus improving the external perceptions of China's normative power.

The successful launch of the AIIB not only complements the current global financial governance structure, but also enhances China's normative diffusion in that existing institutions have taken action to integrate China into this governance structure. For instance, in March 2015, the ADB decided to raise the annual fund for infrastructure and other projects by nearly 40 percent to 18 billion US dollars. This is regarded as a response to the founding of the AIIB. In May 2017, the UN Economic and Social Commission for Asia and Pacific (ESCAP) published "The Asia-Pacific Countries with Special Needs Development Report 2017." This report argues that "a higher policy focus" be placed on "improving availability and access to sustainable infrastructure" for the least developed countries and small island developing countries in this region to achieve economic growth and sustainable development (ESCAP 2017, Foreword). Such focus on infrastructure condition signals that the launch of the AIIB has promoted the norm of infrastructure construction in the Asian region and changed the policy framework of other institutions. In the financial governance area, the AIIB has also caused a series of reactions. In December 2015, after more than half decade of stagnation, US Congress finally approved the reform plan of the IMF, formulated in 2010 to increase the voting rights of China and other emerging economies. This can be regarded as a response to the establishment of the AIIB since the delay in US approval of IMF reform has given China considerable moral weight to build the support of US allies in Asia and Europe for the AIIB (*Economist* 2015b; Weiss 2017, 3). China and other emerging economies have been displeased with the slow process of IMF reform for some time, giving China considerable moral sway in gaining the support of US allies in Asia and Europe (*Economist* 2015b). The formation of the AIIB is partly the result of such an advantage. In the same month, the IMF agreed to add Chinese RMB to the Special Drawing Rights (SDR). This is the first time in over fifteen years that the IMF has made changes to the list of currencies comprising the SDR. Supported by the United States, the IMF believes that the inclusion of RMB will make the SDR more diverse and representative of the international society (IMF 2015).

The analysis of the AIIB's management arrangements reveals that this bank is a manifestation of China's norms regarding governance structure in international institutions. Recent developments indicate that, rather than perceiving the AIIB as a challenge of the WB and IMF, it is more reasonable to regard it as a complement to the existing institutions. Through the cooperation with other institutions, the AIIB can foster China's integration into the international aid structure so it will no longer be treated as the "other" in this area. Moreover, the other international institutions have made changes in their policies to accommodate China's appeals regarding the global financial governance structure. These developments shed light on the spillover effect of the AIIB on the international financial governance structure. Therefore, through the operation of the AIIB, China's preference of infrastructure building will emerge as a fundamental norm in external assistance policies in the Asian region.

CONCLUSION

This chapter highlights the connection between Chinese economic statecraft and China's normative power through analyzing the case of the AIIB. The predominant role of China in the AIIB makes this bank a manifestation of China's use of economic tools to develop its normative influence in international financial governance. This chapter argues that the AIIB, as a new multilateral financial institution initiated by China, inherits Chinese norms regarding external assistance. These norms were set by Zhou Enlai in the 1950s and 1960s and have continued to be the guidelines for Chinese foreign aid programs. In particular, China does not bind political clauses (except the "one-China" policy) with its aid. For most of the time, China has not expressed any preference toward the recipient countries' domestic regimes. Meanwhile, Chinese foreign aid and foreign investment projects concentrate on the infrastructure sector. China argues that compared to other political rights, economic development is more important for people in developing countries. Drawing on Chinese experience, infrastructure building is the foundation for developing countries to obtain steady economic growth. Based on the analysis of the AIIB's policy and Chinese leaders' statements, the AIIB has adopted these norms. More importantly, the endorsement of the AOA by fifty-seven member states significantly enhances the normative influence of China in external assistance area. However, the inclusion of Western developed countries casts a challenge to China's ability to maintain its current preference for these norms during the operation of the AIIB. To cooperate with other members, China has to increase its attention on social security and environmental protection in the infrastructure programs.

In addition to the external assistance area, the formulation of the AIIB is also closely connected to China's normative appeals regarding the existing financial governance structure. The boost in China's economic power has stimulated it well to enhance its role in financial institutions. Together with other emerging economies, especially the BRICS group, China has been actively promoting the reform of governance structure in the IMF and the WB. The key points of China's claim are the redistribution of voting power and the abolishing of unilateral veto power. The AIIB is a manifestation of China's appeals regarding management arrangements. It has a leaner staff structure and a nonresidential board of directors, enhancing the efficiency of policy making. It also has a different formula for voting rights distribution in which the developing countries have the largest share. However, whether or not China will abandon its veto power during the operation of the AIIB still remains uncertain.

The third implication of the AIIB is its future impact on the external perceptions of China's normative power. While China's norms of sovereignty, unconditionality, and infrastructure building are being accepted by developing countries, the preference for sovereignty and noninterference also makes China the "other" in the international normative structure. Furthermore, China's role in international financial governance is perceived as negative by some Western observers. In this regard, the AIIB is an opportunity for China to improve the external perceptions of its normative power. The cooperation between the AIIB and other existing institutions implies that the AIIB is a necessary complement to the external assistance framework in the Asian region. The inclusion of social and environmental framework in the AIIB's policy is a sign that China is willing to converge to the existing normative structure. Moreover, the formulation of the AIIB has triggered a series of policy changes in other institutions.

These recent developments advance China's involvement in international governance structure. They also considerably expand China's normative influence in the Asian region. Both these effects bridge the gap between China's norms and Western norms regarding foreign aid. As a result, the external perceptions of China's normative power will be improved.

The boost of its economic power in the recent decades has enriched the normative power of China in international financial governance area. However, the normative influence of China is still limited, as it has not integrated with the international normative structure. The current structure remains deeply embedded within a value system dominated by the West. Inevitably, China will have to work within the existing structure even if it seeks to expand its normative influence in the international system. The case of the AIIB illustrates how Chinese economic statecraft has contributed to the spread of China's norms in international financial governance structure. China led the creation of the AIIB and has the largest capital share in the bank. Such a position ensures the implementation of Chinese norms in this new institution. The AIIB also gives China a broader platform to diffuse its norms. Meanwhile, the formation of the AIIB increases not only the opportunities, but also the challenges China faces during its norm diffusion. China has to tread carefully to ensure that its normative power is enhanced through the operation of the AIIB. The operations of the AIIB will be a barometer for China's normative power for years to come.

NOTE

1. Philomena Murray deserves a special credit for pushing the authors to write this piece on order in the first place. The authors would like to thank Zhimin Chen, Zhongqi Pan, and two anonymous reviewers for their insightful comments. This research is funded by China's National Humanities and Social Sciences Research Project "China and the International Rule Making" (14BGJ021).

BIBLIOGRAPHY

AIIB. "Articles of Agreement." 2015a. https://www.aiib.org/en/about-aiib/basic-documents/articles-of-agreement/index.html. Accessed January 8, 2018.

———. "Board of Directors." 2015b. https://www.aiib.org/en/about-aiib/governance/board-directors/index.html. Accessed January 8, 2018.

———. "Members and Prospective Members of the Bank." 2015c. https://www.aiib.org/en/about-aiib/governance/members-of-bank/index.html. Accessed January 8, 2018.

———. "Environmental and Social Framework." 2016a. https://www.aiib.org/en/policies-strategies/framework-agreements/environmental-social-framework.htm. Accessed January 8, 2018.

———. "Islamic Republic of Pakistan National Motorway M-4 (Shorkot-Khanewal Section) Project." 2016b. https://www.aiib.org/en/projects/approved/2016/pakistan-national-motorway.html. Accessed January 4, 2018.

———. "The People's Republic of Bangladesh Distribution System Upgrade and Expansion Project." 2016c. https://www.aiib.org/en/projects/approved/2016/bangladesh-distribution-system.html. Accessed January 4, 2018.

———. "Annual Report and Accounts 2016." 2017. https://www.aiib.org/en/news-events/news/2016/annual-report/index.html. Accessed January 4, 2018.

———. "Approved Projects." n.d. https://www.aiib.org/en/projects/approved/index.html. Accessed January 4, 2018.

BBC. "Countries Rating Poll." 2015. http://downloads.bbc.co.uk/mediacentre/country-rating-poll.pdf. Accessed June 2, 2016.

Bhattacharyay, Biswa N. *Estimating Demand for Infrastructure in Energy, Transport, Telecommunications, Water and Sanitation in Asia and the Pacific: 2010–2020*. ADBI Working Paper 248. Tokyo: Asian Development Bank Institute, 2010. http://www.adbi.org/working-paper/2010/09/09/4062. infrastructure.demand.asia.pacific/.

Bräutigam, Deborah. *The Dragon's Gift: The Real Story of China in Africa*. Oxford: Oxford University Press, 2011a.

———. "Aid 'With Chinese Characteristics': Chinese Foreign Aid and Development Finance Meet the OECD-DAC Aid Regime." *Journal of International Development* 23(5) (2011b): 752–64.

BRICS. "Meeting of BRIC Finance Ministers and Central Bank Governors Communiqué." September 4, 2009. London. http://www.brics.utoronto.ca/docs/090904-finance.html. Accessed May 15, 2016.

Chen, Tianyang, and Tan Yu. "Predicaments of the IMF Quota and Voting Rights Reform and its Countermeasures." *Studies of International Finance* 8(3) (2013): 22–32.

China Daily. "China Proposes Establishing Asian Infrastructure Investment Bank." October 3, 2013. http://www.chinadaily.com.cn/xinhua/2013-10-03/content_10245894.html.

———. "AIIB Chief Rules out China Veto Power." 2016. http://www.chinadaily.com.cn/business/2016-01/27/content_23265846.htm.

Condon, Madison. "China in Africa: What the Policy of Nonintervention Adds to the Western Development Dilemma." *PRAXIS: The Fletcher Journal of Human Security* (27) (2012): 5–25.

Cotonou Agreement. "Partnership Agreement between the Members of the African, Caribbean and Pacific Group of States of the One Part, and the European Community and Its Member States, of the Other Part." Cotonou, Benin, 2000.

Cui, J., and T. Chang. "IMF Gaige Kunjing yu Zhongguo de Xianshi Xuanze [The Plight of IMF's Reform and the Feasible Selection of China]." *Dangdai Jingji Kexue [Modern Economic Science]* 35(3) (2013): 23–27.

Diplomat. "The AIIB Is Seen Very Differently in the US, Europe, and China." 2015. http://thediplomat. com/2015/05/the-aiib-is-seen-very-differently-in-the-us-europe-and-china/. Accessed March 10, 2016.

Economist. "The Infrastructure Gap: Development Finance Helps China Win Friends and Influence American Allies." March 15, 2015a. http://www.economist.com/news/asia/21646740-development-finance- helps-china-win-friends-and-influence-american-allies-infrastructure-gap. Accessed March 10, 2016.

———. "Rich But Rash: To Challenge the World Bank and the IMF, China Will Have to Imitate Them." January 29, 2015b. http://www.economist.com/news/finance-and-economics/21641259-challenge-world- bank-and-imf-china-will-have-imitate-them-rich.

ESCAP. "Asia-Pacific Countries with Special Needs Development Report 2017: Investing in Infrastructure for an Inclusive and Sustainable Future." 2017. www.unescap.org/sites/default/files/.../Final%20%28CSN%29%206%20June.pdf.

Financial Times. "China Defends Africa Aid Stance." July 1, 2008. http://www.ft.com/intl/cms/s/0/28a69bd4-479a- 11dd-93ca-000077b07658.html#axzz3qte3ef2w.

———. "UK Move to Join China-led Bank a Surprise Even to Beijing." March 26, 2015. http://www.ft.com/intl/cms/s/0/d33fed8a-d3a1-11e4-a9d3-00144feab7de.html#axzz3qte3ef2w.

Guardian. "US Anger at Britain Joining Chinese-led Investment Bank AIIB." March 13, 2015a. http://www.theguardian.com/us-news/2015/mar/13/white-house-pointedly-asks-uk-to-use-its-voice-as-part- of-chinese-led-bank.

———. "Australia on Brink of Joining China's Asian Infrastructure Investment Bank." March 20, 2015b. http://www.theguardian.com/australia-news/2015/mar/20/australia-on-brink-of-joining-chinas-asian- infrastructure-investment-bank.

G20. "London Summit–Leaders' Statement." April 2009. https://www.imf.org/external/np/sec/pr/ 2009/pdf/g20_040209.pdf.

IMF. "Chinese Renminbi to Be Included in IMF's Special Drawing Right Basket." 2015. http://www.imf. org/external/pubs/ft/survey/so/2015/new120115a.htm . Accessed March 10, 2016.

Japan Times. "Abe Administration Develops Rift Over China's New Development Bank." March 20, 2015. http://www.japantimes.co.jp/news/2015/03/20/business/japan-could-join-china-backed-bank-aso/#VuCtypx96hd.

Kavalski, Emilian. "The Struggle for Recognition of Normative Powers: Normative Power Europe and Normative Power China in Context." *Cooperation & Conflict* 48(2) (2013): 247–67.

Keuleers, Floor. "Explaining External Perceptions: The EU and China in African Public Opinion." *JCMS. Journal of Common Market Studies* 53(4) (2015): 803–21.

Larsen, Henrik. "The EU as a Normative Power and the Research on External Perceptions: The Missing Link." *JCMS: Journal of Common Market Studies* 52(4) (2014): 896–910.

Leonard, Mark. "China's New Intelligentsia." *Prospect Magazine* 144(2) (2008): 1–9.

Lucarelli, Sonia. "The European Union in the Eyes of Others: Towards Filling a Gap in the Literature." *European Foreign Affairs Review* 12(3) (2007): 249–70.

Lu, Z. "Hou Jinrong Weiji Shiqi Zhongguo Canyu Guoji Jinrong Tixi Gaige de Mubiao he Lujing—yi Zhongguo Canyu IMF Gaige Weili [Path and Objectives of China's Participation in the Reform of the International Financial System in

Post-Financial Crisis Period—Taking Chinese Participation in IMF Reforms as A Case Study].” *Dong Nanya Zongheng [Around Southeast Asia]* 8 (2011): 87–91.

Manji, Firoze, and Stephen Marks, eds. *African Perspectives on China in Africa*. Oxford: Fahamu, 2007.

Manners, Ian. “Normative Power Europe: A Contradiction in Terms?” *Journal of Common Market Studies* 40(2) (2002): 235–58.

———. “Normative Power Europe Reconsidered: Beyond the Crossroads.” *Journal of European Public Policy* 13(2) (2006): 182–99.

———. “Assessing the Decennial, Reassessing the Global: Understanding European Union Normative Power in Global Politics.” *Cooperation & Conflict* 48(2) (2013): 304–29.

National Bureau of Statistics of China. “Gross Domestic Product.” 2015. http://www.stats.gov.cn/tjsj/ndsj/ 2015/indexeh.htm. Accessed March 10, 2016.

NDB. “Articles of Agreement.” 2014. http://ndb.int/download/Agreement%20on%20the%20New% 20Development%20Bank.pdf. Accessed March 10, 2016.

Norris, William J. *Chinese Economic Statecraft: Commercial Actors, Grand Strategy, and State Control*. Ithaca, NY: Cornell University Press, 2016.

Noutcheva, Gergana. “Fake, Partial and Imposed Compliance: The Limits of the EU’s Normative Power in the Western Balkans.” *Journal of European Public Policy* 16(7) (2009): 1065–84.

People’s Daily Online. “The AIIB Is a Complement Rather Than a Competitor.” 2014. http://en.people.cn/n/2014/1028/c98649-8800974.html. Accessed March 10, 2016.

Perlez, Jane. “U.S. Opposing China’s Answer to World Bank.” *New York Times*, October 10, 2014. http://www.nytimes.com/2014/10/10/world/asia/chinas-plan-for-regional-development-bank-runs-into-us-opposition.html?ref=world&_r=1.

Renard, Thomas. “The Asian Infrastructure Investment Bank (AIIB): China’s New Multilateralism and the Erosion of the West.” *Security Policy Brief* no. 63, April 2015. http://www.egmontinstitute.be/wp-content/uploads/2015/04/SPB63-Renard.pdf.

Reuters. “China’s AIIB to Offer Loans with Fewer Strings Attached.” September 1, 2015. http://www.reuters.com/article/us- aiib-china-loans-idUSKCN0R14UB20150901.

Sautman, Barry, and Yan Hairong. “African Perspectives on China–Africa Links.” *The China Quarterly* 199 (2009): 728–59.

State Council. *China’s Foreign Aid*. Beijing, People’s Republic of China: Information Office of the State Council, April 2014.

United Kingdom. “UK Announces Plans to Join Asian Infrastructure Investment Bank.” 2015. https://www.gov.uk/government/news/uk-announces-plans-to-join-asian-infrastructure investment-bank. Accessed March 10, 2016.

United Nations. “World Economic Situation and Prospects 2015.” New York, 2015. http://www.un.org/en/development/desa/policy/wesp/wesp_archive/2015wesp-ch3-en.pdf.

Wall Street Journal. “How China Plans to Run AIIB: Leaner, With Veto.” June 8, 2015. http://www.wsj.com/articles/how-china-plans-to-run-aiib-leaner-with-veto-1433764079. Accessed March 10, 2016.

Wan, Ming. *The Asian Infrastructure Investment Bank: The Construction of Power and the Struggle for the East Asian International Order*. New York: Palgrave Macmillan US, 2016.

Weiss, Martin A. "Asian Infrastructure Investment Bank (AIIB)." Congressional Research Service, February 3, 2017.

Wihtol, Robert. "Beijing's Challenge to the Global Financial Architecture." *Georgetown Journal of Asian Affairs* (Spring/Summer 2015). https://asianstudies. georgetown.edu/sites/asianstudies/files/GJAA%202.1%20Wihtol,%20Robert_0.pdf.

Xinhua. "AIIB President Committed to 'Highest Possible Standard,'" January 17, 2016. http://news.xinhuanet.com/ english/2016-01/17/c_135017516.htm. Accessed March 10, 2016.

Zhang, Xiaoming. "A Rising China and the Normative Changes in International Society." *East Asia* 28(3) (2011): 235–46.

Zhou, Enlai. Speech in Accra, Ghana, January 15, 1964.

Zupanc˘ic˘, Rok, and Miha Hribernik. "Normative Power Japan: The European Union's Ideational Successor or Another 'Contradiction in Terms'?" *Romanian Journal of Political Science* 13(2) (Winter 2013): 106–36.

Chapter 10

China's Coherence in International Economic Governance

Marcia Don Harpaz

When and how is China challenging the rules and norms of the prevailing international economic order? Has China adopted the current rules and norms across the board, or is it proceeding in an ad hoc or piecemeal manner? How can its (in)coherence be explained? To address these questions, I compare China's profile vis-à-vis three dimensions of the global economic order: trade, investment, and development aid. I argue that in international trade and investment, China has neither sought nor brought about significant change. China is, however, offering an alternative to the Western norms that until now have dominated the global development aid regime. China's establishment of the Asian Infrastructure Investment Bank (AIIB) and the Belt and Road Initiative (BRI) are notable in this regard. The chapter then considers possible theoretical explanations for the variation in China's behavior across the three areas.

This chapter examines the coherence of China's profile across three dimensions of international economic governance: trade, investment, and development aid.[1] When and how is China challenging the prevailing rules and norms in these three areas? How does China's policy vary in the different areas? Has China adopted the rules and norms of the liberal international economic order they represent, across the board or is China proceeding in an ad hoc or piecemeal manner? How can its (in) coherence be explained?

In the context of the broader debate over China's rising impact on the global order and whether it will lead to conflict or cooperation, it is often claimed that China aspires to change the rules and norms of the liberal economic institutions established after World War II by the West.[2] For example, former US president Obama, in order to promote the Trans-Pacific Partnership (TPP), argued that China presented a serious challenge to the prevailing global economic order, warning that China would be writing the trade rules for the twenty-first century, if nothing was done to stop it (Obama 2015a, 2015b). Trump is taking a different stance, showing less concern with China's broader challenge to Western economic norms and more concern with trade competition. Within a year of Trump's election, the Trump administration had withdrawn from the TPP, self-initiated investigations of China regarding steel and aluminum imports based on rarely used national security legislation found in Section 232 of the Trade Expansion Act of 1962 (United States 1964), and labeled China a strategic competitor in the 2017 National Security Strategy paper (Trump 2017).

Regarding international trade, over a decade has passed since China joined the World Trade Organization (WTO) in 2001. China has also concluded a number of bilateral free trade agreements (FTAs) as well as an important regional trade agreement with the Association of Southeast Asian Nations (ASEAN). Moreover, China has been actively promoting the ASEAN-led Regional Comprehensive Economic Partnership (RCEP) between ASEAN members and the six states with which ASEAN has FTAs (China, Australia, India, Japan, Korea, and New Zealand).[3]

On investment, in addition to signing on to the Convention on Settlement of Investment Disputes between States and Nationals of Other Nations in 1993, China has become one of the world's largest signatories to bilateral investment treaties (BITs) in conjunction with the rise in its inward and outward foreign direct investment (FDI). In 2008, China began negotiating an investment treaty with the United States. More recently, it concluded a trilateral investment treaty with Korea and Japan that went into force in 2014.

I argue that China has neither sought nor brought about significant change in international trade or investment norms and rules (although there may be some disagreement about the former[4]). Regarding development financing, however, China is seriously challenging the status quo and is positioned to continue to do so. It is not only a recipient of aid in the system but has become an important lender within and alongside the World Bank, as well as a contributor to regional development banks. Moreover, China is establishing new, parallel, and possibly competing institutions to Western-dominated institutions. In October 2013, Chinese president Xi Jinping initiated the establishment of the Asia Infrastructure Investment Bank (AIIB) (Xi 2013), with observers predicting that the new bank would compete with the World Bank and the Asian Development Bank.[5] President Xi Jinping has also called for developed country support for developing countries with "no political strings attached" and the establishment of a "more fair and balanced new global development partnership" (Xi 2015). China's Belt and Road Initiative (BRI), an infrastructure plan extending across some sixty-four countries, is part of a broader grand strategy that may present an even bigger challenge to the traditional development aid system. This is somewhat puzzling since it is in development aid that China's process of integration into the international economic order began, with its engagement with the World Bank and the International Monetary Fund in 1980, as participant and beneficiary of these two institutions. Consequently, this is the area in which the longest period of socialization has taken place.[6]

With regard to the variance found in the three areas of global economic governance, this chapter considers two broad types of theoretical explanations: rationalist explanations that focus on cost-benefit calculations and material interests and normative approaches which stress the importance of ideas, beliefs, and socialization. A rationalist state-centric approach would suggest that the variation in China's behavior may be attributed to a disparity in China's national interests in each of the areas. Because different issue areas generate different costs and benefits, policy differences would be anticipated. One strand of such thinking, liberal institutionalism, would further emphasize the role of the institutions/regimes and their different abilities to constrain behavior to explain the variation in China's profile in the three areas.

A domestic politics approach—another strand of rationalist thinking—would highlight the importance of domestic interest groups and their resistance or support in shaping a state's policies in different issue areas. This approach presents a number of problems, some substantive and some methodological. For one, leaders in an authoritarian regime such as China may be less sensitive to domestic interest groups than in a democratic regime. In fact, Chinese leaders have overridden domestic pressure out of foreign policy or broader national interest considerations.[7] While this is changing, as an increasing number of domestic actors contribute to the policy making process,[8] it is still difficult to determine the impact of domestic pressure given the complex and often opaque decision-making process in China. Moreover, as President Xi consolidates his power along with that of the Communist Party,[9] domestic elites are less likely to challenge him. In view of the above, this chapter assumes the state to be a unitary actor in its discussion of rationalist theoretical explanations.

A norms-driven approach would suggest that a social learning dynamic—an interactive process that leads to the domestic internalization of international norms—would explain China's profile in the three areas. Such an approach might predict that the longer the socialization process, the greater the likelihood of China maintaining the status quo. Yet, the findings indicate that the only area of global economic governance in which China challenges the prevailing regime is development financing, the area that has undergone the longest period of socialization. In this chapter, rather than reject a socialization explanation outright, I propose building on Gregory Chin's concept of two-way socialization (Chin 2012a) and consider the possibility that ultimately a socialization process could lead to better understanding of the behavioral norms of other institutional actors, and thus, increased self-confidence to act at times in a nonconforming manner as other key actors do, and finally, to be proactive in promoting institutional norms change that would work to China's advantage.

This analysis begins with China's approach to each of the three issue areas: trade, investment, and development financing, to determine whether it is supporting or challenging the prevailing international order in these areas. The study finds that China's profile varies across the three areas and then discusses possible explanations for the variation. The study concludes that a rationalist state-centric perspective provides an important insight into China's incoherent profile; nevertheless, a normative perspective complements our understanding of China's maintenance of—and challenge to—the status quo in international economic governance.

CHINA AND THE INTERNATIONAL TRADING ORDER

Today China faces a global trading environment based primarily on the highly legalized multilateral WTO system and its rules. Alongside the WTO system is a labyrinth of regional and bilateral trade agreements between countries throughout the world, built on WTO-derived principles. Added to the mix is the emergence of "mega regional" trade and investment agreements, considered "mega" regionals because the negotiating parties comprise such a large volume of global trade and investment.[10]

Two mega-regionals are particularly noteworthy as they were being driven by the historical hegemon in the global trading order—the United States—and they excluded China. These mega-regionals are the TPP[11] and the Transatlantic Trade and Investment Partnership (TTIP).[12] The United States was thought to be pushing them in order to shape twenty-first century trade and investment rules and norms, maintain leadership of the global economy, and as part of its "pivot to Asia" policy aimed at reasserting itself in the region. In response, China was pursuing its own international trade agenda, including a separate set of mega-regionals: the RCEP, and since 2014, a Free Trade Area of Asia Pacific (FTAAP) (Tiezzi 2014). The importance of mega regionals in the global trade and investment landscape have declined significantly since Trump's election to the US presidency in November 2016. At the time of this writing, the United States had withdrawn from the TPP, and it is not clear whether the eleven remaining members will be able to revive it or if the United States will rejoin. And the TTIP negotiations are on hold.

CHINA AND THE WTO

China, like all other WTO members, was required to undertake commitments over a broad range of issue areas when it joined the WTO. But China was also asked to undertake commitments that far exceeded those of other WTO members.[13] For example, China's market access coverage in goods and services went beyond those of other WTO members.[14] More unusually, some of China's rules commitments[15] bound it to a higher standard than that applied to other WTO members (often referred to as WTO-plus commitments), for instance, in areas such as transparency.[16] China also agreed to discriminatory measures where it gave up rights available to all WTO members, such as in anti-dumping and countervailing investigations (often referred to as WTO-minus commitments), in essence, increasing the likelihood of foreign authorities imposing dumping or countervailing duties on Chinese exports.[17]

The discriminatory commitments that China undertook in the WTO (and for which China's chief trade negotiator was labeled by some in China a traitor[18]), its phenomenally rapidly growing importance in world trade, as well as the state's involvement in the economy could conceivably lead it to defy the system by flouting the rules, working to change the rules, creating an alternative framework, or by withdrawing altogether from the organization.[19] Yet this is not happening. China has accepted the current multilateral trading system; it is working within the system; and it is working toward the perpetuation of the system.[20] For one, it is considered to be largely complying with the WTO rules themselves (Gao 2014; Hanlon 2017; Pearson 2006; Kent 2007, 237–38). Moreover, China is generally complying with panel and Appellate Body (AB) rulings, even though the degree of its compliance with the rulings may be debatable.[21] It is making a discernable effort to cooperate in the implementation of rulings against it, is adhering to the time limits set by the WTO, is amending its laws when necessary, and is demonstrating in its rhetoric and behavior that it believes compliance with WTO rulings to be appropriate.[22] Furthermore, China's compliance with dispute settlement rulings stands in sharp contrast with the stalling behavior manifested by other WTO members, such as the United States, when they have lost cases in the WTO.[23]

Regarding the question of if, and how, China may be seeking more generally to change WTO norms and rules, we can also look at China's positions in the WTO's Doha Development Agenda (DDA or Doha Round) negotiations. In its early years in the WTO, China was accused of impeding the progress of the negotiations by maintaining a low profile, not taking on a leadership role, and not offering to make concessions corresponding with its size and importance in the global economy.[24] Indeed, China claimed that as a recently acceded member (RAM), it should not be asked to take on new commitments soon after taking on extensive accession commitments. However, with time, China started to increase its participation in the negotiations (Gao 2014; WTO 2014, 22–24). China's top leaders started expressing their support for the completion of the DDA negotiations and have called for achieving an early harvest in some areas (Fu and Wu 2014). Moreover, accusations that, at times, China had been the cause of the breakdown in the DDA negotiations have been refuted.[25] The large number of China's negotiating proposals[26] also testifies to a high degree of engagement in the negotiating process, and, as such, faith in the WTO system. Moreover, the content of China's proposals suggests its commitment to the basic trade liberalization norm of the current multilateral trading system.[27] China was credited with playing a decisive role in the ministerial in December 2013 that led to the Bali Package (Azêvedo 2014).[28] In the division between WTO members over the continuation or abandonment of the DDA negotiations prior to the Nairobi Ministerial, China called for the completion of the Doha Round (Ministry of Commerce 2015a, 2015b), further underlining China's commitment to the current multilateral trading system. Since Trump's election and the Trump administration's strong criticism of the WTO, China paradoxically seems to be taking over as the champion of the WTO and possibly replacing US leadership in global trade governance.

Other signs of China's active engagement in the WTO include initiating negotiations, along with thirteen other WTO members toward the WTO Environmental Goods Agreement to lower tariffs on an agreed-upon list of environmental goods,[29] participating in WTO negotiations on an expanded deal to cut tariffs on information technology goods,[30] and requesting to join the US- and EU-driven negotiations toward the Trade in Services Agreement (TISA) currently taking place on the sidelines of the WTO.[31]

CHINA AND REGIONAL AND BILATERAL TRADE AGREEMENTS

In addition to operating in the multilateral framework of the WTO, China has, like other countries, established a network of preferential trade agreements (PTAs). If China isn't working to significantly change the WTO system, is it challenging current international trade rules through its bilateral and regional trade pacts?[32]

As of December 2017, China had established fifteen PTAs, with nine more under negotiation and another nine under consideration.[33] China has entered into three basic types of preferential trade pacts.[34] In the first category are special arrangements with areas/economies which are part of Greater China or which it considers to be part of Greater China. China established Closer

Economic Partnership Arrangements (CEPAs) with Hong Kong and Macau in 2003,[35] while the Cross-Straits Economic Framework Agreement (ECFA) between Mainland China and Taipei was established in 2010. The second category of China's preferential trade pacts consists of FTAs negotiated between China and various partners, both developing and developed, including Chile (2006), Pakistan (2007), New Zealand (2008), Peru (2010), Costa Rica (2011), Iceland (2013), South Korea (2015), Australia (2015), Georgia (2017), and Maldives (2017). The third category of trade agreements are China's regional agreements, such the Framework Agreement on Comprehensive Economic Co-operation between ASEAN and China (ACFTA) which was signed in 2002. As part of China's incremental approach to its relations with ASEAN,[36] and further to Article 11 of the Framework Agreement, a separate agreement on dispute settlement was concluded in 2004 and went into effect in 2005 (Agreement 2004).

It may be claimed that China, through its FTAs, is challenging the current global trade rules in areas such as NME status in anti-dumping investigations, where it took on discriminatory provisions when it joined the WTO. As a condition to starting FTA negotiations, China requires its potential FTA partners to renounce the use of NME methodology.[37] While admittedly a gain for China, it does not seem likely that eliminating these discriminatory provisions is China's sole motivation in negotiating new FTAs. Moreover, such provisions are in fact protectionist in nature; thus, by working to eliminate them, China could be viewed as taking a pro-trade liberalization stance.

Taking a broader perspective, while China's PTAs do differ from those of the EU and the United States, in fact, regional/bilateral FTAs generally differ from one another. Regional/bilateral trade agreements typically vary in terms of depth (the degree of harmonization required by the agreement and width (the number of policy areas covered). Some agreements are more interventionist while others are minimalist in terms of the detail of the legal systems imposed on the participating parties. Peter Yu notes that some agreements, such as those of the United States, focus mainly on trade and investment while others such as the economic partnership agreements of the EU expand their agreements beyond trade to non-trade areas.[38]

At the time, and in keeping with its general foreign policy principle of non-intervention, Chinese regional/bilateral FTAs follow a minimalist approach in terms of both depth and width. Unlike the US and EU agreements, the Chinese agreements do not require harmonization or the transposition of laws. Also unlike the template approaches of the United States and the EU, China does not have a standard format for its FTAs—in fact, the market access and the rules coverage of its FTAs are considerably different from one another.[39] For example, as Yu notes, provisions on intellectual property rights vary. China's agreement with Chile mentions the Doha Declaration on the

TRIPS Agreement on Public Health, while the agreement with New Zealand, although concluded later, does not mention the Declaration (Yu 2011, 1011). In certain cases, China has expanded its FTAs on goods to other areas at a later stage, such as services. For example, China's agreement on goods with ASEAN from 2004 was expanded to services in July 2007; its agreement with Chile from 2005 was expanded to services in August 2010 (Kitano and Harada 2014, Table AII.3).[40] Yet its agreement with Peru included a chapter on services from the start [108].

China's FTAs also differ among one another in their tariff elimination schedules. Some call for mutual customs tariff elimination, for example, with Peru, Costa Rica, and Pakistan. In contrast, in the FTA with New Zealand, China was permitted a slightly longer tariff elimination period (up to twelve years for some products from New Zealand to China) while all tariffs on products imported from China to New Zealand were eliminated within nine years. In its FTA with ASEAN, China proposed what was referred to in the agreement as an "early harvest," that is, a shorter tariff reduction period for it and the six original members of ASEAN (by 2010) and a longer phase in period for the four new ASEAN members (by 2015).[41]

Yet, while China's trade agreements admittedly differ from those of the United States and the EU, it would be difficult to conclude that China is challenging the existing rules, since its agreements are based on commonly accepted international trade norms such as progressive trade liberalization, nondiscrimination, and transparency, rather than on weaker or different norms. (Indeed, one of the guiding principles of the RCEP negotiations is compatibility with WTO rules, which are the basis for these norms.) China has even started to adopt rules in areas promoted by the United States and the EU that it had previously rejected, such as competition policy, environmental protection, and more legalized dispute settlement provisions.[42] Domestically, in an unusual move, China has recently demonstrated further commitment to international trade rules by expanding its efforts to ensure compliance with international trade rules (and promote economic reform) at all levels of government (Ministry of Commerce 2014).

CHINA AND THE INTERNATIONAL INVESTMENT TREATY LANDSCAPE

The international investment treaty landscape facing China, and other countries, is more fragmented and multilayered than that of international trade. Investment disciplines may be found in over three thousand different BITs,[43] in WTO investment-related rules in various WTO agreements [e.g., the General Agreement on Trade in Services (GATS), the Agreement on Trade-Related Investment Measures (TRIMS), and the Agreement on Trade-Related Aspects of Intellectual Property Rights (TRIPS)], in a myriad of free trade agreements with investment provisions that vary in scope and depth, and in the World Bank's Convention on the Settlement of Investment Disputes Between States and Nationals of Other States (ICSID).[44] In addition, standards and norms are being shaped in various OECD forums aimed at consensus building to attain uniform meanings of global investment rules.[45]

The difficulty in achieving a less fragmented international investment regime is reflected in several failed attempts to create a multilateral investment framework. At the end of the 1990s, negotiations were launched in the OECD aimed at establishing a multilateral agreement on investment, and at about the same time, some members of the WTO proposed putting investment on the WTO agenda as a new issue; however, both efforts failed.[46] Today, the lack of consensus continues, as many states reevaluate their international investment agreement policies and even terminate their BITs.[47] Both the United States and the EU have formulated new policies; the US policy is embodied in a new model BIT (2012), and the EU policy, in recent negotiating directives (European Union 2012; US Model 2015), both calling for more regulatory policy space. For these and other reasons, the international investment treaty regime is currently in flux.

BITs, and investment chapters in FTAs, typically aim at protecting foreign investors from host state practices such as expropriation and nationalization (through rules on compensation and dispute settlement); in addition, they have also come to facilitate market access by foreign investors into host states by breaking down regulatory barriers (Bath and Nottage 2011, 1). Some BITs grant the host state more regulatory discretion on the entry of foreign investment, while other BITs limit host state regulatory discretion, thereby facilitating foreign investment (Berger 2008, 3). One of the main issues dividing BITs is whether they provide protection such as national treatment or most favored nation (MFN) treatment (both nondiscrimination standards for treatment provided to foreign investors) at the preestablishment stage, or at the post-establishment stage, that is, before or after the investment has been admitted. The preestablishment model has traditionally been applied by the United States, whereas the post-establishment model has been used by China and other developing countries (Berger 2011, 167–68).

Attracting FDI to stimulate growth has long been an important goal of the Chinese government, and in 2014 China became the largest recipient of FDI, surpassing the United States (UNCTAD 2015, 4–5, figure 1.3). China has also come to be one of the world's largest outward investors, in its quest for energy, minerals, and raw materials to support its rapidly developing economy.[48] Along with the tremendous rise in its inward and outward FDI flows, China has become one of the world's largest signatories to BITs, second only to Germany. By the end of May 2015, China had entered into 130 BITs and seventeen other international investment agreements (UNCTAD 2015, Annex 1).

China's BITs have undergone two main stages of development:[49] the first, from 1982, when it signed a BIT with Sweden to 1998, and from 1998 onwards, when its BIT policy changed significantly, becoming less restrictive in terms of governmental regulatory discretion. The change in China's BITs has been attributed, among other things, to its transformation from recipient of FDI to both importer and exporter of FDI (Berger 2008, 7).

This transformation is reflected in a shift from mainly safeguarding domestic regulatory freedom to China's later policy aimed at achieving an open investment environment to facilitate its outward investment in potential host-state countries, particularly since the Chinese government itself is deeply involved in outward foreign investment. China's first generation BITs included MFN provisions but either did not include a national treatment provision at all or contained best effort provisions (with phrases such as, "to the extent possible" and "in accordance with national laws"), and had either weak or no investor-state dispute settlement. In contrast, China's post-1998 BITs (starting with its BIT with Barbados signed in 1998) provide investors with access to international dispute settlement,[50] and since 2000, include stronger provisions on nondiscrimination, including national treatment (Berger 2008). Regarding the question of preestablishment or post-establishment, China's BITs provide for post-establishment national treatment, a standard also applied by European BITs (Berger 2011).

We can see signs of a third generation of Chinese BITs, as China seems to have conceded to the United States in their BIT negotiations. In the United States-China negotiations, China has reportedly agreed to two concepts it had previously rejected: (1) preestablishment national treatment; (2) a negative list approach, which according to a Chinese spokesman, is in accordance with a new trend in the world (Ministry of Commerce 2013). The first concept refers to the stage of the investment to which national treatment would apply, preestablishment or post establishment. China had not previously agreed to preestablishment in its BITs. In a negative list approach, national treatment would apply to all sectors unless explicitly excluded, whereas a positive list approach would imply that only those sectors specifically listed would be subject to national treatment. Thus, by agreeing to the United States' call for a preestablishment, negative list approach, China is agreeing to take on much broader commitments than it had previously. Moreover, the use of the wording, "in accordance with a new trend in the world" in the context of the negative list approach, demonstrates that China seems to be yielding to the United States on investment rules.

Is there any other evidence that China might represent an alternative normative power in the international investment regime? It might be claimed that an example of China promoting change in the international investment system is related to the national security exception in BITs. Apprehensive about the possible rejection of Chinese investment based on national security concerns, China is working to restrict the use of the national security exception, which, in some cases, has been expanded by many countries "from countering military threats to tackling economic crisis and protecting strategic industry" (UNCTAD 2009, viii, 7–24)[51] to justify rejecting investment. Although China has a national security exception in its own legislation (State Council 2011; Ministry of Commerce 2011), one of China's main goals in its BITs is to limit regulatory discretion of the national security exception (Hufbauer, Miner, and Moran 2015).

Recall the case of China National Offshore Oil Corporation's (CNOOC) failed attempt in 2005 to take over US oil firm Unocal after CNOOC was basically forced to abandon its offer following US Congressional intervention or President Obama's 2012 use of executive authority to block Ralls Corporation, a Chinese-owned company, from acquiring wind farms in Oregon, invoking national security, ostensibly because the wind farms were located near US Navy airspace (Younglai 2012; Bath and Nottage 2011).[52] Indeed, the rejection of Chinese investments in the United States may be contrasted with investment by other countries which have not aroused as much opposition or been rejected.[53] Although nondiscrimination and transparency provisions in a future United States-China BIT might provide some protection for the admission of Chinese investment, a broad national security exception providing regulatory flexibility would still constitute a basis for the United States to block such investments. Moreover, given the recent court ruling in the United States where the US government lost to a Chinese-owned company over the US national security review process, US negotiators are likely to be even more wary of limiting the scope of the national security exception in a United States-China BIT. In this case, Ralls Corporation, the abovementioned US company owned by Chinese investors, sued President Obama and CFIUS (Committee on Foreign Investment in the United States) under US domestic law over Obama's executive order requiring Ralls to divest itself of the wind farms in Oregon (Ministry of Commerce 2014). Ralls prevailed in its claim of lack of due process in the US national security review process. At the same time, it should be noted that China is not the only country concerned by the national security exception in BITs, as is evident from the many discussions on freedom of investment and national security, taking place regularly in the OECD (2006–2014).

Is China working more generally to restrict the use of entry barriers to FDI through its BITs, in order to overcome host countries' protectionist measures relating to its investments? While the answer appears to be positive, at the same time, it seems that China is willing to capitulate in order to finalize an agreement. We know that one issue that was reportedly holding up the FTA negotiations between Australia and China was the investment chapter dealing with investment by state-owned enterprises (SOEs) (Murphy 2014).[54] In the final FTA that was concluded in November 2014 (and officially signed in June 2015), China conceded on the issue, and investments by its SOEs and sovereign wealth funds still require approval under Australia's foreign investment procedures (Australian Government). Investment by Chinese SOEs and sovereign wealth funds is also a politically sensitive topic in the United States-China BIT talks, though it is not yet known which side will compromise on this issue (BBC News 2013).[55] As noted above, China reportedly agreed to restart the treaty negotiations in July 2013 (the talks began in 2008, but stalled shortly after) after dropping its demand to protect certain industries and to cover all stages of investment (Eckert and Yukananov 2015).[56] Thus, it seems that the United States and others such as Australia are, for the most part, still dictating the rules on investment provisions, and China is more likely to acquiesce rather than stand its ground in order to finalize these agreements. In the meantime, China-United States talks have come to a standstill as they await Trump's decision whether to continue them.

INTERNATIONAL AID REGIME

Compared to the international trade and investment regimes, it is in the international development aid regime that the Chinese challenge to today's global norms is most noticeable, and where it can be argued that China is already having an important impact (Chin 2012a).[57] Perhaps this is why it is also in development aid that China is generating the most criticism from the West. In particular, China has been harshly criticized for ignoring human rights and environmental sustainability when it does business with, gives loans, grants aid, and provides UN Security Council support for outlier regimes such as Sudan, Zimbabwe, and Qadafi's Libya. It has also been accused of replacing American imperialism, by depleting the valuable natural resources of its clients, while forcing them to buy Chinese products (Krauss and Bradsher 2015).

The norms of today's international development aid system have been shaped by two main international bodies: the World Bank's International Development Association (IDA) and the twenty-nine-member OECD Development Assistance Committee (DAC), both founded in the early 1960s. The norms and rules established by these two bodies guide and monitor the assistance of the World Bank and the bilateral development assistance of members. From the early 1980s, the Western-dominated, neoliberal prescription for economic development that included reforms such as privatization, deregulation, trade liberalization, fiscal discipline, tax reform, and so on, became the dominant approach to development, and in 1989, came to be known as the "Washington Consensus."[58] Conditionality, or the imposition of these macroeconomic reform policies on recipients of grants/aid/loans, has become the most controversial norm of the global development financing system, particularly since conditionality has been expanded further to cover additional areas such as rule of law, human rights, and environmental standards.

At the same time, however, the global aid discourse has moved toward taking into account the needs and interests of both donors and recipients. In March 2005, DAC organized a forum including both donors and recipients that formulated the "Paris Declaration on Aid Effectiveness," calling for the system to be based on the principles of ownership, alignment, harmonization, results, and mutual accountability (OECD 2005).[59] Indeed, the traditional aid regime has been undergoing a shift as nontraditional donors such as China and other BRICS countries become donors as well as recipients. Among other things, this is reflected in the changing discourse regarding development aid. For example, the rising donors prefer to refer to themselves as "southern development partners" rather than "donors," and to "granting aid" as "building development partnerships" (Chin and Quadir 2012, 494). Nonetheless, although a Chinese delegation attended the DAC 2005 meeting, its participation reportedly reflected its role as aid recipient rather than donor (Bräutigam 2009, 133).

China entered this system when it joined the World Bank and the IMF in 1980, as part of its broader strategy of "opening up and reform," starting in the late 1970s. Almost immediately, the World Bank undertook five development projects in China and a comprehensive economic report on the Chinese economy (the latter signifying an important change in China's willingness to agree to outside monitoring). In the early stages of its membership, China was generally thought to have accepted the system, and it quickly became a major recipient of development aid (Jacobson and Oksenberg 1990).

Despite its own domestic economic problems, China has provided foreign aid (although in small amounts) since the 1950s to African states, initially in order to gain support in the international arena. More recently, its aid to African states has been aimed at acquiring the natural resources necessary to foster domestic economic development. Interestingly, China's aid policy is still operating according to principles formulated in 1964: The Eight Principles of Economic Aid and Technical Assistance to Other Countries, which include equality and mutual benefit and unconditioned aid.

China's 2011 White Paper on China's Foreign Aid, with China's first official statistics on its foreign aid, points to a new stage in China's aid program starting in 2004, noting that between 2004 and 2009, China's aid grew by almost 30 percent annually (State Council 2011). In July 2014, China demonstrated increased transparency, when it issued its second White Paper on China's foreign aid, with statistics for 2010–2012 (ibid 2014).[60] Today, China can be considered a major foreign aid donor. Recent estimates by Naohiro Kitano and Yukinori Harada suggest that China's foreign aid ranked sixth in 2012 and 2013 in comparison to that of other DAC members (Kitano and Harada 2014, Abstract).[61]

While on a smaller scale than traditional donor aid, Chinese development aid still makes considerable waves. Aside from claims that China is aiding corrupt regimes, China has also been accused of undercutting Western aid. Gregory Chin, for example, points to the case of Angola in 2004, when in the midst of negotiations with the IMF, the Chinese offered an unconditioned loan which Angola accepted, or similarly, in 2006 when the Chinese intervened during negotiations between Chad and the IMF, over the Chad-Cameroon Pipeline (Chin 2012a, 217). However, Deborah Bräutigam offers an alternative version of the Angola case. After having taken numerous expensive short-term loans, and not being able to repay them, Angola was unable to obtain additional money or reschedule payment without fulfilling a list of reforms dictated by the IMF. It was only after Germany and France made deals with Angola that China entered the picture with an offer of oil for an infrastructure loan. Shortly afterwards, a group of Western banks came in and supplied an oil-backed loan to Angola, and a later loan was organized by a French group with sixteen international participants. Thus, as Bräutigam observes, although traditional donors were also lending money to Angola without requiring transparency and providing cash to a corrupt government through oil exports, it was only China's loans that attracted negative publicity (Bräutigam 2009, 275–76).

What is more significant than the timing of China's aid is that its aid model differs considerably from that of the established international donor community [i.e., the World Bank, the IMF, or the various OECD Development Assistance Committee (DAC) members]. As mentioned above, when established international donors provide foreign aid, it has been based on conditionality and prescribed reform. In contrast, China's foreign assistance is based on a different philosophy. For one, China's aid is not a "one type fits all" model, rather it is geared to the specific needs and requests of the recipient countries. Cheng, Fang, and Lien explain that "the initial step of an aid project is that recipient governments and Chinese embassies in the field propose aid projects to Beijing" (Cheng, Ting, and Hui-Ting 2012, 106).[62] Moreover, the Chinese funded projects focus on infrastructure, education, and manufacturing, rather than on the political and economic reform agenda of the traditional donors (Bräutigam 2009, 11). In line with its historic adherence to the principle of noninterference, China does not condition its aid on "good governance" or on environmental standards as has been common in conventional aid. China's aid is based on the principles of its own model of development—start with economic development and then worry about other areas such as environment.

In addition, China does not typically provide policy advice, and if it does, it is a different sort of advice. As Chin and Thakhur point out, "In the policy advice accompanying its foreign assistance to Africa and Latin America, for example, Beijing has emphasized the importance of state intervention to ensure that national resources can be used to leverage investment and loans from the wealthier parts of the world . . . how to identify and structure revenue and surplus-generating projects so that a stable supply of funds is available to repay loans" (Chin and Thakur 2015, 125).

The very fact that China has developed so rapidly without implementing the neoliberal Western prescription of economic reform gives credence to an alternative to the prevailing development model. China's success not only in weathering the 2008 global financial crisis but also helping pull the rest of the world out of the crisis underscores the challenge China represents to the growth formula that has been put forward by the West.

What's more, China's continued promotion of tied aid, requiring the recipient to use some percentage of the funds to buy from Chinese companies, constitutes a challenge to a norm that traditional donors are trying to change. For example, aid from China Eximbank is tied at 50 percent. While tied aid is a common practice among many countries, including traditional donor countries, the practice is thought to lead to the purchase of overpriced goods and services, and, in 2001, DAC recommended untying aid to least developed countries (OECD 2001).[63] Chinese sources have defended the continued use of tied aid, claiming that disbursing aid directly to Chinese contractors, rather than transferring it into the recipient's national budget, minimizes embezzlement and corruption (Cheng, Ting, and Hui-Ting 2012).

China's success in influencing the development assistance regime is already apparent. Gregory Chin names two tangible effects of China's influence. For one, China has changed the manner in which donor countries work with the World Bank. In contrast to the past, where donors were accustomed to "lining up behind" the World Bank to provide aid, China has succeeded in being accepted by the World Bank as an equal partner and co-donor in providing loans. Moreover, Chin attributes entrenchment of the concept of "appropriate levels of concessionality," that is, varying interest rates often at better than market terms or offering grace periods to China's influence (Chin 2012b).[64]

Chin also points to a third effect: by supporting regional development banks, China is helping to provide an alternative to the traditional donors. For example, it established the PRC Poverty Reduction and Regional Cooperation Fund and the China African Development Fund. In addition, China has been a member of the Asian Development Bank (ADB) since 1986 and has itself borrowed for projects in transport, water, energy agriculture, and finance.[65] China contributes to other regional banks as well such as the Central Asia Regional Cooperation Forum and the Caribbean Development Bank (Chin and Thakur 2010, 126–27). Today, China is deeply involved in the new BRICS Bank.

In this context, the AIIB represents one of the biggest challenges yet to the United States-dominated system.[66] China had long been frustrated by the fact that its influence in the Western financial institutions was not commensurate with its size in the global economy, for example, in increased voting share in the IMF. The establishment of the AIIB, a new and possibly competing financial institution, was one way of responding to this frustration. From the start, the United States was outspoken in its opposition to the AIIB, vigorously lobbying prospective members not to join (Perlez 2014). Only after fifty-seven states—including some of America's closest allies such as the UK, Australia, South Korea, and Germany—joined as founding members did the United States drop its resistance (Dyer 2015) and start proposing collaboration between the new AIIB and the institutions such as the World Bank (Talley 2015). What is presently under debate is whether the AIIB is operating according to Western standards of good governance, transparency, environmental policies, and so on. (Chin 2016). As a result, Chinese officials are working hard to assure other governments that China is committed to "follow the international practice."[67] Indeed, although it seems that the AIIB is largely applying standards consistent with Western standards (Hsu 2017; Hanlon 2017),[68] it is still too soon to tell what the long-term impact the AIIB will have on the global financial order.

Another serious challenge in this regard is China's Belt and Road Initiative (BRI). In 2013, along with the AIIB, Xi Jinping launched the BRI, an enormous infrastructure construction initiative along two historical trade routes to and from China—one over land, the Silk Road Economic Belt, and one over sea, the Maritime Silk Road. It has been compared to the Marshall Plan that involved an expenditure of $800 billion (in today's terms) to rebuild Europe after World War II, although the BRI is expected to expend even more—some $1 trillion over the next decade (Manuel 2017). The importance of the BRI in Xi Jinping's "New Era" vision[69] is reflected in its addition as an amendment to the party constitution by the Nineteenth Congress of the Communist Party in October 2017. Some see the BRI as part of a cohesive grand strategy, while others see it as numerous unconnected bilateral infrastructure projects. *The Economist* has presented the BRI as a particular challenge to the United States in that it treats "Asia and Europe as a single space, and China, not the United States, is its focal point" (*Economist* 2016).

EXPLAINING CHINA'S INCOHERENCE

In this chapter, I have shown that China's profile varies across the different areas of global economic governance. Whereas China seems to have accepted the norms and rules in the international trade and investment regimes and is constructively engaged with them, it is presenting a serious challenge to the existing development aid framework. This is a somewhat surprising finding since China's interaction with the liberal international economic system began with development aid and the World Bank as far back as 1980, and consequently it is in development aid that the longest period of socialization into the Western system has taken place.

Gregory Chin's two-way socialization concept may provide an important insight into the puzzle. In his analysis, Chin suggests that we should "rethink" socialization, arguing that the socialization process is not just a one direction process where China is learning and internalizing norms, but rather a two-way process where China is also contributing to the reshaping of the norms.[70] As an extension of Chin's argument, I maintain that it is precisely because China has undergone such a long period of socialization in this particular regime that it feels comfortable in challenging global norms in order to advance its own interests. Moreover, socialization of a state into a regime does not preclude it from working to change the norms and rules to its advantage. To be sure, as states become further socialized into a regime, their better understanding of the system and increased self-confidence may lead them to challenge it. There are signs that this is occurring in the international trade regime as well as in the development aid regime. As China is socialized into the international trade regime, it seems to be feeling increasingly comfortable in pushing back with alternatives to the TPP and the TTIP such as the RCEP and the FTAAP.

But there is clearly more to understanding this puzzle than a socialization dynamic. We could postulate that the institutions/regimes and their design are constraining China's behavior. Since the institutional frameworks themselves differ considerably from one another, China's policy toward the three economic areas would be expected to diverge as well. The central institution in the international trade regime, the WTO, is an inclusive organization. It encompasses almost all countries in the world, developed and developing alike. China has long expressed its preference for engagement with more inclusive international institutional frameworks and dislike of exclusive ones such as the G7. In addition, the WTO's consensus-based decision-making means that China has veto power over all decisions made. It is not surprising, therefore, that China is adamant about keeping rule-making in the WTO. Regarding investment, the fragmented nature of the international investment treaty framework suggests that no one power completely dominates the rule-making process, particularly now, when the BIT system is in flux. Institutional factors thus support China's engagement within the international investment regime. In contrast, a small group which has imposed its way of thinking on the rest of the world for many years controls the development aid system. This kind of system does not sit well with a rising China that wants to take its proper place at the table.

In accordance with a broader rationalist state-centric approach, cost-benefit calculations would play an important role in explaining China's incoherent profile vis-à-vis the three areas.[71] On trade, China has only gained from joining the existing system, its economy growing tremendously over the past few decades. Why challenge the system from which it has benefited? Regarding investment, China has also succeeded in safeguarding its interests through the existing fragmented system, and with its growing power, it hopes to continue to do so. At the same time, its willingness to compromise on formerly key principles (i.e., China has reportedly agreed to preestablishment national treatment in the investment treaty negotiations with the United States), or at least to display willingness to compromise for the purpose of resuming treaty negotiations, may also be explained by a cost-benefit analysis. Such an analysis would calculate that China's interest in achieving better access for its investments in the US market outweighs the costs of certain concessions. In this context, it will be interesting to see the final outcome of the United States-China BIT negotiations.

In contrast, on aid, China has benefited from bypassing the existing system and by offering an alternative. In doing so, it has succeeded in gaining access to the resources and markets necessary for its continued growth and consequent quiet on the domestic front. Although it can be claimed that China is operating within the development aid system (and perhaps even influencing it in a positive way), it may also be claimed that China is upsetting the status quo. We will only know in time what the long-term effect its behavior will have.

CONCLUSION

Is China challenging the rules and norms of the international economic order? As has been shown, China is not seeking significant change in the international trade order, neither through its behavior in the WTO nor in its PTAs.

It is conforming to the far-reaching commitments it took on when it joined the WTO—it has become an engaged participant (rather than a spoiler) in the WTO Doha Round negotiations after an initial period of reticence, and it has accepted and become an active participant in WTO dispute resolution despite its historical rejection of international adjudication. And to ensure that it has a seat at the table in international trade rule making, China has requested to participate in the multilateral negotiations on trade in the TISA negotiations, even though it had originally objected to negotiations taking place outside the WTO. Its willingness to compromise on the ITA negotiations is another sign that China does not want to be a spoiler in the multilateral trading system.

Like other countries, China has also turned to FTAs to enhance its bilateral and regional economic and political relations. Although its FTAs and regional agreements differ from those of the United States or the EU, those of the United States and the EU do not look the same either. By not taking a template approach, China's agreements permit more sensitivity to the particular needs of its trading partners than those of the United States and the EU. In this context, they allow for incremental liberalization, starting first with goods and later services. In addition, China does not impose WTO-plus rules on its partners as the United States and the EU do. Its bilateral and regional agreements have taken on particular importance in view of the protracted impasse in the WTO negotiations and Western-led mega agreements. It is in its bilateral and regional agreements that China is to some extent, pushing back, among other things, by trying to correct what it considered to be unfairly imposed on it as part of its accession (e.g., NME methodology in anti-dumping investigations) or by promoting its own regional agreements, such as the RCEP and the FTAAP.

Regarding investment, the large number of BITs China has signed (second only to Germany), in addition to the investment chapters it has incorporated into its FTAs, is testimony to China's positive engagement with the existing international investment regime. Nevertheless, China's transformation from being a major importer of FDI to both a major importer *and* exporter of FDI is impacting the international investment system. Developed and developing countries alike are concerned about China's growing outward FDI. While some are worried about the state-owned nature of China's outward investors,[72] others are worried about losing control of their natural resources. Some countries (e.g., South Africa) have gone so far as to terminate their BITs (for reasons unrelated to China per se, but rather for concern with exposure to international arbitration). Both the United States and the EU have formulated new policies; US policy is embodied in a new model BIT (2012), and EU policy in recent negotiating directives. For these and other reasons, the international investment treaty regime is currently in flux.

China's policies regarding BITs are continuing to evolve, in part, as a consequence of its BIT negotiations with the United States. Prior to Trump's election, it appeared that China's BIT evolution was moving in the direction that the United States is pushing for. The negotiations led China to accept new norms—including preestablishment national treatment and a negative list approach to exceptions. In the past, China, like the EU, would only agree to post-establishment national treatment. China's justification for accepting these new norms, that "it wants to go along with the new trend in the world," is another indication of positive engagement within the existing framework.

In contrast with trade and investment where China has adapted to the prevailing norms and is positively engaged with the regimes, China's development aid philosophy and policies are coming into direct conflict with Western norms. China's "no strings attached" approach to providing development aid constitutes a strong challenge to traditional donor aid. Moreover, China is providing an alternative source of loans on better terms, at lower interest rates and with longer repayment periods. China's aid to build infrastructure projects (e.g., roads, railways, bridges) and to support education, agriculture, and health care, all geared to the specific needs and requests of the recipient, goes up against the political and economic reform agenda of traditional donor aid. China is simply not playing by the same rules. In addition, China is in the process of establishing a major development aid institution, the AIIB. We do not know yet whether the AIIB will represent an alternative, and possibly competing aid track, or whether it will complement the traditional development aid institutions. China's rhetoric and early policies indicate that the AIIB is adopting international best practices such as good governance, transparency, and labor and environmental standards, but at the same time China has also stressed the particular needs of the Asian region. In addition, and perhaps an even bigger challenge to the existing global development financing system, is China's BRI, encompassing some sixty-eight countries.

How can the variation in China's profile be explained? A rationalist state-centric approach, based on cost-benefit calculations and interests, plays a crucial role in understanding China's incoherent profile in international economic governance. Such a perspective would suggest that China's profile is based on cost-benefit calculations in each of the three areas, leading to the maintenance of the status quo, wherein the benefits of preserving the status quo outweigh the costs of challenging it. We see this in China's positions toward both international trade and in international investment. To date, China has profited from the prevailing global trading system, particularly in terms of economic growth critical to the present leadership's control. China has also succeeded in safeguarding its interests through the existing fragmented international investment system. A cost-benefit calculation is clearly evident in China's willingness to compromise in its various BIT negotiations, given the potential benefits of better access for its outward foreign investments and interest in attracting FDI. In contrast, regarding the international development aid regime, China has benefited far more from challenging the status quo than from maintaining it. To be sure, circumventing the system with its own development financing model has provided China with access to the natural resources and markets vital to its economic development.

A liberal institutional approach provides additional insight into the variation in China's profile in the three regimes. Just as the regimes differ significantly from one another, so does China's policy vis-à-vis the regimes. The central institution in the international trade regime is the WTO—an inclusive, consensus-based organization, where China has veto power over rules change. China believes strongly in WTO rules and considers the WTO special, unlike other international institutions. The leadership has exploited the constraining effect of the WTO by using its rules as a lever to achieve economic reform and to promote the rule of law. Regarding investment, the fragmented nature of international investment treaty framework suggests that no single power completely dominates the rule-making process, particularly now, when the BIT system is in flux. Institutional factors thus support China's engagement within the international investment regime.

A normative perspective also contributes to our understanding of China's profile in the international economic governance, now and in the future. As China is socialized into the global economic order, it is becomes further entrenched in the existing system and consequently has a larger stake in the perpetuation of the status quo. At the same time, China is gaining a better understanding of how the system works, along with the actors in it. It is therefore not surprising that with increased interaction, China, like other actors, is also working toward making aspects of the system work to its advantage.

What does this imply for China and the broader debate regarding its challenge to the international economic order? My sense is that China's national interests, the constraining effect of the institutions in the liberal international economic order, and China's ongoing socialization will continue to drive it toward upholding the status quo, albeit with modest and incremental efforts for reform from within.

NOTES

1. "Development aid," "development assistance," and "development financing" are used interchangeably in the chapter. China's aid is perhaps best described as "development financing" since much does not fall into the commonly used OECD-DAC definition of overseas development assistance. Shambaugh explains that China's aid "straddles the line between aid and overseas investment, involves private

companies, and [China] gives loans that often do not have a grant element over 25 percent" (Hameiri 2015, 202–5).

2. This chapter makes no judgment as to the merits of maintaining the existing norms and rules of the global economic system. On this, Scott Kennedy argues that the existing system is not perfect and that China should try to promote change (Kennedy 2012).

3. Launched at the Twenty-First ASEAN Summit in Cambodia in November 2012. According to estimates, the trade of participating countries accounts for about 40 percent of world trade.

4. Henry Gao argues that China has gone from rule taker to rule shaker and even rule maker in the WTO (Gao 2011); Peter Yu argues that China's bilateral and regional trade agreements follow a different pattern than those of the dominant players, the United States and the EU (Yu 2011); Nargiza Salidjanova suggests that China is "promoting alternate norms" (Salidjanova 2015, 30–31).

5. On the new bank as a rival to the World Bank and Asian Development Bank, see Feng (2014).

6. China joined the World Bank and the IMF in 1980, after almost a decade of preparation. On China's interaction with the World Bank and the IMF, see Jacobson and Oksenberg (1990).

7. China's willingness to make concessions to its FTA partners to the disadvantage of its domestic industry is well documented, for example, in the case of its agreement with ASEAN. See Chin and Stubbs (2011, 289); Ravenhill and Yang (2009, 31–32, 38–40). In China's WTO accession negotiations, despite expected domestic unrest by farmers and opposition by vested ministerial interests, Wei Liang notes that the drawn out negotiations were only concluded as a result of the personal intervention of China's top leaders (Wei 2002, 716–18).

8. Thomas J. Christensen notes the growing number of bureaucracies that are involved in the foreign policy making process such as the military, energy companies, exporters, and regional party elites (Christensen 2011, 60).

9. For example, it has been suggested that Xi's campaign against corruption is also serving to rid Xi of political rivals. Other measures such as the proposed law on foreign NGOs may impede the development of China's civil society and prevent critique of the government. At the Nineteenth National Congress of the Communist Party in October 2017, Xi Jinping further consolidated his position when the National Congress approved an amendment to the Party Constitution, "Xi Jinping Thought on Socialism with Chinese Characteristics for a New Era" (An 2017).

10. UNCTAD defines mega regional agreements as "broad economic agreements among a group of countries that have a significant combined economic weight" (UNCTAD 2014, XXIV). Whalley refers to such agreements as "large-large" negotiations in contrast to small-small or large-small regional trade agreements (Whalley 2014). Meléndez-Ortiz defines mega regionals as "deep integration partnerships between countries or regions with a major share of world trade and FDI and in which two or more of the parties are in a paramount driver position, or serve as hubs, in global value chains" (Meléndez-Ortiz 2014).

11. Agreement between Australia, Brunei, Chile, Canada, Japan, Malaysia, Mexico, New Zealand, Peru, Singapore, United States, and Vietnam) finalized on October

5, 2015. The agreement covers about one-third of world trade and 40 percent of global GDP (Calmes 2015).

12. Negotiations between the United States and the EU that started in July 2013.

13. The WTO accession process is a one-way negotiating process. Acceding countries are asked to make concessions without being able to make reciprocal demands, while existing WTO members are entitled to make demands without making any concessions, thus subjecting acceding members to enormous pressure.

14. For example, see Kennedy (2012, 79–80); Kong (2012, 299–339); *Reuters* (2014).

15. WTO members make two kinds of commitments—rules-based commitments which are normally uniform for all WTO members and market access commitments which are made on a member-by-member basis and thus differ among members.

16. For example, China agreed to a special transitional review for its first eight years in the WTO, and in its tenth year. For discussion of China's WTO-plus obligations, see Obama (2015a).

17. China agreed to be considered a non-market economy (NME) until the end of 2016 for calculating dumping in anti-dumping investigations (Article 15 of the Protocol of Accession), with the use of a higher cost surrogate country to determine the domestic price, thus making it more likely to find higher dumping margins. Similarly, in countervailing duty investigations, China agreed to an alternative benchmark in calculating its subsidies, thus increasing the probability of WTO members applying countervailing duties. In contrast to the NME provision in anti-dumping, the alterative benchmark provision regarding subsidies does not expire. Now that deadline for the provision regarding NME methodology has passed, China is certain that members are obligated to change their methodology and in December 2016 filed lawsuits in the WTO against the United States and the EU for continuing to apply it.

18. This accusation has been cited in a number of articles. See, for example, Kitano and Harada (2014).

19. Although withdrawing from an international organization or treaty appears far-fetched, in 2013 South Africa terminated its bilateral investment treaties with Germany, the Netherlands, Spain, and Switzerland. Bolivia, Ecuador (2009), and Venezuela (2012) have withdrawn from the ICSID Convention (UNCTAD 2014, 114). Italy recently notified its withdrawal from the Energy Charter, although its obligations will remain in effect for twenty additional years (UNCTAD 2015, 107). At the WTO's Bali Ministerial in 2013, some WTO members, in an unprecedented move, reneged on their original commitment to the Bali Package, although agreement was eventually achieved (*Economic Times* 2014).

20. For more on China's view of its implementation, see Yang (2015a, 2015b).

21. For example, Webster argues that China has only superficially complied with WTO rulings (Webster 2014).

22. For instance, by coming to an agreement for a "reasonable period of time" in a timely manner, by holding discussions toward changing or eliminating its illegal measures and by implementing its commitment in good faith and within the "reasonable period of time" (Mavroidis 2000).

23. The United States has spent years dragging out implementation of the WTO ruling on its Copyright Act, a dispute initiated by the E. C. in 1999. As of August

31, 2017, the United States implementation of the WTO ruling was still on the WTO agenda as a surveillance matter (WTO 2017).

24. For example, see Bergsten (2008).

25. The 2008 mini-ministerial is often cited as an example of China being responsible for the breakdown of the talks because of its support for India against the United States on the Special Safeguard Mechanism. Scott and Wilkenson, based on interviews with participants, argue that China was trying to broker a deal between India and the United States, rather than supporting India (Scott and Rorden 2013, 776).

26. As of July 2008, China had submitted over 100 proposals in the Doha Round negotiations (Gao 2011).

27. China's proposals on anti-dumping are an example of this. China's position might be explained by the fact that it is the world's largest target of anti-dumping action, and therefore its interests lie in stricter anti-dumping rules; nevertheless, the bottom line is that it is promoting a pro-trade liberalization agenda.

28. China, along with India and the Philippines, was particularly supportive of food security, one of the three potential deliverables at Bali (the other two were trade facilitation and development).

29. The agreement is called the Environmental Goods Agreement (EGA). For the official statement, see (Joint statement 2014). Negotiations were launched in July 2014.

30. Though considered to be holding up the negotiations with its request for exemptions on a long list of goods, China and the United States achieved a breakthrough in November 2014 after China agreed to a compromise (*Reuters* 2014).

31. China's request was rejected out of concern that China would hinder the talks (Donnon 2013).

32. The United States, for example, has a history of using PTAs to promote norms that it would like to be incorporated into the multilateral framework. NAFTA is considered an example of this.

33. For a list and description of China's PTAs, see Ministry of Commerce 2018. The Cross-Straits Economic Framework Agreement between Mainland China and Taipei is not included in the twelve PTAs.

34. Articles on China's FTAs include Gao (2011); Kong (2012); Yu (2011); Jun and Webster (2011).

35. China resumed sovereignty over Hong Kong in 1997 and Macao in 1999. Both were members of the WTO prior to the People's Republic of China and are referred to as Hong Kong, China, and Macao, China, respectively in the WTO.

36. For a description of China's incremental approach to ASEAN, see Yu (2011, 1007–1009).

37. The link is implied by the WTO Secretariat (WTO 2006, 45; Kong 2012, 1203).

38. Yu (2011, 962) notes that the EU trade agreements cover "nontrade areas "such as competition policy, investment, improvement of business environment, cooperation in vocational education and training, labor and product standards, environmental protection, tourism, illegal migration, and the resolution of other non-economic cross-border problems." Some of these areas are in fact also covered in

US FTAs. Where the EU model differs is in the political aspects that it includes, for example, the political dialogue it calls for in its association agreements.

39. Yu notes that China does not use a template approach in its FTAs nor is it interested in one (Yu 2011, 1011–18).

40. On China's FTAs and services, see Wang (2012). China's services agreements take the GATS model of positive list approach, rather than NAFTA's negative list approach where all services sectors are included except what is excluded.

41. Six original ASEAN members are Philippines, Singapore, Thailand, Indonesia, Brunei Darussalam, and Malaysia, while the four newer (and less developed) members are Vietnam, Laos, Cambodia, and Myanmar. For an analysis of China's approach to the negotiations, see Chin and Stubbs (2011).

42. China's FTAs with New Zealand, Singapore, and Switzerland include provisions on labor standards and competition. China's FTA with Switzerland refers to sustainable development and devotes an entire chapter to environmental issues (Free Trade Agreement 2013, chapter 12). On the acceptance of increasingly legalized dispute settlement provisions, see Harpaz (2015).

43. At the end of 2013, there were 3,236 BITs and other international investment agreements (UNCTAD 2015, 114).

44. Indeed, Bath and Nottage note that some countries have omitted investment chapters in their FTAs due to reservations about investor-state arbitration (Bath and Nottage 2011, 2). Investor-state arbitration is also one of the issues that held up the ratification of CETA, the Comprehensive Economic and Trade Agreement, concluded in September 2014 between Canada and the EU. The agreement was finally signed by the sides in 2016, and as of this writing is awaiting ratification by the EU member states. In the meantime, most of the provisions are being applied provisionally.

45. For example, OECD Council Recommendation on Recipient Country Policies relating to National Security.

46. Efforts to achieve multilateral agreement on investment in the OECD failed in 1998. Investment, one of the four Singapore issues, was eventually dropped from the negotiating agenda along with government procurement and competition. Negotiations on the fourth, trade facilitation, culminated in the agreement in Bali.

47. According to UNCTAD, in 2014, "at least 50 countries and regions were engaged in reviewing and revising their IIA models. Brazil, India, Norway, and the European Union (EU) published novel approaches. South Africa and Indonesia continued their treaty terminations, while formulating new IIA strategies" (UNCTAD 2015, xi).

48. For a brief description of China's "Going Out" policy, see Shambaugh (2013, 174–83). See also Berger (2008, 6). Berger describes the reasons that China's outward FDI has grown: transfer of plants to lower wage economies, acquisition of technology and knowhow, use of brand names, and access to new markets.

49. Leon Trakmen describes three model BITs: one from the early 1980s, the second from 1992, and the third from 1998 to contribute to its "going out" policy (Trakmen 2013). Shan, Gallagher, and Sheng suggest that the inclusion of a national treatment standard from 1986 in the China UK BIT characterized a new model in Chinese BITs (Shan, Gallagher, and Sheng 2012).

50. Although too soon to tell for certain, it seems that another area where China is considering new norms (in contrast to Washington-dominated ICSID arbitration) is in investor-state arbitration for its BRI arrangements (Peled and Harpaz 2018, 24).

51. For example, Australia's foreign investment regime has a "national interest" exception, which includes national security and also covers impact of investment on the economy (Bath 2013, 87).

52. Under the US foreign investment review system, the Committee on Foreign Investment in the United States (CFIUS) makes a recommendation that is enforced by order of the US President. Headed by the US Treasury Secretary, CFIUS includes representatives of justice, home security, commerce, state, and energy. The Chinese telecom company Huawei backed out of the US market after a 2012 House Intelligence Committee Report came out discouraging US companies from partnering with Huawei, citing security concerns. See Tiezzi (2013).

53. There is some debate about the degree of discrimination toward Chinese investors compared to other foreign investors (Moran 2015, 2).

54. One of the issues raised in the 2010 national elections was investment by Chinese sovereign wealth funds in Australia. In the past, Chinese investment has been blocked in the Australian telecom sector (2012) and mining sector (2009).

55. SOEs, the scope of the national security exception and anti-monopoly law, are the most difficult issues in the US–China BIT negotiations (Inside 2015).

56. The news report suggests that factors driving China's concessions include its increased interest in investing in the United States and the slowdown in its economy.

57. In contrast, Ngair Woods argues that new donors are not challenging the system outright; rather they are bringing competitive pressures into the system (Woods 2008). Deborah Bräutigam argues that, in fact, Chinese practices are not that far from those of traditional donors (Bräutigam 2012).

58. The term was originally coined by John Williamson (1990).

59. Interestingly, despite efforts to coordinate aid among major DAC donors since the Paris Declaration, coordination has declined. Fuchs, Nunenkamp, and Ohler have shown that this can be attributed to competition for export markets and political influence (Fuchs, Nunnenkamp, and Ohler 2013).

60. For analysis, see Zhou (2014).

61. However, Chin notes that estimating China's aid is difficult because China does not use the DAC definitions of foreign aid; various agencies are responsible for providing aid; China may not want to publicize the real amounts of aid, given its domestic poverty; the figures do not include unreported aid to Iran, North Korea, Cuba, and other outlier regimes (Chin 2012b, 581–82).

62. This may be construed as suggesting that domestic politics explain China's aid. Shahar Hameiri argues that because China's aid is driven by "commercial imperatives" it is not operating according to "master plan," implying that a domestic interest paradigm is the main explanation for China's aid policy (Hameiri 2015). However, one does not preclude the other, and in my view, this is a type of mechanism used to implement an overall state strategy.

63. This recommendation was amended in 2006, 2008, and 2011. The OECD rules are only a recommendation, related to LDCs, and some areas, such as food aid and

free-standing technical cooperation, were excluded. Non-DAC donors such as China are considered to be challenges to efforts to untie aid even though China has endorsed the Paris-Accra-Busan Partnership for Effective Development Co-operation in the form of Global Partnership for Effective Development Cooperation.

64. Chin points to the signing of the "Memorandum of Understanding (MOU) on Cooperation between the Export–Import Bank of China and the International Bank for Reconstruction and Development," as evidence of this.

65. For information about the China-Asian Development Bank relationship, see International Monetary Fund, People's Republic of China 2013 Article IV Report (International Monetary Fund 2013, 10–12).

66. For a short history of the AIIB, see Ba (2014, 162–64).

67. For example, see address by Mr. Zhou Ziangwu, the Executive Deputy Director-General of the Asia-Pacific Finance and Development Centre, associated with the Chinese Ministry of Finance at the 2015 Australasian Aid Conference on February 13–14, 2015 (Zhou 2015).

68. For a more critical review, see Chow (2017).

69. Xi Jinping laid out his "New Era" vision for China's future in his speech to the leadership of the Chinese Communist Party at the Nineteenth Party Congress on October 17, 2017 (Xi 2017).

70. Chin concludes that China is not trying to undermine the World Bank, but rather reshape some of the norms (Chin 2012a, 223).

71. Professor Peter Yu, in a private conversation, suggested to me that while there may not be external coherence in China's policies over the three areas, there is internal coherence, and, in fact, China's policies in all three areas are shaped by its development needs.

72. Stemming from concern over subsidies which give the foreign state owned enterprise a competitive advantage or that there might be concern that they will pursue a noncommercial agenda.

BIBLIOGRAPHY

Agreement on Dispute Settlement Mechanism of the Framework Agreement on Comprehensive Economic Co-operation between the Association of Southeast Asian Nations and the People's Republic of China, 2004. http://www.asean.org/communities/asean-economic-community/item/agreement-on-dispute-settlement-mechanism-of-the-framework-agreement-on-comprehensive-economic-co-operation-between-the-association-of-southeast-asian-nations-and-the-people-s-republic-of-china-5.

An, Baijie. "Xi Jinping Thought Approved for Party Constitution." *China Daily*, October 24, 2017. http://www.chinadaily.com.cn/china/19thcpcnationalcongress/2017-10/24/content_33644524.htm.

Azêvedo, Roberto. "Azêvedo Cites China's Crucial Role in Trade Liberalization." Speech by WTO Director-General Roberto Azevêdo on 19 May 2014 at University of Business and Economics, Beijing. https://www.wto.org/english/news_e/spra_e/spra22_e.htm.

Ba, Alice. "Is China Leading? China, Southeast Asia and East Asian Integration." *Political Science* 66(2) (2014): 143–46.

Bath, Vivienne. "National Security and Chinese Investment Policy." *Harvard Business, Law Review Online* 3 (2013): 81–91.

Bath, Vivienne, and Luke R. Nottage. "Foreign Investment and Dispute Settlement Law in Asia: An Overview." Sydney Law School Working Paper, March 2011.

BBC News. "China Agrees to Resume US Investment Treaty Talks." July 12, 2013. http://www.bbc.com/news/business-23267381.

Berger, Axel. "China's New Bilateral Investment Treaty Programme: Substance, Rational and Implications for International Law Making." Paper prepared for the American Society of International Law International Economic Law Interest Group (ASIL IELIG) 2008 biennial conference *The Politics of International Economic Law: The Next Four Years*, Washington, DC, November 14–15, 2008. https://www.die-gdi.de/uploads/media/Berger_ChineseBITs.pdf.

Berger, Axel. "The Politics of China's Investment Treaty-making Program." In Broude, T., Busch, M. L., and Porges, A. (eds.), *The Politics of International Economic Law*. Cambridge: Cambridge University Press, 2011: 162–86.

Bergsten, C. Fred. "Partnership of Equals: How Washington Should Respond to China's Economic Challenge." *Foreign Affairs* 87(4) (July 2008): 57–69.

Bräutigam, Deborah. *The Dragon's Gift: The Real Story of China in Africa*. Oxford: Oxford University Press, 2009.

Bräutigam, Deborah. "Is China a Challenge to the Global Aid Architecture?" APSA 2012 Annual Meeting Paper. http://ssrn.com/abstract=2106387.

Calmes, Jackie. "Trans-Pacific Partnership Is Reached But Faces Scrutiny in Congress." *New York Times*, October 5, 2015.

Cheng, Shuaihua, Ting Fang, and Hui-ting Lien. "China's Foreign Aid Policy." In Kennedy, S. and Cheng, S. (eds.), *The Growing Role of Chinese in Global Governance*. Bloomington, IN: Research Center for Chinese Politics and Business, and Geneva: International Centre for Trade and Sustainable Development, 2012: 103–12.

Chin, Gregory. "Two-Way Socialization: China, the World Bank and Hegemonic Weakening." *Brown Journal of World Affairs* 19(1) (Fall/Winter 2012a): 211–30.

Chin, Gregory. "China as a Net Donor: Tracking Dollars and Sense." *Cambridge Review of International Affairs* 25(4) (2012b): 579–603.

Chin, Gregory. "Asian Infrastructure Investment Bank: Governance Innovation and Prospects." *Global Governance* 22(1) (2016): 11–25.

Chin, Gregory, and Richard Stubbs. "China and Regional Institutional Building and the China-ASEAN Free Trade Agreement." *Review of International Political Economy* 18(3) (2011): 277–98.

Chin, Gregory, and Ramesh Thakur. "Will China Changes the Rules of the Global Order?" *Washington Quarterly* 33(4) (2010): 119–38.

Chin, Gregory, and Fahimul Quadir. "Introduction: Rising States, Rising Donors and the Global Aid Regime." *Cambridge Review of International Affairs* 25(4) (2012): 493–506.

Chow, Lowell. "Is the AIIB Really 'Lean, Clean, and Green'?" *The Diplomat*, August 2, 2017.

Christensen, Thomas J. "The Advantages of an Assertive China." *Foreign Affairs* 90(2) (2011): 54–67.

"Department of Foreign Affairs and Trade, Outcomes at a Glance." *Australian Government* site, n.d. http:///dfat.gov.au/trade/agreements/chafta/fact-sheets/Pages/key-outcomes.aspx.

Donnon, Shawn. "China in Push to Join US-led $4tn Services Trade Talks." *Financial Times*, September 23, 2013.

Dyer, Geoff. "Obama Says AIIB Could Be Positive for Asia." *Financial Times*, April 28, 2015.

Eckert, Paul, and Anna Yukananov. "U.S., China Agree to Restart Investment Treaty Talks." *Reuters*, July 12, 2015. http://www.reuters.com/article/us-usa-china-dialogue-trade-idUSBRE96A0ZD20130712.

Economic Times. "India Says No Trade Facilitation Pact without Solving Food Security Issue." July 3, 2014.

Economist. "Our Bulldozers, Our Rules." July 2, 2016. https://www.economist.com/news/china/21701505-chinas-foreign-policy-could-reshape-good-part-world-economy-our-bulldozers-our-rules.

European Union, Regulation (EU) no. 1219/2012 of the European Parliament and of the Council of 12 December 2012 establishing transitional arrangements for bilateral investment agreements between member states and third countries. http://eur-lex.europa.eu/legal-content/EN/TXT/?uri=CELEX%3A32012R1219.

Feng, Bree. "Deal Set on China-led Infrastructure Bank." *New York Times*, October 24, 2014.

Free Trade Agreement between the Government of the People's Republic of China and the Government of the Republic of Peru, 2009. http://fta.mofcom.gov.cn/bilu/annex/bilu_xdwb_en.pdf.

Free Trade Agreement between the Government of the People's Republic of China and the Swiss Federation, 2013. http://fta.mofcom.gov.cn/topic/enswiss.shtml.

Fu, Jing, and Wu Jiao. "President Calls for World Wide Free Trade." *China Daily*, September 7, 2013. http://europe.chinadaily.com.cn/china/2013-09/07/content_16950983.htm.

Fuchs, Andreas, Peter Nunnenkamp, and Hannes Ohler. "Why Donors of Foreign Aid Do not Coordinate: The Role of Competition for Export Markets and Political Support." *Kiel Working Paper* No. 1825 (February 2013).

Gao, Henry. "China's Strategy for Free Trade Agreements: Political Battle in the Name of Trade." In Buckley, R. P., Hu, R. W., and Arner, D. W. (eds.), *East Asian Economic Integration: Law, Trade and Finance*. Cheltenham, UK: Edward Elgar, 2011: 104–20.

Gao, Henry. "China's Ascent in Global Trade Governance: From Rule Taker to Rule Shaker, and Maybe Rule Maker." In Deere Bierbeek, Carolyn (ed.), *Making Global Trade Governance Work for Development: Perspectives and Priorities from Developing Countries*. Cambridge: Cambridge University Press, 2011: 153–81.

Gao, Hucheng. Statement by H. E. Mr. Hucheng Gao, Minister of Commerce, at Bali Ministerial, WT/MIN(13)/ST/99, January 24, 2014.

Hameiri, Shahar. "China's Charm Offensive in the Pacific and Australia's Regional Order." *The Pacific Review* 28(5) (2015): 631–54.

Hanlon, Robert J. "Thinking about the Asian Infrastructure Investment Bank: Can a China-led Development Bank Improve Sustainability." *Asia and the Pacific Policy Studies* 4(3) (2017): 541–54.

Harpaz, Marcia D. "China's WTO-compliance Plus Anti-dumping Policy." *Journal of World Trade* 45(4) (2011): 727–66.

Harpaz, Marcia D. "Making Sense of China's WTO Compliance." Doctoral thesis, Hebrew University of Jerusalem, 2012.

Harpaz, Marcia D. "China and International Tribunals: Onward from the WTO." In Toohey, L., Picker, C., and Greenacre, J. (eds.), *China in the New International Economic Order: New Directions and Changing Paradigms*. Cambridge: Cambridge University Press, 2015: 43–61.

Hufbauer, Gary Clyde, Sean Miner, and Theodore Moran. "Committee on Foreign Investment in the United States and the US–China Bilateral Investment Treaty: Challenges in Meeting China's Demands." In *Towards a US–China Investment Treaty*. Washington, DC: Peterson Institute for International Economics, 2015: 34–41.

Hsu, Sara. "How China's Asia Infrastructure Bank Fared Its First Year." *Forbes*, January 24, 2017.

Inside US–China Trade. "U.S.–China 'Core Text' Still Outstanding, Beijing 'Negative List' Offer Could Spur Progress: Business Rep." January 26, 2015. https://www.uschina.org/media/inthenews/us-china-bit-core-text-still-outstanding-beijing-negative-list-offer-could-spur.

International Monetary Fund. "People's Republic of China 2013 Article IV Report, Informational Annex." http://www.imf.org/external/pubs/ft/scr/2013/cr13211.pdf.

Jacobson, Harold K., and Michel Oksenberg. *China's Participation in the IMF, the World Bank, and GATT*. Ann Arbor: University of Michigan Press, 1990.

"Joint Statement Regarding Trade in Environmental Goods." January 24, 2014. http://trade.ec.europa.eu/doclib/docs/2014/january/tradoc_152095.pdf.

Kennedy, Scott. "China in Global Governance: What Kind of Status Quo Power?" In Kennedy, Scott and Cheng, Shuaihua (eds.), *The Growing Role of Chinese in Global Governance*. Indiana University, RCCPB and Geneva ICTSD, 2012: 9–22.

Kent, Ann. *Beyond Compliance: China, International Organizations and Global Security*. Palo Alto, CA: Stanford University Press, 2007.

Kitano, Naohiro, and Yukinori Harada. "Estimating China's Foreign Aid 2001–2013." JICA-RI Working Paper No.78 (2014).

Kong, Qingjiang. "China's Uncharted FTA Strategy." *Journal of World Trade* 46(5) (2012): 1191–206.

Krauss, Clifford, and Keith Bradsher. "China's Global Ambitions, with Loans and Strings Attached." *New York Times*, July 24, 2015.

Lardy, Nicholas. *Integrating China into the Global Economy*. Washington, DC: Brookings Institute Press, 2002.

Manuel, Anja. "China Is Quietly Reshaping the World." *Atlantic*, October 17, 2017. https://www.theatlantic.com/international/archive/2017/10/china-belt-and-road/542667/.

Matoo, Aaditya. "China's Accession to the WTO: The Services Dimension." *Journal of International Economic Law* 6(2) (2003): 299–339.

Mavroidis, Petros C. "Remedies in the WTO Legal System." *European Journal of International Law* 11(8) (2000): 793–99.

Meléndez-Ortiz, Ricardo. "Mega Regionals: What Is Going On?" In *Mega Regional Trade Agreements: Game Changers or Costly Distractions for the World Trading System*. Presented in Geneva, Switzerland: World Economic Forum, July 2014. http://www3.weforum.org/docs/GAC/2014/WEF_GAC_TradeFDI_MegaRegionalTradeAgreements_Report_2014.pdf.

Ministry of Commerce, People's Republic of China. "Ministry of Commerce's Regulation on Implementing of the Security Review System for Mergers and Acquisitions of Domestic Enterprises by Foreign Investors." August 25, 2011.

Ministry of Commerce, People's Republic of China. "MOFCOM Spokesman Shen Danyang Comments on China and US to Promote Negotiations on Bilateral Investment Agreement." July 16, 2013. http://english.mofcom.gov.cn/article/newsrelease/policyreleasing/201307/20130700200566.shtml.

Ministry of Commerce, People's Republic of China. "Announcement No. 86 (on Trade Compliance Implementation Measures) (Trial)." December 14, 2014. http://www.e-to-china.com/tariff_changes/Policy_Focus/2014/1219/112637.html.

Ministry of Commerce, People's Republic of China. "Gao Hucheng Attends and Addresses the 10th World Trade Ministerial Conference." December 18, 2015a. http://english.mofcom.gov.cn/article/newsrelease/significantnews/201512/20151201219006.shtml.

Ministry of Commerce, People's Republic of China. "Gao Hucheng Attends WTO Seven Parties Ministers' Meeting." October 9, 2015b. http://english.mofcom.gov.cn/article/newsrelease/significantnews/201510/20151001131740.shtml.

Ministry of Commerce, People's Republic of China. "China FTA Network." 2018. http://fta.mofcom.gov.cn/english/index.shtml.

Moran, Theodore. *Chinese Investment and CFIUS: Time for an Updated (and Revised) Perspective*. Policy brief, Washington, DC: Peterson Institute for International Economics, Number PB15-17, September 2015.

Moynihan, H. 2017. "China's Evolving Approach to International Dispute Settlement." *Chatham House Brief*, March 29, 2017. https://www.chathamhouse.org/publication/chinas-evolving-approach-international-dispute-settlement.

Murphy, Katharine. "Tony Abbott Says Chinese State Owned Enterprises Are Welcome in Australia." *Guardian*, April 11, 2014.

Obama, B. 2012. "Order Regarding the Acquisition of Four U.S. Wind Farm Project Companies by Ralls Corporation." September 28, 2012. https://www.gpo.gov/fdsys/pkg/DCPD-201200764/pdf/DCPD-201200764.pdf.

Obama, Barack. "Remarks by the President in State of the Union Address." Washington, DC, 2015a. http://www.whitehouse.gov/the-press-office/2015/01/20/remarks-president-state-union-address-january-20-2015.

Obama, Barack. "Statement by the President on the Trans-Pacific Partnership." Washington, DC, 2015b. https://www.whitehouse.gov/the-press-office/2015/10/05/statement-president-trans-pacific-partnership/.

OECD. "DAC Recommendation on Untying Official Development Assistance to the Least Developed Countries." Last modified May 2001. www.oecd.org/dac/htm/Untie.htm.

OECD. "Paris Declaration on Aid Effectiveness." Last modified 2005. http://www.oecd.org/dac/effectiveness/34428351.pdf.

OECD. "2006–2014: Summaries of Roundtable on Freedom of Investment, National Security and Strategic Industries." n.d. http://www.oecd.org/investment/investment-policy/oecdroundtablesonfreedomofinvestment.htm.

Pearson, Margaret. "China in Geneva: Lessons from China's Early Years in the World Trade Organization." In Johnston, A. I. and Ross, R. (eds.), *China's Foreign Policy*. Palo Alto, CA: Stanford University Press, 2006: 242–75.

Peled, Hadas, and Marcia D. Harpaz. "Innovation as a Catalyst in the China–Israel Investment Relationship: The China–Israel BIT (2009) and the Prospective FTA." Forthcoming in Chaisse, J. (ed.), *China's Three-prong Investment Strategy: Bilateral, Regional, and Global Tracks*. Oxford University Press, Hebrew University of Jerusalem legal research paper; Hebrew University of Jerusalem international law forum working series 01-18 (2018). https://papers.ssrn.com/sol3/papers.cfm?abstract_id=3109431.

Perlez, Jane. "US Opposing China's Answer to the World Bank." *New York Times*, October 9, 2014.

Ravenhill, John, and Yang Jiang. "China's Move to Preferential Trading: A New Direction in China's Diplomacy." *Journal of Contemporary China* 18(58) (2009): 27–46.

Reuters. "China, U.S. Make Breakthrough on IT Free Trade Deal: U.S. Trade Representative." November 14, 2014. http://www.reuters.com/article/us-apec-china-ita-idUSKCN0IV06E20141111.

Salidjanova, Nargiza. *China's Trade Ambitions: Strategy and Objectives behind China's Pursuit of Free Trade Agreements*. Washington, DC: U.S.–China Economic and Security Review Commission: Staff Research Report, 2015. http://origin.www.uscc.gov/sites/default/files/Research/China%27s%20Trade%20Ambitions%20-%2005.28%2015.pdf.

Scott, James, and Rorden Wilkinson. "China Threat? Evidence from the WTO." *Journal of World Trade* 47(4) (2013): 761–82.

Shambaugh, David. *China Goes Global: The Partial Power*. Oxford: Oxford University Press, 2013.

Shan, Wenhua, Norah Gallagher, and Sheng Zhang. "National Treatment in Foreign Investment in China: A Changing Landscape." *ICSID Review* 27(1) (2012): 120–44.

State Council of the People's Republic of China. "Notice of the General Office of the State Council on Launching the Security Review System for Mergers and Acquisitions of Domestic Enterprises by Foreign Investors." February 3, 2011.

State Council of the People's Republic of China. "China's Foreign Aid." 2011. http://news.xinhuanet.com/english2010/china/2011-04/21/c_13839683.htm.

State Council of the People's Republic of China. "China's Foreign Aid." 2014. http://news.xinhuanet.com/english/china/2014-07/10/c_133474011.htm.

Sun, Zhenyu. "Statement of H. E. Ambassador Sun Zhenyu at the Informal Trade Negotiations Committee Meeting." July 31, 2008. http://wto2.mofcom.gov.cn/article/aboutus/mission/200807/20080705700132.shtml.

Talley, Ian. "U.S. Looks to Work with China-led Infrastructure Fund." *Wall Street Journal*, March 22, 2015.

Tiezzi, Shannon. "Huawei Officially Gives up on the US Market." *Diplomat*, December 5, 2013. http://thediplomat.com/2013/12/huawei-officially-gives-up-on-the-us-market/.

Tiezzi, Shannon. "China's Push for an Asia-Pacific Free Trade Agreement: China Hopes the FTAAP Will Overshadow Less Inclusive Alternatives, Like the Trans-Pacific Partnership." *The Diplomat*, October 30, 2014. http://thediplomat.com/2014/10/chinas-push-for-an-asia-pacific-free-trade-agreement/.

Trakmen, Leon E. "China and Foreign Direct Investment: Looking Ahead." *UNSW Law Research Paper No. 2013–24 (2013)*. http://ssrn.com/abstract=2244634.

Trump, D. J. *National Security Strategy of the United States of America*. WhiteHouse.gov, December 2017. https://www.whitehouse.gov/wp-content/uploads/2017/12/NSS-Final-12-18-2017-0905.pdf.

UNCTAD. *The Protection of National Security in IIAs*. New York and Geneva: United Nations, 2009.

UNCTAD. *World Investment Report 2014*. New York and Geneva: United Nations, 2014.

UNCTAD. *World Investment Report 2015: Reforming International Investment Governance*. New York and Geneva, 2015.

US Model Bilateral Investment Treaty. Accessed December 28, 2015. http://www.state.gov/documents/organization/188371.pdf.

US, Trade Expansion Act of 1962 §232, 19 U.S.C. §1862 (1964).

Wang, Heng. "China, Free Trade Agreements and WTO Law: A Perspective on the Trade in Services." *European University Institute Max Weber Programme Working Papers*, 2012. http://dx.doi.org/10.2139/ssrn.2072974.

Webster, Timothy. "Paper Compliance: How China Implements WTO Decisions." *Michigan Journal of International Law* 35(1) (2014): 525–78.

Wei, Liang. "China's WTO Negotiation Process and Its Implications." *Journal of Contemporary China* 11(33) (2002): 683–729.

Whalley, John. *Global Mega Trade Deals and the Impact on China*. Waterloo, Canada: Centre for International Governance Innovation, 2014. https://www.cigionline.org/sites/default/files/commentary_2.pdf.

Williamson, John. "What Washington Means by Policy Reform." In Williamson, John (ed.), *Latin American Adjustment: How Much Has Happened*. Washington, DC: Institute for International Economics, 1990: 7–20.

Woods, Ngaire. "Whose Aid? Whose Influence? China, the Emerging Donors and the Silent Revolution in Development Assistance." *International Affairs* 84(6) (2008): 1205–21.

WTO. "Trade Policy Review of People's Republic of China." Report by the Secretariat. WT/TPR/S/161, February 28, 2006.

WTO. "Trade Policy Review of People's Republic of China." Report by the Secretariat. WT/TPR/S/264/Rev.1, July 20, 2012.

WTO. "Trade Policy Review of People's Republic of China." Report by China. WT/TPR/G/300, May 27, 2014.

WTO. "Dispute Settlement Body, WT/DSB/M/400." August 31, 2017.

Xi, Jinping. "Carry Forward the Bandung Spirit for Win-Win Cooperation." Xi's speech at Asian–African Conference, April 22, 2015. http://en.theorychina.org/xsqy_2477/201505/t20150511_322108.shtml.

Xi, Jinping. "China Proposes Establishing Asian Infrastructure Investment Bank." *Xinhua*, 2013. Accessed December 22, 2015. http://news.xinhuanet.com/english/china/2013-10/02/c_132769208.htm.

Xi, Jinping. "Full Text of Xi Jinping's Report at the 19th CPC National Congress." *Xinhua*, November 3, 2017. http://www.xinhuanet.com/english/special/2017-11/03/c_136725942.htm.

Yang, Guohua. "China in the WTO Dispute Settlement: A Memoir." *Journal of World Trade* 49(1) (2015): 1–18.

Yang, Guohua. "What Is the WTO in China? A Personal Experience." Unpublished manuscript provided by Professor Yang, June 2015.

Younglai, Rachelle. "Obama Blocks Chinese Wind Farms in Oregon over Security." *Reuters*, September 28, 2012.

Yu, Peter. "Sinic Trade Agreements." *UC Davis Law Review* 44 (2011): 953–1028.

Jun, Zhao, and Timothy Webster. "Taking Stock: China's First Decade of Free Trade." *University of Pennsylvania Journal of International Law* (Fall 2011): 65–119.

Zhou, Taidong. "China's Second White Paper on Foreign Aid Signals Key Shift in Aid Delivery Strategy." *Asia Foundation*, July 23, 2014.

Zhou, Ziangwu. Podcast of address by Mr. Zhou Ziangwu, at the 2015 Australasian Aid Conference, February 13–14, 2015. http://devpolicy.org/podcasts/102-AAC2015.

Chapter 11

Toward a Responsible Great Power?

A Formal Analysis of China's Contributions to UN Peacekeeping Operations

Min Ye and Quan Li

The enormous growth of United Nations peacekeeping operations (UN PKOs) in the past three decades presents perhaps the most revealing evidence of the rise of the UN in maintaining international peace and security. Since the end of the Cold War, UN PKOs have expanded both in quantity and complexity. Within five years from 1989 to 1994, for instance, the total number of peacekeepers increased almost seven times, from 11,000 to 75,000.[1] During the Cold War, the UN never ran more than six PKOs in any given year. By contrast, between 1991 and 2015, on average there are seventeen ongoing PKOs each year under the UN supervision.[2] In the meantime, the nature of UN PKOs also underwent significant changes. While "traditional" UN PKOs were predominantly tasked with cease-fire observation, the "second-generation" PKOs in the post–Cold War era were "multidimensional," broadening their focus to issues such as institutions of governance, human rights protection, combatants disarmament, and demobilization that are considered essential to "ensure the implementation of comprehensive peace agreements and to assist in laying the foundations for sustainable peace."[3] Existing work is overwhelmingly interested in the effects of PKOs to improve peace and stability. Only a few studies touch upon why and how these UN PKOs can be formed in the first place. Because the UN does not have its own armed forces, it must rely on member states' voluntary contributions for those tens of thousands of peacekeepers to be dispatched across the globe. But why countries are willing to sacrifice the lives of their soldiers for operations that might have no direct impacts upon their own countries? In this study, we try to fill the gap by taking on the issue of China's UN PKO personnel contributions.

For scholars on Chinese foreign policy, China's participation in UN PKOs also presents a very unique scenario to examine China's economic statecraft, namely, China's effort to use its growing economic power to pursue its other foreign policy goals (Baldwin 1985). China's quick economic growth is perhaps the most significant feature of the post–Cold War international system. As China ascended to a global economic superpower, scholarly interests in China's economic statecraft soared, leading to a large body of literature on how China wielded its economic clout as well as its impacts upon the dynamics of regional and global international relations. Their critical contributions notwithstanding, our knowledge and understanding about many aspects of China's economic diplomacy are still rather limited. For instance, existing studies overwhelmingly focus on China's economic statecraft in a bilateral setting. Yet little is known about how it is employed in international institutions. Furthermore, as Norris (2016) insightfully points out, a major challenge in our existing studies on China's economic statecraft is how to fathom the true motivation of China's economic behavior. That is, it is very difficult to differentiate between economic statecraft manipulated by the Chinese government from other normal economic activities conducted by China's state-owned and private enterprises. Studies have demonstrated that some of the previous examples of China's economic diplomacy are actually normal business and there exist no significant differences between Chinese companies and their American and European counterparts (Chen 2008; Jiang 2009; Gonzalez-Vicente 2012; Gallagher and Irwin 2015).

Our examination of China UN PKO contributions will enrich our knowledge of China's economic statecraft on these issues. First, our examination of the development of China's participation in UN PKOs represents, to the best our knowledge, one of the first efforts to explore China's employment of economic statecraft in an international organization. As discussed above, UN PKOs have become the hallmark of an assertive UN since the end of the Cold War. Participating in UN PKOs is considered a new norm for major powers in the world (Foot 2001). For an emerging power like China, UN PKOs offer a convenient vehicle for China to overcome its lack of military-projection capabilities beyond its immediate vicinity (Hirono and Lanteigne 2011). As will be discussed below, the post–Cold War era has witnessed the remarkable growth in China's contribution to UN PKOs. Currently, China has become the second largest provider of UN PKOs' budget,[4] and the largest contributor of peacekeepers among the permanent UN Security Council (UNSC) members. Nevertheless, unlike bilateral economic diplomacy, China's decision to contribute to UN PKOs must be made in a multilateral context. China is only one of the participants and its final decision is also determined by the decisions of other participants. Using the language of game theory, the outcome stands for an equilibrium of the interactions among all participants. Therefore, our examination of China's participation in UN PKOs will generate significant insights on China's economic statecraft in a multilateral setting. The second significant distinction of UN PKOs is that, unlike economic activities—such as investment, trade, loans—that largely produce private goods, UN PKOs are essentially mixed goods (Bobrow and Boyer 1997). UN PKOs can generate public goods (e.g., peace and stability) that can be consumed by all countries in the world regardless of their participation. In the meantime, UN PKOs can also create private goods that can be consumed by specific countries (e.g., military training, national profile, protection one's oversea economic interests). Because UN PKOs vary in their public as private goods, China's contributions to these UN PKOs contain critical information about China's assessment of these public and private goods. Therefore, China's participation in these UN PKOs provides an incredible chance for scholars to study the motivations of China's economic statecraft.

In the remainder of the chapter, we first review the development of China's UN PKO policy since the 1970s. Then we introduce the current status of formal analysis of UN PKO personnel contributions. Our analysis leads to a new supply-side rational choice allocation model on China's UN PKO contributions. This model generates a number of hypotheses that are tested using the empirical data between 1990 and 2015. Our findings reveal some interesting features of China's decision on UN PKO contributions.

CHINA AND UN PKOS

Unlike most countries in the world, China's initial impression of UN PKOs was hardly friendly. The bloody Korean War (1950–1953) convinced the Chinese leaders that the so-called peacekeeping operations are nothing but disguises for interventions into other countries' domestic affairs. It therefore comes as no surprise that when the People's Republic of China gained the seat of the permanent member of the UNSC in the 1970s, its UN PKO policy was featured by the principle of "three-NOs": not to vote on, not to pay for, and not to participate in UN PKOs (Chen 2009). Most of the time, Chinese delegates simply refused to cast their votes on Security Council resolutions on PKOs. Such a hostile position started to soften in the 1980s as China switched its primary focus to its own economic development. Seeing the world in a more favorable light, Chinese leaders gradually realized the virtues of UN PKOs to international peace and stability, which is also essential for China's reform and open-up policy. In 1981, China, for the first time, voted in favor of a UN PKO (UNFICYP in Cyprus), marking a formal end to its no-voting policy. Later in the same year, its no-payment policy was dropped when China agreed to share the financial costs of UN PKOs. However, it took a much longer time for China to reverse it nonparticipation policy. Because of the inherent incompatibility between UN PKOs and China's highly cherished principle of nonintervention, China was always very wary of sending any military personnel to other countries. The critical juncture of China's UN PKO policy occurred in the post–Cold War era when both the external and internal conditions for China's assessments of PKOs have undergone dramatic changes. As the UN started to play a more assertive role in international politics, blue-helmet soldiers were more frequently deployed in hotspots across the world. Despite their setbacks and even failures in some occasions, UN PKOs have been more and more widely accepted as a legitimate and effective means to handle threats to peace and security. In the meantime, decades of sustained economic growth have transformed China into a power that is both able and willing to exert more influences in global affairs. In this situation, UN PKOs appear increasingly attractive to Chinese decision makers. In 1989, Chinese civilian officials were sent to the UNTAG (in Namibia). In 1990, China dispatched five military observers to the UNTSO (in Syria). In 1992, another substantial step was made when China sent its first military forces—800 People's Liberation Army engineering troops—to the UNTAC (in Cambodia). The following years witness China's rapid growth in its UN PKO contributions. As showed in Figure 11.1, China's annual average UN PKO contributions have jumped from 5 in 1990 to 2,622 in 2016. In the meantime, its share of total UN peacekeepers has elevated from 0.05 percent in 1990 to 2.74 percent in 2016.

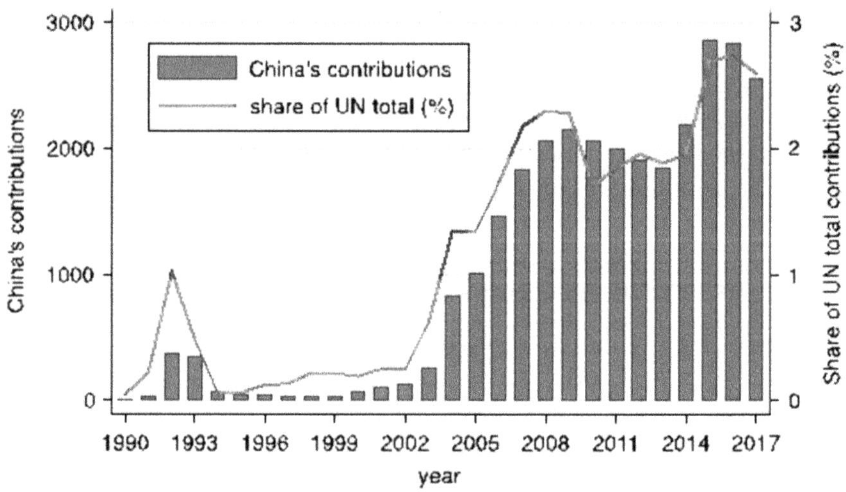

Figure 11.1 China's UN PKO Personnel Contributions (1990–2017). *Source*: IPI Peacekeeping Database.

China's active engagement in UN PKO is also reflected into the structure of its personnel contribution. If we break down China's personnel contributions into three categories: military observers, civilian police, and military troops, Figure 11.2 lists the ratio of Chinese peacekeepers in each category. As we can see from the figure, a conspicuous trend in China's contribution is the increase in China's combat troops. While in the 1990s and early 2000s, China tended to dispatch more civilian police, the focus has shifted to combat troops, another sign of China's deepened involvement in UN PKOs. China has established two training facilities for its peacekeepers. In 2007, Major-General Zhao Jingmin became the first Chinese commander of a UN PKO (MINURSO in Western Sahara). In 2015, at the UN headquarter, Chinese president Xi Jinping announced that China would set up a permanent peacekeeping police squad and build up a peacekeeping standby force of 8,000 troops.[5]

Compared with other major countries in the world, China has become one of the most significant participants of UN PKO in terms of both number of missions and number of peacekeepers. In Figures 11.3 and 11.4, we list the number of PKOs as well as the total peacekeepers contributed by the five UN Security Council permanent members and India since 1990. As we can see, China has replaced France as the UN Security Council permanent member with the widest coverage (numbers of PKOs) and deepest commitment (number of peacekeepers per operation). But China's contribution is still far below the level of India.

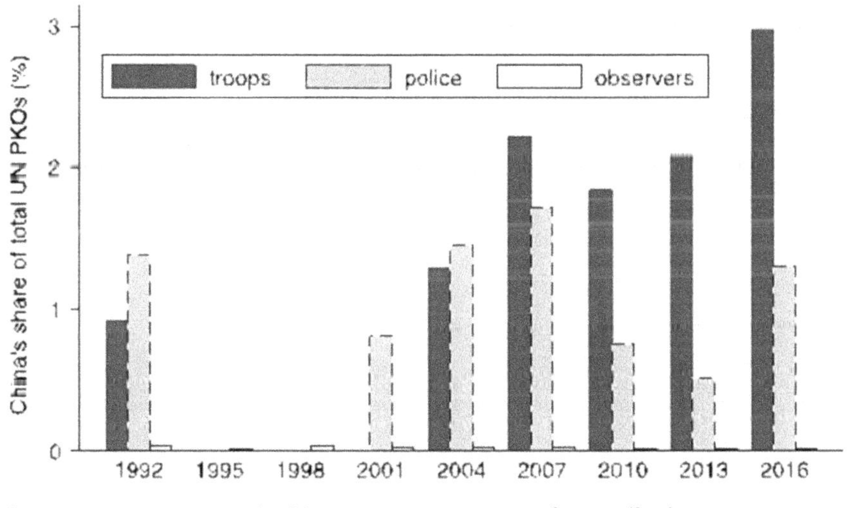

Figure 11.2 Structure of China's UN PKO Personnel Contributions (1992–2016). *Source*: IPI Peacekeeping Database.

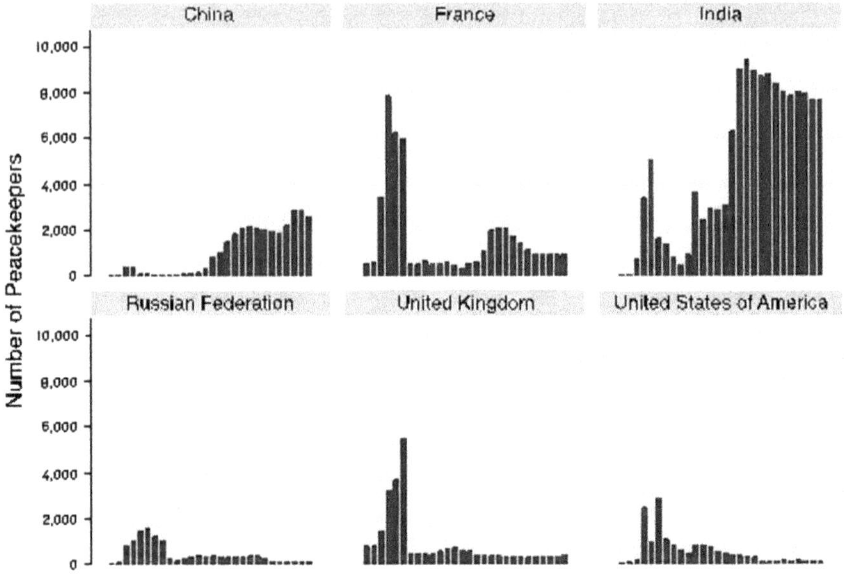

Figure 11.3 Number of Major States' Personnel Contributions to UN PKOs (1990–2017). *Source*: IPI Peacekeeping Database.

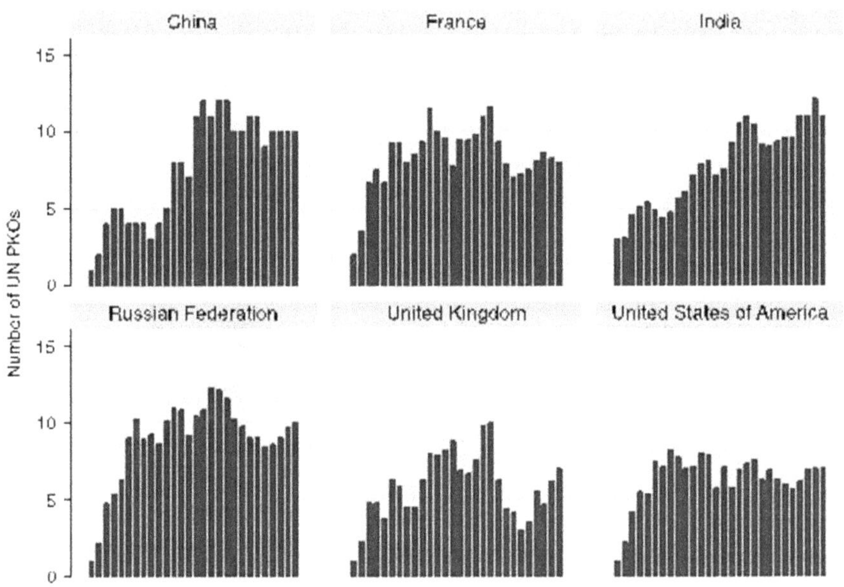

Figure 11.4 Number of PKO Major States Participated In 1990–2017. *Source*: IPI Peacekeeping Database.

It should be pointed out that it is true that Africa has become China's most interested area. In Figure 11.5, it is very clear that China has contributed almost 2.5 percent of peacekeepers deployed in Africa, the highest level since 1990. However, if we compare the way all countries allocate their peacekeepers between Africa and other regions, a different conclusion can be reached. As showed in Figure 11.6, where the percentages of China and other countries' African UN PKO contributions are compared, we can see that whereas China occasionally surpassed the rest of the world in the last century, China's share has been consistently below the average of all other countries in the new century. In conclusion, it is true that China has enhanced its presence in Africa, as many studies correctly point out (Rogers 2007; Huang 2011; Wu and Taylor 2011; Ayenagbo et al. 2012). Yet we should not exaggerate the status of Africa in China's UN PKO strategy. The empirical data show that China also boosts its contributions to UN PKOs in other areas of the world, probably at an even faster pace.

According to *China's Military Strategy* issued in May 2015,[6] China's armed forces will continue to participate in UN peacekeeping missions, strictly observe the mandates of the UN Security Council, maintain its commitment to the peaceful settlement of conflicts, promote development and reconstruction, and safeguard regional peace and security. China's armed

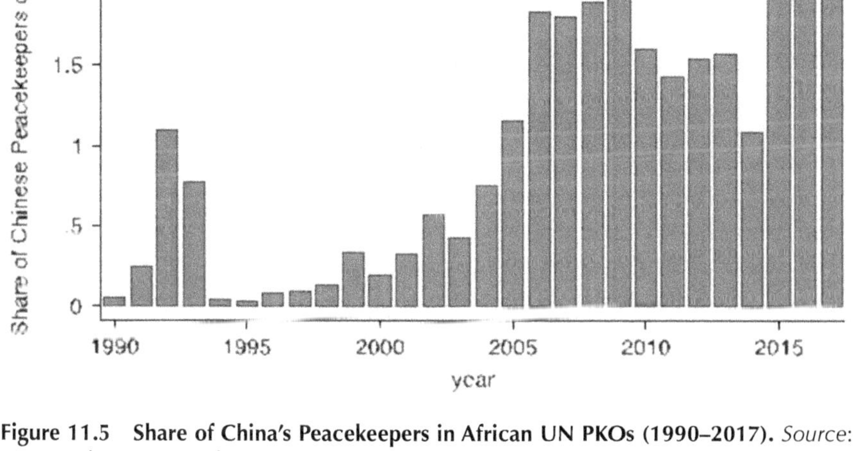

Figure 11.5 Share of China's Peacekeepers in African UN PKOs (1990–2017). *Source*: IPI Peacekeeping Database.

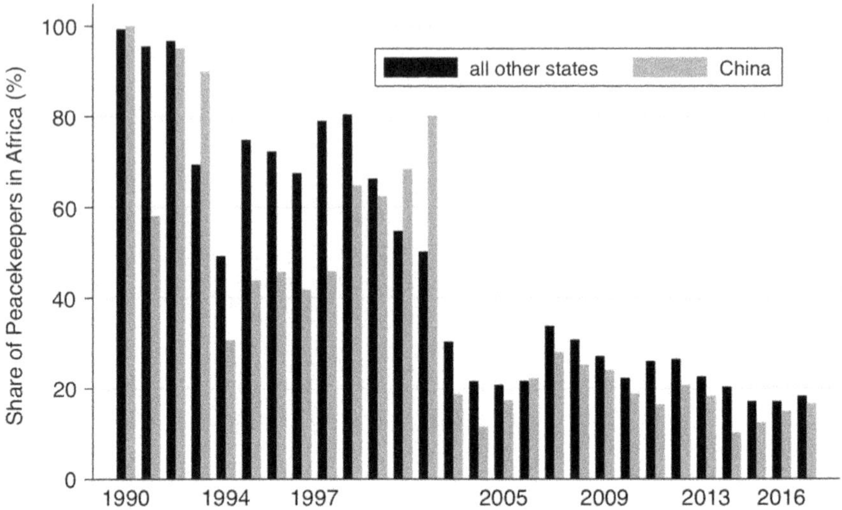

Figure 11.6 Share of Peacekeepers between PKOs in Africa and Other Areas (1990–2017). *Source*: IPI Peacekeeping Database.

forces will engage in extensive regional and international security affairs, and promote the establishment of the mechanisms of emergency notification, military risk precaution, crisis management, and conflict control. With the growth of national strength, China's armed forces will gradually intensify their participation in such operations as international peacekeeping and humanitarian assistance, and do their utmost to shoulder more international responsibilities and obligations, provide more public security goods, and contribute more to world peace and common development.

LITERATURE REVIEW

Even a very brief introduction can clearly reveal the remarkable changes in China's UN PKO policy in the past decades. Existing literature tends to employ two broad approaches in accounting for these changes. Originated from the tradition of constructivism, the first approach tries to ascribe China's changing UN PKO policy to its evolving identity. In the broadest sense, from outright rejections to active engagements, China's changing attitude echoes its evolving grand strategy of foreign policy from "keeping a low profile" to "striving for achievements" (Qin 2014; Yan 2014). Against the backdrop of a shifting grand strategy, studies following this approach endeavor to pinpoint the ideational origin of China's UN PKO policy. For instance, Li (2011) contends that China's new UN PKO policy is driven by its identity as a UNSC permanent member. The "interactive socialization process" with other major powers has gradually reshaped China's identity and policies (Li 2011, 317). In addition to its UNSC permanent membership, Fung (2015) argues that China's another identity as a developing state is also at work. Compared with other UNSC permanent members, this additional identity renders China more subject to influences from its peer group of developing countries. By contrast, Suzuki (2011) attributes China's backing for intrusive UN PKOs to its "sense of superiority and paternalistic attitude" toward those underdeveloped countries where UN PKOs are deployed (271). Studies are also devoted to the process of China's changing identity. For instance, Carlson (2004) observes the gradual acceptance, albeit with caution and reluctance, of the norm of humanitarian intervention—the underpinning principle of nontraditional UN PKOs—among the elites inside Beijing's foreign policy decision circle. Fravel (1996), on the other hand, believes such a change is actually due to "the ambivalence of the China's leadership toward China's position in the world" (1103). Certainly, no one can deny the fact that an emerging superpower like China is prone to play an active role in the global arena, and China's recent active engagements in UN PKOs vividly exemplify China's shifted identity. However, when our interests are in such specific features and patterns of China's UN PKOs as illustrated above, the contribution from this approach is rather limited: it only reveals China's general motivation yet tells little about China's particular tactics and calculations. A prominent drawback of the ideational approach is that while it explains, at the macro level, why China has substantially ramped up its overall participation in UN PKOs, it fails, at the micro level, to address China's selectiveness—namely, why China takes part in only some of the UN PKOs, not to mention how many to contribute to those PKOs. As a result, we are still kept in the dark about China's specific decisions on UN PKO participations. Even scholars turning to China's identity as their main independent variable have to acknowledge China's practical considerations behind their UN PKO participations (Huang 2011). Without the knowledge about China's specific assessment of individual UN PKOs, a comprehensive and in-depth analysis of China's UN PKO policy is almost impossible.

Unlike the first approach, the second approach follows the line of rational choice theory and examines China's UN PKO participations as decisions (1) to select among various UN PKOs and (2) to determine the particular level of personnel contributions. China participates in an UN PKO if and only if the overall benefits outweigh the total costs, and China's contributions stand for the level that most efficiently serves China's interests. Viewed from this lens, China's identity with respect to UN PKOs is not exogenous (Sun 2017), but an outcome of its rational calculation. Every stage in the development of China's UN PKO policy reflects China's rational choice in given domestic and international contexts. For instance, Richardson (2011) calls the choice of the term "responsible power" as a calculated move because the vagueness "enables China to frame the discourse regarding its foreign and security policy" (286). More important, it is possible for China to behave differently than its identity usually suggests. After comparing the multiple identities that motivate China's UN PKO policies, for instance, Hirono and Lanteigne (2011) find that China's behavior is more consistent with a middle power rather than a great power. Studies employing the rational choice approach strive to delve into the practical concerns that drive China's UN PKO participations. Their analysis has unveiled numerous economic, military, and political reasons for China's UN PKO engagements, from establishing China's global power status, shoring up multilateralism, protecting its overseas economic interests, maintaining the one-China policy, building up its national image and soft power, to improving Chinese troops' skills and professionalism (Gill and Reilly 2000; Pang 2005; He 2007; Hirono and Lanteigne 2011; Teitt 2011; Zhao 2011; Ayenagbo et al. 2012; Foot 2014; Sun 2017). Although these studies differ in their focus as well as peculiar explications, they all see UN PKOs as a means for China's other ends in the international arena. The causal links they have uncovered between various aspects of UN PKOs and China's specific interests will undoubtedly help us better understand and predict China's future UN PKO participations.

While the basic logic of rational choice model is rather straightforward, its application is by no means simple. In the past decades, scholars of international relations have developed rigorous methodology of rational choice model (see Bueno de Mesquita 1981; Bueno de Mesquitea and Lalman 1992 for some examples). In a strict sense, rational choice analysis of China's UN PKO participations must address at least two issues. First, when China selects a particular PKO, the potential benefits must be shown to prevail over prospective costs. Second, for a selected PKO, China's contribution must be demonstrated to maximize its expected utility. Unfortunately, neither has been addressed in existing studies. What they have done is no more than simply identifying the potential benefits of a UN PKO. Another methodological flaw of existing literature is their exclusive focus on cases that fit into their arguments (Li 2011). Because both participation and nonparticipation are decisions, bias arises when only part of the cases is focused.[7] To be sure, this is not a criticism of case studies per se. But a complete picture can never be drawn without considering all UN PKOs China has carefully screened. In this chapter we attempt to fill this blank. First, we examine the existing formal analysis of peacekeeping and other types of international military interventions. Our assessment of their contributions and limits gives rise to a supply-side rational choice model on a state's UN PKOs contribution. Then, this model is tested with data for all post–Cold War UN PKOs.

FORMAL ANALYSIS OF UN PKO CONTRIBUTIONS

While formal models are widely used by scholars in their examination about states' behavior in international relations, such as their decision to initiate, continue, and terminate wars,[8] formal analysis of states' contributions to UN PKOs is in short supply. Existing studies usually adopt one of the following two approaches. Nevertheless, as we demonstrate in detail below, neither has offered a satisfactory solution to explain our observations of a state's UN PKO personnel contributions.

The Third-Party Intervention Model

The first approach is based on Regan's (1998) canonical model of third-party intervention. For instance, Bove and Elia (2011) assert, following Regan (1998), the key to understanding a state's decision to contribute to a UN PKO is its calculation about the prospective benefits and costs. Specifically, if we use EU_i^I and EU_i^N to represent a state i's expected utility from intervention and nonintervention, respectively, we have

$$EU_i^I = qU_i^s + (1-q)U_i^f - \Sigma C_i^I, \tag{1}$$

and

$$EU_i^N = pU_i^p + (1-p)U_i^c. \tag{2}$$

In equation (1), U_i^s and U_i^f are i's utility from UN's successful (with probability q) and failed intervention (with probability $1-q$), and C_i^I is the costs of intervention. In equation (2), U_i^p and U_i^c are i's utility from the two outcomes without its participation: successful settlement (with probability p) and continued conflict (with probability $1-p$). The essence of this approach is that the necessary condition for state i to participate in UN PKOs is that the expected utility of doing so must outweigh that of non-participation, or,

$$EU_i^I > EU_i^N. \tag{3}$$

Despite the intuitive sense it makes, Regan's (1998) third-party intervention model is not a good fit for our inquiries into states' personnel contributions to UN PKOs. For Regan's third-party intervention model to work, two preconditions must be satisfied. First, the potential intervening states should have very high stakes in the target conflict. In plain words, the outcomes matter to potential interveners, or using the term in the model, it suggests

$$U_i^s >> U_i^f \text{ and } U_i^p >> U_i^c. \tag{4}$$

Second, their interventions should have significant impacts upon the outcomes, or in plain words, they must be able to make a difference:

$$q >> p. \tag{5}$$

Unfortunately, neither is necessarily the case for states' participation in UN PKOs. For the first condition (equation (4)), according to the IPI Peacekeeping Database, 155 states across the world participate in a total of 78 UN PKOs between 1990 and 2017.[9] It is fair to say few of these countries have vital interests in places further away from their neighboring area. Even Bove and Elia (2011) have acknowledged that most of the countries are indifferent about the outcomes of peacekeeping operations, namely,

$$U_i^s \sim U_i^f \text{ and } U_i^p \sim U_i^c. \tag{6}$$

Furthermore, as showed in Table 11.1, top UN PKO contributors such as Pakistan, Bangladesh, India, and Nepal, and so on dispatched tens of thousands to troops every year to regions (e.g., Africa) where they have little, if any, interests. The situation of the second condition is no less puzzling. Our analysis of the post–Cold War UN PKOs data shows that those 155 states, on average, contribute from 1 to 5,972 peacekeepers to UN PKO.[10] Nevertheless, with 70 states contributing less than 100 peacekeepers and 30 countries less than 10,[11] it is hard to argue that these countries believe their contributions can alter the peacekeeping outcomes in any meaningful ways.

Because most countries fail to meet the two conditions for Regan's third-party intervention model, its application in the analysis of their UN PKO contributions could lead to a conclusion akin to the renowned "paradox of voting" (Downs 1957): since they do not care about the outcomes and do not make any difference, if they are rational, they should not contribute at all. But they do.

The Public-Private Goods Model

Although on the surface, states' decision to participate in the UN PKOs appears a form of third-party intervention, it essentially involves a quite different type of decision: the key is not "whether" but "how many" to contribute.[12] Regan's third-party intervention model is a natural extension of the tradition of rationalist explanation for war (Bueno de Mesquita 1981; Fearon 1995). Its focus is exclusively on the initiation of a war—from the perspective

Table 11.1 UNSC Permanent Members and Other Top Contributors to UN PKOs (Annual Average, 1990–2017)

Ranking	*State*	*Contributions*	*Ranking*	*State*	*Contributions*
1	Pakistan	5972	14	Senegal	1281
2	Bangladesh	5567	15	Morocco	1141
3	India	4857	16	China	1041
4	Ethiopia	3959	17	Indonesia	932
5	Rwanda	3609	18	Kenya	891
6	Nepal	2652	19	Italy	885
7	Nigeria	2562	20	Brazil	879
8	Ghana	2216	21	UK	867
9	Jordan	2074	22	Burkina Faso	800
10	France	1632	23	Saudi Arabia	747
11	Egypt	1517	24	Argentina	745
12	South Africa	1490	38	US	534
13	Uruguay	1371	44	Russia	421

Source: IPI Peacekeeping Database.

of the potential intervener though. By contrast, a state's UN PKO contributions usually do not involve "initiating" the PKOs, which was reserved to the Security Council,[13] but how many to contribute. To a state, a decision not to contribute is essentially a choice of zero personnel contribution, one of the numerous options available to a country. From this perspective, by focusing on the number of contributors, the second approach, the public-private goods model, begins with the right question to ask. In its analysis of states' calculations with respect to its UN PKO contributions, this approach selects to probe into the specific benefits and costs associated with UN PKOs. Without question, the most significant function of UN PKOs is to maintain international peace and security, thereby creating public goods that are universally consumed by all countries in the world. Furthermore, in the post–Cold War era, UN's multidimensional PKOs involve additional tasks such as "facilitating the political process, protecting civilians, assisting in the disarmament, demobilization and reintegration of former combatants; supporting the organization of elections, protecting and promoting human rights and assisting in restoring the rule of law."[14] Although these are largely "impure" public goods that are usually consumed by countries in a quite unequal way (Bobrow and Boyer 1997), they indubitably constitute another component of states' rational calculation. Moreover, UN PKOs can generate private goods attained by specific participants. For instance, the UN compensates states for both their peacekeeping soldiers, equipment, and self-sustainment services, which in the eyes of some developing countries is a significant source of revenue. Some states may have special political and economic interests in countries or regions where a PKO is undertaken. Some states may view UN PKOs as an instrument to elevate its national reputation. According to the pubic-private goods model, the nature of the decision of UN PKO contributions is to figure out the number of peacekeepers that maximizes a state's utility. For instance, Gaibulloeu, Sandler, and Shimizu (2009) develop the following model to examine state *i*'s total PKO contributions:

$$U^i = U^i\left(y^i, x_N^i, Z_N\ E_;^i\right) \tag{7}$$

where *i*'s utility (U^i) is determined by the public goods (Z_N), impure public goods (x_N^i), private goods (E^i) generated by the PKO, as well as its remaining military forces (y^i). Therefore, *i*'s contribution $q^i > 0$ should be the one that maximizes U^i, or

$$q^i = \max\left\{q^i\left(y^i, q^i, q^i + \tilde{Q}^i, E^i\right), 0\right\}, \tag{8}$$

subject to $q^i + y^i = I$, where $\tilde{Q}^i$ is the total contributions from other countries and *I* stands for *i*'s total available armed forces.

Compared with the third-party intervention model, the biggest advantage of the public-private goods model is it presents a theoretical framework to assess states' particular UN PKO contributions. Nevertheless, although Gaibulloeu, Sandler, and Shimizu (2009) correctly point out a state's PKO contribution is eventually an optimization problem—determining the contribution that maximizes its utility, they fail to specify what the optimal contribution is, thereby unable to spell out how this optimal contribution is affected by the contributing country's characteristics and external constraints. As a result, their model is merely a conceptual configuration of states' decision and cannot be tested by empirical data.[15] The main reason for their deficiency is their ignorance of the fact that a state has to decide to contribute to multiple UN PKOs simultaneously. Between 1990 and 2017, on average every year there are more than seven PKOs. States do not select the total (annual) contributions, but the specific contribution to individual operations. In other words, the basic unit of analysis should be individual PKOs (not states), although the contribution to each PKO is constrained by the state's total available peacekeepers. Therefore, states' decision to contribute to UN PKOs is actually how to allocate its scarce resources—namely, their available peacekeepers—among these PKOs. The decision is more similar to an issue of portfolio management: select the best investment mix with limited resources to pursue the optimal return.

The Allocation Model

In their inquiry of South Korea's personnel UN PKO contributions, Ye, Heo, and Li (2017) propose a supply-side rational choice model—the allocation model—to examine how South Korea determines its personnel contributions to various UN PKOs. Compared to the formal models introduced above, their allocation model has at two distinctive advantages. First, the unit of analysis is PKO-year dyads. Since UN PKOs vary widely in location, duration, risk, as well as size, this setup allows researchers to closely check the impacts of these features on states' decision. Second, this is both a conceptual and empirical model. With their model, Ye, Heo, and Li (2017) simulate how South Korean decision makers determine the level of personnel contributions based on the public/private benefits associated with each peacekeeping operation. They also specify the optimal level of contributions and look into its relationship with a handful of factors. Their conclusions generate hypotheses about how various variables affect South Korea's contributions to a given UN PKO in a given year. Although this model is intended to analyze how South Korea, a growing middle power, has played an active role in global affairs, the core of the model does not rely on any presumptions that are unique to South Korea. Since the fundamental rationale for decisions on UN PKO contributions should be similar across nations, their basic research design can be applied to other countries as well. In the remainder of this section, we will present the allocation model in case of China's UN PKOs contributions.

If we use U^j to denote China's utility from a particular UN PKO, say, j, U^j can be written as a function of a series of factors that capture various aspects of China's assessment of UN PKO j:

$$U^j\left(x^j, y^j, z^j, c^j\right). \tag{9}$$

Public Goods (x^j) x^j represents the public goods generated by PKO j, namely, international peace and security. It may also include the enhancement of the status and effectiveness of UN in international politics, as well as the resolution and prevention of humanitarian disasters (Blechman 1995). Let $t^j \geq 0$ and $\tilde{T}^j > 0$ represent the peacekeepers contributed by other countries. The public goods of UN PKO j can be expressed as

$$x^j = \alpha_j\left(t^j + \tilde{T}^j\right)\frac{t^j + \tilde{T}^j}{R^j}. \tag{10}$$

In equation (10), R^j is the level of resistance of the operation, which is proportional to the power of the hostile forces. Therefore, $t^j + \tilde{T}^j / R^j$ denotes the chance of a successful PKO j. Finally, $\alpha_j > 0$ is the coefficient that captures the positive relationship between the public goods and the two factors (total number of peacekeepers, $t^j + \tilde{T}^j$, and the chance of success, $t^j + \tilde{T}^j / R^j$). Recall that, as public goods, x^j should be consumed by all countries regardless of their level of participation of PKO j. However, our above discussions also suggest the public goods might be impure, meaning China may consume the public goods from some PKOs more efficiently than from others. In our model, such a difference is represented by the coefficient: ceteris paribus, a greater α_j implies more public goods from the peacekeeping operation.

Private Goods (y^j) PKO j also creates private goods that are particular to individual contributors. Shimizu and Sandler (2002) specify UN PKOs' three country-specific benefits: enhancing contributors' global status, protecting their neighboring countries' stability, and promoting economic benefits for their trading partners. Nevertheless, for a great power whose economic and political interests are expanding to almost every corner of the world, UN PKOs bring about more private goods, which, as mentioned above, have been thoroughly analyzed by existing literature. Additionally, although there is no evidence about China's sensitivity about the cost to train, dispatch, and deploy its blue-helmet soldiers, the generous monetary compensation to contributing countries may be another factor in China's equation on UN PKOs' economic consequences. To model China's assessment of UN PKOs' private goods, we have

$$y^j = \beta_j t^j \frac{t^j + \tilde{T}^j}{R^j}, \tag{11}$$

where β_j, is the positive coefficient about the relationship between China's contributions (t^j), the chance of success ($t^j + \tilde{T}^j / R^j$), and China's specific benefits from the operation (y^j). Compare equations (11) with (10). We can see China's contributions (t^j) exert independent impact upon its private benefits (y^j), whereas it only matters as one of the contributions in equation (10).

Of course, contributing to UN PKOs is not costless. Our model includes two types of costs in China's calculation.

Opportunity Costs The first is the opportunity cost attached to the contribution to each UN PKO. Like all countries in the world, military forces are a scarce resource in China. The more China contributes to one UN PKO, the fewer troops left for its own national defense and other peacekeeping missions. If we use M to denote China's total armed forces, China's utility from remaining military forces is written as

$$z^j = \gamma_j \left(M - t^j\right), \tag{12}$$

where $\gamma_j > 0$ is the coefficient about the scale of the opportunity costs from PKO j. Note that because the opportunity cost is expressed as an element of China's utility of remaining armed forces, the negative sign of t^j in equation (12) implies z^j decreases in t^j.

Cost of casualties (c^j) The second item of costs regards casualties in UN PKOs. Although the basic principle of UN peacekeeping is "non-use of force except in self-defense and defense of the mandate," no one can deny the reality that peacekeeping operations are a risky business. Since the end of the Cold War, more than 2,400 peacekeeping soldiers have been killed in the UN PKOs.[16] Until 2016, a total of twenty-seven Chinese peacekeepers have scarified their lives. In 2016, the deaths of two Chinese soldiers and injuries of ten more in Mali and South Sudan's PKOs stirred a heated national debate about China's participation in UN PKOs (Sun 2017). To capture how China assesses the possible casualties of its peacekeepers, we present the following equation:

$$c^j = -\delta_j t^j R^j \left(VSL\right). \tag{13}$$

In equation (13), the cost of a peacekeeper's life is measured using the value of a statistical life (VSL), a concept widely adopted in study of public policies. It is true that human life is priceless. But this does not mean decision makers are willing to assign unlimited resources to diminish the risk to people's life. In short, the VSL focuses on "the willingness of people to trade off wealth for a reduction in the probability of death" (Ashenfelter 2006, 10). In addition, the total costs of casualties are affected by the number of peacekeepers (t^j) as well as the level of resistance of the PKO (R^j). The particular relationship is captured by $\delta_j > 0$.[17]

Because each element in equation (9) can be further expressed as a function of China's particular contribution to each PKO in a particular year, t^j, we can figure out China's particular contribution as an optimization problem: China's optimal contribution is the one that maximizes China's utility, U^j. If we adopt the normal assumptions about China's utility function, that is, U^j is continuous, twice differentiable, quasi-concave (Kreps 1990), and strictly increasing in the private and public goods and strictly decreasing in the two cost terms (namely, $\partial U^j / \partial x^j > 0$, $\partial U^j / \partial y^j > 0$, $\partial U^j / \partial z^j > 0$, and $\partial U^j / \partial c^j > 0$), we can spell out the following first-order condition:

$$\frac{2\alpha_j\left(t^j+\tilde{T}^i\right)}{R^j}\frac{\partial U^j}{\partial x^j}+\frac{\beta_j\left(t^j+\tilde{T}^i\right)}{R^j}\frac{\partial U^j}{\partial y^j}-\gamma_j\frac{\partial U^j}{\partial z^j}-\delta_j R^j\left(VSL\right)=0. \quad (14)$$

The solution is China's optimal contribution to PKO *j*:

$$t^{j^*}=\frac{\delta_j\left(R^j\right)^2\left(VSL\right)+\gamma_j R^j\frac{\partial U^j}{\partial z^j}-2\alpha_j\tilde{T}^j\frac{\partial U^j}{\partial x^j}-\beta_j\tilde{T}^j\frac{\partial U^j}{\partial y^j}}{2\alpha_j\frac{\partial U^j}{\partial x^j}+2\beta_j\frac{\partial U^j}{\partial y^j}}, \quad (15)$$

subject to $t^j \geq 0$.

Since equation (15) involves quite a few unknowns, it is unable to tell us how many troops China will contribute to a particular PKO. However, because this equation specifies the relationship between a handful of factors and China's contribution, it will generate significant insights into how these factors would affect China's UN PKO contributions. In the next section, we will probe into the impacts of these factors. Our analysis will lead to a number of hypotheses on China UN PKO contributions.

HYPOTHESES ON CHINA PKO CONTRIBUTIONS

Costs of Casualties (VSL)

Probably the most counterintuitive finding from equation (15) is about the impacts from costs of casualties. Presumably, higher costs of casualties would discourage countries from sending more peacekeepers. This argument is also supported by some empirical analysis of UN personnel contributions (Bove and Elia 2011) and numerous case studies in China (Zhao 2009; Wang 2016). However, the other side of coin is higher VSL is positively related to a state's ability to consume UN PKOs' public and private goods. What is at stake here is how to weigh the positive and negative returns from a state's PKO contributions. In equation (15), it is easy to see that

$$\frac{\partial t^{j^*}}{\partial(VSL)} = \frac{\delta_j\left(R^j\right)^2}{2\alpha_j \dfrac{\partial U^j}{\partial x^j} + 2\beta_j \dfrac{\partial U^j}{\partial y^j}} > 0. \tag{16}$$

It suggests that China's optimal contribution increases in the VSL. Therefore, we have the following hypothesis on the cost of casualties:

Hypothesis 1: China is likely to contribute more peacekeepers to a PKO when its costs of casualties (VSL) are high.

Other Countries' Contributions ($\tilde{T}^j$): When a country determines its level of contributions to a UN PKO (t^j), what is the impact of the contributions from other countries (i.e., $\tilde{T}^j$)? Theoretically, large contributions from other countries create two opposite incentives. On the one hand, the country might be encouraged to contribute more troops because large contributions from other countries make a PKO more likely to succeed (recall the chance of success is $t^j + \tilde{T}^j / R^j$). On the other hand, because the total number of each PKO is fixed, decided by the UN Security Council, large contributions from other countries mean lower level of demand as well as relevance. From equation (15), we can see that

$$\frac{\partial t^{j^*}}{\partial \tilde{T}^j} = \frac{-2\alpha_j - \beta_j}{2\alpha_j \dfrac{\partial U^j}{\partial x^j} + 2\beta_j \dfrac{\partial U^j}{\partial y^j}} < 0, \tag{17}$$

suggesting the negative influence is dominant. Therefore, we have the following hypothesis:

Hypothesis 2: China is likely to contribute fewer peacekeepers to a PKO when there are more contributions from other countries.

Marginal Value of Public/Private Goods ($\partial U^j/\partial x^j$ and $\partial U^j/\partial y^j$): In equation (15), $\partial U^j/\partial x^j$ and $\partial U^j/\partial y^j$ denote the marginal effects of a PKO's public and private goods, or in plain words, how efficiently these goods can be consumed by China. In both cases, we have

$$\frac{\partial t^{j^*}}{\frac{\partial U^j}{\partial x^j}} < 0 \text{ and } \frac{\partial t^{j^*}}{\frac{\partial U^j}{\partial y^j}} < 0, \tag{18}$$

suggesting negative relationships between China's personnel contributions and these two marginal values. Therefore, if we can find out the situations where China's consumption of UN PKOs' public/private goods is more efficient, hypotheses can be derived regarding the relationship between China's personnel contributions and these situations. So the question is: When is China supposed to consume these public and private goods more efficiently? First, as for public goods, we argue that China's efficiency is directly associated with its level of globalization. Despite a permanent member of the UNSC since 1971, until recently China did not have much vital interest in areas beyond its immediate neighboring states. However, since China's economic takeoff in the late 1970s, China quickly grew into a major power in the Asia-Pacific region as well as the whole world. Currently, it is hard to name a major area in the world without significant Chinese economic, political, or military interests. Obviously, as China becomes more globalized, it will get more conscious of threat to regional/global peace and stability across the world. Therefore, we argue that a more globalized China can consume UN PKOs' public goods more efficiently.

Hypothesis 3: China is likely to contribute fewer peacekeepers to a PKO as China becomes more globalized.

Let us now turn to country-specific private interests. While some of the aforementioned private goods—such as military training, national image, or advocacy of multilateralism—can be largely invariably consumed in nearly all sorts of UN PKOs, three types of private goods are sensitive to the selection of PKOs: oversea economic interests, the one-China policy, and neighborhood security. Understandably as the world's largest exporter and second largest importer and investor, China has economic interests across the world. But these interests are not uniformly distributed. The efficiency is higher in countries where China has more foreign trade and investment. Second, the one-China policy is undoubtedly one of the most cherished goals of Chinese foreign policy. Compared to other states, states with diplomatic relations with

Taiwan or newly established countries pondering over their choice across the Taiwan Strait matter more to Chinese decision makers. Finally, China always attached the utmost significance to the peace and stability in its neighboring region, considering it as the core of China's national interests. Therefore, the private goods of border security are more relevant in China's neighboring states. These discussions lead to the following three hypotheses:

Hypothesis 4: China is likely to contribute fewer peacekeepers to a PKO when China has more economic interests in the state.

Hypothesis 5: China is likely to contribute fewer peacekeepers to a PKO in states with diplomatic relations or more likely to established one with Taiwan.

Hypothesis 6: China is likely to contribute fewer peacekeepers to a PKO in its neighboring states.

While the negative relationships suggested in the above four hypotheses sound counterintuitive, they do have solid rationale. First, from the perspective of economics, higher efficacy suggests the same amount of private/public goods can be generated with a smaller number of contributions. There is therefore no need to send more peacekeepers. Second, recall the nature of UN PKO contributions which is to allocate scarce resources (peacekeeper) among available options (UN PKOs). Because a UN PKO does not have unlimited benefits, in order to maximize total net benefits, the rational way to allocate peacekeepers is to send additional peacekeepers to other missions.

DATA AND METHOD

Dependent Variable

Recall that our unit of analysis is a PKO-year dyad. Therefore, the dependent variable is China's annual PKO contributions to a particular mission. However, the size of PKOs varies dramatically from mission to mission and from year to year, ranging from single digits to as many as tens of thousands. The same amount of peacekeepers may have different implications in a small PKO operation than in a huge one. To make China's personnel contributions comparable across PKOs, we use the share of Chinese peacekeepers in a PKO in a year as the dependent variable. The data are from the IPI Peacekeeping Database. The original IPI data only include states' monthly personnel contributions. The annual data used in the study are based on the average of all the months of a year when the data are reported.[18] Since China did not send its first peacekeeper until the end of the Cold War, our empirical analysis actually covers the whole post–Cold War period. For a UN PKO, a country can contribute three different types of peacekeepers: "contingent troop," "experts

Table 11.2 China's Contributions to UN PKOs (1990–2017)

Mission	*Country*	*Starting Year*	*Ending Year*	*Annual Contributions (Average)*
MINUSRSO	West Sahara	1991	ongoing	14.8
MINUSMA	Mali	2013	ongoing	332.5
MINUSTAH	Haiti	2004	2012	93.2
MONUC	DR Congo	2001	2010	178.6
MONUSCO	DR Congo	2010	ongoing	230.2
ONUB	Burundi	2004	2006	2.6
ONUCI	Cote d'Ivoire	2005	2006	7
ONUMOZ	Mozambique	1993	1994	10
UNAMA	Afghanistan	2004	ongoing	1
UNAMIC	Cambodia	1991	1992	3
UNAMID	Sudan	2007	ongoing	248
UNAMSIL	Sierra Leone	1999	2005	5.3
UNFICYP	Cyprus	2011	ongoing	3
UNIFIL	Lebanon	2006	ongoing	332
UNIKOM	Iraq	1991	2003	12.9
UNIOSIL	Sierra Leone	2007	2008	1
UNISFA	Sudan	2011	2011	1
UNMEE	Eritrea	2000	2008	5.7
UNMIBH	Bosnia	1999	2002	17
UNMIK	Serbia	2004	2008	17.1
UNMIL	Liberia	2003	ongoing	527.3
UNMIS	Sudan	2005	2011	382
UNMISET	Timor-Leste	2002	2004	36.8
UNMISS	South Sudan	2011	ongoing	646.4
UNMIT	Timor-Leste	2006	2012	20.6
UNOCI	Cote d'Ivoire	2004	ongoing	5.5
UNOMIL	Liberia	1993	1997	8.5
UNOMSIL	Sierra Leone	1998	1999	2.5
UNOTIL	Timor-Leste	2005	2006	6.6
UNSMIS	Syria	2012	2012	5.5
UNTAC	Cambodia	1992	1993	359.2
UNTAET	Timor-Leste	2000	2002	44
UNTSO	Israel	1990	2017	4.3

Source: IPI Peacekeeping Database.

on mission," and "individual police."[19] A state's personnel contribution is based on the sum of all three types of contributions. In Table 11.2, we list all China's PKO contributions since 1990.

Independent Variables

Costs of Casualties (VSL): Comparable national VSL data at the global level is not available (Miller 2000). However, studies have demonstrated that VSL is very sensitive to a country's income level (Viscusi and Aldy 2003).

Therefore, in this study we follow Bove and Elia (2011) and use China's per capita GDP as the proxy of the costs of casualties. In particular, we use the data of per capita GDP in 2010 constant U.S. dollars from the World Bank's *World Development Indicators* (WDI).[20] This variable is lagged by one year.

Other Countries' Contributions: The contributions from other UN members are from the IPI Peacekeeping Database. For each UN PKO, the number of other countries' contributions is calculated by subtracting China's contributions from the total number of peacekeepers. This variable is lagged one year.

Globalization: We use the KOF Index of Globalization to measure the level of China's globalization. Developed by Dreher (2006), a country's overall globalization index is calculated as a weighted sum of its economic, political and social globalization indexes.[21] The index runs from 0 to 100, with a higher value corresponding to a higher level of political globalization. This variable is lagged one year.

China's Economic Interests in the State of PKO: China's economic interest in the state where a PKO is deployed is measured by the bilateral trade between the state and China. The data are from Correlates of Wars (COW). In particular, for each country, we use its share of the annual bilateral trade with respect to China's total foreign trade of the year.[22] This variable is lagged one year.

Diplomatic Relationship with Taiwan: A dummy variable is created to indicate whether a state has a formal diplomatic relationship with Taiwan in a year. Furthermore, when a new state is established, the first three years since its establishment are also coded 1 due to its high probability of a formal tie with Taiwan.

China's Neighboring States: If a state shares land border with China, this country is coded 1.

Control Variables

Other UN PKO Contributions: The first control variable is China's contributions to other UN PKOs in the same year. Understandably, China's ability to contribute to a specific UN PKO will be restrained if it has already contributed to other UN PKOs. This variable is the sum of China's personnel contributions to all other UN PKOs in the same year. Since China can only know its contributions from the previous year, this variable is lagged one year.

Size of Chinese Military Forces: The second control variable is China's total military forces. A larger size of armed forces will allow more contributions to UN PKOs and vice versa. The armed forces personnel data is from the World Bank.[23]

Stationarity

Since our panel data are not balanced, we conduct a Fisher-type unit root test (Choi 2001). If a unit root is detected, the time series are differenced. Four variables included in our model are not stationary: Cost of Casualties, Other Countries' Contributions, Economic Interests, and China's Other PKO Contributions. Accordingly, first differencing is employed.

Method

A statistical model with the following functional form is used:

$$y_{it} = \alpha_i + x'_{it}\beta + \epsilon_{it}. \tag{19}$$

Given that we have a panel data structure, we need to control for intra-mission correlation across years. In addition, α_i in the above equation controls for the individual mission effects. Depending on whether α_i is correlated with the independent variables, we could use either fixed or random effects estimation. Since some of our independent variables are time invariant plus China's personnel contributions in some PKOs lack variations,[24] we surmise the random effect estimation should be more appropriate. Our conjecture is confirmed by the Hausman test, in which the null hypothesis cannot be rejected, indicating that random effect estimator is consistent. Furthermore, errors (ϵ_{it}) may have panel heteroskedasticity (i.e., $Var\left(\epsilon_{it}^2\right) = \sigma_i^2$), contemporaneous correlation (i.e., $E\left(\epsilon_{it}\epsilon_{jt}\right) = \sigma_{ij}$), and serial correlation (i.e., $\epsilon_{it} = \rho\epsilon_{it-1} + v_{it}$).[25] Our test confirms panel heteroskedasticity and serial correlation. We follow Beck and Katz (1996) to address serial correlation by adding a lagged dependent variable (LDV). Then, we run the random effect estimation with robust standard errors to address the issue of panel heteroskedasticity.

FINDINGS

The outcomes of our empirical analysis are listed in Table 11.3.

As indicated in the table, all coefficients are as expected and three of them are statistically significant. First, hypothesis 1 is supported. Higher costs of casualties do not deter China from sending more troops to dangerous UN PKOs. Specifically, for each \$100 increase in China's per capita GDP (in 2010 constant dollars), the share of Chinese peacekeepers in a PKO will increase about 0.2 percentage. Note that this finding runs directly against the outcome from those systemic examination of states' peacekeeping contributions (Bove and Elia 2011), which contend that states are usually very

Table 11.3 Outcome of Empirical Analysis (1990–2015)

Variable	*Coefficient (Std. Err.)*
Lagged Dependent Variable (LDV)	0.974** (0.081)
Costs of Casualties (VSL)	0.002† (0.001)
Other Countries' Contributions	−0.000135 (0.000)
Globalization	−0.011 (0.014)
Economic Interests	−1.398† (0.842)
Taiwan	−0.182 (0.177)
Neighboring States	−0.133* (0.057)
Other PKO Contributions	0.000565 (0.000)
Size of Military	4.79e-07† (0.000)
Intercept	−1.333† (0.700)
N	299
Log-likelihood	
Chi-squared (9)	918.307

Significance levels: †10%, *5%, **1%.

sensitive to the costs of casualties and high costs will curtail a state's ability to dispatch more blue-helmet soldiers. China's very high level of tolerance to cost of casualties may be due to the fact that China's top-town decision-making procedure renders its decision makers less vulnerable to the influences of public opinion (Sun 2017).

Second, hypothesis 4 is supported. China's economic interests in a country do not boost China's contributions to PKOs in the country. On the contrary, accordingly to the outcome, when the share of a country's bilateral trade increases one percentage, we will expect about 1.4 percentage drop in the share of Chinese peacekeepers in the PKO in the country. According to the allocation model, this drop is due to the rise of China's efficiency to consume the private benefits for this country. Translated into plain language of global politics, when China has more influences in a country, it is less reliant on the UN to handle security issues in the country. By contrast, when China can barely exert any direct impact on a state, UN PKOs appears more appealing and more personnel contributions can be expected from China.

Third, hypothesis 6 is supported. Our outcomes show that China tends to contribute fewer troops to PKOs in its border states. In particular, for a PKO in a state that borders on China, the share of Chinese peacekeepers will be 0.13 percentage lower than a PKO conducted in other countries. The reason is the same as hypothesis 4: when China has more influences and multiple conduits to affect a country, there is no need to devote more valuable resources to UN PKOs.

There is no evidence for the other three hypotheses: hypotheses 2, 3, and 5. Even though the negative coefficients are in line with our prediction, they are not statistically significant. Therefore, we fail to reject the null hypotheses at the 5 percent level. We find no evidence to support hypothesis 2, which suggests a negative relationship between China's contribution and contributions from other countries to the same PKO. The reason, we conjure, might be twofold. One, while the allocation model assumes China's full knowledge of countries' contribution when it decides its own contribution, the reality for countries to determine their personnel contributions is akin to a simultaneous game: they usually have to make the decision at about the same time. Errors may occur if China's estimate of other countries' contributions is not correct. This is extremely likely when some countries' actual contributions sharply deviate from the pledged number or they dramatically alter their contributions from the previous year. Moreover, although most UN PKOs have never reached the upper limit set by the Security Council, it is possible that the upper limit restrains the number of peacekeepers China (and other countries) can actually dispatch. For instance, studies have reported at least two occasions that the lack of vacancies causes China's absences: East Timor (UNTAET) in 2000 and Lebanon (UNIFIL II) in 2008 (Gill and Reilly 2000; Hirono and Lanteigne 2011).

There is no evidence to support a negative impact from the level of China's globalization, as suggested by hypothesis 3. We suspect that the negative but insignificant relationship is caused by China's low overall level of globalization. Although China's overall globalization index has almost doubled from 36.49 in 1990 to 60.15 in 2015, China's ranking is still very low. According to the 2016 Report of KOF Index of Globalization, China ranks 73rd in the world, behind countries like Peru and Georgia.[26] At such a low level, China is still not very sensitive to the public goods—peace and stability—from remote areas.

Hypothesis 5 is not verified, either. No significant proof is found about fewer contributions to PKOs in countries that already have or are more likely to have formal relations with Taiwan. One possible reason is China's evolving tactics to handle the Taiwan issue using UN PKOs. As observed by Sun (2017), the post–Cold War era has witnessed a gradual reversal of China's attitude with regard to UN PKOs and the one-China policy. During the early years, UN PKOs are mainly used as a punishment against countries that recognized Taiwan. The best example is China's veto to renew the UNPREDEP in Macedonia in 1999 after the host country cut off the tie with China and turned to Taiwan in the same year. However, in the new century, China seems to adopt a more flexible policy. As the case of UMINUSTAH in Haiti—a state with a diplomatic tie with Taiwan—has manifested, China not only approved the PKO in the UNSC, but also actively participated in it, a sign to use UN PKO as an allurement. Note that the key is not whether China sees UN PKOs as a stick or a carrot, which does not matter for the allocation model because both confirm the higher efficiency for those states to serve China's national interests. The question is this may cause some selection bias in the empirical analysis: When China vetoed a PKO because of Taiwan, we will not have the chance to observe whether China is likely to contribute more or fewer peacekeepers. Finally, as for the two control variables, only one, the size of China's military, is significant. As we reasoned, China can contribute more peacekeepers when China has a larger pool of armed forces. The observed influence is minuscule but statistically significant.

CONCLUSION

Despite its relatively short history in UN PKO participation, without any doubt, China has already become a significant sponsor of UN PKOs. To scholars, China's UN PKO contributions offer an invaluable opportunity to observe how a rising power can effectively translate its economic resources into global influence. While this study is not the first to examine China's personnel UN PKO contributions, it is the first attempt to scrutinize this country's UN PKO decision with some vigorous empirical models and data. Our findings reveal some interesting patterns and mechanisms of how China strives to maximize its interests with its limited resources. Some of our findings, for instance, the effect of personnel costs of UN PKOs, run directly against some conventional understanding of UN PKOs participations.

With numerous empirical examinations of UN PKO contributions being published at the systemic level (Shimizu and Sandler 2002; Bellamy, Williams, and Griffin 2010; Bove and Elia 2011), little has been done for individual states. Our study joins the effort by Ye, Heo, and Li (2018) to bridge our knowledge of the global peacekeeping endeavors and individual countries' self-interested calculation. Our empirical model can be adjusted to examine other countries' UN PKO contributions.

Our study also fills the gap of our knowledge on China's economic statecraft. Our examination of China's contributions to UN PKOs shows that when employing economic statecraft China faces more restraints in a multilateral setting. Unlike bilateral economic diplomacy, China has only limited choices in UN PKOs. The location, size, and mandates of PKOs are set up by the UNSC. What China can decide is the level of contributions, which, as discussed above, is also contingent upon the decisions of other contributors. However, these restraints have their payoffs. UN PKOs provide a vehicle to pool together scarce resources to achieve something that is beyond the means of individual countries. It is akin to the "leverage effect": the same purpose can be served with much smaller input. Therefore, UN PKOs, along with other multilateral activities, present both an opportunity and a challenge to employ China's economic statecraft.

Our analysis also exemplifies multiple motivations behind China's economic statecraft. China contributes to UN PKOs to pursue both public goods and private benefits. The outcomes reveal China's different decisions toward PKOs in regions where China has special interests. But this does not mean China is a free-rider and only concerns its own private benefits. Our study demonstrates that China is actually also enthusiast about creating pubic goods, which is evidenced by the sheer size of China's total contribution. Brautigam and Tang (2012) have summarized three major objectives for China's economic statecraft: resource security, soft power, commercial opportunities for national firms. Apart from those objectives, our study adds one more goal to the list: creating public goods.

NOTES

1. The data are from the United Nations Department of Peacekeeping Operations (DPKO). Available at http://www.un.org/en/peacekeeping/resources/statistics/contributors_archive.shtml (last accessed on January 3, 2017).
2. Ibid.
3. United Nations Peacekeeping, "Honoring 60 years of United Nations Peacekeeping." Available at http://www.un.org/en/events/peacekeepersday/2008/60years.shtml (last accessed on January 3, 2017).
4. In the 2017–2018 fiscal year, China contributed about 10.25 percent of the total UN peacekeeping budget, next only to the United States (28.47 percent).
5. Xi Jinping's speech at the UN General Assembly on September 27, 2015. Available at http://www.reuters.com/article/us-un-assembly-china-idUSKCN0RS1Z120150929 (last accessed on August 1, 2017).
6. The State Council Information Office of the People's Republic of China. Available at http://www.scio.gov.cn/zfbps/gfbps/Document/1435341/1435341.htm (last accessed on May 5, 2017).
7. Not surprisingly, all case studies are those that China selects to join. We are not aware of any case studies on China's nonparticipation in a UN PKO.
8. See Ye (2012) for a complete literature review.
9. The latest data are in March 2017.
10. Note that the average contributions only involve those years they participated in at least one UN PKO.
11. The national average annual contributions are badly skewed with the mean of 470 and the median of 145.
12. Note that the difference between the two is not absolute. In the case of multistate joint intervention, such as intervention by regional IGOs, the state's decision involves both. See Mullenback (2005) for more information on different types of intervention.

13. For the specific procedure to form a PKO, see "Forming a New Operation." United Nations Department of Peacekeeping Operations. Available at http://www.un.org/en/peacekeeping/operations/peacekeeping.shtml (last accessed on May 16, 2017).

14. United Nations Department of Peacekeeping Operations. "What Is Peacekeeping?" Available at http://www.un.org/en/peacekeeping/operations/peacekeeping.shtml (last accessed on May 16, 2017).

15. Gaibulloeu, Sandler, and Shimizu (2009) have to establish a separate statistical model for empirical analysis.

16. The data are available at http://www.un.org/en/peacekeeping/resources/statistics/fatalities.shtml.

17. It is worth reiterating that since the UN compensates member states for their personnel contributions, equation (13) does not include economic costs.

18. For instance, if China contributes a certain number of troops in two months of a certain year, that year's contribution is calculated as the average of the two months (rather than twelve months).

19. Before October 2009, the UN had three contribution categories: "military observers," "civilian police," and "troops." Since November 2009, "military observers" was replaced by "experts on mission"; "civilian police" was replaced by "formed police units" and "individual police"; and "troops" now includes both traditional "troops" and "contingent troops."

20. The data set is available at http://data.worldbank.org/data-catalog/world-development-indicators (last accessed on March 13, 2017).

21. The data set is available at http://globalization.kof.ethz.ch (last accessed on March 13, 2017).

22. Another significant indicator is foreign direct investment (FDI). However, China's FDI has a very short history (less than ten years). Furthermore, China only publishes the FDI data for a small number of countries. See for instance, National Bureau of Statistics of China, available at http://data.stats.gov.cn/easyquery.htm?cn=C01 (last accessed on October 16, 2017).

23. Data can be found at https://data.worldbank.org/indicator/MS.MIL.TOTL.P1 (last accessed on October 18, 2017).

24. This is especially so if China does not participate in a PKO, namely, zero contribution.

25. $|\rho| < 1$ and v_{it} are independent, identically distributed, and zero-mean random variables.

26. The Report can be found at http://globalization.kof.ethz.ch/media/filer_public/2016/03/03/rankings_2016.pdf (last accessed on October 18, 2017).

BIBLIOGRAPHY

Ashenfelter, Orley. 2006. "Measuring the Value of a Statistical Life: Problems and Prospects." *The Economic Journal* 116 (510): 10–23.

Ayenagbo, Kossi, Tommie Njobvu, James Sossou, and Biossey Tozoun. 2012. "China's Peacekeeping Operations in Africa: From Unwilling Participation to

Responsible Contribution." *African Journal of Political Science and International Relations* 6 (2): 22–32.

Baldwin, David Allen. 1985. *Economic Statecraft*. Princeton, NJ: Princeton University Press.

Beck, Nathaniel, and Jonathan Katz. 1996. "Nuisance vs. Substance: Specifying and Estimating Time-Series-Cross-Section Models." *Political Analysis* 6: 1–36.

Bellanmy, Alex, Paul Williams, and Stuart Griffin. 2010. *Understanding Peacekeeping*. 2nd ed. Cambridge: Polity.

Blechman, Barry. 1995. "The Intervention Dilemma." In *The United Nations, Peacekeeping, and American Foreign Policy*, edited by Dick Clark, 620–29. Washington, DC: The Aspen Institute.

Bobrow, Davis, and Mark Boyer. 1997. "Maintaining System Stability: Contributions to Peacemaking Operations." *Journal of Conflict Resolution* 41 (6): 723–48.

Bove, Vincenzo, and Leandro Elia. 2011. "Supplying Peace: Participation in and Troop Contribution to Peacekeeping Missions." *Journal of Peace Research* 48 (6): 699–714.

Brautigam, Deborah, and Xiaoyang Tang. 2012. "Economic Statecraft in China's New Overseas Special Economic Zones: Soft Power, Business or Resource Security?" *International Affairs* 88 (4): 799–816.

Bueno de Mesquita, Bruce. 1981. *The War Trap*. New Haven, CT: Yale University Press.

Carlson, Allen. 2004. "Helping to Keep the Peace (Albeit Reluctantly): China's Recent Stance on Sovereignty and Multilateral Intervention." *Pacific Affairs* 77 (1): 9–27.

Chen, Jing. 2009. "Explaining the Change in China's Attitude toward UN Peacekeeping: A Norm Change Perspective." *Journal of Contemporary China* 18 (58): 157–73.

Chen, Shaofeng. 2008. "Motivations behind China's Foreign Oil Quest: A Perspective from the Chinese Government and the Oil Companies." *Journal of Chinese Political Science* 13 (1): 79–104.

Choi, In. 2001. "Unit Root Tests for Panel Data." *Journal of International Money and Finance* 20 (2): 249–72.

Downs, Anthony. 1957. "An Economic Theory of Political Action in a Democracy." *Journal of Political Economy* 65 (2): 135–50.

Dreher, Axel. 2006. "Does Globalization Affect Growth? Evidence from a New Index of Globalization." *Applied Economics* 38 (10): 1091–110.

Fearon, James. 1995. "Rationalist Explanations for War." *International Organization* 49 (3): 379–414.

Foot, Rosemary. 2001. "Chinese Power and the Idea of a Responsible State." *China Journal* 45: 1–19.

Foot, Rosemary. 2014. "'Doing Some Things' in the Xi Jinping Era: the United Nations as China's Venue of Choice." *International Affairs* 90 (5): 1085–100.

Fravel, M. Taylor. 1996. "China's Attitude Toward U.N. Peacekeeping Operations Since 1989." *Asian Survey* 36 (11): 1102–121.

Fung, Courtney. 2015. "What Explains China's Deployment to UN Peacekeeping Operations?" *International Relations of the Asia-Pacific* 16 (3): 409–41.
Gaibulloeu, Khusrav, Todd Sandler, and Hirofumi Shimizu. 2009. "Demands for UN and Non-UN Peacekeeping: Nonvoluntary Versus Voluntary Contributions to a Public Good." *Journal of Conflict Resolution* 53 (6): 827–52.
Gallagher, Kevin, and Amos Irwin. 2015. "China's Economic Statecraft in Latin America: Evidence from China's Policy Banks." *Pacific Affairs* 88 (1): 99–121.
Gill, Bates, and James Reilly. 2000. "Sovereignty, Intervention, and Peacekeeping: The View from Beijing." *Survival* 42 (3): 41–59.
Gonzalez-Vicente, Ruben. 2012. "Mapping Chinese Mining Investment in Latin America: Politics or Market?" *China Quarterly* 209 (March): 35–58.
He, Yin. 2007. *China's Changing Policy on UN Peacekeeping Operations*. Stockholm: Institute for Security and Development Policy.
Hirono, Miwa, and Marc Lanteigne. 2011. "Introduction: China and UN Peacekeeping." *International Peacekeeping* 18 (3): 243–56.
Huang, Chin-hao. 2011. "Principles and Praxis of China's Peacekeeping." *International Peacekeeping* 18 (3): 257–70.
Jiang, Wenran. 2009. "Fueling the Dragon: China's Rise and Its Energy and Resources Extraction in Africa." *China Quarterly* 199: 595–609.
Kreps, David. 1990. *A Course in Microeconomic Theory*. Princeton, NJ: Princeton University Press.
Li, Chien-pin. 2011. "Norm Entrepreneur or Interest Maximiser? China's Participation in UN Peacekeeping Operations, 2001–2010." *China: An International Journal* 9 (2): 313–27.
Miller, Ted. 2000. "Variations between Countries in Values of Statistical Life." *Journal of Transport Economics and Policy* 34 (2): 169–88.
Mullenback, Mark. 2005. "Deciding to Keep Peace: An Analysis of International Influences on the Establishment of Third-Party Peacekeeping Missions." *International Studies Quarterly* 49 (3): 529–55.
Norris, William. 2016. *Chinese Economic Statecraft: Commercial Actors, Grand Strategy, and State Control*. Ithaca, NY: Cornell University Press.
Pang, Zhongying. 2005. "China's Changing Attitude to UN Peacekeeping." *International Peacekeeping* 12 (1): 87–104.
Qin, Yaqing. 2014. "Continuity through Change: Background Knowledge and China's International Strategy." *Chinese Journal of International Politics* 7 (3): 285–314.
Regan, Patrick. 1998. "Choosing to Intervene: Outside Interventions in Internal Conflicts." *Journal of Politics* 60 (3): 754–79.
Richardson, Courtney. 2011. "A Responsible Power? China and the UN Peacekeeping Regime." *International Peacekeeping* 18 (3): 286–97.
Rogers, Philippe. 2007. "China and United Nations Peacekeeping Operations in Africa." *Naval War College Review* 60 (2): 73–93.
Shimizu, Hirofumi, and Todd Sandler. 2002. "Peacekeeping and Burden-Sharing, 1994–2000." *Journal of Peace Research* 39 (6): 651–68.

Sun, Meicen. 2017. "A Bigger Bang for a Bigger Buck: What China's Changing Attitude Toward UN Peacekeeping Says About Its Evolving Approach to International Institutions." *Foreign Policy Analysis* 13: 338–60.

Suzuki, Shogo. 2011. "Why Does China Participate in Intrusive Peacekeeping? Understanding Paternalistic Chinese Discourses on Development and Intervention." *International Peacekeeping* 18 (3): 271–85.

Teitt, Sarah. 2011. "The Responsibility to Protect and China's Peacekeeping Policy." *International Peacekeeping* 18 (3): 298–312.

Urdinez, Francisco, Fernando Mouron, Luis Schenoni, and Amancio de Oliveira. 2016. "Chinese Economic Statecraft and U.S. Hegemony in Latin America: An Empirical Analysis, 2003–2014." *Latin American Political and Society* 58 (4): 3–30.

Viscusi, Kip, and Joseph Aldy. 2003. "The Value of a Statistical Life: A Critical Review of Market Estimates Throughout the World." *Journal of Risk and Uncertainty* 27 (1): 5–76.

Wang, Peng. 2016. "Zhongguo Weihe Fuchu Daijia, Zhide Ma? [China's Sacrifice for Peacekeeping: Is It Worth It?]." *Xinhua News*, June 7, 2016. http://news.china.com.cn/world/2016-06/07/content_38618184_2.htm.

Wu, Zhengyu, and Ian Taylor. 2011. "From Refusal to Engagement: Chinese Contributions to Peacekeeping in Africa." *Journal of Contemporary African Studies* 29 (2): 137–54.

Yan, Xuetong. 2014. "From Keeping a Low Profile to Striving for Achievement." *Chinese Journal of International Politics* 7 (2): 153–84.

Ye, Min. 2012. "Bargaining and Rationalist Explanations for War." *Korean Journal of Social Science* 39 (1): 37–58.

Ye, Min, Uk Heo, and Quan Li. 2018. "Economic Development and South Korea's UN PKO Participation." *Journal of Asian and African Studies* 53 (5): 666–84.

Zhao, Lei. 2009. "Zhongguo Canyu Lianheguo Weihexingdong De Leixing Ji Diyu Fenxi [Analysis of China's Participation in UN PKO by Type and Region]." *Dangdai Yatai [Journal of Contemporary Asia-Pacific Studies]* 2: 54–72.

Zhao, Lei. 2011. "Two Pillars of China's Global Peace Engagement Strategy: UN Peace- keeping and International Peacebuilding." *International Peacekeeping* 18 (3): 344–62.

Index

About the Contributors

Laura Bunting holds a master's degree in international relations and politics from the University of Auckland. She currently works for the North Asia Centre of Asia-Pacific Excellence. Her research focuses on political economy, democratic theory, and Chinese politics.

Charles Burton is associate professor at Brock University specializing in comparative politics, government, and politics of China, Canada-China relations, and human rights. He served as counselor at the Canadian Embassy to China in 1991–1993 and 1998–2000. Prior to coming to Brock, he worked at the Communications Security Establishment of the Canadian Department of National Defence. He earned his PhD in 1987 from the University of Toronto after studying at Cambridge University (Oriental studies) and Fudan University (History of Ancient Chinese Thought Program, Department of Philosophy, class of '77). He was Izaak Walton Killam Memorial Post-Doctoral Scholar in political science at University of Alberta, 1986–1988. He has published extensively on Chinese and North Korean affairs and Canada-China relations and has been commissioned to write reports on matters relating to Canada's relations with China for agencies of the Government of Canada. He is a frequent commentator on Chinese affairs in newspapers, radio, and TV.

Jonathan Fulton is assistant professor of political science in the College of Humanities and Social Sciences at Zayed University in Abu Dhabi, UAE. He received his PhD in international relations from the University of Leicester, UK, where his dissertation focused on China's relations with the Gulf Cooperation Council member states. He has written widely on China-Middle East relations for both academic and popular publications and presented his research at several international conferences. He is the author of the forthcoming *China's Relations with the Gulf Monarchies* and co-editor of the forthcoming *External Power and the Gulf Monarchies*.

Marcia Don Harpaz is adjunct lecturer in the International Relations Department and the Faculty of Law at the Hebrew University of Jerusalem. She previously served as director of the International Agreements Division in Israel's Ministry of Economy, and earlier as senior economist-investigator in its Trade Levies Unit. She is currently a member of Israel's Trade Levies Commission and on Israel's Roster of Panelists for Dispute Settlement under the Free Trade Agreement between Israel and Mexico, and between Israel and Mercosur. Her primary research interests are the WTO, China, and the international economic system, and Israel's foreign trade policy.

Bas Hooijmaaijers is assistant professor and Chenhui Research Fellow in the School of Advanced International and Area Studies at East China Normal University (Shanghai, China), and affiliated scholar at the LINES Institute at KU Leuven (Leuven, Belgium). Dr. Hooijmaaijers also serves as Assistant Director at the Mr. and Mrs. S. H. Wong Center for the Study of Multinational Corporations (Los Gatos, CA, USA). He obtained his PhD from Shanghai Jiao Tong University's School of International and Public Affairs, where he was named an "Excellent International Ph.D. Student" in both 2015 and 2016. From 2011 to 2013 he worked as a researcher and assistant of Professor Stephan Keukeleire at the Institute for International and European Policy, KU Leuven. During this period he also held a part-time position as teaching assistant at the KU Leuven's Centre for European Studies. He has published in leading journals including the *Journal of Common Market Studies*, *Global Governance*, and *Journal of European Integration*, and has contributed to ad hoc studies for the European Parliament. His research activities include projects on European Union foreign policy-making toward China, Chinese investment in Europe, and the BRICS and the global power shift toward the Asia-Pacific Region. Dr. Hooijmaaijers is fluent in multiple languages and has a functional proficiency in Mandarin.

Quan Li is professor in the College of Political Science and Public Administration at Wuhan University in Wuhan, China. He is a skilled methodologist and has published works on a variety of topics related to American politics and foreign policy analysis.

Wei Liang is professor of international policy at the Middlebury Institute of International Studies, Monterey, California. Her research interests include international political economy of East Asia, Asian regionalism, international trade negotiation, and global governance. She is the coauthor of *China and*

East Asia's Post-Crises Community: A Region in Flux? (2012), co-editor of *China and Global Trade Governance* (2013), in addition, a number of journal articles and book chapters.

Pippa Morgan is a PhD candidate in international politics at Fudan University. Her research interests include China's foreign policy and foreign economic relations, international political economy, and Sino-Africa relations. Her dissertation project analyses changes in patterns of Chinese aid in Africa over time. She is also assistant editor of the *Chinese Political Science Review* and the *Fudan Journal of the Humanities and Social Sciences*.

Stephen Noakes is senior lecturer of Chinese politics, jointly appointed to politics and international relations and Asian studies. His research has appeared in journals such *China Quarterly*, *Pacific Affairs*, *Voluntas*, *Journal of Chinese Political Science*, *Problems of Postcommunism*, *Political Science Quarterly*, and elsewhere. He is also the author of *The Advocacy Trap: Transnational Activism and State Power in China* (2017), a regular commentator on China's role in international affairs, and a frequent advisor to the aid community on governance issues in the PRC. Prior to joining the University of Auckland, he was a SSHRC postdoctoral fellow at the University of Toronto's Munk School of Global Affairs, and a visiting research scholar at Fudan University's School of International Relations and Public Affairs in Shanghai. In 2018, he was a visiting New Zealand-China Fellow at the School of International Studies at Peking University.

James F. Paradise is assistant professor at Yonsei University in Wonju, South Korea. He did his graduate studies at the London School of Economics and Political Science and the University of California, Los Angeles, where he obtained two master's degrees and a PhD, respectively. He also worked as a journalist for United Press International and Dow Jones Newswires in Tokyo, Japan, for many years and spent a year as a University of Hawaii Asia Fellow. His academic writings have appeared in *Korean Political Science Review*, *Journal of Chinese Political Science*, *Fudan Journal of the Humanities and Social Sciences*, *Asian Journal of Social Science*, *The Brown Journal of World Affairs*, *Asian Survey*, *The China Quarterly*, *Chinese Law & Government*, and *Millennium: Journal of International Studies*.

Zhongzhou Peng is a PhD candidate of international relations in the School of Social and Political Science, University of Melbourne, Australia. His research focuses on the EU-China relationship, with a particular interest on the normative power of these two actors in global governance.

Sow Keat Tok joined as lecturer at the Asia Institute, the University of Melbourne, in May 2012. His research interests span the Asia-Pacific region and covers in particular China's foreign relations and domestic politics, and issues on sovereignty, nationalism, and historical narratives.

Yi Edward Yang is professor of political science at James Madison University in Harrisonburg, Virginia. He specializes in foreign policy decision-making, political psychology, and Chinese foreign policy. His research has appeared in several edited volumes and peer-reviewed scholarly journals including the *Journal of Conflict Resolution*, *International Studies Quarterly*, *Political Psychology*, *Journal of Contemporary China*, and the *Chinese Journal of International Politics*. He served as President of the Association of Chinese Political Studies (ACPS) in 2016–2018, a US-based organization dedicated to academic and professional activities relating to Chinese politics.

Min Ye is professor in the Department of Politics at Coastal Carolina University. His research interests include international conflict, foreign policy analysis, East Asian politics, and formal modeling. He is the author of the book *China-South Korea Relations in the New Era: Challenges and Opportunities* and numerous journal articles.

Biao Zhang was educated at the universities of Beijing, Warwick, and Exeter, and is currently a lecturer of international relations in the School of Political Science and Public Administration, China University of Political Science and Law. He is interested in IR theory and China-EU relations (with a special focus on China-UK relations). Intrigued by the Chinese involvement in the Hinkley Point C project, he is also interested in the political economy of nuclear energy. His latest publications include "Hans Morgenthau, Realist Theory of International Leadership, and the Future of Global Order" (*Chinese Political Science Review*) and "Global Britain: UK's Foreign Policy Choice after Brexit" (*Contemporary International Relations* [in Chinese]).

www.ingramcontent.com/pod-product-compliance
Ingram Content Group UK Ltd.
Pitfield, Milton Keynes, MK11 3LW, UK
UKHW020219290926
15470UKWH00001B/281

9 781498 583442